Migration and Social Upheaval as the Face of Globalization in Central Asia

Social Sciences in Asia

Edited by

Vineeta Sinha
Syed Farid Alatas
Kelvin Low

VOLUME 34

The titles published in this series are listed at brill.com/ssa

Migration and Social Upheaval as the Face of Globalization in Central Asia

Edited by

Marlene Laruelle

BRILL

LEIDEN • BOSTON
2013

Cover illustration: photo made by the editor.

Library of Congress Cataloging-in-Publication Data

Migration and social upheaval as the face of globalization in Central Asia / edited by Marlene Laruelle.
p. cm. — (Social sciences in Asia ; v. 34)
Includes bibliographical references and index.
ISBN 978-90-04-22681-4 (pbk. : alk. paper) — ISBN 978-90-04-24950-9 (e-book) 1. Migration, Internal—Asia, Central. 2. Asia, Central—Social conditions—1991– 3. Asia, Central—Economic conditions—1991– 4. Globalization—Asia, Central. I. Laruelle, Marlène.

HB2096.42.A3M54 2013
304.80958—dc23

2012051264

This publication has been typeset in the multilingual "Brill" typeface. With over 5,100 characters covering Latin, IPA, Greek, and Cyrillic, this typeface is especially suitable for use in the humanities. For more information, please see www.brill.com/brill-typeface.

ISSN 1567-2794
ISBN 978-90-04-22681-4 (hardback)
ISBN 978-90-04-24950-9 (e-book)

This book is printed on acid-free paper.

CONTENTS

PART 4

IMPACT ON GENDER RELATIONS: MASCULINITY AND FEMININITY IN FLUX

ABOUT THE AUTHORS

Aida Aaly Alymbaeva. Formerly a senior researcher at the Aigine Cultural Research Center in Kyrgyzstan from 2005 to 2010, Aida is a PhD candidate at the Max Plank Institute for Social Anthropology in Germany. Her main research interests include ethnicity, migration, and state-minority relations.

Stéphanie Belouin. Graduate of the Institut d'Études Politiques of Grenoble, Stéphanie Bélouin was a cultural attaché at the French Embassy in Uzbekistan. She is now writing a doctorate in sociology on Central Asian migration at the MIGRINTER laboratory of the University of Poitiers, and is working in the Asian division of the French Office for the Protection of Refugees and Stateless Persons.

Adeline Braux holds a PhD from Sciences Po-Paris. Her dissertation, titled "Migrations, Transnationalism and New Diasporas in the Post-Soviet Space: South-Caucasian Migrants in the Russian Federation," focuses on strategies of migration, integration, and vectors of co-presence of Armenian, Azerbaijani, and Georgian immigrants in Russia, as well as on the policies of these immigrants' countries of origin in this regard. She is currently working on a new project titled "Ex-Soviet Migrations in Turkey: New Forms of Migratory Movement in the Eurasian Space," which aims to contribute to the study of migration within the space consisting of the Russian Federation, Ukraine, Southern Caucasus, and Turkey.

Olivier Ferrando holds a PhD in Political Science from Sciences Po-Paris, which he carried out under the supervision of Prof. Olivier Roy. His research explores the minority question in post-Soviet Central Asia, focusing on political mobilization and ethnic violence in the Ferghana valley. He has published various articles and book chapters on this topic and teaches international politics, including geopolitics of Central Asia and the Caucasus. He is presently Director of the French Institute for Central Asian Studies (IFEAC) in Bishkek.

Asel Dolotkeldieva is a PhD candidate and Teaching Assistant at the Department of Politics at the University of Exeter, UK. She received her Research Master degree in Post-Soviet studies from Sciences-Po-Paris,

France. Currently, she is studying the use of contentious politics in Kyrgyzstan, looking in particular at the nature of the mobilizations during the two Revolutions of 2005 and 2010. Her current research interests include: social movements, rebellions, and various forms of political contention; and Central Asian and post-communist politics.

Nafisa Khusenova. After completing a Master in Development studies at the EHESS in Paris, Nafisa worked in agriculture development for the OSCE and GIZ offices in Tajikistan from 2009 to 2012. Since August 2012, she has been working for the French NGO GERES as Country Director in Tajikistan.

Sophie Hohmann holds a PhD in Social Science at the EHESS, Paris, and is an Associate Scholar at CERCEC in Paris. Her research focuses on sociological and demographical approach of healthcare issues, migration, and the relationship between state and society in Central Asia and the South Caucasus. She has published various papers on these topics and has authored a book on the issue of infant mortality in Soviet and post-Soviet Uzbekistan: *La mortalité chez les jeunes enfants en Ouzbékistan. Des particularismes soviétiques aux réalités contemporaines*, Editions universitaires européennes, 2010.

Marlene Laruelle is a Director of the Central Asia Program, and a Research Professor of International Affairs, The Institute for European, Russian and Eurasian Studies (IERES), The Elliott School of International Affairs, George Washington University, Washington DC. She holds a Ph.D. at the National Institute for Oriental Languages and Cultures in Paris. She has published many titles including *Russian Eurasianism: An Ideology of Empire* (Woodrow Wilson Press/Johns Hopkins University Press, 2008), *In the Name of the Nation: Nationalism and Politics in Contemporary Russia* (Palgrave, 2009), and has co-authored *The 'Chinese Question' in Central Asia: Domestic Order, Social Changes, and the Chinese Factor* (Hurst/Columbia University Press, 2012). She works on national identity, nationalism, citizenship, and migration in Central Asia and Russia.

Erica Marat, PhD, teaches Central Asia at the American University in Washington, DC. She has extensive field work experience in Central Asia researching crime, corruption, and state-crime relations. She is currently working on a project comparing police reforms in Georgia, Kyrgyzstan, and Mongolia.

Sophie Massot holds a PhD in Political Science from Sciences Po-Paris, devoted to Uzbek labor migrations to Seoul, Moscow, and New York. She has taught Political Sciences at the University of St Denis de la Réunion (France), and currently teaches history and geography at the Lycée Français in Cali (Columbia).

Saodat Olimova is a political scientist and head of the public opinion services at the SHARQ (ORIENS) Research Center. Her interests are migration, Islam, and political and social issues in Tajikistan. Among other titles, she has published *Environmental Degradation, Migration, Internal Displacement, and Rural Vulnerabilities in Tajikistan* (IOM, 2012); *The Impact of Labour Migration on Human Capital: The Case of Tajikistan* (Sharq, 2012), "The Multifaceted Chinese Presence in Tajikistan" (*China and Eurasia Forum Quarterly*, 7, No. 1, 2009), and "Opposition in Tajikistan: Pro et Contra" (in *Democracy and Pluralism in Muslim Eurasia*, Routledge, 2004).

Sebastien Peyrouse is a Research Professor of International Affairs, The Institute for European, Russian and Eurasian Studies (IERES), The Elliott School of International Affairs, George Washington University, Washington, DC. He holds a PhD at the National Institute for Oriental Languages and Cultures in Paris. He is the author of *Turkmenistan: Strategies of Power, Dilemmas of Development* (M. E. Sharpe, 2011), and the co-author of *The 'Chinese Question' in Central Asia: Domestic Order, Social Changes, and the Chinese Factor* (Hurst, Columbia University Press, 2012). He has also co-edited *China and India in Central Asia: A new "Great Game"?* (Palgrave Macmillan, 2010), and *Mapping Central Asia: Indian Perceptions and Strategies* (Ashgate, 2011).

Luisa Piart is an anthropologist with an MA in Migration Studies from the University of Poitiers. She is currently completing a PhD in Anthropology at the University of Vienna and the EHESS in Paris. Her chapter in this volume is based on ethnographic material collected with Uzbek female shuttle traders in Turkey and Uzbekistan between 2004 and 2006. She is interested in processes of economization and globalization in urban contexts, as well as issues of waste and branding. Starting in 2013 she will be a research assistant at the Institute of Social Anthropology of the University of Bern.

Madeleine Reeves is a University lecturer in Social Anthropology at the University of Manchester, where she was previously a RCUK Research

Fellow in Culture, Cohesion and Change. Her interests lie in the anthropology of the state, borders, conflict and transnational livelihoods. She is the editor of *Movement, Power and Place in Central Asia: Contested Trajectories* (Routledge, 2012) and, with Johan Rasanayagam and Judith Beyer, of *Ethnographies of the State in Central Asia: Performing Politics* (forthcoming with Indiana University Press). She is currently completing a manuscript on the everyday working of new borders in the Ferghana valley.

Elena Sadovskaya is an international consultant on migration and migration policies. She has conducted research on migration and migration policies in Kazakhstan and Central Asia for the International Organization for Migration, UNHCR, the World Bank, ILO, UNFPA, EU, the MacArthur Foundation, the Ford Foundation, The Norwegian Institute of International Affairs, as well as governmental bodies of Kazakhstan, particularly Ministry of Economics and Trade and Ministry of Labour and Social Protection. She has published extensively on migrations in Central Asia.

INTRODUCTION

Marlene Laruelle

A symbol of globalization, migration is one of the most studied phenomena, effacing as it does state borders, transforming cultural boundaries, and accelerating the mobility of people across the globe. Moreover, the economic and technological changes that have brought about globalization have been aided by the fluidity of population movements and the creation of a globalized labor market.[1] However, migration is also in the media spotlight for more negative reasons, with reporting inevitably playing on the card of xenophobia, fear of migrant numbers, as well as its illegal character and links with the shadow economy.

According to the International Organization for Migration (IOM), the global stock of migrants has doubled in the past 40 years; in 2010, it amounted to around 214 million persons living outside of their countries of birth, representing 3 percent of the world population.[2] However, the precise figure is difficult to gauge; indeed, approximately 20 to 30 million people should be added to this number given that much migration goes undocumented.[3] Furthermore, the number of migrants could increase to 405 million by 2050 as a result of growing demographic disparities, the effects of environmental change, new global political and economic dynamics, technological revolutions, and social networks. Migration flows are no longer uniquely south-north directed; they are also east-west, and above all, south-south. The sociological profile of migrants has also changed: half of all migrants are women, and an increasing number of them have attained secondary or tertiary levels of education.[4] The circumstances under which they migrate have also become more diversified. Migrants may be competitive, skilled professionals who have left one country for another to pursue better job opportunities. Conversely, they

---

[1] P. Stalker, *Workers without Frontiers* (Boulder: Lynne Rienner, 2000).

[2] *World Migration Report 2010. The Future of Migration: Building Capacities for Change* (Geneva: IOM, 2010), 3.

[3] P. Dicken, *Global Shift. Mapping the Changing Contours of the World Economy* (New York, London: The Guilford Press, 2011, 6th edition), 515.

[4] S. Castles and J.M. Miller, *The Age of Migration: International Population Movements in the Modern World* (London: Macmillan, 1993).

may be impoverished individuals in desperate circumstances, migrating at their own peril, sometimes becoming the victims of human trafficking. It should also be noted that the figure of 214 million includes only international migration, and therefore excludes the large number of people who migrate within their own countries from rural to urban areas, or from remote areas to the coasts, which often offer better infrastructure and prospects for social promotion. China alone, for instance, has about 130 million domestic migrants.

International migration has had profound and transformative effects on both recipient and sending countries—not only on their social and state structures, but also in terms of their economies and governance. Migration also transforms individuals, family bonds, gender relations, community networks, traditional senses of belonging, and the self-identities of citizens. The policy-oriented community is not alone in trying to understand these phenomena. Social science disciplines have been exploring the subject for quite some time. Economics, demography, human geography, political science, international relations, sociology, and anthropology—all are concerned with issues related to migration. Particularly pertinent for migration issues are multidisciplinary areas of study, including cultural studies, gender studies, labor market studies, post-colonial studies, network/community studies, and trans-nationalism, among others.[5]

The Forgotten Post-Soviet World

Long forgotten, the post-Soviet world has been largely overlooked by major international studies on migration, which have instead focused primarily on the historical migration routes from the area south of the Mediterranean basin to Europe, and from Latin America to the United States. However, migration in the post-Soviet space has taken place on an immense scale. Approximately 10 percent of former Soviet citizens (or 28 million out of a total of 287 million in the last Soviet census of 1989) have moved to another country since the collapse of the Soviet regime in 1991. About six to seven million people, mostly Russians, Germans, and Jews, have left the post-Soviet space for Europe, North America, Israel, or Australia. More

[5] S. Vertovec, ed., *Migration. Critical Concepts in the Social Sciences* (London: Routledge, 2009). Most of the articles cited here are taken from this collection. See also C.B. Brettell and J.F. Hollifield, eds., *Migration Theory: Talking across Disciplines* (New York and London: Routledge, 2000).

than 20 million have relocated within the post-Soviet space. According to IOM data, Russia received 12.3 million migrants in 2010—second in the world in terms of inflows after the United States[6]—whereas the Ukraine received 5.3 million, and Kazakhstan three million.[7]

What is unique about these three post-Soviet states is that they are simultaneously sending, receiving, and transit countries. They are, in fact, so called crossroads-countries, situated along a larger migration route from Asia toward Europe, from the south toward the north.[8] Added to this are the millions of internal migrants in each of the post-Soviet states: rural populations seeking to flee poverty by moving to the cities; those abandoning regions in full industrial crisis for new centers of development; massive population displacements from Siberia and the Far East toward the European regions of Russia; refugees that have fled the Tajik civil war and the conflicts in the Caucasus; and those displaced due to environmental reasons.

Within the post-Soviet space, Central Asia occupies a unique place. Since the beginning of the 1990s, it has been the main supplier of migrants due not only to the "return" of Russians and Russian-speaking populations to their kin-state, but also the large-scale labor migration of Central Asians themselves. Throughout the twentieth century, the Soviet regime strove to increase the mobility of its population within the Soviet space, with the exception of specific policies aimed at peasants, who were considered to be "attached" to the land until the Khrushchev era. The aim of this intra-Soviet mobility was ideological (mixing ethnic groups in order to weaken longstanding solidarities and to form a uniform *homo sovieticus*), social (pushing country dwellers to move to towns), and economic (using the workforce in regions subject to intensive development strategies). Under this framework, Central Asia was decried as being rather unreceptive to the logic of territorial mobility and social promotion. While the region received millions of Russians, Ukrainians, and Belarusians—as well as the so-called punished peoples deported under Stalin—the indigenous groups seemed immobile and uninterested in massive linguistic and cultural Russification, which was a prerequisite for social promotion and territorial

---

[6] See "Facts and Figures" on the IOM website, http://www.iom.int/jahia/Jahia/about-migration/facts-and-figures/regional-and-country-figures/cache/offonce/.

[7] *World Migration Report 2010*, 191.

[8] On the role of Europe as a receiving migration space, see F. Duvell, "Crossing the Fringes of Europe: Transit Migration in the EU Neighbourhood," COMPAS Working Paper 06–33, 2006; P. Ireland, *Becoming Europe: Immigration, Integration and the Welfare State* (Pittsburgh, PA: University of Pittsburgh Press, 2004).

mobility.[9] Whereas the Soviet regime seemed to have failed on this front, the rise of the market economy, or at least the dismantling of the Soviet welfare state, has proven successful in pushing people to relocate. Today Central Asia is experiencing large-scale patterns of migration, the impact of which can be compared to the major "exporter" regions of migrants such as Central America.

The chronology of migration in Central Asia not only reveals the underlying dynamics, but also replicates chosen directions and strategies. Since the 1970s, inflows toward Central Asia have slowed, and the region experienced net negative migration in the 1980s. While Germans and Jews were the first to emigrate from the Soviet Union and the former "punished peoples" fled the pogroms against them, Russians "returned" to Russia. The period from 1992 to 1994 saw an emigration of Russophone speakers that would eventually reach epic proportions. Refugees, displaced persons, and economic migrants fleeing the civil war in Tajikistan (1992–97) quickly followed. At the end of the 1990s, Tajiks accounted for the largest number of migrants to Russia, while Kyrgyz were flocking to Kazakhstan, which emerged as their second most preferred destination in the Commonwealth of Independent States (CIS). Over the course of the 2000s, Uzbeks also partook in labor migration on a massive scale, indicative of the deterioration of socioeconomic conditions in the country. Today, about five million Tajiks, Kyrgyz, and Uzbeks work seasonally in Russia, and between one and two million in Kazakhstan. The slowdown of flows in 2008–9 was due to the impact of the economic and financial crisis in Russia and Kazakhstan, and represents only a slight fluctuation in what is a long-term migration process; the volume of flows resumed in 2010 without any fall in numbers.

Russia remains the primary destination for Central Asian migrants seeking work, followed by Kazakhstan, whose rise as a recipient country confirms its standing as a regional leader in Central Asia. The more adventurous try their luck in major global immigration destinations such as the United States, Canada, and Israel. Thanks to its repatriation policy for Soviet co-ethnics, Germany also became a popular destination for labor migrants, and the leading one among European countries.[10] Often, the choice of destination depends to a large extent on the financial capacity

---

[9] H. Carrère d'Encausse, *Decline of An Empire (The Soviet Socialist Republics in Revolt)* (New York: HarperCollins, 1981).

[10] On flows from the Soviet Union to Europe, see A. de Tinguy, *La Grande Migration. La Russie et les Russes depuis l'ouverture du rideau de fer* (Paris: Plon, 2004).

of the migrant's family. While the richest look to migrate to developed Western countries, those with smaller savings cross the border into Kazakhstan or Russia. Poorer migrants are forced to wait at market places or at bus and railway stations, where they hope to be hired for work, and are paid only by the day or the hour. In a more recent trend, the flow of some Uzbek migrants to South Korea signals a new form of migration to countries with which historical links are tenuous. Such countries are not among major receiving states on an international level, but have nonetheless set up strategies to attract workers. The Gulf countries are also proving an increasingly attractive destination for migrant workers from Central Asia. Dubai, Abu Dhabi, and Saudi Arabia have already signed modest contracts with Uzbekistan, Tajikistan, and Turkmenistan for the provision of workers. Although largely confined to the post-Soviet space for the moment, the migration of Central Asian workers is expected to go global in the next decade.

One of a Kind

In the world of policy studies, the IOM has long been the sole institution to have done in-depth studies on population movements in the former Soviet Union. In 2006, furthermore, the World Bank decided to fully integrate the post-Soviet region into its yearly reports on world migration.[11] In the area of the social sciences, the first studies were carried out by Russian researchers, notably by the Analysis and Forecasting of Migration team at the Center for Demography and Human Ecology, and the Russian Research Center for Migration, both led by Zhanna Zayonchkovskaya.[12] The team conducted detailed sociological surveys on all population flows following the collapse of the Soviet regime, in particular on Russians "returning" from Central Asia to Russia and refugees from the Tajik civil war.

In Central Asia, meanwhile, few local studies on migration have thus far been published. Those that have been carried out were linked to Zayonchkovskaya's team, while others were IOM-commissioned field studies by the Sharq Analytical Center in Dushanbe. Internal migration has been better studied, especially in Kyrgyzstan thanks to the Social Research Center of the Bishkek-based American University of Central

[11] A. Mansoor and B. Quillin, eds., *Migration and Remittances. Eastern Europe and the Former Soviet Union* (Washington, D.C.: The World Bank, 2006).

[12] See their website, http://migrocenter.ru.

Asia. Since these research studies were published mainly in Russian, their circulation was limited to the circle of researchers specializing in the region and has, by and large, not reached Western institutions working on global migration. It was not until a second wave of research was carried out in the 2000s that the phenomenon came to be perceived as one of the drivers of contemporary post-Soviet societies, similar in scope to migration issues affecting Latin America or Africa. Today, academic research on migration in Central Asia is mostly conducted within the disciplines of sociology and anthropology, and is oriented toward the analysis of social and cultural transformations, and personal and familial experiences in both recipient and host countries.

This collection of studies, the first of its kind to be published in English, covers several issues related to migration by scholars from diverse backgrounds. Among the contributors are well-known Central Asian experts specializing in migratory phenomena (Saodat Olimova, Elena Sadovskaya), as well as a team of mostly French social science specialists. The methodological tools they use primarily come from the fields of political science, sociology, and anthropology. The information provided here does not aim to be statistically representative; instead, it is of a qualitative nature, and does not seek to provide any quantitative analysis of migration. It must be stressed that compared to other, better-known regions of the world, the statistical information available on Central Asia remains limited. Until now, there have been no major sociological studies on Central Asian migration that would have allowed researchers to cross-check statistical and biographical data, similar, for example, to the one which exists on migrant flows from the area south of the Mediterranean to Europe (the MAFE project).[13] As much of this work is grounded in field studies, some of the chapters in this volume could even be charged with lacking sufficient theoretical content. As often happens in area studies, especially "new" regions such as Central Asia, the researchers are not always closely connected with the theoretical debates of their discipline. Nevertheless, all the field data presented here is original. Most of it could only be collected through months of field research conducted alongside the migrants themselves and their families, whether in the sending or receiving country. These valuable analyses will therefore form the basis upon which new generations of researchers can build their studies.

---

13 See the website http://mafeproject.site.ined.fr/en/.

Plan of the Work

At the very core of this collection is the transformation of Central Asian societies that migration has brought about. Although the majority of Central Asian migrants have headed toward Russia, only a few of the contributions to this volume—such as those by Adeline Braux, Asel Dolotkeldieva, and Nafisa Khusenova—are focused on the recipient country. Examining the economic, social, and cultural impact of the massive migratory flow to Russia requires its own separate work in light of the number of issues it raises, from Russia's migration policy to the integration of migrants and the rise of xenophobia.[14] Rather, this collection accords priority to an analysis of the Central Asian societies themselves and the evolution they have undergone over the last 20 years due to social upheavals, which have been one of the causes of migration. In so doing, it concentrates on the three main source countries—Tajikistan, Uzbekistan, and Kyrgyzstan—as well as includes a case study on Kazakhstan as a recipient country. We have also deemed it useful to include Azerbaijan, even though it is situated in the South Caucasus and not in Central Asia, as the migratory processes in both regions are similar. Furthermore, it is not the intention of this work to address the entire gamut of questions that the social sciences raise in relation to migration. Rather, it seeks to concentrate on a few key topics, namely: issues of governance, patterns of social adaptation, individual and collective identity transformations, and gender studies.

Accordingly, the first section of this work discusses governance-related issues through studying the major migration trends (Elena Sadovskaya), the impact of the 2008–9 economic crisis, the issue of remittances and return migration (Saodat Olimova and Erica Marat), and government policies on migration in the case of Kazakhstan (Marlene Laruelle).[15] The questions raised by these first set of authors revolve around the existing legislative systems in both the sending and receiving countries. They point out the need to study migration not only at a macro-level (revenues generated via remittances), but also at a micro-level. In fact, the decision to migrate is taken by individuals, households, and/or communities as they adapt to market changes through their own cost-benefit analyses. The importance for the Central Asian case of the "meso-level," a topic

---

[14] W. Kymlicka, "Immigration, Citizenship, Multiculturalism: Exploring the Links," in S. Spencer, ed., *The Politics of Immigration* (Malden: Blackwell, 2003), 195–208.

[15] W. Cornelius and T. Tsuda, eds., *Controlling Immigration. A Global Perspective* (Stanford: Stanford University Press, 2004).

regularly discussed in the social sciences, is highlighted in this collection.[16] This first section not only demonstrates the need to better understand the "push-pull" mechanisms[17] existing in Central Asia, but also the role of migrants and their contributions to the Russian and Kazakh economies, which are in need of guest workers in both unskilled jobs[18] as well as highly-skilled occupations.[19] Moreover, although Central Asia represents only 1.5 percent of the world's total labor-migrant population, its economies are heavily dependent on migrant workers. Remittances represent half of Tajikistan's GDP (the highest in the world), and 28 percent in Kyrgyzstan, but their role in local economic development has yet to be fully determined.[20]

The second section of this work studies migration as an adaptation to post-Soviet social upheavals. Whether it is internal migration from rural areas to cities (Aida Aaly Alymbaeva), or international migration, these movements not only have an impact on the urban landscape but also on family issues, including profoundly modifying the traditional health and reproduction patterns of Central Asian societies (Sophie Hohmann).[21] The meso-level enables us to understand how people rebuild their collective and individual identity in migration, and the interactions of personal and familial decisions with ones based on traditional kinship networks. Among new identity patterns that have taken shape, the concept of "diaspora" is one of the most widespread. Very common in the post-Soviet era, it is used to describe not only the traditional diasporas (Jews and Armenians), but also the longstanding ethnic minorities residing in the territory of a neighboring state (the Uzbeks in Kazakhstan or Kyrgyzstan, for instance)

---

16 T. Faist, "The Crucial Meso-Level," in T. Hammar, G. Brochmann, and K. Tamas, eds., *International Migration, Immobility and Development: Multidisciplinary Perspectives* (Berg, 1997), 187–217.

17 G. Dorigo and W. Tobler, "Push-Pull Migration Laws," *Annals of the Association of American Geographers* 73, no. 1 (1983): 1–17.

18 S. Castles, "Guestworkers in Europe: A Resurrection?" *International Migration Review* 40, no. 4 (2006): 741–766.

19 K. Koser and J. Salt, "The Geography of Highly Skilled International Migration," *International Journal of Population Geography*, no. 3 (1997): 285–303.

20 N. Nyberg-Sørensen, N. Van Hear, and P. Engberg-Pedersen, "The Migration-Development Nexus: Evidence and Policy Options," *International Migration* 40, no. 5 (2002): 49–73; J. Durand, E.E. Parrado, and D.S. Massey, "Migradollars and Development: A Reconsideration of the Mexican Case," *International Migration Review* 30, no. 2 (1996): 423–444; R.E.B. Lucas, *International Migration and Economic Development: Lessons from Low-Income Countries* (Northampton: Edward Elgar, 2005).

21 To compare with Shao-hua Liu, *Passage to Manhood: Youth Migration, Heroin, and AIDS in Southwest China* (Stanford: Stanford University Press, 2010).

and the migrant communities. Constructing an entity such as "the Azeri diaspora of Russia" thus makes it possible to establish strategies that are simultaneously individual and collective, which both the Russian and the Azeri states can also invest in (Adeline Braux).[22] Migrants also learn to make rational choices when searching for jobs, maneuvering within the Russian bureaucratic system, negotiating with law enforcement agencies, and interacting with the complex aims of the organizations claiming to represent them (Asel Dolotkeldieva). Using their networks as social capital is one of the key traits that defines migrants' logic of integration and their attempts to create a world that straddles two countries.[23]

The third section of this work explores the parallels between spatial mobility and identity mobility. The population flows in the last two decades have deeply transformed the cultural landscape of the Central Asian states, which are moving toward greater mono-ethnicization. At the same time, the population flows have more clearly demarcated the urban and rural division among titular populations. As the flow of the former colonizers—that is, the Russians and other so-called European minorities—has gradually dried up, it has drastically modified the Central Asian ethnic map and forced those European minorities remaining to define the nature of their two homelands—the Central Asian one and the kin-state one (Sebastien Peyrouse). Similarly, the governments' interest in diasporas, specifically their co-ethnics abroad, and the logic of ethnic repatriation have advanced the idea that these states are the preserve of a single ethnic group (Olivier Ferrando).[24] This section also examines the way in which individuals have to manage the transformation of their identities through perpetual renegotiations of the relations between the individual and the group: rural/urban identities, ethnic identities, family identities, and identities as migrants or as *nouveau riche* (two articles by Sophie Massot). Migrants' attitudes profoundly shape the shared myths on migration, which create new perceptions of the world and also serve to legitimate new behaviors. Whereas the Soviet Union partly failed to export perceptions rooted in the daily life of the former colonial metropole to

---

[22] R. Cohen, *Global Diasporas: An Introduction* (London: UCL Press, 1997); G. Sheffer, ed., *Modern Diasporas in International Politics* (New York: St. Martin's Press, 1986).

[23] D.S. Massey, J. Arango, G. Hugo, A. Kouaouci, A. Pellegrino, and J.E. Taylor, *Worlds in motion. Understanding International Migration at the End of the Millennium* (Oxford: Clarendon Press, 1998), 17–59.

[24] T. Tsuda, ed., *Diasporic Homecomings: Ethnic Return Migration in Comparative Perspective* (Stanford: Stanford University Press, 2009).

Central Asian rural cultures, today's migrants spread knowledge of Russia to their villages by means of memories, conversations, consumer goods, and standards of living. By constructing migratory narratives, they transform their societies of origin and create new cultural dynamics.

The last section of this work delves into the gender aspect of migration. While there have been numerous studies that focus on the impact of male migration on women's living conditions, the evolution of masculinity remains poorly understood. The in-depth transformation of a twofold masculinity, that of men departed and that of those who remained behind, is therefore discussed here (Madeleine Reeves). Among gender-related changes linked to migration, three case studies are analyzed: women's specialization in shuttle trade throughout the post-socialist era and the links that it creates between petty trade and women's lives (Luisa Piart); the increasingly important role that Central Asian women play in Russia's bazaar economy (Nafisa Khusenova); and the emigration strategies of highly skilled women, which range from studying abroad to marriage migration (Stéphanie Bélouin).

Analyzing the reciprocal influences between internal political orders and external ones will be an increasingly important research topic over the next few years. It will encourage future studies to re-examine the interactions between Central Asia and its external environment. Labor migration is creating a dynamic matrix of economic, social, and also—potentially—political change.[25] The research contained in this volume thus raises a host of questions concerning Central Asia. How, for instance, do differences in age, gender, class, family situation, professional occupation, and ethnicity shape one's experiences of migration and trans-nationalism? How will migration transform domestic politics in the coming decades? How will the growing number of migrants who want to settle permanently in Russia affect relations between the two regions? How will the local and the global interact in Central Asia, especially in terms of cultural changes? An awareness that state borders can be bypassed, the establishment of mobility as an accepted and even valued social norm, the creation of both intra-and supra-state solidarities, and the deterritorialization of national spaces are all factors that contribute to major changes in the societal

---

[25] H. Donnan and T.M. Wilson, *Borders: Frontiers of Identity, Nation and State* (Oxford: Berg, 1999); M. Anderson, *Frontiers: Territory and State Formation in the Modern World* (Cambridge: Polity Press, 1996).

fabric.[26] Although peripheral on many counts, when it comes to migration Central Asia finds itself at the heart of international dynamics and globalization, which are radically changing the concept of the contemporary political order.[27]

[26] A. Appadurai, *Modernity at Large. Cultural Dimensions of Globalization* (Minneapolis: University of Minnesota Press, 1996).

[27] C. de Wenden, "The Frontiers of Mobility," in A. Pécoud and P. de Gutcheneire, eds., *Migration without Borders. Essays on the Free Movement of People* (Oxford, New York: Bergham Press, 2007), 51–64; B. Badie, R. Brauman, and E. Decaux, *Pour un autre regard sur les migrations. Construire une gouvernance mondiale* (Paris: La découverte, 2008).

PART ONE

FLOWS, REMITTANCES, AND GOVERNMENT POLICIES

INTRODUCTION

Marlene Laruelle

The phenomenon of migration is often studied at a macro-level, where it has an impact on interstate relations between receiving and sending countries, and on the way governments perceive migration, both as an economic opportunity and as a threat to what they define as their national or economic security. Statistical analyses on the phenomenon are complex and sometimes contradictory; there is no single, universally accepted definition of the term "migrant" (it depends on seasonality, legal status, and so on). Nor are there any means of precisely calculating undocumented movements of populations. In the post-Soviet space, as in the rest of the world, migrants have to deal with a large number of informal and institutional constraints, which often serve to keep them and their activities undocumented. The irregular nature of their revenues and the remittances they send to their families, which often do not go through official banking channels, make it difficult to gauge the exact scale of these sources of income. Nonetheless, so-called migra-dollars are the most significant consequence of international labor migration. They constitute one of the more stable sources of capital inflows for Tajik, Kyrgyz, and Uzbek households, and their impact on the long-term evolution of the social fabric cannot be overlooked.

Some post-Soviet migrant-supplying states like Kyrgyzstan, Tajikistan, and Azerbaijan are beginning to understand the necessity of lobbying Moscow to support the interests of their migrant communities in Russia. The migration issue has thus become an element of interstate relations in the CIS. Only Uzbekistan still denies the significance of its migrant laborers, particularly as they are an indirect disavowal of the country's unfavorable socio-economic situation. While Tashkent continues to value the conventional definition of state power by declaring that it is "in control" of its own citizens, quite to the contrary the Tajik and Kyrgyz governments have recognized not only their inability to operate with closed borders, but also exert political influence over the formation of both intra- and supranational groups. The message sent by the Tajik and Kyrgyz authorities is very clear: their states cannot meet the needs of their citizens, and therefore encourage them to take care of themselves by finding jobs abroad. Kyrgyzstan even wishes to follow the same model as the Philippines in terms of making official the export of workers as one of the main sources of state income. In coming years, Uzbekistan, Kyrgyzstan, and Tajikistan will find themselves partially bereft of their very small middle classes, unless they are able to develop service economies on a national scale, replicating what Bishkek has done by positioning itself as a platform for the re-export of Chinese products. On the other hand, Russia and Kazakhstan will find themselves competing for Central Asian graduates and unskilled laborers in order to inexpensively feed their own economic growth.

Mass migration also changes the relationship between individuals, the state, and economic development strategies. Some texts that focus on remittances appear to imply that the individual financial self-sufficiency that migration can create is able to compensate for the absence of the state as the manager of the common good. This is a principle based on the neoliberal idea that the market economy regulates itself naturally. And yet, the political, social, and cultural costs of massive labor migration on the sending society are more complex than a simple mathematic calculation of revenue per household. What is more, migration in Central Asia appears to be more a matter of survival than a strategy of capturing market share; it includes almost no macroeconomic investment. Migrants send money back home to meet the immediate need for food, medicine, clothing, debt repayment, and to strengthen social bonds. Remittances, however, have not been able to create new revenues for long-term sustainability, such as for opening small businesses, improving plots of land, or purchasing cattle. On another level, the labor drain of productive men and women of working age deprives the agricultural sector of a much needed workforce, as well as stifles opportunities for small enterprises to be created. Thus, one can call into question whether the remittances migrants send can be considered sufficient replacement for state aid or a counter to the failure of basic social services.

Remittances also impact the everyday social fabric and interactions. In the space of less than two decades, spatial mobility, something which had not previously been valued, has come to be viewed as a normal way of life and even as a positive experience. Young men are sent abroad as a rite of passage into adulthood, and long-term settlement strategies in the receiving country have taken shape, the plan generally being to return home at around the age of 50, when the family unit has become independent. Once the migration process is under way, it becomes part of the norm. Higher incomes raise the living standards of families, albeit if not leading to the creation of local jobs. In sum, it would seem rather unlikely that the phenomenon of migration in the region will peter out.

In this first section of the volume, Elena Sadovskaya provides a broad overview of the manifold stakes of current migratory flows. The majority of Central Asian migrants have headed for other CIS countries, mainly Russia and Kazakhstan, while Uzbekistan leads in terms of outside-CIS flows. The destination chosen often depends upon the revenues at the migrants' disposal. Poorer migrants tend to choose to go to a neighboring country, while those who have accumulated more substantial funds aim for developed countries farther away, which are seen to offer more professional opportunities. In her analysis, Sadovskaya shows that migrants within a single national/ethnic community comprise a variety of social and legal statuses, ranging from undocumented, unqualified, and impoverished, to prosperous, legal residents, qualified specialists, and university students. She focuses on the growing role of networks in the structures of migration. Those who have settled in Russia for several years tend to organize the arrival of the most recent migrants and facilitate their entry into the labor market. There are also many systems of mutual aid based on regional solidarity, particularly in fighting violations of migrants' rights. Finally, while the community network makes it possible to cope with the Russian bureaucratic system, it can also have a negative impact, with some ethnically-based criminal groups specializing in trafficking and blackmailing migrants through the exploitation of their illegal status.

The 2008 economic crisis has had an impact on migration in the post-Soviet space. But whilst what were mostly alarmist discourses warned of the risk of a sudden drop in migrant numbers and therefore of a fall in remittances to the sending countries, Erica Marat's chapter shows that these fears were largely unsubstantiated. The economic slowdown experienced in Russia and Kazakhstan did not actually reduce the demand for labor. On the contrary, there has been an increase in employers' demands for unskilled migrant laborers, largely because they are deemed to be more cost-efficient than employing national workers. With the exception of the construction sector, which was most affected by the crisis, the market for other unskilled jobs normally taken up by migrants, namely drivers, retailers, and street sweepers, did not evaporate. However, the crisis did accentuate the dysfunctionalities of the labor market in receiving countries, and revealed in a more acute way the need for regional legislation on labor migration and, therefore, for greater interstate cooperation on the issue.

The 2008 crisis has to be considered as a single historical moment in the evolutionary ebb and flow of post-Soviet migrations. Thanks to fieldwork undertaken by the Sharq Analytical Center, Saodat Olimova provides a very detailed analysis of how Tajik migrants have coped with the crisis. Her analysis ought not to be understood as limited to the crisis period; it also discloses the rationales behind migrants' global behavior. They managed to cope with the difficulties, largely by accepting salary cuts and changing jobs. They also avoided returning home during the off-season winter months not only to save on the cost of returning, but also to ensure that they would be in Russia to resume business. For those who decided to return home, their social and economic reintegration has been challenging. Most returned as self-employed with their own family businesses, preferring not to engage in the administration and private enterprises. They have complained about the lack of locally based networks that would enable them to use the skills they have learned in Russia.

While Russia is the main destination for Central Asian migrants, Kazakhstan, as Marlene Laruelle's chapter shows, is both a receiving and a sending country. As is the case with migrants headed for Russia, Kyrgyz and Uzbek, and to a lesser extent Tajik, migrants going to Kazakhstan come from diverse social backgrounds, ranging from highly skilled individuals seeking better-paid work to impoverished villagers from rural areas. Some of them plan to stay in Kazakhstan for the long term and thus tend to develop strategies of integration (migrating with their families, educating their children), while others are there only for seasonal work. The majority of them look for jobs in the construction and service industries, although they are also drawn to the agricultural sector in the southern part of the country. Kazakhstan must therefore manage growing regional differences in terms of migration flows. The authorities have attempted, albeit rather unsuccessfully, to provide a legal framework for migration, but up until now only one interstate agreement has been reached—with Kyrgyzstan. Although xenophobia is less rampant in Kazakhstan than in Russia, Astana has so far failed to regulate the opportunities offered to its economy through this imported workforce, and thus has yet to develop concrete strategies of integrating migrants from neighboring countries.

CONTEMPORARY INTERNATIONAL MIGRATION IN CENTRAL ASIA AND THE RISE OF MIGRANTS' DIASPORAS AND NETWORKS

Elena Y. Sadovskaya

The nature of migratory movements in the post-Soviet republics, including those in Central Asia, has changed dramatically over the last 20 years. Previously characterized by internal movement within a single state (the Soviet Union), international migration between sovereign states is now the dominant trend. Whereas populations were effectively pushed to migrate in the 1990s, this gave way to more labor-driven flows in the 2000s. Due to favorable economic conditions and relatively dynamic macroeconomic reforms, the socioeconomic situation in Russia and Kazakhstan has improved, with the result that they have become major recipient countries for migrant labor. Russia and Kazakhstan are also, albeit to a lesser extent, transit and labor-sending states. Migrant flows from Central Asia are changing, however, and are increasingly directed beyond the CIS states; nevertheless, the global economic crisis of 2008–9 has impacted international migration. It has had a negative effect not only on the "shrinking" domestic labor markets of the recipient countries, but also on the "secondary," "tertiary," and "enclave" labor markets, where labor immigrants are mostly engaged.

Large-scale migration at the end of the twentieth and the beginning of the twenty-first centuries has resulted in the emergence of numerous migrant diasporas in destination countries. Moreover, it can be observed that the role of diasporas in contemporary international migration in Central Asia is growing. Networking between migrants in origin and destination countries is developing rapidly, facilitating further migration; however, this has not yet been studied in depth. The major issues this chapter will address are thus identifying the major trends in international migration, including labor migration, in contemporary Central Asia and the role of diasporas in migration. The goal is to analyze the latest trends in international migration in Central Asia, including its causes, regional and global trends, and main patterns. It will also consider the role of migrant diasporas and networks in international migration in Central Asia. It will not attempt to cover all ethnic diasporas in the region, instead focusing on issues relevant to the emerging diasporas of temporary labor migrants and newly arrived permanent residents in receiving countries.

Some of the propositions here may be considered to be "formulations of research questions."

Research Methodology

This chapter summarizes the author's ongoing research on migration in Central Asia, with a particular focus on Kazakhstan, during which pioneering analysis has been undertaken in regard to international labor and illegal migration in Kazakhstan, the emerging regional migration subsystem in Central Asia, remittances and their role in migrant households, and contemporary Chinese migration in Kazakhstan and Central Asia. The methodologies employed include analysis of official statistics (state statistics on international migration in the republics of Kazakhstan, Kyrgyzstan, Tajikistan, and Uzbekistan), expert interviews, applied sociological surveys conducted by the author, or under her supervision, between 2000 and 2008, and analysis of secondary sources such as other scholarly research or mass media publications.

Drawing on a number of theories of international migration and diasporas, research tools from various disciplines, including economics, sociology, political science, and international relations, will be employed. The analysis of contemporary migration in Central Asia, furthermore, reveals the applicability of nearly all contemporary theories of international migration: world systems theory (Simmons, Massey), macro and micro studies of neoclassical economics (Ranis, Fei, Lewis, Harris, Todaro, Maruszko, and Borjas), the new economics of migration theory (Stark, Levhari, Katz, Taylor, and Lauby), social capital (Loury, Bourdieu, Harker, and Coleman), theories of social and migrant networks (Thomas and Znaniecki, Tilly, Brown, MacDonald, Levi, and Taylor), cumulative causation (Myrdal, Massey), and other theories and concepts that are mutually complementary in understanding the causes of international migration and its development and "perpetuation" in Central Asia.[1]

World systems theory, for example, can be applied to the analysis of the post-Soviet migration system. Emerging after the break-up of the Soviet Union, the CIS is a regional structure which, in terms of migration processes, represents a common system. Former Soviet Union countries once

---

[1] D.S. Massey, J. Arango, G. Hugo, A. Kouaouci, A. Pellegrino, and J.E. Taylor, *Worlds in Motion. Understanding International Migration at the End of the Millennium* (Oxford: Clarendon Press, 1998), 17–59.

shared a single economic system, unified working standards in production and service industries, and standardized quality controls, as well as a single system of secondary, higher, and professional education featuring the obligatory use of the Russian language. Furthermore, the former Soviet republics are still connected by a common infrastructure, including transportation and communication systems, as well as sharing many economic, financial, and socio-cultural ties. It is therefore no surprise that 90 to 95 percent of migration exchanges take place between CIS states. Modern economic and trade relations and visa-free regimes between CIS countries stimulate migration and professional mobility across economic sectors, where the demand for workers and specialists is growing. The Russian language, a lingua franca, creates a common linguistic space for horizontal and vertical mobility, thus easing adaption to a new, or similar, socio-cultural environment in different countries within the CIS.

Russia sits at the center of the post-Soviet migration system. As the most socially and economically advanced state, Russia's labor market attracts migrants from all the CIS states. Among other "pull" factors to Russia are its depopulation and the consequent ageing and shrinking of its labor force. Migration flows to Russia come mainly from Uzbekistan, Ukraine, Tajikistan, Kyrgyzstan, Moldova, and the South Caucasian states. Indeed, international migrants have become an important labor resource in Russia. According to various assessments, between 8 and 12 percent of Russia's GDP is generated by migrant labor.

Macro and micro studies of neoclassical economics add further perspective in analyzing international migration in Central Asia and Russia. Macroeconomic theories explain labor migration by means of geographic differences in the supply of and demand for labor in the sending and receiving countries, as well as by differences in wages. Labor migration in Central Asia is caused both by the demand for workers in Kazakhstan, and the supply of surplus human resources in Kyrgyzstan and Uzbekistan. The demand for labor in Kazakhstan is a consequence of the large-scale emigration and "brain drain" of the 1990s, when net migration numbered more than two million people. Consequently, when Kazakhstan's economy started picking up in the 2000s, the country suffered from a lack of qualified specialists and workers. The difference in wages is also decisive in bringing in workers from labor excess and low-wage countries like Kyrgyzstan, Tajikistan, and Uzbekistan, to labor scarce and higher-wage countries such as Kazakhstan and Russia.

Micro theories are instrumental for studying the level—individual or household—at which decisions to migrate are made. According to them, the decision is modeled as an individual choice to move to a place where skilled migrants can be more productive and thus expect improved remuneration. At the same time, the "cost-benefit" migration formula is associated with certain investments such as the cost of travel and lodging, learning a new language and culture, and adapting to a new labor market.

Proponents of a new "economics of migration" theory point to the importance of considering the decision-making level in migration, not only on the individual level, but also larger units of related people (the migrant household or group of households, and sometimes communities) within which people act collectively to maximize profit (benefit) from migration, and minimize the risks and losses.[2]

Diasporas are an important albeit controversial issue in migration discourse. There are many theoretical frameworks and approaches to diaspora analysis. Notable scholars, to name but a few, include Brubaker, Castles, Clifford, Cohen, Sheffer, and Tololyan.[3] The concept of a diaspora varies greatly. According to Cohen, all diasporic communities settled outside their natal (or imagined natal) territories acknowledge that "the old country"—a notion often deeply embedded in language, religion, custom, or folklore—always lays some claim to their loyalty and emotions. That claim may be strong or weak, and boldly or meekly articulated in a given circumstance or historical period, but the adherence of a member to a diasporic community is demonstrated by the acceptance of an inescapable link to a past migration history and a sense of co-ethnicity with others from a similar background.[4]

The initial concept of a diaspora implied a forced movement of people who then lived in exile. The "ideal" notion of diaspora is presented by the Jewish tradition. Cohen points out that contrary to the ancient Greeks, who thought of a diaspora in terms of migration and colonization, and to Jews, Africans, Palestinians, and Armenians for whom diasporas signified collective traumas, contemporary diasporas are populations living abroad

---

[2] Quoted in *Ibid.*, 17–19, 21–22.

[3] M. Boyd, "Family and Personal Networks in International Migration: Recent Developments and New Agendas," *International Migration Review* 23, no. 3 (1989): 638–670; S. Castles and J.M. Miller, *The Age of Migration: International Population Movements in the Modern World* (London: Macmillan, 1993); R. Cohen, *Global Diasporas: An Introduction* (London: UCL Press, 1997); G. Sheffer, ed., *Modern Diasporas in International Politics* (New York: St. Martin's Press, 1986); W. Safran, "Comparing Diasporas: A Review Essay," *Diaspora* 8, no. 3 (1999): 255–291; K. Tololyan, "Rethinking Diaspora(s): Stateless Power in the Transnational Moment," *Diaspora* 5, no. 1 (1996): 3–35; and others.

[4] Cohen, *Global Diasporas: An Introduction*, IX.

who, in many cases, are neither active agents of colonization nor passive victims of persecution. Notwithstanding, they do maintain strong collective identities.[5]

Cohen identifies the following types of diasporas based on the initial cause/incentive to migrate. Victim diasporas are created as a result of persecution, massacres, and exile—for example, the Jewish, African, and Armenian diasporas. An imperial diaspora, like that of Great Britain, maintains ties of loyalty and deference to the mother country and can become what he terms a quasi-diaspora through a process of creolization, in which new settlers marry into the local community or actually turn against their homelands. The obvious paradigm here is what could broadly be described as the Latin American model. Other types are labor diasporas (Indians), trade diasporas (Chinese and Lebanese, active in entrepreneurship and trade), and cultural diasporas (Caribbean peoples).[6] Cohen identifies the Indian and Chinese diasporas as formed by voluntary, rather than forced, labor through ethnic entrepreneurship and trade migration. There are numerous examples of labor migrant diasporas that have emerged in the second half of the twentieth century: Turkish *gastarbeiter* in Germany that arrived in the 1950s, Filipino and Chinese migrants in Southeast Asia since the 1970s and 1980s, and Mexican workers in the United States since the 1970s. The emergence of a new type of labor diaspora from Central Asia in the post-Soviet states can currently be observed, particularly Tajik, Uzbek, and Kyrgyz diasporas in Russia and Kazakhstan, and trade and entrepreneurship diasporas, such as the Han Chinese in Russia, and the Chinese and Uyghur diasporas in Kazakhstan and Kyrgyzstan.[7]

In his analytic overview of the various types of diasporas, Cohen identifies them according to specific ethnicities and causes/incentives to migrate. It is essential to explore these types of diasporas and how they structure communities and attempt to preserve their ethnic, cultural, and collective identity. He also argues that it is important to understand the challenges diasporas face in the globalized world, especially in the midst of a deepening economic crisis, when issues of survival (jobs, shelter, and safety) become of paramount importance for migrant groups.

---

[5] *Ibid.*

[6] *Ibid.*, 151–54.

[7] E. Sadovskaia, "Kitaiskaia migratsiia v Tsentral'noi Azii: Kazakhstan, Kyrgyzstan, i dalee vezde?" in E.I. Safonova, ed., *China in the Regional and World Politics* (Moscow: The Far East Institute of the Russian Academy of Sciences, 2009).

Contemporary diasporas and labor migration in the former Soviet Union are a new social phenomenon,[8] emerging against a backdrop of a number of more well-established ethnic diasporas. The latter appeared as a result of the forced, spontaneous, and mass migrations that followed the dissolution of the Soviet Union in December 1991, and a number of violent conflicts prior to or shortly after its collapse. These forced migrations and diasporas have been extensively studied by Russian scholars, including Arutyunayan, Astvatsaturova, Drobizheva, Kosmarskaya, Poloskova, Tishkov, and Zayonchkovskaya, among others. Conventionally defined, a diaspora generally refers to an ethnic migrant community dispersed in a different environment outside of its country of origin. The people in this community typically share a common history, cultural traditions, and language. In-depth studies of emergent post-Soviet labor migrant diasporas are relatively new.[9]

Rather than conceptualizing the notion of the diaspora or exploring the multiethnic composition and history of diasporic communities in Central Asia, the aim here is to study some of the aspects of temporary labor migrant diasporas and newly arrived permanent residents from Central Asian countries over the last 10 to 20 years. These migrant diasporas are a new phenomenon in the post-Soviet destination countries—primarily limited to Kazakhstan and Russia—and as such remain largely unstudied. Among a variety of existing concepts and definitions, Cohen's appears to be the most relevant to the analysis of post-Soviet migrations and diasporas.

---

[8] The free movement of individuals per se is a new phenomenon in post-Soviet states, which came about through the adoption of new laws and the simplification of the *propiska* regime (residence permit and obligatory registration) at the end of the 1980s and beginning of the 1990s.

[9] The reader may find more details on diaspora formation in the works of Brusina, Diatlov, Kuznetsov, Mukomel', Popkov, and Zotova. V. Diatlov, *Sovremennye torgovye men'shinstva: faktor stabil'nosti ili konflikta? (Kitaitsy i kavkaztsy v Irkutske)* (Moscow: Natalis, 2000); V. Diatlov, "Trudovye migratsii i protsess diasporalizatsii v sovremennoi Rossii," in Zh. Zaionchkovskaia, ed., *Trudovaia migratsiia v SNG: Sotsial'nye i economicheskie effekty* (Moscow: Adamant, 2003); I.M. Kuznetsov and V.I. Mukomel', *Adaptatsionnye vozmozhnosti i setevye sviazi migrantskikh etnicheskikh men'shinstv* (Moscow: Institut sotsiologii RAN, 2005); V. Popkov, *Fenomen etnicheskikh diaspor* (Moscow: Institut sotsiologii RAN, 2003); and others.

Central Asia: Mixed Regional and Global Trends

Regionalization Trends

While the CIS remains a common migration system that unites nearly all post-Soviet countries, Kazakhstan in particular, especially since 2000, has emerged as a recipient state,[10] becoming the center for the sub-regional migration system in Central Asia. Conversely, Kyrgyzstan, Tajikistan, Turkmenistan, and Uzbekistan have mainly served as sending countries.[11] Formation of this regional migratory subsystem can be attributed to a number of factors: disparities in economic development among the republics of Central Asia; lack of balance in the regional labor market (with a demand for labor in Kazakhstan and an excess of labor resources in the remaining countries of the region); differences in the countries' demographic potential (with populations of 26.3 million in Uzbekistan, 15.4 million in Kazakhstan, 5.1 million in Kyrgyzstan, 6.9 million in Tajikistan, and 5.3 million (author's estimate) in Turkmenistan in 2006).

According to the author's assessments, the number of undocumented immigrants in Kazakhstan ranged from 500,000 to 700,000, and even up to 1 million, in the 2005–8 period, and presumably more when shuttle traders are taken into account. Migrant labor flows to Kazakhstan from the neighboring republics are, however, eclipsed by Russia, which receives the lion's share of migrants within the CIS. According to the latest estimates by the Committee on Migration and Employment of Kyrgyzstan, the overall number of labor emigrants from Kyrgyzstan amounted to 500,000 people in 2008, while experts estimate this figure to be higher still—up

---

[10] E. Sadovskaia, *Migratsiia v Kazakhstane na rubezhe XXI veka: novye tendentsii i perspektivy* (Almaty: Galym, 2001), 165–186; E. Sadovskaia, "Respublika Kazakhstan kak strana immigratsii: novye tendentsii v razvitii trudovykh migratsii v Tsentral'noi Azii," in *Ekonomicheskie i pravovye problemy garmonizatsii zakonodatel'stva v oblasti zashchity prav i obespecheniia interesov lichnosti v usloviakh globalizatsii: teoriia i praktika stran SNG* (Almaty: Kazakh State University, 2005), 45–50; E. Sadovskaia, "Trudovaia migratsiia v stranakh Tsentral'noi Azii: noveishie tendentsii," in *Migratsiia v Tsentral'noi Azii: problemy i perspektivy* (Almaty: Daik-Press, 2005), 17–31.

[11] E. Sadovskaia, et al., *Trudovaia migratsiia v stranakh Tsentralnoi Azii, Rossiiskoi Federatsii, Afganistane i Pakistane* (Almaty: European Commission, IOM, 2005); E. Sadovskaia, "Novye tendentsii v migratsionnykh protsessakh v Tsentral'noi Azii i podkhody v ikh kontseptualizatsii," in *Globalization and socio-cultural adaptation. Proceedings of the II Congress of Kazakhstan Sociologists* (Astana: Kazakhstan Sociologists' Association, 2006), 220–224; E. Sadovskaia, "International Labor Migration, Remittances and Development in Central Asia: towards Regionalization or Globalization?" in *Migration and Development. Proceedings of Moscow State Lomonosov University International Conference* (Moscow: Moscow State Lomonosov University, 2007).

to 1 million.[12] Two-thirds of them work in Russia whereas one-third work in Kazakhstan. This means that 25 to 35 percent of Kyrgyzstan's economically active population is abroad. It is a similar story in Tajikistan, where this figure ranges from 25 to 30 percent, or even more, according to some experts.

Expert estimates of the number of labor migrants from Uzbekistan range from two to three million, and from three to five million, even.[13] The share of the economically active population annually working abroad has risen rapidly in the past several years: from 5 to 10 percent in 2003–4, to 20–25 percent in 2007–8. The "migration wave" from Uzbekistan to Kazakhstan and Russia is on the rise and is expected to peak in the near future; following the arrival on the job market of the new generation. In 2006–7, the annual inflow of labor immigrants was equivalent to up to 12 percent of the economically active population of Kazakhstan.[14]

The distribution of migration flows among Central Asian states confirms existing regional trends. According to the Border Service of the State Security Committee of Kazakhstan, the major migration exchange in Kazakhstan takes place between CIS states. For instance, in 2004, 95.7 percent of foreign nationals arrived in Kazakhstan from former Soviet countries and only 4.3 percent from outside of the CIS. Nationals of Kyrgyzstan (36.4 percent), Russia (30.6 percent), Uzbekistan (24.6 percent), and Tajikistan (4.7 percent) made up an overwhelming majority of the CIS arrivals; other CIS countries accounted for 3.7 percent. Citizens from China, Germany, and Turkey accounted for 22.6 percent, 21.4 percent, and 12.4 percent of non-CIS arrivals, respectively, with other countries making up the remaining 43.6 percent.[15]

The major destination countries for Kyrgyz migrants are Russia and Kazakhstan: 98.1 percent of migrants move to these two countries, seeking permanent residence, and only 1 percent emigrate to countries outside of

---

[12] Expert interviews conducted by the author using a standard semi-structured questionnaire in Almaty and Bishkek, from 2004 to 2008, in the framework of various international projects.

[13] F. Djani, "Goskomstat Uzbekistana poobeshchal chto budet i vpred' povyshat' kachestvo zhizni naseleniia," *Ferghana.ru*, March 4, 2009, http://www.ferghana.ru/article.php?id=6083.

[14] As far as the major migration flows are illegal migrants, no registrations or official statistics exist on their numbers. The assessment is based on expert estimates, the results of sociological surveys, comparative migrant household surveys, ministerial statistics, and indirect indicators.

[15] Calculated by the author according to the current statistical data of border crossings by the Border Service of the State Security Committee of Kazakhstan.

the CIS. Bearing in mind the future socio-demographic prospects of such countries as Kazakhstan and Kyrgyzstan, growing Chinese migration and the forming of Chinese communities in Central Asia may also be considered as a newly emergent regional trend.[16]

Formation of the regional migration subsystem in Central Asia has been facilitated by geographical proximity, the liberalization of regulations pertaining to migration, and other favorable factors such as similar climates and socio-cultural environments, including language and religion. The majority of the populations in all five of the Central Asian states are associated with Sunni Islam and speak Turkic languages (with the exception of Tajikistan). The Russian language is also still widely used as a lingua franca for interstate and international communication in the region. Socio-cultural similarities and a common linguistic space serve as important factors in the emergence of a (so far) largely unregulated "common migration space" and of migrant diasporas in the destination countries.

Transportation and communications infrastructure in the destination country or region, and the relatively low costs of travel and communication, are additional factors that households take into consideration when making the choice to migrate. Poverty-stricken rural families often cannot afford to pay for an expensive flight to Russia or further afield. Labor migration is mainly temporary and circular in nature, following a pattern of seasonal migrations. It allows families with many children, common in Kyrgyzstan and Uzbekistan, to send the head of the household to work for several months and to join him (or her) for a period in the summer or autumn in order to maximize profits from their migration. Migrants also find it easier to make short visits back to their homes during the season if and when the need arises.

The above is confirmed by the responses of migrant laborers from Central Asian republics working in Kazakhstan. According to a 2004–6 sociological survey, the most important motivating factor for deciding to migrate was related to income. This was stated by an average of 40 percent

---

[16] E. Sadovskaia, "Kitaiskaia migratsiia v Kazakhstane: sovremennye tendentsii i perspektivy," *Analytic,* no. 6 (2007): 33–45; E. Sadovskaia, "Chinese Migration to Kazakhstan: a Silk Road for Cooperation or a Thorny Road of Prejudice?" *The China and Eurasia Forum Quarterly* 8, no. 4 (2007): 147–170; E. Sadovskaia, "Etnicheskaia struktura sovremennykh migratsii iz Kitaia v Kazakhstan i problem prinimaiushchego obshchestva," *Eurasia News,* no. 2 (2008).

of respondents in three countries: Kyrgyzstan, Tajikistan, and Uzbekistan.[17] Additionally, migrants mentioned that it was easier (25.2 percent) and cheaper (23.8 percent) for them to get back home for visits from their current destination areas. In terms of earnings, higher remuneration was the main motivation for immigrants from Kyrgyzstan (57 percent) and Tajikistan (41.2 percent). For Uzbek immigrants, cheap travel ranked first (49.2 percent), and Kazakhstan's proximity and ease of return visits to their families was second (44.4 percent).

Contemporary migration in Central Asia now has a "younger" face. Those born in the favorable demographic period of the 1980s, and who have tried and failed to find jobs in their home cities or villages, have been forced to move abroad; and it is the titular populations of the countries sending migrants (Kyrgyz, Tajiks, and Uzbeks) that are predominant in labor migrant flows. Their level of Russian tends to be relatively low, and they have limited knowledge of the laws and their rights. This impedes their adaptation to and integration in local communities in the destination countries and exacerbates violations of their rights.

One cannot predict how the post-crisis situation will affect labor migration in sending and receiving countries in the near term, but it will undoubtedly have an impact on migration size and structure, remittances, and development issues.[18]

Globalization Trends in Central Asia

Alongside regionalization, contemporary labor migration in Central Asia has become increasingly affected by trends of globalization. The globalization of economic production, growing foreign investment, and the

[17] Sociological surveys among labor migrants in the southern region of Kazakhstan in April–May 2005, in which 255 people were interviewed using a personal standardized questionnaire. Respondents were selected through snowball sampling. The sampling was targeted and homogenous. The geographic scope of the research included the cities of Almaty and Shilik, localities in the Shilik district of the Almaty oblast, the city of Shymkent, and some localities in the Dzhetysai district of the Southern Kazakhstan oblast. The project was funded by the John D. and Katherine T. MacArthur Foundation in 2004–6.

[18] The August 2007 subprime mortgage crisis in the United States and the financial crisis of 2008, which spun off into global economic crisis, have affected the banking and construction sectors in Kazakhstan. The construction sector was the first to decline followed by the industrial sector. According to Minister of Industry and Trade Vladimir Shkolnik, 283 Kazakhstan enterprises had fully or partially stopped their production by March 2009. Many construction sites were "frozen" and labor migrants fired. V. Panfilova, "Kazakhstan gets rid of migrant workers," *Nezavisimaia gazeta*, March 10, 2009, http://asiaplus.tj/articles/39/3173.html.

activities of transnational corporations stimulate the mobility of capital, goods, and services in Russia and Central Asia, particularly in Kazakhstan, but increasingly in Turkmenistan and Uzbekistan, which are becoming strategically significant due to their oil and gas reserves. International labor emigration from Central Asia has been increasing in response to capital flows and the emergence of new technologies, providing transportation and communication services in even the most remote parts of the region. For example, a number of electronic money transfer systems have sprung up, with thousands of service bureaus dotted across the Central Asian republics.[19]

The mobility of Central Asian labor forces increased in the first decade of the twenty-first century, both in terms of the number of migrants and the range of destination countries, including also the diversity of employment sectors and professions. Destination countries are not limited to the CIS, but now include Eastern and Western Europe, and North America. According to the State Committee on Migration of Kyrgyzstan, around 30,000 Kyrgyz citizens traveled outside the CIS in 2005. Some media sources report that around 10,000 were illegally employed in the United Kingdom alone.[20] Labor migrants from Tajikistan, meanwhile, tend to find jobs almost exclusively in CIS countries; however, there are skilled contractors working in Canada, and some Tajik and Kyrgyz drivers and housekeepers have been working in Saudi Arabia since 2008. In fact, the government of Tajikistan signed an agreement with Saudi Arabia on labor force recruitment.

In the poorest countries of the region—Kyrgyzstan, Tajikistan, and Uzbekistan—unskilled labor forces are "pushed" to countries situated in close proximity, while highly qualified specialists are motivated to move to more developed countries. The strategies of these two groups are based on "cost" and "benefit" considerations. According to the well-known Uzbekistan expert Maksakova, 10–15 percent of contemporary Uzbek labor migration is directed to countries beyond the CIS, such as the United States, Israel, Turkey, Greece, and other European countries; however, the majority still migrate to Russia and Kazakhstan.[21] Shuttle trade

---

19 E. Sadovskaia, "Denezhnye perevody trudovykh migrantov i ikh rol' v migrantskikh domokhoziaistvakh Tsentral'noi Azii," *Central Asia and the Caucasus*, no. 3 (2006): 109–123.

20 Sadovskaia, et al., *Trudovaia migratsiia v stranakh Tsentralnoi Azii, Rossiiskoi Federatsii, Afganistane i Pakistane v 2000e gody*, 40.

21 L.P. Maksakova, "Eksport rabochei sily iz Uzbekistana," in Zaionchkovskaia, ed., *Trudovaia migratsiia v SNG: sotsial'nye i economicheskie effekty*.

has an even larger geographical scope: Canada, China, Germany, Greece, India, Italy, the Netherlands, Pakistan, Poland, Turkey, United Arab Emirates, and the United States.

To give an example of the combination of regional and global trends, as well as the applicability of different theoretical and conceptual approaches to the analysis of international migration in Central Asia, it is worth considering the movement of temporary (predominantly seasonal) workers from the Osh oblast in southern Kyrgyzstan to tobacco farms in the Almaty region of Kazakhstan. Macro- and micro-level economic factors that influence the decision of a Kyrgyz migrant to find a job in Kazakhstan include: dynamic economic growth in Kazakhstan from 2000 to 2007, as a result of favorable prices for Kazakhstan's oil in the global market; the development of the tobacco industry in the Almaty oblast through the reconstruction of existing infrastructure as well as reinvigorated international investment by transnational tobacco companies such as Philip Morris; higher wages in Kazakhstan; high unemployment and low wages in the southern areas of Kyrgyzstan; relatively liberal legislation; bilateral agreements between Kazakhstan and Kyrgyzstan on cross-border labor migration and quotas for officially recruited, semi-skilled Kyrgyz agricultural workers; demand for labor in the agrarian sector in and around the city of Almaty; geographical proximity to Kazakhstan, which facilitates migration (for instance, low transportation and communication costs, opportunities to visit relatives throughout the season, opportunity to employ family members as seasonal labor during the summer, and the easy use of unofficial channels to send back money); a more developed social infrastructure in Kazakhstan, and access to medical and educational facilities (some pregnant Kyrgyz women arrive in the last weeks of their pregnancies, give birth to their babies, and resume work in the tobacco fields shortly thereafter);[22] and the presence of diasporas and migrant networks with informal ties among Kyrgyz compatriots or even fellow-villagers who often work at the same farms and are able to assist one another in finding jobs and housing.

All these factors influence not only the individual decision to migrate, but also the decision by an entire household or several households in seeking to minimize the costs of and maximize the profits from their

[22] According to the data (for nine months in 2008) of the health department of Almaty, 27,448 babies were born; 5,324 mothers were not residents of the city; 2 percent of them, or 106 persons, were nationals of foreign states. Sh. Dandybaeva, "Meditsinskaia pomoshch' migrantam v meditsinskikh organizatsiiakh goroda," in *Snizhenie riskov trudovoi migratsii i torgovli liud'mi* (Almaty, Eretpes NGO seminar materials, 2009), 25.

move. Obviously, the existence of diasporas in the destination countries is not decisive among the reasons to migrate, but diasporas and networks undoubtedly do play an important role in establishing migration routes.

Migrant Diasporas and Networks: Dynamic Changes, Diverse Manifestations

Newly Emergent Migrant Diasporas

As defined here, migrant diasporas encompass migrants of the same ethnicity or citizenship (for instance, ethnic Kyrgyz permanently residing in Russia, or Kyrgyzstani citizens but of different ethnicities temporarily employed in Russia) permanently or temporarily residing, whether compactly or dispersedly settled, on the territory of another country for different purposes (employment, permanent residence, or political asylum).

The rising role of diasporas in facilitating and stimulating migration, as well as promoting business cooperation, can be observed. For example, as many as one million ethnic Germans from Kazakhstan and Kyrgyzstan, and about half a million from Russia and other CIS states, as well as members of mixed interethnic marriages, have formed a "wave" of resettlement—*aussiedler* and *spätaussiedler*—to Germany since the end of the 1980s. With the exception of CIS states, Germany is the main destination country for migrants from Kazakhstan, with Germany also ranking among Kazakhstan's top three international trade partners. Diasporic links with ethnic Germans in the country of origin are conducive to migration, including trade and business migration, and private travel and tourism between Germany and former Soviet republics.

In the last 20 years, over 2.5 million former citizens of Kazakhstan have moved permanently to Russia. In addition to historically based links, there are other motivators spurring migration, such as family reunification, entrepreneurship, and trade, between the two states. Russia's top ranking among Kazakhstan's international trade partners can be attributed primarily to long-term economic and trade ties; however, trade and business links between individual entrepreneurs are also developing rapidly. The considerable share of remittances sent back from Russia and Germany to Kazakhstan also points to intensive cooperation between diasporas and their countries of origin, indicative of rising transnational trends on the Eurasian continent.

Kazakhstan has a large Uzbek diaspora (370,663 people), but relatively small Tajik (25,659) and Kyrgyz (10,897, according to the 1999 census) diasporas. Uzbeks constitute the third-largest ethnic minority of Kazakhstan, numbering 90 percent of those populations residing in the southern oblasts of Kazakhstan neighboring Uzbekistan. The deterioration of the economy in Uzbekistan in the 1990s and kinship relations stimulated migration from Uzbekistan to Kazakhstan. Migrant communities in the receiving country and networking with fellow compatriots in the sending country have further spurred labor migration to Kazakhstan.

As previously stated, the most stable annual migration in-flow to Kazakhstan is comprised of Kyrgyz labor migrants, who have gradually formed an ethnic diaspora by using the routine mechanisms common to many receiving countries. Since in Kazakhstan a Kyrgyz migrant may lease land, subsequent "waves" of migration have included relatives and other compatriots, where together they grow tobacco and cultivate land. Some Kyrgyz migrants have even got married or gained Kazakh citizenship. No empirical studies have been done, however, to explore what role, if any, the Kyrgyz diaspora in Kazakhstan plays in this process.

The emerging Tajik and Kyrgyz migrant diasporas in the Russian Federation (both permanent and temporary residents) promote the expansion of all types of migration to Russia.[23] Migrant diasporas and networks are especially important in more "traditional" societies, where relations are built around family or kinship groups, and are especially important in conflict or post-conflict situations, such as Tajikistan. During and after the civil war in the 1990s, hundreds of thousands of Tajik nationals fled the country and formed compact settlements and spheres of employment, the majority electing to go to Russia while the remainder went to different CIS countries. *Avlod*, the traditional kinship-based community, plays a vital role in Tajik life. It forms migrant networks ready to help new Tajik migrants in finding jobs and apartments, and provides support and protection in the case that migrants are detained or put into prison for working illegally.[24]

Interviews by the author in 2007 with a group of Tajik migrants, who had been working in Moscow and were planning to apply for permanent

---

[23] According to the data of Kyrgyz State Statistics Committee in 2007, the share of ethnic Kyrgyz among the total number of emigrants from the country comprised 50.2 percent (27,437 people), Russians 24.1 percent (13,143 people), and all other ethnic groups 25.7 percent. The overwhelming majority of them emigrated to Russia and Kazakhstan. The high share of ethnic Kyrgyz should be compared with the share of Kyrgyz in total emigration flows in previous years: 31 percent in 2006, 20.5 percent in 2005, and 12.4 percent in 2004.

[24] S. Olimova and I. Bosc, *Trudovaia migratsiia iz Tadzhikistana* (Dushanbe: IOM and Research Center Sharq, 2003), 51.

residence in Russia, revealed that the oldest among them was 40 years old and had migrated to Moscow in the mid-1990s. And whilst he held a specialized professional certificate and had experience in electro-technical services, he had been employed only on an unofficial basis. When in the 2000s the construction boom took off in Moscow, he informed his relatives of the new opportunities available and some of them joined him at different job sites in the Moscow area. The next group of relatives and fellow villagers arrived later, some of them without a specialized professional education. One did not speak Russian at all. However, this older and more experienced migrant helped them to find a cheap apartment and jobs as cleaners, unskilled laborers at the construction site, and as traders at the wholesale bazaar. He also made money transfers as a consolidated sum from several unregistered migrant workers in his circle and helped them out in other difficult situations. They also celebrated their national holidays together.

A human rights activist and leader of the Tajikistan Fund in Moscow, Gavkhar Djuraeva, said that when faced with extremely difficult situations, she usually went to where a Tajik diaspora from a specific region of Tajikistan was compactly living or working, and appealed to them to render assistance to a fellow villager from Badakhshan, Sogd, Khatlon, or any other region, who found himself in trouble. There were no cases, Djuraeva admitted, where people refused to assist a fellow compatriot where they could. Ties of kinship and community are very important, and relatives or fellow-villagers are invariably helpful when members are faced with a difficult situation.[25]

Migrant diasporas can be identified not only by ethnicity and country of origin, but also by the purpose of their migration, duration of stay, and the adaptation dynamics at play in the receiving community. For example, the majority of Russians from Central Asia who moved to Russia to seek permanent residence there in the last 15 to 20 years may be perceived as "other Russians" by the recipient communities upon their arrival.[26] As a rule, however, the adaptation and integration of Russians in Russia is comparatively fast. On the other hand, the integration of Germans from Kazakhstan, Kyrgyzstan, and Russia in Germany, within the frame-

---

[25] Expert interview with human rights activist Gavkhar Djuraeva, the leader of the Tajikistan Fund, Moscow, October 2006.

[26] "Drugie russkie: mobilizovannaia mental'nost'," Research project led by Boris Firsov at the European University of St. Petersburg, 2000–2, http://www.cisr.ru/complete_etnos.en.html.

work of the latter's repatriation policy, will most likely take one or two generations.

Migrant diaspora formation is also influenced by the period migrants stay in the destination country, and their individual and group strategies. Some plan to stay and seek permanent residence in the destination country, while others plan to return to their country of origin. Some still are seasonal migrants and try to be independent and rely on themselves. Many Tajik, Kyrgyz, and Uzbek migrants remain undocumented in Kazakhstan and Russia, deprived of rights and opportunities. Their illegal status may serve as an impediment to their adaptation and integration; however, the existing diaspora may prove helpful in a number of dangerous and "sensitive" situations such as detentions and deportations.[27]

The spectrum of social and legal statuses of different migrant groups within one diaspora is considerable, ranging from illegal, unqualified, and impoverished migrants to prosperous, legally residing, or qualified specialists and university students.[28] With rare exceptions, no representative studies have been undertaken to explore whether more educated and successful first wave immigrants, who have access to savings, credit, or government assistance—in other words, to cultural, social, and financial capital—help the newly arrived, or if, on the contrary, stratification has increased alienation. Migrant diasporas from Tajikistan could serve as a case study, since their history and contemporary status represents a variety of strategies and the continuum of stratified migrant communities. Another case is those many thousands of Kazakh citizens who have obtained Russian citizenship without renouncing their Kazakh citizenship, though both states forbid dual citizenship. Similar to the situation with illegal migrants, they are difficult to evaluate, but nonetheless remain a very important phenomenon to study in terms of diaspora resources for adaptation and integration.

Since the beginning of the 2000s, and especially during the economic crisis of 2008–9, members of the Central Asian diasporas have undertaken intensive efforts to organize formal social associations to protect their

---

27 O. Brusina, "Migranty iz Srednei Azii v Rossii: etapy i prichiny priezda, sotsial'nye tipy, organizatsii diaspor," *Vestnik Evrazii* 40, no. 2 (2008): 66–95; N. Zotova, "Mekhanizmy adaptatsii migrantov iz Tsentralnoi Azii v Rossii," *APN.kz*, November 7, 2006, http://www.apn.kz/publications/article6823.htm.

28 For one of these "success stories," see: A. Kaipova, "Uzbek iz Tadzhikistana prodolzhil dinastiiu vrachei. No uzhe v Rossii," *Ferghana.ru*, March 19, 2009, www.ferghana.ru/article.php?id=6102.

rights.[29] These social organizations serve both to assist group communication and develop relationships with local communities, authorities, and the mass media. An example of this kind of consolidation of contemporary diasporas is the establishment of the International Union of Labor Migrants Support in Yekaterinburg in March 2009. According to Geydar Djemal', the leader of the Union, the major goal of this social movement is the protection of labor migrants' rights, the consolidation of diasporas irrespective of religious and cultural differences, and the promotion of ethnic minorities as active participants in political life.[30]

The current economic crisis raises a number of questions. Will it speed up the process of migrants' "atomization," or on the contrary, provide an opportunity to unite the most active to protect those migrants most in need? Will the crisis pave the way for the establishment of social organizations for diaspora viability and development? Do these newly established non-governmental organizations and, potentially, professional trade unions testify to a "shift" in diasporas from relying on ethnic consolidation toward social and political activism? These are the transformations that require more scholarly attention and in-depth study.

The Role of "Migrant Networks" in Organizing Migrations in Kazakhstan

Alongside diasporas, migrant networks are also very important in facilitating migration in Central Asia and the post-Soviet space in general. They consist of sets of interpersonal ties that connect migrants, former migrants, and non-migrants in receiving and sending areas through bonds of kinship, friendship, and shared community origin.[31] Migrant diasporas in the receiving country networking with compatriots in the sending country can help migrants to find jobs and housing, assist in difficult economic and legal situations, and send money via unofficial channels. The emergence of such informal networks between migrants, communities, and regions enhances human capital and facilitates mobility.

---

[29] "Fond Tadzhikistan pomogaet vernut' zarplaty gastarbaiteram," *Ferghana.ru*, December 22, 2008, http://www.ferghana.ru/index.php?did=4&bracket_flag=; "*Yiyntymak*—kirgizskaia diaspora v Tatarstane," *Ferghana.ru*, May 4, 2007, http://www.ferghana.ru/index.php?did=4&bracket_flag=1.

[30] "V Rossii sozdan internatsional'nyi soiuz podderzhki trudovykh migrantov," *Ferghana.ru*, February 22, 2009, www.ferghana.ru/article.php?id=6075.

[31] Massey, Arango, Hugo, Kouaouci, Pellegrino, and Taylor, *Worlds in Motion. Understanding International Migration at the End of the Millennium*, 42.

According to a sociological survey on labor migration, conducted by the author in southern Kazakhstan in 2005, 60 percent of respondents obtained information about potential jobs from friends, acquaintances, and neighbors, 35.7 percent from relatives, 20 percent from colleagues, 16.1 percent on their own initiative, 9 percent from middlemen, 6.7 percent from the state employment service, and 1.2 percent from newspapers or the Internet (the total sum of the responses exceeds 100 percent because respondents could choose several options).[32]

In terms of those who had assisted them to travel, surveyed migrants mentioned acquaintances and fellow villagers in the countries of origin (25 percent), recruiting agencies (7.1 percent) and employers (1.3 percent), and relatives (3.5 percent). The majority—66 percent of respondents—indicated that they had traveled to the destination area by themselves. 14.8 percent didn't give any answer; presumably, some of them crossed the border and worked illegally in Kazakhstan.

According to the survey, many labor migrants found employment through informal channels. The majority, 31 percent, found jobs via friends and acquaintances, 22 percent via relatives, and 20 percent on their own. Middlemen in spontaneous labor markets, through "black" exchanges, facilitate illegal employment. Furthermore, the institutional mechanisms of legal employment are weak: only 5 to 7 percent of migrants find jobs via recruiting agencies.

That informal ties among migrants play a significant role is reflected in their responses to the question regarding who assists them once they reach the destination area: relatives are mentioned most frequently (43.1 percent), followed by migrants in destination communities (34.9 percent), and fellow compatriots (32.5 percent). Employers were mentioned by only 10.2 percent of respondents and local residents by 9.8 percent. Just 0.4 percent of respondents mentioned the participation of recruiting agencies in supporting and resolving migrants' problems (see Table 1).

Remittances of Labor Migrants and the Role of Networks

Remittances are an important outcome of labor migration. The International Organization for Migration (IOM) defines migrant remittances broadly as monetary transfers that a migrant makes to the country of origin, or in other words, the financial flows associated with migration.

---

32 Data unpublished.

Table 1. Who Supports Labor Immigrants at the Destination Area in South Kazakhstan? (2005)

Who supports you at the place of destination?	Respondents	Percent
Relatives	110	43.1
Other immigrants in the destination area	89	34.9
Compatriots from the same *aul, kishlak* (village) in the country of origin	83	32.5
Employer	26	10.2
Local residents	25	9.8
Friends, acquaintances	6	2.4
Recruiting agency's staff	1	0.4
Nobody	23	9
No answer	5	2
Sample	255	100

Note: respondents could choose several response options, thus the sum is more than 100 percent.

Most of the time, remittances take the form of personal cash transfers from a migrant worker or immigrant to a relative in the country of origin. Remittances can also be funds invested in, deposited in, or donated by the migrant to the country of origin. The definition could possibly be further broadened to include personal transfers and donations made in-kind.

There are two basic types of remittances by labor migrants: official and "unofficial." Various international and national money transfer systems are used as official channels to send money. However, many migrants still bring money home by themselves or send their earnings unofficially via friends, relatives, or through informal money transfer systems such as *hawala.*

Currently used in many countries, hawala is an alternative money transfer system that operates parallel to the common banking system. It differs from other money transfer systems in that it is based on trust and the extensive use of family connections and regional affiliations. Money transfers are carried out thanks to the ties between the members of the networks of hawala dealers, usually relatives or representatives of one clan.[33] In countries like Tajikistan, and according to some experts Uzbekistan, many migrants still hand over earned money unofficially via friends, relatives, or the hawala system.

[33] "The hawala alternative remittance system and its role in money laundering," Interpol General Secretariat, Lyon, January 2000, http://www.interpol.int/Public/FinancialCrime/MoneyLaundering/hawala/.

Diasporas and networks play an important role in ensuring safe channels for sending money home unofficially. The spread of unofficial means to transmit funds and the amount of remittances sent depends on such parameters as follows: the number of labor migrants, their employment sectors, wage levels, the duration of the working period, the share of wages transferred to the household, the level of development of the (inter) national money transfer systems, the access of migrants to money transfer services, geographical closeness, the share of legal versus undocumented migrants, migrant networks, and the potential opportunity to send money by unofficial means.[34]

According to the sociological survey in southern Kazakhstan, 41.2 percent of labor migrants take back money they have earned by themselves, 23.9 percent send it back with friends, and 14.9 percent with relatives. Only 17.6 percent, or less than one-fifth of the total number, regularly transfer money by post (see Table 2).

Table 2. Means of Transferring Money to Families

How do you transfer money to your families?	Respondents	Percent
I carry it on my own	105	41.2
I send it with friends	61	23.9
I send it with relatives	38	14.9
Western Union money transfer	24	9.4
Postal remittance	21	8.2
I don't send it	12	4.7
I use it to buy goods and carry them by myself	4	1.6
I have not sent any money yet, since it's my first visit	4	1.6
I send it with a special person	3	1.2
I don't know / no answer	37	14.5
Sample	255	100

Note: Respondents could choose more than one option, therefore the total is more than 100 percent.

[34] For more details, see E. Sadovskaia, "Denezhnye perevody trudovykh migrantov: rol' v migrantskikh domokhoziaistvakh i soobshchestvakh Tsentral'noi Azii," in V. Tishkov and E. Fillipova, eds., *Etnicheskaia situatsiia i konflikty v SNG i gosudarstvakh Baltii* (Moscow: Institute of Ethnology and Anthropology of the Russian Academy of Sciences, 2006), 48–60; E. Sadovskaia, "Remittances and their role for labor migrants' households in the Republics of Central Asia," *Central Asian Affairs*, no. 3 (2006): 36–40.

It should be noted that the above survey was conducted in 2005, and that since then, the share of those who use money transfer systems has risen considerably. However, the irregular and illegal component of migration between migrant-recipient Kazakhstan and neighboring Uzbekistan remains high. The majority of Uzbek immigrants to Kazakhstan, and especially to the region of South Kazakhstan, are impoverished and engaged in the agrarian sector, where wages are low and remuneration for migrants therefore modest. These migrants try to preserve their earnings by not paying commission for sending them via transfer systems, but rather pass them to relatives, fellow villagers, and acquaintances, or more often, carry the money themselves.

Contrary to Uzbek migrants coming back from Russia, who typically bring back expensive household (electric) appliances, clothes, footwear, and other goods (usually for private use by families, and rarely for sale),[35] only 1.6 percent of respondents returning from South Kazakhstan, and presumably some of the 14.5 percent respondents who gave no answer, bring back goods to their households. Money earned in Kazakhstan is used mostly for satisfying everyday needs. Both personal interviews with migrants and official statistics confirm this.

In terms of flows to Uzbekistan, experts estimate that the amount of income from migration in 2002, including remittances, money brought back independently, and the value of imported goods, amounted to at least $225 million. Five years later, in 2007, remittances totaled more than $1 billion. According to the Central Bank of Uzbekistan, the amount of remittances sent via the Unistream money transfer system alone amounted to $787 million in 2008.[36] Bearing in mind that according to UN assessments more than 40 percent of remittances are sent through "unofficial" channels, the total amount of remittances is much higher and equivalent to a significant portion of Uzbekistan's GDP.

The amount of remittances flowing back to Kyrgyzstan has also grown steadily: from $120 million in 2003 to $1.2 billion in 2008, just before the world crisis. Yet, according to the National Bank of Kazakhstan, residents and non-residents transferred only $774,000 from Kazakhstan to Kyrgyzstan in 2004. Moreover, its data indicates that only $4.761 million was

[35] *Uzbekistan: problemy trudovoi migratsii i vozmozhnye podkhody k formirovaniiu politiki* (Tashkent: Center for Human Resources Development, 2004), 31.

[36] "UNISTREAM: V 2008 g. migranty otpravili na rodinu gorazdo bol'she deneg chem v 2007," *Ferghana.ru*, February 19, 2009, www.ferghana.ru/news.php?id=11338.

sent back to Kyrgyzstan in remittances in 2008.[37] This does not tally with the author's field study which has shown that even semi-skilled Kyrgyz workers earned 800–1,500 dollars each for one season working on tobacco plantations around Almaty in 2005, thus generating a sizeable volume of remittances. The figures of the National Bank, therefore, do not reflect the fact that most Kyrgyz migrants send money earned in Kazakhstan through unofficial channels.

Whereas further research and verification is necessary, at least two propositions may be put forward. One is that the role of diasporas and networks is decisive in the self-organization and self-regulation of international labor migrations, considering the large number of informal channels for obtaining initial information about jobs, actually finding jobs, and solving problems with the help of relatives, friends, acquaintances, fellow villagers, or compatriots. The role of diasporas and networks notwithstanding, according to the survey 16.1 percent of respondents find information about potential job placements themselves, 66 percent of respondents traveled to the destination area alone, 20 percent found work on their own, and 42 percent transfer their money themselves, bearing full responsibility for their employment and the associated difficulties. Another proposition is that migrants acquire new social norms and standards specific to market practices in out-migration and employment.

Labor Migrants' Remittances: A Survival Strategy for Migrant Households

Migrant remittances are having an increasing impact on the living standards of migrant households. It could even be contended that this is the most significant outcome of international labor migration. A survey on the way remittances are spent in the households of migrants from Central Asian republics demonstrated that "migradollars" earned abroad are spent mainly on food (55.7 percent) and clothing (47.2 percent). Of the respondents, 30.3 percent reported that the money they earned provides them only with the bare essentials, 22.5 percent said the earnings helped them pay for medicines and medical treatment, and 25.5 percent said they financially supported their parents and children.

[37] On remittances in Kazakhstan see E. Todoroki, K. Celik, and M. Kholmatov, *Alternative Remittance Systems In Kazakhstan* (Washington, D.C.: The World Bank, 2011).

The spending of migrants' remittances differs from country to country. Lower-income migrants from Kyrgyzstan and Uzbekistan spend their money on daily necessities. Migrants from Tajikistan who have been working in Kazakhstan for many years (71 percent of the Tajik respondents have been migrants for more than five years) provide material assistance to relatives (47.1 percent), pay for medical services (35.3 percent), and purchase more expensive goods. The share of respondents who invest in the education of their children, especially girls, is relatively small.

Research has demonstrated that remittances are predominantly used for purchasing consumer goods by migrant households, and to a lesser degree for paying for health services and education. The positive impact of labor migration includes the accumulation of initial capital for starting up new businesses for some and improvement of migrants' qualifications, which consequently increases the quality of the labor force in the countries of origin.

International labor migration in the past decade has played a positive stabilizing role in the prevention of social and political tensions and conflicts in both the recipient and origin countries. To give only one example, money earned by Uzbek migrants in Kazakhstan helps hundreds of thousands of households survive in the poor agrarian regions of the Ferghana Valley in Uzbekistan. Furthermore, migration of labor surplus mitigates the situation of the local labor markets, reducing social tension and unrest.

Migrant Diasporas and Networks: Contradictory Manifestations

To analyze only the positive role of diasporas and networks would be to give a one-dimensional picture of the reality. Whereas these informal ties are helpful in finding jobs or apartments, they are also conducive to the emergence of secondary and tertiary labor markets and ethnic enclaves where immigrants are often illegally employed en masse. During steps undertaken to legalize illegal migrant workers in Kazakhstan in 2006, whole brigades of Uzbek citizens were involved in constructing residences for the large number of Uzbek families living in Shymkent and other cities and villages of the South Kazakhstan oblast (region). However, the heads of the households refused to legalize them, stating they were their relatives assisting in home renovation or preparations for weddings, thus preventing the legalization push from being successfully implemented.

Moreover, members of the migrant diaspora may be involved in criminal activities against their own compatriots, as a sociological survey revealed.[38] Investigating a rising mortality among Uzbek labor migrants, it was found that two oblasts alone in 2008, Khorezm and Bukhara, saw the deaths of 24 migrants registered with the regional authorities.[39] A large number of deaths are not included in official statistics: bodies are concealed or moved illegally because of the high official transportation costs of repatriation.

While the causes of deaths are various, the most frequently reported are the result of conflicts with law enforcement bodies, negative attitudes of the local population, and quite unexpectedly, the Uzbek diaspora in Russia, a fact confirmed by recent publications in the Russian mass media and by Uzbek migrants themselves. A survey conducted (see Table 3) among migrants who returned to Uzbekistan from Russia for the winter season offered interesting insights into threats to their personal security. Three large Russian regions harboring significant migrant populations—Primorie, Ural, and Podmoskovi'e (Moscow city and the Moscow oblast)—were represented in the poll through interviews with migrants employed there. The total number of respondents was 300 (100 migrants from each region) and their average age was 35.

Threats from nationalist groups and law enforcement bodies in Russia are commonplace and, unsurprisingly therefore, are strongly reflected in the poll results. However, threats from compatriots in each region (28, 32, and 40 percent, respectively) indicate a new trend in social and criminal relations between migrants and receiving communities, as well as between migrant groups. Interviewees admitted anonymously that Uzbek organized criminal groups (OCG) are "specializing" in trafficking, blackmailing, establishing illegal underground workshops (*podpolnyi tchekh*), smuggling, and "peacefully co-existing" with local law enforcement bodies in the Uzbek enclaves in different regions of Russia.

These OCGs consist mainly of current or former Uzbek citizens who arrived early and established "sustainable ties" with law enforcement bodies and local administrations. Migrants' responses indicated that the most substantial OCG activities are found in Moscow and its wider region. In fact, it would seem that OCGs control all labor migrants. According to one

---

[38] The "Analytic Group of Rapid Response—Uzbekistan" held a number of studies among Uzbek migrants. One of the surveys on physical threats against the personal security of Uzbek labor migrants in the Russian Federation was conducted in 2008, "Guest workers from Uzbekistan in Russia are afraid of their countrymen and skinheads most of all," *UzMetronom.com*, September 9, 2008.

[39] *Ibid.*

Table 3. Threats to the Personal Security of Uzbek Migrants in Russia

No	Geographical areas of employment of Uzbek labor migrants	Threat Options	Percentage of respondents
1.	Primorie region (Vladivostok and Khabarovsk)	law enforcement bodies	25
		skinheads	30
		compatriots	28
		local criminal groups	12
		working conditions	5
2.	Ural region: Chelyabinsk, Yekaterinburg, Perm	law enforcement bodies	20
		skinheads	20
		compatriots	32
		local criminal groups	21
		working conditions	7
3.	Moscow city and the Moscow oblast (Podmoskov'e region)	law enforcement bodies	18
		skinheads	30
		compatriots	40
		local criminal groups	4
		working conditions	8

migrant, and indicative of the sentiment of the overwhelming majority of Uzbek migrants working in Moscow, "The most dangerous moment for us is salary time: you are lucky if you manage to send money home via Western Union the same day, if not, you shall give half of your salary to your countrymen-bandits."

Thus the role of diasporas and networks seems to be somewhat contradictory. While they help migrants to find jobs and housing, assist in difficult economic situations and in the case of violations of their rights, and as such are very important in the self-organization and self-regulation of labor migrations, migrants often find themselves exploited and discriminated against by members of "their own" ethnic diaspora. Corruption accompanies the informal or "shadow" sector of the economy, and diasporas may even facilitate the criminalization of economic activities and community life.

The criminal component of labor migration is increasing. According to expert estimates, approximately 10 percent of income in Tajikistan from émigré job activities is derived from drug trafficking.[40] No study has been undertaken to explore in-depth what role diasporas and their

40 Olimova and Bosc, *Trudovaia migratsiia iz Tadzhikistana*, 97.

transnational criminal groups play in drug trafficking and other criminal activities, such as using international money transfer systems for the purposes of money laundering and terrorist financing. In any case, the level of these criminal activities is so high in Central Asia and Russia that mechanisms are being created to prevent the usage of transfer systems in such illicit activities.[41]

* * * * *

International migration will continue apace with globalization. Indeed, after the economic crisis of 2008–9, the movement of people, capital, goods, and ideas has resumed with a new intensity. Migration will continue across territorial borders when households face challenges to their survival, which is particularly the case in some Central Asian countries. Geopolitical and geo-economic factors stimulate international migration in the region, and migrant diasporas and networks are conducive to this process. This chapter has analyzed some of the issues relevant to the emerging diasporas composed of temporary labor migrants and newly arrived residents in Russia and Kazakhstan seeking permanent residence. Some of the author's considerations and interpretations are merely prudent hypotheses, which may be formulated as "research questions."

A specificity of Central Asian migrant diasporas is that the latter are strongly defined by both ethnic and kinship relations. However, the transformation of migrant communities as a result of acquired social norms and the practices of modernized society, which trend toward individualism and transnational action, may be a phenomenon worthy of future study. It is also interesting to note that migrant communities are being formed in social and cultural environments that are largely similar to their countries of origin, which can be attributed to the legacy of the Soviet Union. What is more, "virtual diasporas" may be in the process of emerging in cyberspace. One such example is the website www.odnoklassniki.ru, which unites 28 million former classmates and university graduates from all of the former Soviet republics, and facilitates their communication irrespective of ethnicity, profession, and social status. While it is most strikingly migrant diasporas from former Soviet countries that are emerging, so are such groups from countries outside of the CIS, especially China.

---

[41] See reports by Euroasiangroup, the Eurasian group on combating money laundering and financing of terrorism (EAG), which is a FATF-style regional body uniting Belarus, Kazakhstan, China, Kyrgyzstan, Russia, Tajikistan, and Uzbekistan, http://www.euroasiangroup.org.

A further research challenge, therefore, is to explore more in-depth the relationships between Han Chinese migration communities and the receiving societies in Russia and Central Asia.

Migrant diasporas and networks from Central Asia remain poorly studied, and their emergence and development must be studied using quantitative and qualitative methods. Challenging issues identified here, to name but a few, that necessitate further applied research are as follows: the self-identity of diaspora members; differences between migrant groups, communities, and diasporas; the economic and political, as well as national and cultural (religious, linguistic), dimensions of migrant diasporas and their role in the construction of diasporas; networking/communication of diaspora members with the sending and receiving communities; individual and diasporic strategies, adaptation, and integration; tolerance and inclusion versus intolerance and exclusion practiced in the receiving communities; and the various diasporas' viewpoints.

LABOR MIGRATION DURING THE 2008–9 GLOBAL ECONOMIC CRISIS

Erica Marat

In late 2008, as a result of the global economic crisis, countries around the world reported a significant decrease in the level of remittances sent by their citizens working abroad. Tajikistan alone reported a decrease of almost 25 percent.[1] This sharp decline alarmed Central Asian experts, who warned that the lack of jobs overseas would force migrants to return en masse to their countries of origin and create social and political instability. However, November 2009 data showed that remittances in Tajikistan fell by only 6.1 percent, lower than the 7.3 percent that had been forecast in late 2008.[2] Yet, the sudden drop in remittances reported globally could reflect a familiar cycle in labor migration whereby remittances surge during the summer months, followed by a burst of remittances sent home before the school year begins.

The latest data also indicates that the drop in remittances did not affect the number of migrants from Tajikistan and other Central Asian countries seeking jobs abroad. In fact, the number of people migrating abroad during the global economic crisis remained stable. Despite earlier predictions, most migrants were unwilling to travel to their country of origin because they feared that tighter immigration regulations would prevent them from going abroad again. Furthermore, although remittance levels shrank globally in 2009, it was only for a relatively short period of time. In South Asia, for example, the economic crisis only slowed down the overall increase in remittances; it did not trigger a decline. Importantly, the remittances returned to their 2008 level by late 2010, while by early 2011 they had grown in the whole of Central Asia by an average of 20 percent.[3]

---

1 "Tajikistan: Remittances Take a Dive," *Eurasia Insight*, January 7, 2009, www.eurasianet.org/departments/briefs/eav010708c.shtml.

2 See *The World Bank Migration and Development Brief*, November 1, 2009.

3 A. Bravi, "Remittances in Central Asia Three Times Higher than in Europe," *UNDP*, March 5, 2012, http://europeandcis.undp.org/blog/2012/03/05/remittances-in-central-asia-three-times-higher-than-in-europe/.

This chapter argues that labor migrants continued to be an important economic force in Central Asia during the years of global financial crisis. The latter forced more Central Asians to look for jobs abroad in spite of facing greater uncertainty and challenges in finding a stable income in Russia and beyond. Unless domestic economies in poor countries like Kyrgyzstan, Tajikistan, and Uzbekistan create enough incentives to entice workers in their own countries to take up jobs domestically, the current trend of out-migration will continue to increase. Contrary to predictions by regional experts, labor migrants will not demand political changes at home because they will not return unless they see attractive opportunities in their homeland. The roughly two million Central Asian migrants currently residing in Russia have already built extensive networks there, and these connections will encourage more people to emigrate. Partly as a result of the crisis, Central Asian diasporas are now scattered across many Russian cities. This, coupled with opportunities for land and air travel, as well as a general knowledge among the region's population of how to travel and live in Russia and Kazakhstan, make labor migration an entrenched process that cannot simply be overturned by government decrees.

According to World Bank data, in the late 2000s migrants faced increased personal risks. Their ability to work and send remittances largely depended on the availability of jobs, strict immigration controls and Russia's imposition quota on the foreign labor force, as well as unpredictable exchange rates. Still, remittances remain a stable source of capital inflow to developing countries compared to foreign direct investments. National governments also see labor migrants as a convenient financial resource that can help sustain the majority of the population. The global economic crisis has demonstrated to the local governments the benefits that labor migration brings. The main challenge to them, though, is how to direct remittances into economic and social development, rather than being channeled into personal consumption.

This chapter offers three differing viewpoints about labor migration during the economic crisis. These viewpoints were compiled from interviews conducted between late 2008 and early 2009 with several dozen experts in Central Asia. It discusses how the lack of cooperation between migrant-receiving and migrant-exporting states affects the daily lives of labor migrants, in addition to examining how national governments deal with issues of labor migration. Finally, it offers recommendations to the Central Asian governments on how to reap the potential benefits from migration, as well as how to improve the lives of those who have migrated.

Economic Crisis and Migration

History suggests that remittances tend to rise during economic crises, as a greater outflow of labor migrants seek to help their relatives at home. While many forms of financial capital inflow drop during recession, remittance levels tend to remain the same or, in some cases, even increase.[4] Thus, remittances are often considered a bulwark in ameliorating economic shocks—or prevent them altogether. As migrants seek to maximize their earnings, they will set aside more of their wages to be sent back home. The past decade has shown that remittances in Eurasia increased at a much faster rate than in other regions. The fall in the remittances received during the crisis subsequently hurt the economies of recipient countries.

Forecasts on remittance patterns in 2010 were affected by a number of factors, particularly in light of the economic downturn which impacted both migrant-sending and migrant-receiving countries.[5] Fluctuating oil prices and exchange rates further complicated forecasts. In Central Asia, Russia's dramatic cut in its quota of guest workers was the key factor that affected the 2009–10 outlook. Such policy changes could have several different effects. Central Asian migrants could prefer to remain in Russia to work in menial jobs outside the construction sector, which has been hardest hit by the Russian government's slashed quotas in major cities. Although overly pessimistic forecasts prevailed, there are three schools of thought on how the global crisis has affected labor migrants' remittances.

The first approach warned that the crisis would shake the very fundamentals of the migrant-sending countries. Kyrgyzstan and Tajikistan, and to a lesser extent Uzbekistan, would suffer tremendously from an abrupt decrease in remittances, it was argued. Some Central Asian experts predicted at least a 15–20 percent drop in the number of labor migrants who traveled to Russia and Kazakhstan in spring 2010, and were bracing for the corresponding drop in capital.[6] It was argued that returning migrants would increase unemployment and exacerbate the ongoing energy crisis in Kyrgyzstan and Tajikistan. But the most feared implication of returning migrants would be their potential to mobilize against the ruling regimes in the three states, which could consequently lead to instability or even

---

[4] Remittances increased during the financial crisis in Mexico in 1995 and in South Asia in 1998. See *The International Migration Agenda and the World Bank. Managing Risks, Enhancing Benefits* (Washington, D.C.: The World Bank, 2006).

[5] *The World Bank Migration and Development Brief*, November 11, 2008.

[6] Interview with Muzafar Zaripov, IOM, Dushanbe, February 2009.

government collapse. As one Tajik opposition leader commented in the spring of 2008, the migrants "will either join our party or turn against us. It is an unpredictable crowd."[7] According to him, migrants who were unable to find jobs upon returning home would turn against the government.

The second group argued that migrants would not return from Russia and Kazakhstan en masse, and thus remittances would decrease only gradually. And although the impact of the economic crisis would still be significant, they contended that there would be no strong, sudden shocks. Labor migrants who had lost jobs in Russia, for instance, would try to stay there and find jobs in other sectors. Only a small number of migrants would return, which could result in a reduction in remittances, thus putting pressure on the domestic economy.

Finally, the third group contended that although the effects of the global economic crisis would be felt on labor migrants' remittances for a few months in 2009, the overall volume of remittances would subsequently stabilize in late 2009 and into 2010. This, they argued, was a result of new migrants traveling to Russia and Kazakhstan to find jobs whose remittances would substitute the shrinking revenues from other family members. According to the third school, the economic crisis would also see a reduction in job opportunities abroad and a decrease in salaries. As such, migrants would seek to maximize their earnings and allocate larger sums for remittances. The poorest people, the hardest hit by the global economic crisis, would feel the greatest pressure to earn money.

The Positive Impact of Migration

November 2009 World Bank data on migration and remittances confirmed that labor migration trends could weather the economic crisis. In fact, the number of migrants leaving Kyrgyzstan, Tajikistan, and Uzbekistan for Russia increased when the economic downturn began in the late fall of 2008. The data showed that more young men bought one-way tickets to Russian cities during the period from November 2008 through to January 2009 compared to the same period in the previous year. They headed mostly to Moscow, Yuzhnyi Sakhalin, and Yekaterinburg.[8] Migrants working in Kazakhstan's construction sector had to move into the agricultural and retail sectors as building projects dried up. The initial crisis shock

[7] Interview with a Tajik political activist, Dushanbe, February 2009.
[8] Interview with Shukhrat Ganiyev, Bukhara, January 2009.

resulted in a sharp decline in remittances in late 2008, which propelled more migrants to go abroad. Many migrants, determined to find jobs abroad, decided to remain in Russia or Kazakhstan for an extended period of time without making plans to return. Experts in both Kazakhstan and Russia, however, argued that unskilled labor migrants were in greater demand by employers since they are more cost-efficient than national workers.

Indeed, remittances fell dramatically during the period from late 2008 to early 2009. But this was not due to the loss of jobs but rather employers' delays in paying salaries to guest workers. Remittances to Tajikistan continued to decline by about 30 percent in the first half of 2009, while remittances to Kyrgyzstan increased by 2 percent during the same period. The differences were attributed to the growing number of Kyrgyz labor migrants in the last few years, whereas in Tajikistan migrants had already left en masse since the 1990s. Labor migration became a common phenomenon in the case of Kyrgyzstan in the mid-2000s, when Russian and Kazakhstan labor markets were ready to offer more jobs, and it has continued to grow to the present day.

The Russian government's efforts to stop the devaluation of the ruble has also had an effect on the volume of remittances. As of fall 2008, migrants could transfer money only in rubles, a problem exacerbated by the fact that Uzbek banks do not accept deposits in rubles. The 25 to 30 percent decline in the value of the ruble between the fall of 2008 and the winter of 2009 further reduced the value of remittances sent from Russia. In Tajikistan, a 30 percent loss against the U.S. dollar translated into a less than 10 percent decrease in the ruble.[9] In other words, if a migrant sent 2,500 rubles or roughly 100 dollars in late 2008, this was equivalent to 70 dollars in early 2009. A similar comparison between the U.S. dollar and ruble in Kyrgyzstan shows a 17 percent increase in remittances. In 2009, the volume of remittances in Kyrgyzstan increased by almost 50 percent compared to 2007. Comparing the same period in Tajikistan, the overall volume of remittances was also higher in 2009. In Uzbekistan, meanwhile, the currency market became flooded with rubles and sums, and the value of the U.S. dollar also increased. In a matter of a few months, the dollar strengthened by 40 percent in Uzbekistan, and to a lesser extent in Tajikistan, Kyrgyzstan, and Kazakhstan.

---

[9] *The World Bank Migration and Development Brief*, November 3, 2009.

The job market in migration-receiving countries changes with migrants shifting to other sectors during economic crises, since for many the process of finding jobs largely depends on market availability. With the construction sector shrinking, migrants seek employment in private or public services. As many as 80 percent of Kyrgyz migrants, for instance, leave for Russia without a specific job in mind.[10] Labor migrants typically take up jobs that are often not attractive to Russian citizens. Migrants are sometimes stereotyped as working in specific jobs because of their nationality. In large cities like Moscow and St. Petersburg, where the cost of living is high, the jobs occupied by migrants such as drivers, construction workers, retailers, and street sweepers are unpopular among the local population due to the low wages. Kyrgyz and Tajiks are known to prefer the construction and retail sectors, but Kyrgyz also take up street sweeper jobs. According to the IOM office in Dushanbe, construction contractors prefer Tajiks to other Central Asians because they were the first wave of post-Soviet labor migrants and often have more experience in the construction sector.

The high number of returning migrants, as well as the declining level of remittances during the period from winter 2008 to early 2009, largely reflects the annual tendency of the vast majority of migrants to travel home during the coldest months, and does not necessarily indicate that the economic crisis affected the migrant labor market.[11] Competition has intensified among migrants, and a possible outcome could be an increase in cases of abuse among migrants, including more cases of slavery and human trafficking. Some illegal migrants are either sent to a different destination than the one they had paid to go to, or are forced to work for very low wages—and sometimes none at all—to pay off debts supposedly accrued during the migration process.

The Kyrgyz, Tajik, and Uzbek governments have also not taken constructive steps to alleviate the impact of the crisis on domestic economies, such as by creating more jobs or reducing taxes. Their continuous focus on raising revenues has forced more people to seek earnings abroad. For instance, in January 2009, the Kyrgyz government increased taxes on small businesses, and custom fees jumped almost tenfold. This resulted in some small businesses delaying in paying off credits, while others folded

---

10 "Kyrgyzskie migranty edut na zarabotki vslepuiu," *Azattyk RFE/RL*, October 14, 2008, www.azattyk.org/content/News/1334585.html.

11 K. Mikhailov, "Kto, esli ne oni: problemy vneshnei i vnutrennei migratsii," *Nezavisimaia gazeta*, December 23, 2008.

their businesses altogether. The Tajik government, however, did show interest in creating jobs for returning migrants. Several roundtables featuring international organizations and government employees were held in January and February 2009. The government announced that returning migrants would be needed to build new hydropower sites, especially the huge Rogun dam project. They also announced that new roads and electric gridlines financed by China would give priority to Tajik citizens instead of Chinese nationals.[12] In spite of this, few of the government's promises have been realized.

Since some of the larger cities in Russia proved to be too inhospitable for Central Asian migrants during the economic hardship of 2008–9, they looked for other less accessible destinations such as Europe, the United States, and Southeast Asia. At the same time, the shrinking job market also forced Russian citizens to look for jobs abroad in Europe, Turkey, and North America. Overall, the year 2009 proved to be the most difficult for Central Asian migrants in their search for jobs abroad. Whereas remittances per capita have slightly declined, the overall volume of remittances has remained roughly the same with more migrants working abroad. Importantly, by the first half of 2011, a new labor market had already re-emerged throughout Russia and other migrant destination countries.

Lack of Interstate Cooperation

The problem of labor migration in Central Asia reached a critical mass in 2003–4, when it became impossible to deny the significance of these migration trends. By then, hundreds of thousands of migrants were traveling to Russia and Kazakhstan and sending substantial remittances home. Human trafficking and slavery were booming as well. Migrants faced discrimination in Russia, while law enforcement structures abused their rights rather than protecting them. However, there were no statistics on the number of migrants or the volume of remittances collected because national governments and international organizations had failed to notice the growing problem.

To date, Central Asian governments have failed to encourage migrants to put their remittances into some form of investment such as by offering them micro-grants, lifting taxes, encouraging bank savings, or decreasing

[12] Interview with Muzafar Zaripov, IOM, Dushanbe, February 2009.

customs fees. Most Central Asian public officials lack even a basic understanding of migration issues. In order to create conditions favorable to small businesses, governments must realize that migrant remittances are just another type of foreign investment.[13] However, across all Central Asian states migration is—if addressed at all—treated as a social problem, not an economic opportunity that has the potential to become a powerful driver of national development. Furthermore, Central Asian special committees on migration are designed as social programs and are excluded from decision-making processes in the economic sector. In the meantime, several government institutions deal one way or another with migration issues—from customs control to financial and health issues. Typically, they prefer to act unilaterally than to collaborate or even communicate among one another.

At the regional level, labor migration has become a highly politicized issue. At CIS meetings, migration issues such as work contracts, pensions, and health insurance are typically raised by sending countries. Meanwhile, receiving countries see the issue as an opportunity to exert political leverage to pressure Kyrgyzstan and Tajikistan to comply with policies set by Astana and Moscow.[14] Although this is a fairly common problem among migrant-sending and receiving countries worldwide, Russia and the Central Asian states are extremely slow in changing this dynamic. Kyrgyzstan usually brings up the issue at interstate meetings of the CIS, Collective Security Treaty Organization (CSTO), Shanghai Cooperation Organization (SCO), and Customs Union. Tajikistan joins Kyrgyzstan's pleas occasionally, but usually Uzbekistan blocks discussions of the issue, even though it has the highest number of migrants working abroad. Furthermore, in spite of these meetings yielding agreements that could potentially benefit both receiving and sending countries, efforts that seek to arrive at some form of agreement are blocked at the national level in Russia and Kazakhstan. Parliaments in both countries often see interstate agreements on migration as contradicting domestic legislation on labor and social protection. Both countries treat labor migrants as pawns, often demonstrating their power by deporting undocumented migrants en masse.

Russia and the Central Asian countries must treat the interstate regulation of migration as an economic issue that benefits both migrant-sending

[13] Interview with Bermet Moldobaeva, IOM National Program Officer, Bishkek, January 2009.

[14] *Ibid.*

and receiving countries. Legalization of migrants could potentially reduce corruption in law enforcement structures that benefit from illegal migrants' bribes. Sending countries, on the other hand, will be better able to protect their citizens abroad and help them find jobs. Since the early 2000s, Russia has moved to reinforce security and military cooperation with the Central Asian states. Most of the signed bilateral agreements have increased the Kremlin's influence in the region. Kyrgyzstan and Tajikistan, in particular, regularly receive economic, political, and military aid from the Kremlin. Yet, despite regular collective activities of the CIS, CSTO, and Customs Union, labor migration issues are rarely addressed. And whereas in 2002 Russia began to conclude bilateral agreements with the CIS states on labor migration, these agreements allow migrant-recipient countries to use their leverage over sending countries. In other words, bilateral documents have failed to ease migrants' registration woes or protect their rights in Russia.

Only the governments of Kyrgyzstan and Kazakhstan have taken into account some of the international community's recommendations. For its part, in the run-up to the OSCE chairmanship in 2010, Kazakhstan tried to present itself as a multi-ethnic state and major regional recipient of migrants. Kyrgyzstan, on the other hand, has more independent public servants able to collaborate with international organizations and local NGOs. For instance, since migration is not considered a political issue, representatives of the Committee on Migration are able to collaborate with external donors. Most of the bilateral agreements are therefore signed between Russia and Kazakhstan, Kyrgyzstan or Tajikistan. Despite its large migrant population, Astana only has an agreement with Kyrgyzstan.[15] Uzbekistan, in turn, has only one elaborate agreement on labor migrants—with South Korea. These agreements are usually reactions to existing migration trends. Short-termist and tending to lack in vision and strategy for periods longer than a year, they fail to provide for extraordinary situations, such as the changing structure of the labor market or economic downturns.

[15] A. Mansoor and B. Quillin, eds., *Migration and Remittances: Eastern Europe and the Former Soviet Union* (Washington, D.C.: The World Bank, 2006).

Working Conditions and Health Issues of Migrants

The lack of interstate cooperation on labor migration and the corresponding low interest among public officials has led to the widespread abuse of migrants' rights. Without official procedures, both Russian employers and labor migrants are forced to establish informal contracts. Over 65 percent of employment agreements among Tajik migrants in Russia are brokered without any written contract.[16] Among them, only one-third have legal employment authorization in Russia. The employers, in order to legally employ guest workers, must pay a deposit to the authorities that would cover the deportation costs for migrants who break the law. They must also pay higher taxes and take responsibility for the civic rights of these workers.[17]

According to sociological surveys, most Central Asian migrants in Russia work up to 9 hours per day, with over 10 percent working more than 12 hours. Moscow and Saint Petersburg are the highest-paying cities, with monthly salaries ranging between 3,000 and 9,000 rubles (100 to 300 dollars). Higher salaries in both cities, however, also make them prime places for fraud and corruption. Roughly 35 to 50 percent of migrants in these cities are not paid for their work. In Yekaterinburg, 80 percent of the migrants reported being short-changed at least once. Migrants in Astrakhan receive the lowest salaries (less than 3,000 rubles/month) and live in the worst conditions.[18] Over 44 percent of all migrants live in adverse conditions, while 80 percent of them lack access to healthcare.

The registration process in Russia for citizens from former Soviet republics is lengthy, taking up to 30 days. However, a migrant must register within three days upon arrival in Russia if he or she wants to continue the legal registration process. Labor migrants arriving by airplane or train from Kyrgyzstan, Tajikistan, and Uzbekistan are accustomed to paying bribes to the customs control officers. When they leave Russia, they are again pressured into paying bribes, often with their remaining wages, if they want to travel back home. Surveys of migrants show that most would indeed prefer legal registration.[19]

---

[16] N.N. Nuraliev, *Problemy trudovoi migratsii iz Tadzhikistana v Rossiiu*, 2005, 68–72, http://www.ecsocman.edu.ru/images/pubs/2006/07/06/0000281728/009.NOURALIEV.pdf.

[17] *Ibid.*

[18] *Ibid.*

[19] Interview, experts from Tajikistan, Dushanbe, February 2009.

Starting in 2003–4, several international organizations began to work with NGOs in sending countries to develop special manuals for migrants, informing them of their rights and responsibilities, the necessary documents for legal registration, and pertinent immigration regulations in Russia. Such attention to migrant needs was provoked after death and deportation rates among migrants in Russia spiked in the early 2000s. Between 400 to 1,000 migrants die in Russia and Kazakhstan each year, due to poor working conditions, a lack of access to health care, and violence. Labor migration also damages migrants' health. According to the Bishkek IOM office, half of all migrants return home with worse health than when they departed.[20] Heavy lifting, freezing temperatures, insufficient health care, and poor living conditions are the leading causes of deteriorating health. Indeed, after working in Siberia, where temperatures can drop to as low as minus 60 degrees celcius, most returning migrants meet government criteria usually applied to handicapped people. Moreover, in the first decade of the twenty-first century many young men migrated to Russia straight after finishing secondary school, which has led to the creation of a generation of young citizens with severe health problems.

As winters in Russia are colder than in Central Asia, along with the slowdown in the construction sector, most labor migrants who travel without families return home during the winter period, usually for one to two months.[21] But the energy crisis and abnormally prolonged sub-zero temperatures during the winters from 2007 to 2009 led most migrants to remain in Russia, with some of them summoning their families from Central Asia. In fact, it is common among migrants who have worked for over five years in Russia to bring their families over. Tajik and Uzbek women tend to stay within the home and not find a job even after moving to Russia, with the lack of a second income often affecting the family's living standards.

To obtain a legal work permit in Russia and Kazakhstan, migrants must prove that they are in good health. Any person harboring a potentially infectious disease is not able to work legally. Although migrants are required to collect the necessary medical documents prior to leaving their home country to work abroad, they are not required to have a medical examination upon their return home. Yet, as previously stated,

---

20 *Trudovaia migratsiia iz Kyrgyzstana* (Bishkek: IOM, 2008), 150.

21 N.A. Zotova, "Trudovaia migratsiia iz Tadzhikistana. Po materialam polevogo issledovaniia v Samare i Moskve," *Ferghana.ru*, May 30, 2006, www.ferghana.ru/article.php?id=4424.

many return with far worse health than when they departed.[22] Since the majority of labor migrants are young, often unmarried males, they may be exposed to a number of sexually transmitted diseases from paid sex services. Respiratory transmitted infections such as tuberculosis are also a common problem among migrants living in cramped quarters. Lacking access to health care abroad, they might be unaware of their diseases, delay treatment, and spread infectious diseases among their fellow co-workers and families. Compulsory medical examinations for returning migrants are essential and will act as a prevention.

* * * * *

The global economic crisis has shown that migrants represent a powerful stabilizing force for the Central Asian states. Because local governments are not able to create jobs at home, the number of migrants seeking jobs abroad continues to grow. The crisis further demonstrates that Central Asian countries and Russia must seek to sign bilateral and multilateral agreements to ease the burdens of migrants. Yet challenges remain. Receiving countries tend to prefer unilateral decisions, disregarding the implications for sending countries. Migrant-sending countries, on the other hand, are mostly concerned with the political implications of potentially large flows of returning migrants, as they seek to further centralize their power.

The cases of Tajikistan and Kyrgyzstan show that remittances contribute to the development of domestic banking systems as well as increase the scope of services and credit lines. Migrants' remittances also help the state in providing support to families in rural areas. Hard labor on foreign soil changes the work ethics of migrants. Returning migrants tend to be more industrious and innovative in their search for a market niche as well as in their investment strategies. However, the governments of Central Asia and Russia remain passive about migration, failing to act on several fronts. Post-factum agreements between migrant-sending and receiving countries—or the lack of them—promote slavery, trafficking, and organized crime. The absence of clear state policies also fuels corruption among customs workers and law enforcement agents.

Central Asian states fail to ease migrants' burdens or capitalize on remittances by encouraging small- and medium-sized businesses. Remittances are instead spent on consumption or on certain goods such as real

[22] Interview with Bermet Moldobaeva, IOM National Program Officer, Bishkek, January 2009.

estate, the prices of which tend to fluctuate. Governments of migrant-sending countries must encourage investment by allowing remittances to be channeled to that cause, as seen during the recent economic crisis. International practice shows that increasing deposit interest rates, as well as decreasing customs fees and taxes, will motivate investment. The practice of micro-lending has a vast potential in Tajikistan and Uzbekistan. Furthermore, special training workshops on how to invest should be conducted for migrants' families. Central Asian governments must understand that labor migration is an important economic phenomenon that can potentially facilitate local development.

In light of the above, Russia and Kazakhstan must continue to develop more efficient immigration policies, while the Uzbek government must recognize the issue of migration at the regional level. Kazakhstan and Uzbekistan have traditionally competed at a regional level for political influence and recognition, but it is Kazakhstan's rapid economic development that has made it attractive to foreign workers and investors, becoming the main receiving country in Central Asia for migrant labor. Uzbekistan, on the other hand, has quickly become a migrant-sending country. Although local NGOs and IOM offices have been addressing the problem, there is a need for an international mediator to foster an interstate dialogue between countries. The issue of labor migration must be depoliticized, and migrants' rights and safety must be prioritized when countries discuss migrants' conditions.

Furthermore, the international community must train government employees and parliamentarians to help them gain a better understanding of migration issues and how to deal with them. To date, only a few government experts are knowledgeable about the legal and economic aspects of labor migration. Strong efforts are also needed to educate people in rural and urban areas about human trafficking. Kyrgyzstan is the only Central Asian migrant-sending country that lacks funding for such information campaigns. Along with trafficking for sexual exploitation, labor and child exploitation must also be actively addressed through legal means and public campaigns.

The international community should help Central Asian governments to improve technical and vocational education as opposed to only fostering the social sciences. The current education system in Kyrgyzstan and Tajikistan is currently overcrowded with social science departments and is unable to satisfy the local demand for skilled workers, who are also more in demand in Russia and Kazakhstan. Moreover, girls and young women must be encouraged to attend schools and universities. The value of formal education must be promoted, not just within families but also at the community level. Technical and vocational education must be introduced to young women to help them become financially and psychologically independent. Very often, the lack of education forces women into early marriage (under the age of 16), making them economically dependent. Last but not least, special attention should be paid to the pervasive corruption prevalent in law enforcement structures that often cover up cases of slavery and human trafficking. Reducing corruption among the police in larger cities, passport-issuing agencies, as well as among customs control officers, will decrease human trafficking.

TO STAY OR NOT TO STAY: THE GLOBAL ECONOMIC CRISIS AND RETURN MIGRATION TO TAJIKISTAN[1]

Saodat Olimova

The financial and economic crisis that the world has experienced since 2008 has had a great impact on labor migration, including return migration. Unsurprisingly, the connection between the global financial crisis and migration has also aroused academic interest. Previous studies of return migration have been motivated by the rapid growth of international migration and remittances, the toughening of migratory legislation in the destination countries, discussion of "voluntary repatriation," growth theory, unresolved questions of readmission between sending and receiving countries, and debates about the influence of labor migration on the development of the countries of origin. But more recently, return migration as a consequence of the world crisis has been receiving additional attention. This question is critical in the countries of Central Asia, which have been witness to international labor migration for two decades. Of particular significance is the case of Tajikistan where the highest levels of migration can be observed.

Despite the fact that the history of labor migration on the territory of modern Tajikistan goes back several centuries, modern labor migration from Tajikistan is a phenomenon of post-Soviet independence. The most significant drivers of labor migration from Tajikistan have been the civil war of 1992–97 and the extremely high social price exacted by the country's transition to independence. Indeed, the scale and socio-economic impact of this migration has been extraordinary. One in four households in the country has at least one member who is working abroad. According to a study conducted by the Asian Development Bank (ADB) in 2007, the number of labor migrants amounted to 700,000 people.[2] This is a significant

[1] This chapter was written in the framework of the research project "Return migration in Tajikistan," which was funded by the Foundation Maison des sciences de L'Homme, France.

[2] R. Brown, S. Olimova, and M. Boboev, *A Study on International Migrant Remittances in Central Asia and South Caucasus: Country Report on Remittances of International Migrants in Tajikistan* (Asian Development Bank, 2008), http://www.adb.org/Documents/Reports/Consultant/40038-REG/40038-04-REG-TACR.pdf, 4.

share of the total population of Tajikistan, which totals about seven million. Half of the total population is younger than 18 years of age. In addition, 75 percent of the population live in rural areas, and more than half can be classified as poor.

Although the range of migratory flows from Tajikistan encompasses several CIS countries, labor migration from Tajikistan is almost exclusively directed toward the Russian Federation (97 percent of all migrants). Migrants usually work in such areas as construction, transportation, trade, and utilities. A large number of them (73.1 percent) are seasonal migrants, defined as those who work abroad temporarily (from March through November) and who return home for the winter months.[3] Seasonal migration is encouraged by a visa-free regime between Tajikistan and recipient countries, the existence of transportation links connecting Tajikistan and Russia, and engagement in subsistence farming in Tajikistan during the slack winter months.

It is difficult to overestimate the influence of labor migration on all aspects of life in Tajikistan. Migrants make critical contributions to the development of both recipient and host economies. According to data from the National Bank of Tajikistan, the size of remittances through official channels in 2008 amounted to 46 percent of the gross domestic product (GDP) of Tajikistan. The rapid growth of labor migration from Tajikistan, its extraordinary size, and its importance, has caused a boom in migration research in Tajikistan and, since the beginning of the 2000s, there has been an active accumulation of empirical data.[4] To a certain degree the basic trends and patterns of migration, remittances, and social and economic influence of migration have already been documented and studied. However, return migration has not been examined as closely. This is not surprising, since labor migration from Tajikistan only became significant 12 to 14 years ago. However, the radically changed situation by the end of 2008, with a stream of returning migrants because of the effects

[3] *Ibid.*, 33–34.

[4] S. Olimova and I. Bosc, *Labour migration from Tajikistan* (Dushanbe: IOM, 2003); A. Kireyev, "The Macroeconomics of Remittances: The Case of Tajikistan," *International Monetary Fund Working Paper*, January 2006; *Tajikistan Policy note: enhancing the development impact of remittances*, World Bank Report No 35771-TJ April 2006; Kh. Umarov and R. Ulmasov, *Vneshniaia trudovaia migratsiia v Tadzhikistane (prichiny, problemy, posledstviia, regulirovanie)* (Dushanbe: Irfon, 2006); S. Olimova and J. Quddusov, *Families of Migrants in Tajikistan: Problems and Ways of Their Solution* (Dushanbe: Irfon, 2007); A. Mansoor and B. Quillin, eds., *Migration and Remittances: Eastern Europe and the former Soviet Union* (Washington, D.C.: The World Bank, 2007).

of the world financial and economic crises, presented new problems for researchers studying migration.

Accordingly, these new developments raise a host of questions. Why do some migrants leave after losing their jobs in Russia while others stay? How have migration and return strategies changed as a result of the financial crisis? Who are the returning migrants, why do they return, what sort of lives do they lead, and where do they work? To what extent are they reintegrated in their local communities? How do they influence the host country and its path of development? Finally, what happens to migrants who depart for Russia despite the crisis?

These questions still do not have answers. Unlike in Lebanon, Jordan, Algeria, and other countries that are used to accommodating returning migrants, the states of Central Asia do not have any experience in dealing with large numbers of returnees. It is not known how returnees will affect social stability, economic well-being, social life, religious revival, and gender relations, as well as the development of the countries of the region more generally. It is also not known to what degree return migration in Central Asia can be compared to other countries with similar circumstances. This chapter attempts to answer these questions, providing an overview of the current situation and explaining the impact of the financial crisis on labor migration, both now and in the future.

Theory and Empirical Basis

Empirical researchers typically use several theoretical models to study migration. Economists often rely on neoclassical theory and the New Economics of Labor Migration (NELM). Sociologists, anthropologists, and social geographers prefer to use structuralism, trans-nationalism, and the theory of social and economic networks.[5]

It is assumed here that in the case of return migration to Tajikistan, the most pertinent theory is structuralism. The choice of methodology in the collection of empirical data presents a considerable difficulty in the study of migration. The quantitative methods that are most popular in migration research cannot provide the necessary depth of analysis. On the other hand, qualitative methods, which are used more often in anthropological

[5] See, for example, J.P. Cassarino, "Theorising Return Migration: the Conceptual Approach to Return Migrants Revisited," *International Journal of Multi-Cultural Society* 6, no. 2 (2004): 253–279.

research, can provide descriptive and analytical explanation to a single phenomenon, but cannot give consistent explanation to phenomena involving large groups of people, such as those found in labor migration or migrant household analyses. All these factors are the reason why several methodological approaches are used in an interdisciplinary fashion.

Several sources of data are utilized here. One of the sources was data obtained in March and April 2009, when the Sharq Research Center conducted an express study of the effects of the financial crisis on labor migration and remittances in Tajikistan; it consisted of 133 interviews with Tajik migrants in Moscow, returnees in Tajikistan, and migrants who departed to Russia in spite of the crisis. The study attempted to address the following issues: the protectionist policies of destination countries, the decreasing numbers of migrants, the decreasing volume of remittances, changes in the behavioral patterns of migrant workers, and especially return migration. This chapter also utilizes surveys, focus group discussions, and interviews from the Migration and Development Project, funded by the International Labor Organization in 2008, and results of the household surveys from the Migration and Poverty Project, funded by the Asian Development Bank (ADB) in 2007.[6]

Over the last decade, the presence of Tajik labor migrants in Russia has rapidly increased, attaining its peak level in 2008. Out of an estimated total number of 800,000 migrant workers from Tajikistan, 97 percent were working in Russia. However, the slump in business activity in construction, manufacturing, agricultural production, financial services, trade, and tourism has had a negative impact on migrants, since the majority of them worked in these sectors of the Russian economy.

Usually governments adopt protectionist policies to shield domestic labor markets in an effort to overcome financial crisis. The widespread belief among local populations that migrants "take away" jobs forces the governments of destination countries to toughen their migratory policies. Since these beliefs are broadcast by the mass media, they promote discrimination and xenophobia, and increase tensions between countries of destination and origin. As a result, labor migrants face increasing political

[6] The project "Migration and Development" included a survey of 1,000 returnees from 2003 to 2007. A "snow ball" sample with a regional composition was created. The project also included a survey of 100 top managers of firms that employ returnees, ten focus group discussions, and expert interviews. The period of the survey and the interviews spanned from April to June 2008. The "Migration and Poverty" ADB project included a survey of 3,300 households.

and administrative risks in their countries of destination. For instance, in Russia the administrative barriers to labor migrants obtaining registration and other legal documents have recently become stricter. This is compounded by a seven to ten-fold increase in the size of informal fees that migrant workers have to pay to Russian law enforcement authorities (Federal Migration Service and local police officers) in order to obtain temporary residence permits on the territory of the Russian Federation.

The Dynamics of Labor Migration

The first stage of the financial crisis in October 2008, which directly affected the labor market in Russia, coincided with the period when labor migrants from Tajikistan usually returned home. These seasonal migrants, who comprise 73 percent of all Tajik migrants, usually work in Russia from March or April until October or November. However, in 2008, local authorities and transport companies pointed out that the number of returning migrants was three times less than in previous years. For instance, according to the Ministry of Transport of Tajikistan, the number of passengers in the period between November and December 2008 was three times less than the same period in 2007. One of the reasons for this slowdown was the inability of seasonal workers to gather enough money to return home, since many of them either did not get paid at all or experienced delays in the payments of their salaries. Another reason is that some migrants preferred to stay and more closely monitor the situation on the Russian labor market in an attempt to obtain better employment the following year. Seasonal workers started to go back to Russia only at the very end of February 2009, continuing to return there for several months until June. Yet the number of seasonal workers was 35 to 40 percent less than in 2008.

In general, estimates show that the total number of migrants from Tajikistan working in Russia in the summer of 2009 decreased by 20 percent. This figure correlates with the data from the Department of Migration of the Ministry of Internal Affairs of Tajikistan, which estimates that the number of Tajik migrant workers in Russia decreased by 120,000 people. Despite the constraints of the financial crisis, however, migrants obviously continue to go abroad to seek employment. In 2011 the total number of Tajik migrants working in Russia had recovered its pre-crisis level.

Changes in Migrants' Living Conditions in Russia Due to the Crisis

Prior to analyzing the impact of the financial crisis on migrants from Tajikistan, there must be an overview of the main recipient countries for Tajik migrants, since the financial crisis has had different impacts on them. The findings of Sharq 2008 Migration and Development study indicate that the overwhelming majority of migrants from Tajikistan worked in the Russian Federation (94.9 percent). A small number have returned from Kazakhstan (1 percent), the United Arab Emirates (1 percent), Ukraine (0.6 percent), Uzbekistan (0.5 percent), and Iran (0.4 percent). Only a very small percentage of people worked in other countries, including Kyrgyzstan, Belarus, Germany, the United States, Afghanistan, and China. Other survey materials confirm this data. According to the ADB study cited earlier, 97 percent of migrants worked in Russia. A small number of migrants from Tajikistan worked in other countries such as Kazakhstan (0.8 percent), China (0.6 percent), Uzbekistan (0.4 percent), Afghanistan (0.2 percent), the United Arab Emirates (0.3 percent), and Turkey (0.2 percent).

Along with other similar studies, this survey shows that the most popular location for Tajik migrants in Russia is the Moscow metropolitan area. Of those migrants who returned from Russia, 46.3 percent had worked in the greater Moscow region. The main sphere of employment was construction, and to a lesser extent, trade and services. The Siberian Federal District is the second most significant host territory for Tajik migrants.[7] A significant concentration of Tajik migrants can be observed in Yekaterinburg (4.3 percent), Tyumen (2.7 percent), Nizhnevartovsk (1.2 percent), Surgut (1.4 percent), and other Siberian cities. Here, migrants tend to work in the oil and gas industry, construction, chemical production, and industrial enterprises. Large industrial centers such as St. Petersburg (6.4 percent), Samara (4.4 percent), and Rostov-on-Don (2.9 percent) are other areas where many Tajik migrants find employment.

The survey showed that Moscow and the Moscow region, St. Petersburg, and Yekaterinburg account for the largest job losses for Tajik migrants. Conversely, the rate of job losses barely increased in smaller cities in the European part of Russia, like Samara, Saratov, and Volgograd, or the Southern Federal District, Siberia, and the Far East. As a result, migrant networks are quite actively collecting information about labor opportunities elsewhere and sending their representatives there. Therefore, it can

[7] Significantly less attractive for migrants are the Ural and Privolga districts.

be observed that internal migration within Russia, that is, from Moscow and St. Petersburg to other cities in Russia, is already taking shape.

Legal Status

Although the rate of informal employment among Tajik migrants is already high, it has been rising still higher, along with incidences of labor abuse. This can be explained by the fact that the reduction in formal quotas for foreign labor in Russia, and sharp increases in formal and informal payments for employment of foreign employees, forces employers to avoid legal employment practices when dealing with migrant workers. Indeed, the legal status of migrants is one of the most important factors determining migrant behavior, income, and the efficiency of migration for the countries of destination and origin. Although labor migration brings huge economic and social benefits to both Tajikistan and the destination countries, tremendous informal and institutional constraints affect labor migrants in the CIS. This has resulted in the violation by most migrants of the legislation regulating the duration of stay and employment in the destination country. This is the main reason why informal employment exceeds that of formal employment. In light of the above, although Tajikistan enjoys a visa-free regime with a number of destination countries, including the Russian Federation, it has a significant number of illegally or informally employed migrant workers abroad.

Obstacles related to residence registration are particularly acute: 12.8 percent of the sample returnees had resided illegally or without being registered by the OVIR (the department for the issuance of visas and permits), and 12.5 percent reported that they only registered on a sporadic basis. The most oft-cited reason (given by every fourth migrant worker living abroad) for having no residential registration was the fact that in order to obtain legal status, bribes needed to be paid to the police to reside in a specific area. The same number noted that payment for registration was so expensive that they could not afford it. Nearly 70 percent of migrants did not leave their workplaces, which doubled up as their places of residence. Frequently, employers do not allow their employees to leave their workplaces on account that they are not registered. When necessary (arrivals, departures, travel to the market, or medical appointments), employers provide their workers with transport enabling them to avoid contact with law enforcement bodies.

The survey findings prove that, in the majority of cases, informal status stems from informal employment. However, the data on legal and illegal employment is quite different for returnees compared with other migrants.

A large number of returnees legalized their labor by signing contracts: 34.8 percent of returnees versus 18.4 percent of migrants.[8] Among returnees, there were also more who worked according to a verbal agreement (32 percent) compared to the figure for all migrants (25.6 percent). These differences result from labor market particularities in the CIS. Despite the efforts of government officials to legalize labor relations, labor markets in CIS countries remain shadowy for the most part. One can assume that one of the reasons for the increased share of informally employed migrants among returnees is their deportation as well as dissatisfaction with the pay and/or working conditions abroad.

Changes in Salaries and Working Conditions

Since the beginning of the crisis, wages in some cases have been cut by as much as half. To make matters worse, the practice of non-payment of salaries is quite widespread. There are cases in which salaries have not been paid for four or five months. Migrants who lose their jobs are also forced to accept menial unskilled jobs and reside in poor living conditions. This consequently leads to alcohol abuse, with unskilled youths turning to petty theft and fraud.

Besides all the difficulties of being a migrant, in particular in Russia, the increased rate of job losses has forced migrants to look extensively for new jobs, even in those sectors normally associated with lower salaries and harsher working conditions. As a result, migrants increasingly face deteriorating conditions of employment in addition to rising administrative barriers and hostile attitudes from local populations, including abuse and harassment. It is calculated that around 40 percent of Tajik labor migrants in Russia have had to change jobs due to cuts or changing work environments. Sixty percent of those who changed jobs faced salary cuts, with 40 percent of respondents stating that their living conditions had gotten worse as a result of having to share their living space with a greater number of people. The vast majority—85 percent—stated that the current situation in Russia had affected them in one way or another. Social and living conditions continue to be far from desirable with 25 percent of all interviewed migrants actually living on their worksite and another 35 percent in hostels, sharing with at least three to four other people.

---

[8] S. Olimova and R. Kurbonova, *Povedencheskoe issledovanie sredy trudovykh migrantov iz Tazhikistana i chlenov ikh semei po voprosam VICH i IPPP* (Dushanbe: IOM, 2006), 14.

Seventy percent of all respondents also stated that as a result of the crisis, the attitudes of both employers and law enforcement bodies had become less tolerant. They cited increasing incidences of harassment and abuse, and unsubstantiated monetary extortions even if the relevant paperwork was in place.

The survey also showed a strong correlation between the level of income in Russia and the decision to return to Tajikistan. Those migrants with insufficient funds were most likely to stay in Russia despite losing their jobs, compared to their better-off peers who had some savings. As a rule, the latter lowered their job expectations, agreeing to positions with lower pay and worse conditions. In a worse-case scenario, these groups of people lived off their earnings and reduced their consumption to a bare minimum. Some of these migrants still returned home and the rest continued living off their prior earnings. While continuing to send home remittances, these had become substantially smaller in size.

According to the National Bank of Tajikistan, the amount of remittances to Tajikistan decreased by more than 30 percent in the first half of 2009. One-third of all migrants continued to send home the same amount of money as before, whereas 40 percent sent smaller amounts, 20 percent failed to send any money at all, and only 5 percent actually increased their remittances. Among those who lost their jobs, 25 percent continued to send money from their own savings, and 10 percent took out loans to send money to their families. The rest, more than half, did not send anything.

Migrants' Responses to the Crisis

For the most part, migrants attempt to adapt to new conditions in destination countries. Only 3.8 percent of migrants who lost their jobs decided to return to Tajikistan immediately afterward; the rest started looking for another job. Most of the migrants continue to rely heavily on extensive familial networks, using friends and relatives as their first and most important resource in seeking employment. Half of all returning migrants have tried this channel alone, while a third of returning migrants looked for jobs in newspaper announcements; a further 20 percent took it upon themselves to look for jobs. That only 5 percent of all respondents looked for a job outside of Moscow shows that job opportunities are much higher there. It is also interesting to note that around 10 percent of those who had lost their jobs stated that it was useless to look for another one, as getting another work permit had become a major challenge. Of those who looked for another job, 60 percent could not get one, as they did not have a work permit or citizenship; at the same time, 40 percent *could* get new jobs in spite of lacking the necessary paperwork. The financial crisis also reduced the savings of migrants and increased the time of involuntary job hunting. Forty percent of returnees unsuccessfully looked for a job for up to a month before they decided to leave for Tajikistan, 30 percent spent more than two months, and a further one-third of returnees remained over three months in Russia before they left for home.

Almost half of the migrants stated that their wages had been cut and that, even so, they were willing to temporarily work for a lower wage. Over half of all respondents also stated that there was nothing they could do apart from tolerating the situation. Meanwhile, a quarter of all migrants had searched for another job. Although only a small percentage of migrants looked for a job outside of the greater Moscow region, the majority of migrants stated they did not mind moving to other regions, provided they knew where they could find a job without being subject to harassment. Also discernible was a shift of migrants from the construction sector to catering, transportation, and agriculture as a temporary measure to weather the crisis. These sectors are less regulated and require more unskilled labor.

Changes in Behavioral Patterns of Migrant Workers

In order to analyze behavioral changes, this section focuses on three different categories of migrant workers: those who decided to stay in Russia, those who returned to Tajikistan, and those who left for work in Russia during the period of the financial crisis.

Migrants Who Stayed in Russia During the Crisis

In general, older migrants with relatively higher levels of education, skills, and salary, and more experience of labor migration, were more likely to stay in Russia during the crisis. Close to two-thirds of all those staying in Russia had been migrants for over two years, while among those who returned, two-thirds had worked in Russia for only a year or less. Almost half of the more experienced migrants deciding to stay in Russia were between the ages of 25 and 39, whilst returnees tended to be younger: over half were under 24 years of age. On average, moreover, the former are more likely to be earning higher salaries. In spite of this, around half of all migrants stated that their income was lower than average, suggesting that salaries might have been cut substantially, or not paid, even.

Nevertheless, the decision to stay in Russia did not depend so much on the current salary level, but rather on the ability to retain one's position or find a new job. Such qualities as entrepreneurship, skills, activeness, low risk aversion, and the ability to change one's specialty or move to another region appeared to be important factors determining the likelihood of staying in Russia. Other qualities such as patience, willingness to work in harsh conditions, and the readiness to accept lower salaries may appear to be even more important. Among those who stayed in Russia, 60 percent said that they would be ready to accept lower salaries, while among those who returned to Tajikistan only 30 percent would have accepted such conditions.

The results of the survey show that those who stay behind show greater resilience or tolerance in the face of adversity, as only 25 percent of those staying stated they had done nothing in response to a job loss or other "crisis" situation, as opposed to over half of those who returned. This contrasts with the information that over two-thirds of surveyed migrants from both groups stated that their life had in fact changed in the last three to five months due to the crisis. However, the remarkable difference in the behavior of these two types of migrants is in the approaches and strategies undertaken to cope with job losses and worsening working conditions. Migrants from both groups used generally the same channels to find new jobs; in over half of all cases, migrants went to friends and relatives, utilized various media channels where jobs are advertized, or searched on their own. Over 40 percent of all surveyed migrants stated that they were offered (and accepted) lower salaries. Among those who changed jobs, the share of those who were offered and accepted lower salaries increases to over 60 percent. Almost 20 percent of all surveyed migrants stated they were ready to work in other regions of Russia, as opposed to only 5 percent among those who returned; and another 40 percent actually changed their sector of employment.

In the case of worsened working conditions, only 25 percent of those deciding to remain in Russia expressed their intention to return home. And even where working conditions were particularly harsh, the percentage of those intending to return increased to only 30 percent. In both cases, over half of the surveyed migrants stated they would stay in Russia regardless, accepting other jobs in different sectors or regions with lower salaries if need be. Another important factor determining the likelihood of staying in Russia was a positive attitude toward the country. Two-thirds of those who managed to stay in Russia stated that they would like to get Russian citizenship. Only a third of respondents said they would like to return to Tajikistan. Half of the respondents indicated that they were not planning to return, with 10 percent stating that they would like to go back to Tajikistan only when they had earned more money and the situation in their home country had improved.

Migrants Who Returned to Tajikistan During the Crisis

The first wave of return migration to Tajikistan took place in March 2009. The survey showed that two-thirds of all returning migrants came back because of work-related reasons and only a third returned for family reasons or holidays. Among those who returned due to work-related issues, roughly a third returned because of having lost their job, half due to "cheating" on the part of their employer such as underpaying, and 15 percent due to wage cuts. A worrisome increase was also observed in the share of migrants returning due to worsening health and deportation (almost 10 percent each). This situation is very different in comparison to IOM data obtained in April and May 2008,[9] when well over half of all returning migrants came back due to family reasons, only 5 percent due to deportation, and 10 percent due to health reasons. The rate of job losses in the services sector, including catering, comes second to the rate of job losses in construction, but the number of losses is equally significant in absolute terms.

Only 10 percent of returning migrants clearly stated that they did not want to go back to Russia. On the contrary, 90 percent planned to return to Russia to work. In addition, almost half of all interviewed migrants planned to stay in Tajikistan for a maximum of only two months, a quarter of migrants up to three months, another 10 percent planning to stay until the crisis is over, with a remaining 20 percent unsure. When asked exactly what they would do if they stayed at home and could not find a job, a third indicated that they would return to Russia, another third stated that they would wait out the crisis, 10 percent answered that they were not sure what they would do, while 15 percent said that they would start a business or revert to agriculture as a survival strategy. In terms of what they actually do upon their return, over half of all migrants go home to rest, 25 percent attend to some sort of family affair (wedding, funeral, or construction work on a home), 5 percent work, and only a further 5 percent engage in business.

---

[9] *Migration and Development in Tajikistan. Emigration, Return and Diaspora* (Moscow: International Labor Organization, 2010), 17–18.

Two large sub-groups can be distinguished among the returnees. The first group consists of those young individuals between 18 and 26 years of age, accounting for 20 percent of all returnees, who have only made one trip to Russia to work. Typically they do not speak Russian, have no prior migration experience, and have low or no professional skills. During the financial crisis, members of this group were the first to lose their jobs. The second group, on the other hand, consists of highly skilled workers who lost their high-paying jobs and returned to Tajikistan in order to rest and await the end of the crisis. One example of such a group was a brigade of six skilled welders, all with a higher education and aged 29 to 42, who had worked legally in Russia for over nine years. They lost their jobs when their employer went bankrupt. The group waited initially for three months without pay—they had yet to be paid by the time of the survey—and did not look for other jobs, whereupon they decided to return home. Similarly, a brigade of 17 finishing construction workers (in high-end jobs) were paid only two months after their company had stopped their projects. However, they were told by the company that they would resume work in five to six months' time.

Respondents pointed out that many employers appreciated highly skilled specialists and tried to give them work even during the crisis. Most employers maintained connections with these workers even after their return to Tajikistan, intending to invite them back as soon as the industry started picking up again. Migrants of this second group consider their return to Tajikistan only as a temporary "rest" and do not plan to look for permanent jobs at home. In this group only 10 percent of the respondents claimed that they would never work abroad again.

In general, it is clear that although the crisis did hit migrants badly, equally important is the impact of worsening attitudes on the part of law enforcement agencies and migration authorities (via stringent statements and actions with respect to quotas) as well as employers (via their efforts to cover their losses at the expense of the labor migrants and outright abuse), all of which has led to an increase in the amount of both formal and informal payments. Such a situation means that it is harder for migrants to "break even" and makes migration less economically beneficial and also more dangerous to their personal security. It is not surprising that better-off migrants prefer to return home and wait until the crisis is over. Relatively less well-off migrants remain in Russia and agree to take on more menial jobs. Meanwhile, the most mobile groups even change regions or seek employment in other countries such as the United States,

European Union, or the United Arab Emirates, or try to learn new skills so as to meet demands in the Russian labor market.

Migrants Who Departed for Russia During the Crisis

Various features of current Tajik migration to Russia were studied, including socio-demographic characteristics, preferences, values, and strategies. The data revealed that 64 percent of respondents arranged their work before they departed for Russia. Members of this group included qualified workers in manufacturing, construction, trade, catering, transportation, housing, as well as public and other types of services. Two-thirds of these workers were above the age of 30, spoke Russian, and had between two and nine years of experience in labor migration. As for those migrants who departed for Russia without any prior job arrangement (36 percent), they intended to do any work regardless of salary and working conditions. They planned to wait in Russia until the end of the crisis and then to seek better jobs once the economic situation improved. Half of the migrants from this group did not care at all about the type of work, the salary, or working conditions. They were labeled "hopeless" because they had the lowest salaries and resided in extreme poverty.

One of the respondents was a 56-year-old stonemason from Rasht valley who had worked in Russia for six years, but had quit three years ago when his three sons started working in Moscow with the Donstroi construction company. At the time of the survey, his sons had lost their jobs three months previously as construction work dried up, leading to a situation in which they had not been paid for four months and had not been sending money home. The employer only paid for their food and let them live in a mobile home at the construction site. The father indicated that he would help his newly impoverished household by any means possible, stating "I cannot see [my] children suffer and stay at home listening to women all the time."

Migration strategies have changed noticeably since the beginning of the crisis. Currently only 50 percent of migrants are willing to do seasonal work in Russia; the other half plan to look for long-term employment ranging from one to two years in duration. As a 46-year-old carpenter stated during the survey, "There is always some work in Russia. It may be better or worse, but it will be some work anyway. While here in Tajikistan there is nothing." Migrants quickly adapt to the changing labor conditions of the Russian market, as is demonstrated by the fact that 36 percent of migrants are willing to do any type of work. This implies that one of the most crucial strategies for migrants is their ability to change occupations and acquire various professional skills. Thus, those who depart for Russia have different qualifications and can quickly respond to changing demands for labor there.

The Reintegration of Migrants Who Stay in Tajikistan

One can conditionally divide returning migrants into two general categories: successful and unsuccessful migrants. Successful returning migrants often start their own businesses, as private entrepreneurs in most cases. Unsuccessful returning migrants, on the other hand, fail to reintegrate well or cannot find suitable jobs. Having exhausted their savings, they go back to Russia again, agreeing to undertake any kind of work for low wages in view of a lack of decent job opportunities—ironically the same circumstances that push them to migrate in the first place. In addition to this, there is a large group of people consisting of both "older" migrants and those whose health has substantially deteriorated. However, a large share of those who return are actually highly skilled and highly paid contractors in Russia, mainly in high-end construction. These individuals do not plan to find work in Tajikistan and prefer to stay away from the crisis, wait, and return to Russia at a more opportune moment. In terms of economic behavior, all returning migrants reduced their consumption and tried to save money, assuming that the crisis period would be a prolonged one. Most of the savings were in the form of foreign currency or investments in land, cattle, or food supplies.

Results of the survey show that over two-thirds of all returning migrants find employment in Tajikistan. Many, if they have the choice, prefer to start their own business or work as individual contractors. Of all those employed upon return, 20 percent are either owners of their own businesses or are self-employed, another 15 percent are in public service, another 10 percent work for private companies, and 7 percent work as short-term contractors.

The study revealed that the experience and knowledge acquired abroad improved the status of some returnees on the labor market in Tajikistan. Thus, 39.1 percent of respondents said that after migration, it was easier for them to find a well-paid job. However, for 42.7 percent, nothing had changed, and 18.2 percent stated that after their return, it had become even more difficult for them to find a well-paid job.

> I am a returned migrant, but I do not want to find a job. Because my education is not enough to find a position with a good salary, and it is not profitable to become an ordinary worker, the salary is not enough to sustain a

> family. Therefore, currently I work as a taxi driver with my personal car. *Yokubkhoja, taxi driver, 27 years old, Isfara.*

The majority of the respondents who stated that it had become easier to find a job with a good salary in Tajikistan work in private businesses or are self-employed. Typical responses from such returnees include the following sample, all of whom started their own businesses:

> It is almost impossible to find a well-paid job; therefore I started my own business.
>
> I have created a job myself and am currently earning bread for my family through it.
>
> I've got good experience, improved my knowledge, professionalism, acquired entrepreneurial skills, and started my own business.
>
> I have brought a motor car with me [from Russia] and now work as a taxi driver and earn for the family.
>
> I am working as a hairdresser with the equipment I have brought, my hairdressing salon is bringing me profit.
>
> I opened an Internet café and earn good money.
>
> I brought a modern incubator from Russia, created a chicken farm at home, and work there.

Meanwhile, a small portion of returnees, predominantly those who obtained an education abroad, found well-paid jobs in state-owned organizations and enterprises. This category of returnee less frequently finds employment in private companies. When asked about their jobs, the survey elicited some of the following responses:

> Now I am working in the militia forces in a trained specialty.
>
> Now I am working as a second pilot in our air company.
>
> I train my apprentices in modern construction techniques and skills I acquired when I was a labor migrant, but presently I work as a teacher in the vocational school and share my experience with the youth.
>
> I am a geologist. After returning, through my acquaintances, I succeeded in finding a job for which I was trained.

In analyzing the answers of those who had more difficulties in finding a well-paid job, however, it is noticeable that returnees encounter the same set of problems they had before deciding to migrate—namely, unemployment and low salaries. Among this category of returnees are also "elderly" people and those with poor health.

Abdumavlon, a 38-year-old handyman from Isfara, stated: "It is very difficult for a returning migrant to find a job in Tajikistan. For instance, migrants, who before migration used to work on a farm, presently do not want to work on the same farms, which do not pay wages to the farmers at all. In Russia, they were paid on time and much more, and in the homeland they have to work for free. After returning they are either idle or leave for Russia again. It makes no sense to get a job here."

Another respondent, Abdughaffor, a 38-year-old driver from Khorog said: "Khorog is a small town. It is very hard for a migrant to find a job in such a city—all jobs are occupied. In our area, a migrant can only find a job as a teacher or a physician with a very low salary. Nobody wants to work for that money. Only women have remained to work here. And I earned 18–20,000 rubles [nearly 600 dollars] when I worked in Russia. If it were my will I would have left long ago."

What is more, if a migrant is already employed prior to migrating, his departure often interrupts his career development. This is the case because migrants seldom get a job abroad for which they were trained. During their absence abroad, many lose their professional skills—or, conversely, gain such skills and experience which, however, are of little use in Tajikistan due to the technological lag—and social capital (the necessary acquaintances and contacts that would help them find a decent job in their home country) without accumulating new ones. Some of the disadvantages and obstacles are illustrated in the quotations from respondents below.

> If a migrant formerly worked in a responsible and profitable position, of course, after his return, he will not be able to occupy this job, as someone else has taken it. *Salim, teacher, 45 years old, Bokhar.*
>
> Starting work for a migrant after his return from Russia is very difficult because influential acquaintances or big money is required to get a good job or to start one's own business. *Homidjon, welder, 42 years old, Isfara.*
>
> Many migrants fail to find a job after their return, since there are no jobs here that they had abroad. They are used to working with new technologies. Introduction of technologies, which are being used in Russia, needs much time, money, and effort. *Abdunabi, businessman, 30 years old, Isfara.*

Notwithstanding the above, returning migrants nevertheless do have an important role to play in the modernization of many industries and the introduction of new technologies, instruments, and skills. This is constrained, however, by the fact that this is often only possible in the sphere of smaller enterprises. This is not only because returnees prefer starting their own businesses or getting involved in the businesses of their relatives, friends, and acquaintances, but also because in spite of bringing back cheap tools, machines, and means of production, they do not have money for big investment projects and have no possibility to access such funds. Secondly, the business environment is not friendly in Tajikistan and overcoming bureaucratic obstacles necessitates informal protection from criminals or officials. This represents a major problem for migrants, as studies show that migrants are often marginalized people who do not have access to such protection, resources, or power.[10]

Given all these considerations, returnees make the most significant impact on the following economic sectors in Tajikistan: services, where migrants bring new and effective cheap tools and technologies; construction, especially finishing construction, as migrants bring instruments and machines, provide information on new finishing materials on the market, new technological methods, and modern trends in construction; and agricultural production, storage, and processing.

The survey revealed that in these spheres of activity, employers better compensate returnees for their labor as compared to those without migration experience. However, migrants do not have significant impact where modernization or reconstruction of larger-scale production is necessary or where big investments are required. Such companies, which do not need technological and organizational innovations, often do not hire returnees. There are also employers who refuse to recruit returnees. These employers usually run enterprises with outdated production equipment and cannot afford to introduce the latest technologies. Top managers at such enterprises avoid returning migrants, since they demand the replacement of old equipment and the introduction of new and better working methods. Managers emphasize that they cannot do so because of the business environment in Tajikistan:

> The state of the enterprise does not allow hiring migrants, since they want to work on modern machines, and we have no such equipment [sewing machines]. If we replace equipment and expand production following their recommendations, tax rates will increase drastically and we will go bankrupt. *Tailors' workshop, Dushanbe.*

---

[10] Brown, Olimova, and Boboev, *A Study on International Migrant Remittances in Central Asia and South Caucasus: Country Report on Remittances of International Migrants in Tajikistan*, 60–61.

> We have no conditions and means for modernization and introduction of technologies that the returned migrants demand, for instance, buying cars. Therefore, to avoid dissatisfaction of the staff, I try not to recruit the returned migrants. *Director of a wholesale depot.*

On the other hand, returnees do make a strong impact on businesses in Tajikistan, especially those where there is a clearly expressed family organization. Most frequently, returnees start their businesses with the involvement and support of their family members and relatives: 43 percent of 279 respondents had their own businesses or managed relatives' businesses, which do not pay salaries to employees. In these types of businesses, the income of the workers is distributed within a family budget managed by the returnee.

> If I start my own business, first of all I will attract my family members and friends. Then, to the extent possible, I will hire workers, but smart and knowledgeable ones. *Jonsho, technician, 44 years old, Khorog.*

> You should recruit persons whom you trust. Of course, you will hire people close to you. They will not demand a salary when the business has become 'stuck.' *Alijon, handyman, 23 years old, Khorog.*

Of returning migrants who are businessmen, 55.5 percent *do* hire staff and pay them a wage. At the same time, many of their employees are related to them. Almost 4 percent of business owners said that they simultaneously had wageworkers to whom they paid salaries as well as family members working for free.

There are substantial differences in the employment trends and starting of businesses across different regions of Tajikistan. Most of the returning migrants finding employment are in Khatlon region (over 80 percent), while the smallest number of them are in the Gorno-Badakhshan Autonomous Oblast (GBAO) (only 20 percent). This is mainly explained by the size of the labor market and employment opportunities in the regions. The so-called Region of Republican Subordination (RRS region), which includes Karategin, has the largest share of migrants who open their own businesses (70 percent), followed by Khatlon (60 percent), Dushanbe (50 percent), Sogd (around 30 percent), and only 5 percent in the GBAO. Some migrants with their own businesses in Russia, mainly residents of the Dushanbe and Sogd regions, have started moving their businesses to Tajikistan. These businesses are mainly concentrated in chains of small street shops or transport services (public transport or private taxis).

The key barriers to the successful reintegration of returnees are as follows: difficulties in starting businesses (including lack of knowledge, lack of access to credit, and corruption); exclusion from social networks (especially for "long-term" migrants); and a lack of information and access to available information about job vacancies. The survey also shows that, in general, returning migrants are not inclined to be mobile—less than 10 percent of returnees move to different areas within Tajikistan upon their return—or are prepared to change their citizenship. Only 5 percent of returnees, all of whom were young people under the age of 30, stated they had thought of moving permanently and changing citizenship.

* * * * *

The current developments in labor migration make it clear that the main factor determining changes in labor migration are Russian protectionist policies rather than the financial crisis itself. These protectionist policies include increasingly intolerant attitudes on the part of police authorities toward migrants, employers' attempts to reduce their losses by underpaying migrants, and the increasing proportion of formal and informal payments. All such factors raise the risks of migration and make employment in Russia less profitable.

In response to this, some migrants prefer to return home, cut their expenditures, and wait until the end of the crisis. Other migrants prefer to stay in Russia, accepting lower wages and deteriorating working and living conditions. Young labor migrants without professional skills have been laid off first, and most of them decide to return to Tajikistan. The most skilled workers, however, continue to work, despite worsening conditions in Russia. Thus, the major impact of the crisis on Tajikistan is likely to manifest itself through lower volumes of remittances, rather than through socio-demographic indicators such as an increased number of returnees.

The studies also find that migrants form clearly defined pre-, post-, and in-migration strategies. These strategies are shaped not only on the basis of the individual experiences of migrants, but also upon consideration of social and institutional factors in both the host and destination countries. The survey of returning migrants shows that during the global financial and economic crisis, different groups of migrants have developed different strategies of migration. Comparisons of the data on migrants collected in April and May 2008 suggest that the share of young low-skilled and unskilled returning migrants (with no Russian-language ability) has increased substantially since the start of the crisis. This category of migrant was the first to be hit by the crisis, to lose their jobs and to return home. Twenty percent of all returning migrants fall into this category. Women are least affected, however. Only a small percentage of female migrants were in the sample, and those who were came back due to family reasons and were better off in general. Well over two-thirds of all returning migrants only have high school or vocational training. At the same time, there is also quite a large number of highly skilled migrants (high-level welders, for instance) who have lost their high-paying jobs.

The comparison of the group of Tajik migrants who stayed in Russia with those who returned home during the crisis shows that the most significant difference between these two groups is their migration and return strategies. Whereas groups used the same channels to find jobs, such as friends and relatives, and relied less on newspapers and independent searches, migrants that stayed in Russia are more active in looking for jobs and are prepared to be more flexible, and to work for a lower salary. Twenty percent of staying migrants were willing to relocate to other regions of Russia in search of a job in contrast to only 5 percent of returnees. Aside from the dynamism of migration, the main distinctions between different groups of migrants can be found in the duration of migration, language skills, professional skills, position in the household (son, father), and the intensity of connections with their local community in Tajikistan.

KAZAKHSTAN: CENTRAL ASIA'S NEW MIGRATION CROSSROADS

Marlene Laruelle

In the short span of just a few years, Kazakhstan has become a unique migration crossroads in Central Asia. In 2007, it experienced the paradox of becoming simultaneously the world's ninth-largest migrant-receiving country whilst also being the seventh-largest migrant-sending country.[1] The emigration of its so-called European population, which has been considerable, especially in the 1990s, declined through the second half of the 2000s. But the country has had to contend with the massive arrival of migrants from neighboring Central Asian states, as well as some Russian-speaking "return" migrants.[2] At the same time a country of departure and arrival, Kazakhstan is also a transit country hosting a growing number of non-CIS migrants, mostly Afghans, Turks, Chinese, and Indians, all of whom see it as the gateway to Russia and subsequently to Europe. This chapter focuses mainly on labor migration from the neighboring countries of Kyrgyzstan and Uzbekistan, and to a lesser extent Tajikistan.

After Russia, Kazakhstan has the second-largest intake of migrants from Central Asia. Attracted by its economic dynamism, Uzbek, Kyrgyz, and Tajik migrants are continuing to grow in number. They are distributed geographically according to their professions, and are very diverse in terms of their social backgrounds and professional qualifications. As Kazakhstan seeks to position itself as a regional leader for the whole of Central Asia, it is aware that its migratory appeal works in its favor. In an address made in February 2008, President Nursultan Nazarbayev pledged that his country would set up a special labor transfer scheme for the countries of the Central Asian region. However, the Kazakh authorities were not able to formulate adequate legislation, oscillating between taking a more liberal approach to migration and protecting the national employment market.

---

[1] A. Mansoor and B. Quillin, eds., *Migration and Remittances. Eastern Europe and the Former Soviet Union* (Washington, D.C.: The World Bank, 2006), 3.

[2] Return migrations to Kazakhstan are very rarely documented. On the global issue of return migration, see J.-P. Cassarino, "Theorising Return Migration: The Conceptual Approach to Return Migrants Revisited," *International Journal on Multicultural Societies* 6, no. 2 (2004): 253–279.

Contrary to the hopes raised, Kazakhstan failed to become a welcoming place for migrant workforces, even if its legislation improved in 2011. Yet, the growing number of Uzbeks and, to a lesser extent, of Kyrgyz, who are settling in its southern border regions, coupled with the departure of its Russophone population, entails changes in how Kazakhstani identity will be defined in the years to come, as well as how it will manage its current "Central-Asianization."

A Pillar of Development for all Central Asia

While Kazakhstan was the world's ninth-largest migrant-receiving country in 2007,[3] it has since relinquished this position to Ukraine. By 2010, it was ranked tenth internationally, and third inside the CIS, after Russia and Ukraine.[4] According to the International Organization for Migration (IOM), Kazakhstan has about three million migrants and remains an especially attractive destination for people from the southern parts of the former Soviet Union.

There are many explanations for the country's appeal. For one, the immense territory of Kazakhstan (2.7 million km^2) combined with its small population (16 million people according to the 2009 census, or 5.6 inhabitants per km^2) makes it a potentially promising land for immigration. Since the beginning of the 1990s, the Kazakh authorities have also kept their borders open, following the signing of agreements for free movement inside the CIS. As a result, citizens from Uzbekistan, Kyrgyzstan, and Tajikistan have been able to enter Kazakhstan without requiring a visa. The politics of migration are far from smooth, however. The coming into effect of the Customs Union in 2011 has served to intensify tensions across the border between Kazakhstan and Kyrgyzstan. Moreover, relations between Kazakhstan and Uzbekistan have always been testing, but their 780-kilometer-long common border nonetheless allows for numerous unmonitored crossings.

[3] Mansoor and Quillin, *Migration and Remittances. Eastern Europe and the Former Soviet Union*, 3.

[4] See "Facts and Figures" on the IOM website, http://www.iom.int/jahia/Jahia/about-migration/facts-and-figures/regional-and-country-figures/cache/offonce/.

The main reason for Kazakhstan's success as a receiving country can be attributed to its economic dynamism, which stands in great contrast to the stagnation—and sometimes even recession, as in the case of the Kyrgyz economy—that has affected its southern neighbors. Since the beginning of the 2000s, the country has had economic growth rates of around 8 percent a year and, according to the figures of the National Bureau of Statistics, only 13 percent of the population lived below the poverty line in 2010.[5] This figure, however, conceals significant regional disparities, with over a quarter of citizens in Mangystau province, the country's least developed, classified as poor. It is therefore likely that the actual number of people living below the poverty line is higher.[6] Nevertheless, compared with its neighboring countries to the south, Kazakhstan would appear to be an oasis of wealth. Somewhere between 40 to 60 percent of Kyrgyz, Uzbek, and Tajik citizens live below the poverty line, and the GDP per capita in these three countries ranges from 2,100 to 2,600 dollars,[7] far below Kazakhstan's GDP per capita, which increased to 12,800 dollars in 2010, second only after Russia within the CIS.[8]

Since 2004, Kazakhstan's yearly migration balance has been positive, despite a still notable outflow of citizens (668,000 persons departed from Kazakhstan in the first decade of the twenty-first century).[9] In 2004 alone, emigration reduced sevenfold compared to its peak a decade previously. The same year, Kazakhstan saw its first—modest but symbolically important—positive migration balance in 36 years. In 2011, the number of people who emigrated increased again (by 22.8%) compared to 2010, but the country was still able to claim a positive migration balance of 5,400 people.

---

[5] See http://www.stat.kz.

[6] V. Ivanov, "Nepriatnaia statistika. Podavliaiushchee bol'shinstvo kazakhstantsev, po standartam sosedei, zhivut za chertoi bednosti," *Delovaia nedelia*, June 3, 2011, http://www.dn.kz/.

[7] For more on the poverty affecting these countries, see R. Jha and Tu Dang, "Vulnerability to Poverty in selected Central Asian Countries," *The Australian National University Working Paper*, no. 10, August 2008.

[8] See European statistics, http://ec.europa.eu/trade/creating-opportunities/bilateral-relations/statistics/.

[9] "Over half a million left Kazakhstan for other countries for permanent residency in the recent decade," *Tengri.news*, April 13, 2012, http://en.tengrinews.kz/people/9144/.

Table 1. Kazakhstan Migration Balance 2001–11[10]

Year	Number of arrivals (in thousands)	Number of departures (in thousands)	Migration balance
2001	34.4	104.3	−69.9
2002	58.2	120.2	−62.0
2003	65.6	73.9	−8.3
2004	68.3	65.5	+2.8
2005	74.3	52.2	+22.1
2006	67.4	33.9	+33.5
2007	53.3	42.4	+11.0
2008	47.6	45.2	+2.4
2009	33.9	41.4	+7.5
2011	32.7	38.1	+5.4

According to official Kazakh reports, the country was host to approximately one million illegal workers in 2010.[11] Taking seasonal flows and shuttle trade into account, some experts have put forward a more plausible figure of about one-and-a-half to two million migrants.[12] At the end of the 1990s, Kyrgyz migrants were the first to take advantage of the opportunities presented by Kazakhstan.[13] The number of Kyrgyz migrants working seasonally overseas is calculated to be between half a million and one million (the figure of one million would appear to be more realistic, especially in

[10] Source: For 2000–8: National Bureau of Statistics. Information compiled from *Kontseptsiia migratsionnoi politiki respubliki Kazakhstan na 2007-2015 gody*, http://www.enbek.kz/law/lawdetail.php?recordID=364; and Ju.K. Shokamalov, "Demograficheskoe razvitie Kazakhstana: sostoianie i perspektivy," *Informatsionno-analiticheskii tsentr izucheniia obshchestvennykh politicheskikh protsessov na postsovetskom prostranstve*, March 10, 2009, http://www.ia-centr.ru/expert/3879/. For 2009: *Basic indicators for 2003–2009: migration of population*, The Agency of Statistics of the Republic of Kazakhstan, http://www.stat.kz/digital/naselsenie/Pages/default.aspx. For 2011: "Number of Emigrants from Kazakhstan Rose by over 20% in 2011—Statistics Agency," Interfax Agency, 2011, http://www.interfax.kz/?lang=eng&int_id=expert_opinions&news_id=826.

[11] N. Zhiger, "Kak 'perevarit,' million. V Kazakhstane gotovitsia novaia redaktsiia zakona 'o Migratsii,'" *CentrAsia*, April 5, 2011, http://www.centrasia.ru/newsA.php?st=1301986920.

[12] E. Eshamanova, "Tendentsii i puti sotrudnichestva Kazakhstana i Rossii v reshenii problem trudovoi migratsii iz stran Tsentral'noi Azii," *Informatsionno-analiticheskii tsentr izucheniia obshchestvennykh politicheskikh protsessov na postsovetskom prostranstve*, March 5, 2008, http://www.ia-centr.ru/expert/578/; "Cross Border Migration Probe: Critical Study Aims to Protect Migrants' Rights," UNESCO, July 15, 2009, http://www.unesco.kz/?sector=&region=&lang=&newsid=2373&announce=.

[13] R. Abazov, "Economic Migration in Post-Soviet Central Asia: The Case of Kyrgyzstan," *Post-Communist Economies* 11, no. 2 (1999): 237–252.

light of the new wave of departures following the 2010 crisis).[14] Of that number, about two-thirds have left for Russia, while a third have headed for Kazakhstan, which would mean that about 300,000 Kyrgyz would be working in the latter country. The flows from Tajikistan are smaller; an overwhelming majority of Tajik migrants choose Russia as their primary destination and have no Turkic language links with Kazakhstan, unlike the other states of the region. In 2007, it is thought that there were only about 50,000 Tajiks in Kazakhstan, including close to 10,000 in Almaty; this can party be explained by the fact that the latter is well-serviced by air with Dushanbe.[15]

Uzbeks began to migrate en masse at the start of the 2000s and now constitute about two-thirds of the so-called *gastarbeitery*. Although Uzbekistan is the largest migrant-sending country of Central Asia (in gross figures, not proportionally), calculating the exact numbers is hampered due to the fact that the Uzbek authorities refuse to recognize the importance of informal migration flows; only a very small minority of people emigrate through legal channels. According to rough estimates, anywhere from between two to five million people leave Uzbekistan on a seasonal basis, half of whom head to Russia while approximatively the other half go to Kazakhstan. Of those who leave for Kazakhstan, between 200,000 and 1 million go to its southern regions.[16] A 2005 survey conducted by the IOM in South Kazakhstan revealed that 55 percent of Uzbek migrants surveyed cited the lack of jobs in Uzbekistan as the reason for their departure, while 35 percent left because of the low salaries they received at home, which, they claim, were insufficient to feed their families.[17]

During the period 2007–8, before Russia and Kazakhstan had been fully hit by the world financial crisis, between 25–35 percent of the working-age population in Kyrgyzstan, Tajikistan, and Uzbekistan were working abroad. The financial impact of migration on the economies of those three

---

[14] L. Ormonbekova, "Equivocal Claims. Examining Labour Migration Regimes with Ambivalent Control Claims—Central Asian States' Policies on Migration Control," in E. Guild and S. Mantu, eds., *Constructing and Imagining Labour Migration. Perspectives of Control from Five Continents* (Farhnam: Asghate, 2011), 281.

[15] A. Dosmanbetova, "O problemakh trudovykh migrantov Tadzhikistana na territorii Kazakhstana," *Analitika.org*, June 1, 2007, http://www.analitika.org/article.php?story=20070524234253285.

[16] F. Djani, "Goskomstat Uzbekistana poobeshchal chto budet i vpred' povyshat' kachestvo zhizni naseleniia," *Ferghana.ru*, March 4, 2009, http://www.ferghana.ru/article.php?id=6083.

[17] V.V. Chupik and K.Z. Alimov, *Trudovye migranty iz Uzbekistana v iuzhnykh regionakh respubliki Kazakhstana* (Almaty: International Organization for Migration, 2005), 16.

countries is therefore significant.[18] Remittances sent by migrants working in Kazakhstan during the period from 1995 to 2006 are said to have multiplied six-fold (from $500 million to $3 billion, representing 3.9 percent of Kazakhstan's GDP). Nearly 40 percent of remittances were reportedly sent to Uzbekistan, 25 percent to Kyrgyzstan, and 16 percent to Tajikistan.[19] After the world crisis, the diversity of remittances sent to and from Kazakhstan increased, a visible trend being, among others, an increasing "Islamic" community-type sharing of remittances.[20]

Industrial Sectors and Host Regions

For Central Asian migrant workers, Kazakhstan is easily reachable by relatively affordable public transport (mostly by bus) that allows for maintaining close family links back at home. In addition, the effectiveness of cross-border familial contacts can be reinforced by the presence of Kyrgyz or Uzbek minorities settled on Kazakh territory. Far greater cultural links between Central Asian migrants and Kazakhs, as well as the absence of violent xenophobia in Kazakhstan, also make the country an attractive destination, especially in comparison to Russia.[21] Lastly, the country's liberal legislation governing work-related matters, its developed social infrastructure (including access to medical care and schools for children), and its higher salaries relative to those available in neighboring labor markets are deciding factors for many migrants when choosing Kazakhstan.

Kazakh industries are in need of recruiting large numbers of migrants to compensate for the dearth of local workforce or the refusal of Kazakh citizens to accept poorly paid employment, notably in the construction sector (both energy-related and housing). However, unlike Russia, Kazakh agriculture also offers many job opportunities to migrants, as it is facing a shortage of workers, particularly in the cotton fields and tobacco plantations. Thanks to international investments by Philip Morris, which have given a new lease of life to ageing Soviet infrastructure, the tobacco

---

18 On the impact of remittances, see E. Sadovskaia, "Mezhdunarodnaia trudovaia migratsiia i denezhnye perevody v respublikakh Tsentral'noi Azii: strategiia vyzhivaniia ili strategiia razvitiia?" in V.A. Iuntsev, ed., *Mezhdunarodnaia migratsiia: ekonomika i politika* (Moscow: TEIS, 2006), 68–84.

19 Eshamanova, "Tendentsii i puti sotrudnichestva Kazakhstana i Rossii v reshenii problem trudovoi migratsii iz stran Tsentral'noi Azii."

20 E. Todoroki, K. Celik, and M. Kholmatov, *Alternative Remittance Systems in Kazakhstan* (Washington, D.C.: The World Bank, 2011).

21 Interviews with migrants, Almaty, June 2009.

industry has grown in prominence, especially in the Chui region near the Kyrgyz border. Furthermore, the booming hydrocarbons sector is also attractive to migrants, although here they compete not only with Kazakh nationals, but also with Turkish and Chinese migrants who are employed on the extraction sites. The service sector (mostly catering and caring) is another migrant-attracting sector, offering numerous positions such as for waiters and waitresses in cafés and restaurants, cooks, domestic help, and child care for wealthy Kazakh families.[22]

The country is undergoing increasing economic differentiation between its regions, and this diversity also emerges with regard to labor migrants. The regions with the largest migrant intake are those with the most developed industrial sectors. They include the Almaty region (especially the Enbekshikazakh district) for tobacco plantations, the Zhambul region for market produce, southern Kazakhstan for cotton, both capital cities (the former one, Almaty, and the new one, Astana) for the construction sector and services, and the western regions (Atyrau and Mangystau) for hydrocarbons.[23] With different regions specializing in specific sectors, and some districts being dominated by mono-production or mono-industry, market enclaves for migrants have appeared: the Almaty region for canned fruit factories and wine factories, Karaganda for its automobile industry, and Shymkent for furniture manufacturing.[24] Pay varies greatly: the construction sector is considered well-paid (at least 200 dollars per month), while working in the cotton fields yields around only 100 dollars per month.

Although there are no precise figures available, it appears that some national specialization among migrants is taking shape in different sectors. The Uzbeks are, for instance, renowned for their competence in cotton production and market produce. The Kyrgyz have been particularly noticeable in tobacco cultivation since the mid-2000s; around 30,000 Kyrgyz are estimated to work in this sector alone.[25] The Tajiks have

---

[22] *Trudovaia migratsiia v stranakh Tsentral'noi Azii, Rossiiskoi Federatsii, Afganistane i Pakistane* (Almaty: International Organization for Migration, 2005), 14–16.

[23] E. Sadovskaia, "Vneshnie trudovye migratsii v Tsentral'noi Azii: formirovanie regional'noi migratsionnoi sistemy" (Moscow: Tsentr migratsionnykh issledovanii, no date), http://www.migrocenter.ru/publ/konfer/suzdal/m_suzdal02.php.

[24] Iu. Semykina, "Trudovaia migratsiia v Kazakhstan. Drugaia storona medali," *Centr Asia*, July 13, 2006, http://www.centrasia.ru/newsA.php?st=1152772440.

[25] "Solntse uzhe vysoko? 30,000 kyrgyzstantsev rabotaiut na tabachnykh plantatsiiakh Kazakhstana," *CentrAsia*, April 20, 2004, http://www.centrasia.ru/newsA.php?st=1082407620.

dominated the construction sector since the 1990s, as well as the food industries. A significant number of migrants also work in the local markets. Depending on the products transported, such work entails more regular migration between the country of origin and the host country. Many Central Asians are hired to work in the bazaars, in particular in the wholesale markets of Almaty, Altyn Orda, and Bolashak, where they resell products from China, Iran, and Turkey, and specialize in running fruit stalls (the fruit juices from the Khudjand factory, for example, are sold in Kazakhstan by Tajiks).[26] Some migrants have also been successful in running their own businesses overseas. The Tajik migrant associations of Kazakhstan, for example, boast about the success of their compatriot, Mirazin Usmanov, who runs the Asyl Arman cereals company and who intends to open a flour factory in Chkalov. Another "success" in this regard is Tolib Sanakulov, who exports Kazakh products to Tajikistan and as far away as Afghanistan.[27]

The Social Status of Migrants and Short- and Long-Term Strategies

Migration flows into Kazakhstan are extremely diverse. What is more, migration is not always considered permanent; indeed far from it, as many migrants aim to return to Uzbekistan or Kyrgyzstan after having accumulated sufficient capital to build houses and improve the everyday lives of their extended families. Their length of stay, therefore, varies depending on the opportunities offered by the Kazakh job market. In most cases, the migration period lasts between two to eight months, or is dependent on the length of a particular construction project or harvest. In most cases, construction work takes place in the spring and summer, while the harvesting period starts in the fall.[28] The winter months are predominantly spent at home.

While some migrants only work seasonally and return to their country of origin during the winter months, a growing number are settling in Kazakhstan for longer periods of time—for up to several years. Some of these long-term migrants search for jobs that are located close to the border, so

---

[26] Field work observations, Almaty, Astana, Shymkent, 2008; Almaty, June 2009.

[27] S. Mirzorakhmatov, "Kak zhivut tadzhiki v Kazakhstane?" *Asia Plus*, May 4, 2006, http://www.asiaplus.tj/articles/39/391.html.

[28] Chupik and Alimov, *Trudovye migranty iz Uzbekistana v iuzhnykh regionakh respubliki Kazakhstana*, 24.

that they can return home regularly to visit their families and friends. They also develop strategies to cope with their long-term absence: for instance, while some family members leave for annual work, other members of the family travel abroad only for occasional jobs. Further, it is common for a worker with experience in cotton production to have other members of his family assist during the harvesting season.[29] Also increasingly discernible is a trend toward family migration, especially among the Kyrgyz. Kazakh employers sometimes hire the services of an entire Uzbek or Kyrgyz family who have come to Kazakhstan to work in the cotton fields or in building construction. Rather than pay individual migrants, which sometimes causes tensions, employers therefore choose to negotiate a group price for several workers.[30] As Kyrgyz citizens have the right to rent property in Kazakhstan, some extended families have settled for good in the Chui region, and rent land that has been left fallow.[31] In South Kazakhstan, about 45 percent of Uzbek migrants have migrated as part of a family network.[32]

Although extremely varied, the social status of migrants falls into three broad categories. First are those migrants with a higher education or diplomas from technical colleges, but who are unable to find work at home, and who are attracted by the higher salaries and job opportunities offered in Kazakhstan. Many Kazakh firms tend to employ Kyrgyz or Uzbek specialists, as they are more willing to accept lower pay than their Kazakh counterparts, who have the choice of going to Russia for higher wages. The "brain drain" from Uzbekistan and Kyrgyzstan is therefore considerable, in particular prompting those younger generations from provincial cities not part of the political or economic elites to move away.[33] Often these migrants enjoy a legal status due to having been hired though the official quota system.

The second category of migrants forms the majority and represents those from the rural areas of Uzbekistan and Kyrgyzstan. These workers

---

[29] See E. Sadovskaya's chapter in this volume.

[30] Fieldwork observations, Almaty, Astana, Shymkent, 2008; Almaty, June 2009.

[31] "Polozhenie trudovykh migrantov iz Kyrgyzstana v respublike Kazakhstana: pravovye, ekonomicheskie, sotsial'nye aspekty," *Ekspert.kz*, August 2005, http://www.expert.kg/content/social/9.

[32] Chupik and Alimov, *Trudovye migranty iz Uzbekistana v iuzhnykh regionakh respubliki Kazakhstana*, 18.

[33] The figure of qualified Uzbek migrants in Kazakhstan is less than that of qualified Uzbek migrants in Russia because statistically the proportion of migrants working in agriculture is, by and large, greater in Kazakhstan than in Russia. Chupik and Alimov, *Trudovye migranty iz Uzbekistana v iuzhnykh regionakh respubliki Kazakhstana*, 20.

are mostly employed without the proper papers and frequently shuttle back and forth to obtain new entry stamps. Many of them are unskilled and are either trying to escape situations of chronic unemployment in their own regions of origin or are looking to earn higher salaries abroad. They do not belong to the poorest rural strata, however, as they typically finance their own migration, but they do seek to accumulate greater wealth and, if possible, climb up the social ladder.

A third category migrates simply in order to survive. Known as the *mardikory*, meaning "masculine work" in Persian, this group of men and women live in precarious conditions. Every morning, they gather in designated locations, often in areas near the bazaars, and sell their labor by the hour, the day, or the week, to those who have come to hire them.[34] While these practices have become extremely common throughout Central Asia, their migration is often small in geographical scale. Those living near the border with Kazakhstan take advantage of neighboring markets to find work and wait at the train stations to be sought out by intermediaries. A similar phenomenon has been noted in Karakalpakstan, where the *mardikory* wait for passing trains heading toward Kazakhstan and Russia in the hope of being hired for several days of work.[35] In the border regions, an increasing number of Uzbeks work on the Kazakh side during the day and return to their village in the evening.[36] Such cross-border movements on a daily basis partly explain the tension that commonly erupts whenever the border is closed or its crossing made more difficult.

A further factor is the feminization of migration, a trend which has been accelerating since 2002–3. Women now represent nearly half of all Kyrgyz migrants and about a quarter of Uzbek migrants in the southern part of Kazakhstan. Their migrating to Kazakhstan is supposedly more socially acceptable than going to Russia, as gender codes and segregations are relatively similar between their culture of origin and that of Kazakh society. In general, female migrants are older than male migrants, as they tend to migrate only after their children have grown up.[37] Those who migrate with their families generally work in the fields, while those who migrate

[34] K. Kalanov, "Vnutrenniaia migratsiia na neformal'nom rynke truda v Uzbekistane," *Informatsionno-analiticheskii tsentr izucheniia obshchestvennykh politicheskikh protsessov na postsovetskom prostranstve*, May 15, 2008, http://www.ia-centr.ru/expert/1119/.

[35] Chupik and Alimov, *Trudovye migranty iz Uzbekistana v iuzhnykh regionakh respubliki Kazakhstana*, 45.

[36] Field work observations, Almaty, Astana, Shymkent, 2008; Almaty, June 2009.

[37] Chupik and Alimov, *Trudovye migranty iz Uzbekistana v iuzhnykh regionakh respubliki Kazakhstana*, 17.

alone are involved mostly in shuttle trade or are hired in service-related sectors.[38] Women migrants are particularly vulnerable to sexual abuse, especially when they are not surrounded by men from their family.

Working Conditions, Forced Work, and Exploitation

Globally, migration issues are linked to those of labor exploitation and human trafficking. But migrants are far from being mere victims and passive pawns; instead they should be regarded as individuals equipped with strategies for survival and development. Yet, undocumented migration often puts them in vulnerable situations.[39] Like in Russia, the working conditions of migrants in Kazakhstan are generally poor, and sometimes even hazardous to their health. Migrants often sleep in rudimentary shelters close to the fields or construction sites where they work. These barracks are often crowded, and migrants are forced to sleep in shifts by rotation. They are often undernourished, even though money for food is taken out of their salaries. A large number of them have no work contracts, health insurance, or other forms of protection. As a result, they are sometimes exploited or even assaulted by their employers and left without legal recourse.[40]

In 2005, nearly a third of Uzbek migrants working in Kazakhstan claimed that they were not paid salaries, and only 13 percent have reportedly signed work contracts.[41] Official restrictions on working hours (40 hours per week, 36 hours for dangerous or hard labor, five days maximum per week) are very rarely adhered to, despite the fact that the work outdoors is particularly arduous, especially in summer. The average working week for a migrant is said to be about 60 hours, the record being held by employees in the Kzyl-Orda region, who reportedly worked more than a 100 hours per week on a construction site. The number of cases of forced labor (use of physical and other forms of violence, confinement to the work premises, retention of identity papers, and slavery) have increased

[38] Field work observations, Almaty, Astana, Shymkent, 2008; Almaty, June 2009.

[39] B. Anderson and B. Hancilová, "Migrant Labour in Kazakhstan: A Cause for Concern?" *Journal of Ethnic and Migration Studies* 37, no. 3 (2011): 467–483.

[40] "Kyrgyzskie batraki na plantatsiiakh Kazakhstana," *IWPR-Kazakhstan*, August 27, 2003, http://www.adic.org.ua/nosmoking/2003/10/kz-20030827.htm.

[41] Chupik and Alimov, *Trudovye migranty iz Uzbekistana v iuzhnykh regionakh respubliki Kazakhstana*, 30.

significantly in recent years.[42] What is more, because family migration is booming, children are being removed from school and made to work alongside their parents. In 2010, for instance, the tobacco company Philip Morris was criticized for letting children work in the tobacco fields with their parents.[43]

A very common form of exploitation is linked to the need for intermediaries. Indeed, migrants who lack sufficiently developed networks have to go through intermediaries (*brigadir*) in order to contact employers. Their first salaries are therefore used to pay fees in the reimbursement of various kinds of service providers, from recruiters to passport carriers, and to pay for a number of levels of protection (*krysha*).[44] Those who manage to join their friends or relatives, or who migrate as part of a family, may well work in strenuous conditions, but they at least manage to avoid any form of violence. A large majority of Kyrgyz and Uzbek migrants in Kazakhstan use their own family and regional networks to find jobs. In a survey conducted in 2005 in the southern part of Kazakhstan, 60 percent of those interviewed said that they had obtained information about job opportunities from friends or relatives; 16 percent looked for jobs on their own; 9 percent said they used intermediaries; and only 6 percent went through official placement agencies.[45]

Increasingly, some organized criminal groups have tried to seize control of the illegal migration channels, especially those to Russia, but also those to Kazakhstan. Migrants can therefore be exploited for purposes of money laundering or drug trafficking, but information on this issue is scarce. Organized prostitution rings servicing migrants or local consumers have become rampant.[46] Although Kazakhstan is part of the Combat Trafficking in Persons in Central Asia program, run by the IOM, the program is limited in its legal capacity, which makes it hard to pursue suspicious cases and bring culprits to justice. Neither does the program offer much in the way of protection to victims of drug trafficking or prostitution. Nevertheless, compared to Moldova or Albania, Kazakhstan is still considered to be fairly marginal in terms of the prostitution flows bound for Europe or the Gulf countries.

---

42 There is a wealth of information on this topic available on the sites of migrant and information associations such as *Ferghana.ru*, *CentrAsia*, and so on.

43 *"Hellish Work". Exploitation of Migrant Tobacco Workers in Kazakhstan*, Human Rights Watch, July 2010.

44 Field work observations, Almaty, Astana, Shymkent, 2008; Almaty, June 2009.

45 See E. Sadovskaya's chapter in this volume.

46 L. Kelly, "Fertile Fields: Trafficking in Persons in Central Asia," *Child and Woman Abuse Studies Unit London Metropolitan University*, April 2005.

The Contradictory Logics of Migration Legislation

The Kazakh authorities are increasingly aware of the need to regulate migration. In 2007, the Ministry of Labor and Social Welfare forecast that it would need to increase its intake by a minimum of 60,000 migrants per year to meet its labor needs.[47] As for the National Statistics Office, it estimated that Kazakhstan would need an additional two million people to meet its labor requirements by 2015. The country, however, faces many challenges. It needs to implement adequate legislation, address the needs of its national job market, but also to regulate migration flows toward Russia and Europe. Migrants' rights and protection have therefore to be framed not only by domestic legislative bodies, but also by bilateral agreements with supplying countries, as well as with Russia, at the regional level.

Hitherto, all decisions by the Kazakh government have been in favor of taking a hardline approach to quotas and making it impossible to legalize the majority of migrants. The security dimension of migration, also very visible in the case of Russia, dominates local narratives and ideological frames. Migration remains the purview of several institutions including the Ministry of Labor and Social Welfare and its Committee on Migration and Employment, the Ministry of Foreign Affairs (which deals with international agreements), and the Ministry of Interior (which deals with undocumented immigrants). Dating back to 1997 and amended in 2002, migration was regulated by the first migration law (*Zakon o migratsii*), which was superseded by a new law passed in 2011. A further law governing employment of the population (*Zakon o zaniatosti naseleniia*), as well as several presidential decrees, have sought to introduce quotas on the import of foreign labor.

The notion of legality is particularly difficult to define in the post-Soviet space, due to still large patterns of free movement among the CIS countries, and endemic corruption among agencies in charge of regulating migration. CIS migrants can enter Kazakh territory legally without the need for a visa, but they have to register their place of residence within five days; they are not allowed to stay in the country for more than one month (six months in the past); and they are not supposed to work. Obtaining a work permit is not their responsibility, but rather that of their

---

[47] "Mezhdu vygodoi i natsional'noi bezopasnost'iu: vzgliad na uzbekskuiu migratsiiu v Kazakhstane," *Regnum.ru*, July 4, 2007, http://www.regnum.ru/news/economy/852465.html.

employers who have to receive licenses that permit them to import foreign laborers.[48] However, the bureaucratic and time-consuming process to gain such licenses, in particular the need to justify why it is impossible to employ a national, in addition to the high cost involved in granting rights and insurance to the migrants, are all disincentives to companies to legalize their workers; in their eyes, adhering to such measures would only make them less profitable.[49] Furthermore, the entire administrative process profits from keeping migrants undocumented, and police officers are themselves sometimes involved in arranging false documents.[50]

Although the Kazakh authorities have tried to follow in the footsteps of Russia by launching a reform of their migration policy, it failed to take the liberal turn initiated by Moscow after 2007, which had contributed to legalizing many migrants in the Russian Federation. In 2007, Kazakhstan decided to set a legal work quota of 55,000 people, principally for those migrants with specific professional qualifications. Yet, the figure fails to reflect reality; in the same year migrants are reported to have made up as much as 12 percent of the country's working population, a significantly large figure.[51] In 2008, the legal work quota increased to 120,000, representing 2.4 percent of the working-age population. There was, however, a sharp decline in 2009 to 66,000 (representing 0.75 percent of the working-age population), which constituted a 50 percent decrease from the previous year, largely in anticipation of a slowdown in the country's economy due to the global financial crisis.[52] In 2011, the quota increased to 72,000, representing a slight increase to 0.85 percent of the national workforce.[53]

The Kazakh quota system identifies four categories of foreign workers: executive personnel; highly qualified specialists; skilled workers; and

48 E. Sadovskaya, "Prava trudiashchikhsia-migrantov i perspektivy prisoedineniia k Konventsii OON 1990 g. po ikh zashchite v respublike Kazakhstana," in Zh.A. Zhaionchkovskaia ed., *Zashchita prav trudiashchikhsia-migrantov v stranakh CBE i SNG i perspektivy prisoedineniia k Konventsii OON 1990 g.* (UNESCO, 2005), 59–79.

49 Semykina, "Trudovaia migratsiia v Kazakhstan. Drugaia storona medali."

50 See Transparency International, *Korruptsiia i nezakonnaia migratsiia* (Almaty: Transparency International, 2005).

51 See E. Sadovskaya's contribution in this volume.

52 Resolution of the Government of Kazakhstan, no. 1197, December 22, 2008, "On establishing of a quota for Foreign Labor Force Industrial Intake for the Labor Activity in the Republic of Kazakhstan for 2009." See also "Kazakhstan snizil na 2009 g. kvotu na privlechenie inostrannoi rabochei sily v 3,2 raza," *Investkz.com*, December 26, 2008, http://www.investkz.com/articles/5212.html.

53 N. Zhiger, "Kak 'perevarit' million. V Kazakhstane gotovitsia novaia redaktsiia zakona 'o Migratsii.'"

workers employed in seasonal agricultural work.[54] The share of workers in each category is unequal, as a large majority of migrants belong to the fourth category or to the absent category of unskilled workers engaged outside of the agriculture sector. In 2009, out of the fourth category of workers, only 4,000 foreign migrants were authorized to work. Not only that, but they had to come from countries with which Kazakhstan has signed a labor supply contract—so far only Kyrgyzstan. The quota system thus contributes to keeping migrants undocumented, and does not allow them to find ways that would help them to become legalized.

Moreover, the Kazakh authorities have largely contradictory objectives. On the one hand, they aim to attract qualified personnel and increase the country's pool of human capital, but on the other, they seek to reduce the supposed competition for work created by foreigners. The Supervisory Commission for Employment Legislation, set up in 2008, has a mission to protect the rights of Kazakh workers, essentially by ensuring that their pay is equivalent to those of foreigners.[55] The biggest foreign companies are now required to put aside 1 percent of their budget into training local specialists, and will have to replace foreign workers with Kazakhs within a few years. Defensive measures that seek to protect the domestic labor market target mainly the big foreign companies, particularly those in the hydrocarbons and extraction sectors, who often employ a lot of Turkish or Chinese employees as well as technical specialists from Europe or the Middle East.[56] Since the mid-2000s, Kazakhstan has had to contend with increasing tensions between workers from different nationalities. Social discontent has also become widespread in many regions, including Atyrau and Mangystau, where locals consider themselves to have been excluded from the oil wealth. The Zhanaozen riots organized by Kazakh workers in December 2011, for instance, were confirmation of the deteriorating social and political climate in the oil-rich west of Kazakhstan.[57]

---

[54] Kazakhstan International Bureau for Human Rights and the Rule of Law (KBHR), "Analysis of the Laws of the Republic of Kazakhstan Regarding Employment of Foreign Workers on the Territory of Kazakhstan," Almaty, 2007.

[55] "Rukovodstvo Kazakhstana obespechit sobliudenie trudovogo zakonodatel'stva s svoei strane," *AkiPress*, June 6, 2008, kz.akipress.org/news/17628.

[56] On the competition with Chinese workers, see M. Laruelle and S. Peyrouse, *The Chinese Question in Central Asia. Domestic Order, Social Changes and the Chinese Factor* (London/New York: Columbia University Press, and Hurst, 2012), 105–107.

[57] A. Kourmanova, "Lessons from Zhanaozen. Bringing Business, Government and Society Together," *Voices from Central Asia*, no. 6, September 2012.

The fact that two antonymic logics are at work in the drafting of legislation is hardly expedient to the implementation of a consistent migration policy. The Kazakh authorities have adopted a global restrictive migration policy in the name of protecting their skilled specialists from competition from highly qualified expatriates, while the reality on the ground is that of massive unskilled migration which occupies specific niches in the job market. Some measures aimed at legalizing migrant laborers have nonetheless been taken. In 2005, the Ministry of Interior granted Kazakh citizenship to more than 20,000 people, three-quarters of whom were of Uzbek origin, while 10 percent were from Kyrgyzstan and 5 percent from Tajikistan. The following year, more than 160,000 people were legalized and received a work permit.[58] However, the 2008 global financial and economic crisis served as a pretext for the Kazakh authorities to toughen their migration legislation. Thus the expulsion procedures for undocumented migrants became more stringent in 2009.[59] Since then, about 20,000 undocumented migrants have been deported from Kazakhstan each year.[60]

More recently, in 2011, it could be noted that some progress was being made in regard to reform of migrant labor legislation, with several meetings held with the European Union and the International Labor Organization to discuss bigger quotas for migrant laborers, as well as the legalization of some of them every five years.[61] In the same year, Kazakhstan eventually passed a new bill on migration,[62] but it failed to clearly define the different categories of migrants and their rights. The text confuses legality and undocumented status, ethnic repatriation, and labor migration; and it also pursues a narrative on the need for differentiating titulars from non-titulars, who are often confused with non-citizens. The country has still to ratify the UN Convention on the Protection of the Rights of All Migrant Workers and Members of their Families, and to build a more

---

58 Eshamanova, "Tendentsii i puti sotrudnichestva Kazakhstana i Rossii v reshenii problem trudovoi migratsii iz stran Tsentral'noi Azii."

59 A. Abdullina, "Kyrgyzstanskim trudovym migrantam uzhestochaiut 'pravila igry' v Kazakhstane," *Kginfo.ru*, June 6, 2009, http://www.kginfo.ru/diasporas/kz/news/kyrgyzstanskim-trudovym-migrantam-uzhestochayut-pravila-igry-v-kazakhstane/; O. Dosybieva, "Kazakhstan: Migrant Workers Face Deportation," *IWPR.net*, January 23, 2007, http://www.iwpr.net/?p=rca&s=f&o=328709&apc_state=henirca7aa85b1eb3060919efb8d3b6046e9250.

60 N. Zhiger, "V Kazakhstane gotovitsia novaia redaktsiia zakona o migratsii," *Liter*, April 5, 2011, http://www.nomad.su/?a=3-201104060026.

61 N. Zhiger, "Kak 'perevarit', million. V Kazakhstane gotovitsia novaia redaktsiia zakona 'o Migratsii.'"

62 *Zakon Respubliki Kazakhstana o migratsii naseleniia*, August 2011, http://www.zakon.kz/top_law_news/228002-zakon-respubliki-kazakhstan-ot-22.html.

efficient migration strategy, especially in changing the quota categories. Notwithstanding the limitations, at least a first step toward establishing a proper legal base has been taken.

Given the economic revival of Kazakhstan witnessed in 2010–12 in the aftermath of the crisis, the country's need for cheap labor continues to grow. Leaving hundreds of thousands of workers with undocumented status is very much a way of meeting the economic interests of the companies that employ them, which are in no hurry to legalize their workforce, as this would increase their costs. In a country where business circles form a close nexus with the political decision-making process, it is difficult to create incentives for legalizing what is a very profitable, unregulated migrant market.

The Issue of Bilateral Agreements: The Uzbek Case versus the Kyrgyz Case

One of Kazakhstan's main difficulties concerns the implementation of legislation that is consistent with migrant-supply countries. The 1994 bill on cooperation between CIS states concerning work migration never came into force. Although Astana initiated new discussions in 2008, which led to an agreement among CIS countries on the protection of migrant workers, it has yet to be ratified. In addition, Uzbekistan, which has been the main migrant supplier to Kazakhstan and Russia in recent years, has refused to negotiate regional and bilateral agreements with both countries. To date, Tashkent has limited itself to signing two documents from the International Labor Organization against human trafficking in 2008.[63] The absence of any bilateral legal mechanisms has therefore hindered Kazakhstan's ability to manage its primary source of migrants, namely from Uzbekistan.

The migration of Uzbek workers to Kazakhstan started in the beginning of the 1990s and peaked in the early 2000s. Migration numbers in 2002 alone multiplied threefold. Between 1999 and 2004, more than 130,000 Uzbeks were reported to have settled permanently in Kazakhstan. Even the poorest also started to embark on migration: during the period from 2002 and 2004, the number of Uzbek migrants defined as very poor rose

63 "Uzbekistan predprinial konkretnye shagi v bor'be s liudskim trafikom," *Oasis*, June 5, 2008, www.ca-oasis.info/news/?c=5&id=31398.

from less than 60 percent to 75 percent.[64] Although the majority of them settled just over the other side of the border, some managed to make it as far as Atyrau. In fact, more than 30,000 Uzbek citizens were reported to be working illegally in oil companies in this town, therefore constituting a considerable proportion of its 160,000 inhabitants. In the first half of the 2000s, Uzbek migrants who arrived in Kazakhstan came mostly from the Autonomous Republic of Karakalpakstan. Bordering Kazakhstan, it is in the midst of a grave environmental and industrial crisis, which has forced many to settle in the border region of Mangystau. These migrants were followed by those from the Ferghana Valley and Khorezm, most of whom chose to settle in southern Kazakhstan and the Kzyl-Orda region, while those from Samarkand generally headed toward the Almaty region.[65]

Uzbek migrants find themselves in an awkward situation as they are considered illegal both by the Kazakh authorities and by their own government, which only recognizes persons that migrate through official channels.[66] Following the decree of 2003, only the qualified state organs of Uzbekistan—the National Agency for External Labor Migration under the Ministry of Labor and Social Protection, and the Center for the Adaptation and Education of Citizens Going Abroad—are officially able to supply workers to foreign countries. The National Agency has signed contracts for workforce exports with South Korea and some Gulf countries, in turn pocketing part of the financial windfall from these exports. However, it refuses to look after migrants who leave by themselves, because they refuse to pay for state services.[67] Uzbek migrants who have been subjected to discrimination in the host country thus have no legal means of requesting aid from their state agencies.

Kyrgyz migrants are, at least in theory, better protected under the agreements ratified between Kazakhstan and Kyrgyzstan. In 2002, both countries signed an agreement on the employment of migrants in the agricultural sector in the border regions, with provisions of social protection accorded

---

64 Chupik and Alimov, *Trudovye migranty iz Uzbekistana v iuzhnykh regionakh respubliki Kazakhstana*, 18.

65 *Ibid.*, 21.

66 A. Ilkhamov, "Geographic Mobility of Uzbeks: the Emergence of Crossnational Communities vs. Nation-State Control," Paper Prepared for NBR Conference on Generational Change and Leadership Succession in Uzbekistan, March 2, 2006, Washington, D.C., www.nbr.org/programs/eurasia/Ilkhamov.pdf, 7.

67 S. Ganiev, S. Ismoilov, and A. Ergashev, *Rapid Response Group (RRG) For Prevention of Torture In Uzbekistan. The Government Of Uzbekistan Should Change Its Policy On The Uzbek Labor Migrants Abroad*, December 2007, http://www.labournet.de/internationales/uz/migranten.pdf.

to them.[68] Another document validated in 2009 protects the individual entrepreneurial activities of Kyrgyz migrants in Kazakhstan, thus making life easier for those Kyrgyz working in the bazaars. Kyrgyz migrants can also visit the consultation offices located at the Kyrgyz consulates that have been opened in the main migrant-receiving cities to address legal concerns. The Kyrgyz authorities have been relatively active in trying to implement regional legislation to protect their migrants. The situation is similar, albeit to a lesser extent, for Tajikistan, although Dushanbe is chiefly concerned with protecting its migrants in Russia.[69] The case is much worse for Uzbeks. Tashkent's refusal to recognize the importance of migration, not to mention the generally poor state of Uzbek–Kazakh relations, have detrimental consequences for the protection of migrants.

Migrants, Diasporas, and Identity Construction in Kazakhstan

One of the main issues related to labor migration in Kazakhstan is the presence of contiguous ethnic minorities along its borders. These minorities have not arrived from other countries, but rather are made up of Uzbeks and Kyrgyz populations cut off from their titular republics by the territorial divisions made during the Soviet era. Uzbeks in Kazakhstan consider themselves an indigenous population (*korennoe naselenie*), although the Kazakh state tends to classify them as a "diaspora," a term that implies outsider status, and thus a weakened legitimacy in terms of political participation. Current migration reinforces this confusing terminology: the "diaspora" terminology is often used throughout the post-Soviet space to designate migrant communities, often failing to distinguish between minority groups, which, in some regions, have always been present, and newcomers.

Uzbeks are the third-largest minority in Kazakhstan after Russians and Ukrainians. According to the 1999 census, there were around 370,000 of them in the country, representing 2.5 percent of the total population. They are heavily concentrated in certain parts of the country: more than 90 percent of them live in the southern regions, where they make up

---

[68] Agreement between the Government of the Republic of Kazakhstan and the Government of Kyrgyzstan concerning labor activity and social protection of migrant workers, employed in agricultural work in border regions, July 9, 2002. http://www.base.spinform.ru/show_doc.fwx?Regnom=4873.

[69] *Tadzhikistan: problem trudovoi migratsii i vozmozhnye podkhody k formirovaniiu politiki* (Dushanbe: Panorama, 2004).

17 percent of the population (they constitute 60 percent of the population in the Sairam district, and 42 percent in the town of Turkestan), while the others have settled in the Dzhambul region.[70] According to the same census, there were only 25,000 Tajiks and even fewer Kyrgyz, at around 10,000. This can be attributed to the fact that a large number of the latter declared themselves to be Kazakhs in the census so as to enjoy the same rights as the titular majority.

The relationship between the existing Uzbek minority and the newly arrived migrants is a complex one. On the one hand, family links with people living in Kazakhstan work to the advantage of new migrants. Those based in Kazakhstan can easily invite their family members or people from their villages to join them. They also play an important and relatively reliable intermediary role in helping to facilitate the peaceful integration of these newcomers. However, such relationships are not without their problems. During the legalization campaign of 2006, for instance, many Uzbek farmers chose not to declare the migrants who worked for them, claiming that they were family members who had come over to help out for a short time. Furthermore, local criminal networks such as those founded on ethnic solidarities sometimes force migrants to participate in the shadow economy against their will.[71]

Given the cultural proximity between the Kazakhs and Kyrgyz, their historical interactions, and their relatively good interstate relations, that a growing proportion of Kyrgyz are settling in Kazakhstan is not perceived by Kazakh public opinion to be problematic. Relations with the Uzbek minority, however, cannot be deemed as harmonious. The growing "Uzbekization" of the country's south is of increasing concern to the Kazakh authorities. The arrival of hundreds of thousands of Uzbek migrants, some of whom will seek to settle in Kazakhstan permanently, risks accentuating a trend toward the "ghettoization" of the country's south. Localized tensions between Kazakh and Uzbek villages or farmers, due to rising competition for market produce and farming, is interpreted by the Kazakh authorities as a risk for long-term interethnic tensions.[72] Relations between Astana and Tashkent are also complicated, and any

---

70 A. Alekseenko, "O nekotorykh itogakh perepisi naseleniia Kazakhstana," *Demoscope*, no. 57–58, March 4–17, 2002, http://www.demoscope.ru/weekly/2002/057/analit04.php.

71 Interviews with migrants, Shymkent, March 2008.

72 "Luchshe kak luchshe ili kak vsegda? (o kazakho-uzbekskikh otnosheniiakh)," *Uzland*, October 18, 2002, http://www.uzland.info/2002/october/18/04.htm; A. Zhumabaev, "Ty uzbek, a ia kazakh. Pochemu stradaet uzbekskaia diaspora v Kazakhstane?" *Geokz.tv*, July 1, 2007, http://www.geokz.tv/article.php?aid=8772.

destabilization that occurs in Uzbekistan would have inevitable repercussions among the so-called Uzbek diaspora. In spite of the above, the latter has not been politicized, and the Uzbek authorities have never played the diaspora card, nor have they tried to manipulate their minorities abroad by using them as a fifth column.[73]

These identity concerns have to be placed in their historical context. Since independence, Kazakhstan's population has undergone drastic changes. Between 1992 and 2002, the country lost 10 percent of its population.[74] Over the last 20 years, about three million people identified as European or Russian-speaking have emigrated. The majority of the emigrants were of working-age and nearly half of them possessed higher or technical qualifications. The country faces an ongoing shortage of qualified human capital in the industrial, agricultural, and service sectors. In 2006, the regions of northern and eastern Kazakhstan still displayed negative migration figures numbering in the thousands. While the emigration trend of those headed toward Russia and Europe has ebbed, internal migration from the countryside to the city has led to significant changes in urban areas.[75] Due to the repatriation program, the arrival of about 600,000 ethnic Kazakhs from Mongolia, Afghanistan, and China has further intensified the transformation of the urban culture in terms of ethnic make-up and social practices.[76] This identity reshaping is expected to become even more apparent as Kazakhstan transforms itself into a leading migration destination for Uzbeks, Kyrgyz, and Tajiks.

* * * * *

In the years to come, the Kazakh authorities will have to manage growing migratory flows, be they transitory flows toward Russia and Europe, seasonal workers seeking temporary work, or migrants looking to settle in the country in the long run. Competition between Kazakhstan and Russia for the intake of Central Asian migrants will intensify as they play

[73] M. Fumagalli, "Ethnicity, State Formation and Foreign Policy: Uzbekistan and Uzbeks abroad," *Central Asian Survey* 26, no. 1 (2007): 105–122; by the same author, "Framing Ethnic Minority Mobilization in Central Asia: The Cases of Uzbeks in Kyrgyzstan and Tajikistan," *Europe-Asia Studies* 59, no. 4 (2007): 565–588.

[74] M. Laruelle and S. Peyrouse, *Les Russes du Kazakhstan. Identités nationales et nouveaux États dans l'espace post-soviétique* (Paris: Maisonneuve & Larose—IFEAC, 2004).

[75] S. Yessenova, "Routes and Roots of Kazakh Identity: Urban Migration in Postsocialist Kazakhstan," *The Russian Review* 64, no. 4 (2005): 2–20.

[76] A. Danenova and A. Formanek, *Sravnitel'nyi opyt integratsii immigrantov v zarubezhnykh stranakh i Kazakhstane* (Almaty: International Organization for Migration, 2004).

an instrumental role in the Russian and Kazakh economies, and in helping to raise the living standards of their own nationals. Both Kazakhstan and Russia will have to find a balance between allowing the arrival of unqualified migrants destined for unskilled employment and managing the "brain drain" from the southern republics. The implications for the supplying countries will also be complex. Migration may offer Uzbekistan, Kyrgyzstan, and Tajikistan some degree of social stability through the remittances received from migrant workers abroad, which may provide temporary alleviation for local socio-economic difficulties. In the long run, however, these countries may lose out as their qualified urban elites seek better employment opportunities elsewhere.

Kazakhstan's status as the regional leader of Central Asia lies partly in its ability to integrate migrants from neighboring countries. The population changes of the last two decades have had a drastic effect on formulating a new civic identity. Cultural tensions among the established urban elite, marked by a largely Russified culture, and the new urbanites coming from provincial and rural regions, already challenge the cohesiveness of the nation. Xenophobia could emerge in reaction to the massive migration flows, especially as Kazakhstan already views its southern neighbors with a mixture of condescension and fear. Often regarded by its own citizens as a bridge between the Russian North and the Central Asian South, Kazakhstan today is in a process of "Central-Asianizing," especially as the Russians still living there are getting older and will progressively fade from the national landscape. In the coming years, the Kazakh authorities will therefore have to manage these vast social changes and offer new identity references for their citizens that take these complex migration evolutions into account.

PART TWO

MIGRATORY STRATEGIES AS PATTERNS OF ADAPTATION TO SOCIAL UPHEAVAL

INTRODUCTION

Marlene Laruelle

Central Asian migration is occurring in societies that are increasingly spatially mobile. Domestic circumstances have been a decisive "push" factor in this migration. The Tajik civil war, for example, triggered a massive population displacement. In the other republics, population movements within regions, between regions, and above all toward big cities, also became key elements of spatial reconfigurations during the upheaval of the 1990s. These phenomena may appear somewhat contradictory. Central Asian societies have undergone a process of de-urbanization due to the mass exodus of Russian speakers, but the social promotion offered by independence (in particular in the countries' respective civil services) and the expansion of tertiary services encourage those in rural areas to escape poverty by moving to cities. Migration is therefore part of the complex reconfiguration of the Central Asian urban and rural landscape, one that occurred even more rapidly in Kyrgyzstan and Tajikistan, where, unlike in Uzbekistan or Turkmenistan, the registration system has been relaxed or abolished, thus accelerating the influx of newcomers to cities.

Inhabitants from rural areas are the most prominent in these migratory flows. The consequent breakdown of the social fabric with the collapse of the Soviet Union, which led to the almost complete ruin of the industrial sector, not to mention widespread rural poverty, has created a situation ripe for labor migration. For Central Asia the arrival of a market economy has meant the impoverishment of a still largely rural population dependent on subsistence agriculture. Pressures on the land are acute and birth rates remain high, especially in the countryside, where more than half of the population of the four southern republics (Kazakhstan excluded) resides.[1] Rural populations suffer from high unemployment rates and a scarcity of land. And in spite of its overall low population density,[2] Central Asia is experiencing severe overcrowding in its agricultural areas.

[1] According to 2003 figures, 65 percent in Kyrgyzstan, 72 percent in Tajikistan, 55 percent in Turkmenistan, 58 percent in Uzbekistan, and 44 percent in Kazakhstan.

[2] There are 5.5 people per km^2 in Kazakhstan, 10 in Turkmenistan, 28 in Kyrgyzstan, 49 in Tajikistan, and 64 in Uzbekistan; detailed annual figures are available at http://perspective.usherbrooke.ca.

The situation is particularly serious in the Ferghana Valley, where more than ten million inhabitants live, or nearly 20 percent of the entire population of Central Asia. Population density near Andijan is close to 559 persons per square kilometer.[3]

Trapped by the false dilemma of cotton cultivation versus food self-sufficiency, some Central Asian states like Uzbekistan are reluctant to undertake land reforms. They also have to cope with many other structural problems, such as the massive corruption of the agricultural administrative structures, in particular those for credit and input deliveries; opaque decision-making structures for exports; child labor; and grave environmental problems related to extensive over-use of the soil. Kyrgyzstan and Tajikistan are classified among the poorest countries in the world, with a GDP per capita of about 2,000–2,200 dollars per year. According to UN data, about 60 percent of the population of Tajikistan live below the poverty line, equal to earning less than a dollar a day. The situation is hardly better in Kyrgyzstan and Uzbekistan—just under 50 percent live below the poverty line in these countries—where many rural areas remain on the brink of economic collapse, for instance Naryn, Khorezm, and Karakalpakstan.[4] Adversarial conditions contribute to the strengthening of traditional domestic economies, that is, patriarchal social function, withdrawal into the family (growth of endogamy), subsistence production centered on working plots of land, and partially demonetarized economies. The only cash resources available come from remittances and the sale of products at markets, with part of the economy operating on a system of subsistence and barter.

However, migration does not only affect rural areas. The growing unemployment among recent university graduates is equally if not more disturbing. The middle classes consider higher education opportunities to be strategies of social promotion. They largely invest in technical colleges and new, provincial universities (many former training colleges for secondary school teachers have been promoted to university status), but the lack of jobs leads to migration in search of employment opportunities elsewhere. Given the appeal of the Russian and Kazakh labor markets—where working conditions are better, wages more competitive, and the atmosphere more dynamic—Uzbekistan, Kyrgyzstan, and Tajikistan simply

---

[3] *Chislennost' Naseleniia Respubliki Uzbekistan na 1.1.2005* (Tashkent: Goskomstat, 2005), 5–15.

[4] See *Central Asia Human Development* (Washington, D.C.: UNDP, 2005).

cannot compete. Acting as a safety valve to relieve the pressure on their own sclerotic labor markets, in the short run the latter three states benefit from the social stability afforded by migration. However, in the longer term, they will lose out from the disappearance of their already small pool of qualified urban elites.

Although migration in Central Asia is a phenomenon that the states do not have full control over, it is increasingly affecting interstate relations. The more migrant communities become entrenched in the destination country, the more they organize themselves in order to influence the politics of both the host country and their homeland. For example, there have been demands made to Russia that it pay the pensions of Kyrgyz workers once they have returned to Kyrgyzstan. Migrant associations are often funded by businessmen wanting to invest money in building social networks, hoping to legitimize their political role as intermediaries between the state structures and the migrants. They can be regarded as "identity entrepreneurs," seeking to reinforce ethnic affiliation among migrants. Migrant associations remain rooted in their ethnic origin and, at least for the moment, do not aim to be transnational or corporatist. Ethnicity is therefore used by them as a tool to justify communitarian practices. However, it is also connected to marketing activities, as these practices often operate through the sale of legal services to migrants, who are seen as a captive market. Migration also has the potential to become a driving force for the democratization of Central Asian societies. Migrants essentially comprise a new social force, wielding a certain financial power that is in theory capable of competing with the state. Although little has been achieved hitherto by the few attempts at politicizing migrant communities in Kyrgyzstan and Tajikistan, it can be assumed that social and political legitimacy will evolve.

Internal migration, which preceded international migration and played a central role in making rural populations more dynamic, is the topic of the first two chapters of this section. Both focus on the effects of this sudden acquisition of mobility. Aida Aaly Alymbaeva's chapter sheds very detailed light on the internal dynamics of mobility in Kyrgyzstan; that is, on the motivations driving the massive rural exodus to small- and medium-size towns and, even more so, to Bishkek. The author offers a historical perspective, analyzing the division between rural and urban dwellers, ethnic population distribution, and the ethnic division of labor in the Soviet period, all of which have shaped contemporary phenomena. This internal migration is essentially that of the titular Kyrgyz nationality. The so-called European populations have emigrated abroad, whereas the

Uzbek minority in the country's south has up until recently proven not very mobile—excepting after the ethnic riots of Osh in June 2010. In two decades, the rural-urban and center-periphery balance has been drastically modified: internal migration involved around 700–800,000 people per year from 2003 to 2005. The peculiarity here is the increasing number of older people involved compared with the 1990s when it was mainly only younger people on the move. Today the capital Bishkek appears as the archetypal illustration of the country's urbanization resulting from internal migration. The city's suburban districts are home to migrants seeking work as well as plots of land on which to build houses, resulting in numerous cases of undocumented land occupation. Even without employment, they do not envisage returning to their villages of origin, instead continuing to see in their new urban identity the only prospect for social promotion.

In Tajikistan, internal migration has also contributed to emigration out of the country. The civil war of 1992–97 precipitated the departure of the so-called European minorities, the flight of 250,000 persons seeking refugee status abroad, as well as the forced displacement of about 20 percent of the population within the republic itself. These displacements are in fact part of a longer history, since the areas that were most affected by the civil war often coincided with those that had experienced massive and organized displacements during the Stalinist period. The newer phenomenon of labor migration has emerged only since the mid-1990s. Moreover, different regions of the country are host to different strategies of migration. Departures from high-altitude regions such as the Pamirs, for example, seem to be more permanent than those from the plains, where migration is attributable to seasonal logics. Against this background, Sophie Hohmann examines the impact on people's health of the displacements caused both by the civil war and labor migration, at a time when the Tajik public health system is deteriorating markedly. Among the most vulnerable groups are young male migrants abroad, who run a high risk of contracting sexually transmitted diseases. However, internal migrants are also in danger as their displacement from one region to another prevents medical follow-ups from being carried out, especially any epidemiological prevention such as vaccination. Lastly, the social fabric has been transformed by migration: the increase in the number of non-registered early marriages means that young pregnant women are not monitored and the rate of deaths in childbirth is on the rise. Migration therefore is a social driver that will shape the human development of these societies over the long term.

Exploring the Azeri and the Kyrgyz cases, the last two chapters of this section examine migrants' adaptation strategies once settled in Russia, and analyze the logics of integration, as well as the migrant communities' relation to the state of origin and to the host state. Whereas the term diaspora is widely used in the post-Soviet space with very different meanings, Adeline Braux's contribution to this volume enables the reader to gain a precise grasp of the individual and collective articulations of the term's use and the adaptation strategies of one of Russia's oldest diasporas, the Azeris. During the Soviet period, many Azeris took advantage of internal mobility within the Soviet Union and sought prospects for social promotion by settling in Russia, mainly in Moscow, but also in the oil-rich towns of western Siberia. With the collapse of the Soviet Union, new flows followed as less educated youths searched for work. The so-called Azeri diaspora is therefore particularly socially diverse, which is reflected in the archetypal categories discussed by Braux, ranging from the "notable" to the "pioneer" and "adventurer." Her findings show that the better qualified one is, the more one is likely to want to settle permanently in Russia, and, therefore, less likely to send remittances to family left behind. Settlement creates new issues, in particular self-organization into competing associations, a process that is intensified by the strategies of businessmen seeking to make a name for themselves in the community. A key question also arises in regard to the mediation role between the state of origin and the country of settlement. Here, associations have been trying to gain legitimacy among the Azeri diaspora, as well as with the authorities in Azerbaijan and Russia, since both Baku and Moscow are looking for "go-betweens" who are able to relay their interests.

Focusing on the Kyrgyz migrants of Moscow, Asel Dolotkeldieva's chapter discusses migration as a strategy of adaptation and mediation. These migrants are also diverse, divided between those with a higher or specialized education but unable to find a job in Kyrgyzstan, such as medical personnel and teachers, and completely unskilled laborers. Despite sometimes very difficult circumstances, these migrants have adapted by targeting jobs such as waiting in restaurants and hotels, or as concierges. They also cope with Russian bureaucracy and endemic corruption by trying to gain protection from local district policemen or buying "authentic counterfeit" registrations granted by law enforcement agencies. They live largely disconnected from the aid offered by the Kyrgyz embassy, and so instead favor informal circuits and personal networks. The multitude of associations that are supposed to represent migrants and help them with legal matters are often commercial operations that may contribute to keeping them in various forms of illegality. Lastly, Dolotkeldieva addresses a nascent development, but nonetheless one that is bound to grow in magnitude in the future: the use of revenues accumulated during migration and of migrant social networks in Russia to gain political influence in the country of origin.

INTERNAL MIGRATION IN KYRGYZSTAN: A GEOGRAPHICAL AND SOCIOLOGICAL STUDY OF RURAL MIGRATION

Aida Aaly Alymbaeva

"We all knew each other before; almost everyone greeted each other. It was such a good time. It was clean everywhere. Houses were nice and green. However, now there are so many unknown faces. They came here from the mountains, uncivilized, rude, and uneducated. No one says hello to you. Our settlement changed a lot and for the worse" (N63, interview from October 2, 2001, Kemin settlement).

The extract above expresses an oft heard sentiment during the time of "the great movement" of Kyrgyz people within the country. The words were uttered by a woman living in a settlement two hours by car from the capital, Bishkek. She was speaking about the process by which the majority of Russian-speaking people had left the country to be replaced by ethnic Kyrgyz people from remote areas moving into the formers' houses. These words epitomize the majority of narratives from the "old" inhabitants of a settlement or town about "newcomers". The statement also exposes the results of 70 years of Soviet policy, according to which the mobility of the indigenous populations was constrained, and to some extent the hidden but consistent state intervention into the (national and civic) identity sphere.

I observed attempts to squat on the territory of Pobedy Park, in the south of Bishkek, in the week following the Tulip revolution of March 24, 2005. Despite widespread talk of "migrants"—in this case, those from remote areas—occupying the land, I saw people who were of a decidedly "urban" appearance or who had lived in the city for a relatively long period of time. Everyone there was hoping to get a plot of land. Territory had already been divided into plots and people were sitting on "theirs" ready to defend them. I joined one the groups that was making a list of names staking claims to a plot of land. Elbowing my way through a crowd and being jostled, I asked to be included on the list. A person wrote my name on a piece of paper, giving me the name and phone number of another individual who would have the "necessary connections" to answer further questions. Conversations I overheard were typically as follows: *They promised to accommodate everyone who needs it . . .* or *In a year, the cost of this land will rise and we can then profit.* This indicated to me that not all of the people there were recent migrants who needed the land for accommodation, but rather there were those who already had a place to live and were hoping to benefit opportunistically from the situation. Later, the city government managed to evict these people and protect the park, promising land in another part around the city, though this remains only a pledge.

However, squatting in other areas proved more successful. The "establishment" of Fifteenth Street in Kelechek[1] (there were 14 officially recognized streets there before 2005) came about in the short period of time after the events of March 24. It consists of territory between the road and bazaar that officials had not previously recognized as a residential area. During my visit to Kelechek, in September 2005, I saw the foundations or even walls of houses under construction in this area that had previously been empty. In October 2007, during a further visit, I interviewed a woman in one of the finished small houses on Fifteenth Street. She told that she had two more plots of land there for her sons who were currently in Russia. She had moved with her family (a husband and four small children) to Kelechek in 1993, for a better life. Their life in her place of origin, Batken, had become too difficult, almost hopeless. They lived in Kelechek permanently, renting rooms and working hard, performing the most tiring and dirtiest jobs. However, she stated that she was now happy and proud of the achievement of her family: they now had a house and her sons in Russia had given a car to their father (even if it was secondhand). They now aimed to legalize their houses, which she believed they would do together with their neighbors. Later, other contacts stated that this woman was one of the most active squatters on this land. While she and others now living on Fifteenth Street had previously lived in Kelechek, they had not had the chance to actually legally own a house.

Migration, both foreign and domestic, is a litmus test that reflects political, economic, and social changes over the long term. By following the main flows and directions of migration over time, one can paint a chronological picture of the development of Kyrgyzstan and understand why internal migration is so prevalent in the country, including the processes and reasons that drive it. Accordingly, this chapter considers the process of internal migration in Kyrgyzstan from a chronological

[1] Kelechek is a suburban area of Bishkek, established at the end of the 1980s and inhabited by internal migrants, that forms one of my research "subjects" in examining the influence of urbanization on Kyrgyz identity, 2004–7.

perspective to identify the reasons for the large flows of rural Kyrgyz to urban areas during the post-Soviet period. To understand migration processes in Kyrgyzstan, it will consider the relationship and dynamics between rural and urban populations, ethnic population distribution, and the ethnic division of labor. Furthermore, it provides a historical overview to portray Kyrgyzstan's population growth from Czarist times until independence. With this background on migration processes, the chapter reviews the process of internal migration in Kyrgyzstan since independence, along with its motivations and impacts. Finally, it presents a short overview of the growth of the capital Bishkek as an illustration of the extensive urbanization resulting from internal migration.

Internal migration is understood as the movement of people within one country. It can be multidirectional: rural to urban, rural to rural, and urban to rural. In the case of Kyrgyzstan, the main flow is rural to urban, though a smaller number of people also move in the two other directions. Internal migration is typically permanent or long term. However, rural to urban, and to a lesser extent, rural to rural, migration can also include other, more temporary types of migration, which may take place according to regular or irregular intervals or seasonally. Another type is circular migration, when people move to a city for a short period, for work or other reasons, but do not change their place of residence. Commuting on a daily basis for work or study is another category; this has become one of the main strategies for inhabitants of districts adjoining Bishkek.[2]

I argue in this chapter that intensive internal migration over the last 15 years is the result of policies developed during Soviet times and has gradually sharpened rural-urban and center-periphery imbalances, and correspondingly, has led to an unequal correlation between rural and urban populations and resulted in specificities of ethnic distribution.

Methodology

This study is based on observations and interviews conducted during research on the issue of identity as a function of urbanization resulting from internal migration, which was carried out in two suburban areas of

[2] Cited by Yap Kioe Sheng, "Urbanization and Internal Migration," *Population Studies Series No. 158: Fifth Asian and Pacific Population Conference's Selected Papers* (Bangkok: UNESCAP, 2003), 139.

the capital city from 2004 to 2007. It also utilizes and builds upon the work of Kyrgyz scholars who have done sociological research over the past ten years. Indeed, one of the intentions of this chapter is to provide a thorough review of Kyrgyz studies hitherto limited to a domestic (or wider Russian-speaking) audience. There are several works in the scholarly oeuvre of Kyrgyzstan dedicated to the study of internal migration; however, this type of migration was not a focal point for scholars during the first years of independence, as attention was directed instead toward studying the big emigration flows out of the country. Two scholars, Baktygul Bekturganova and Nuratbek Mendibaev, were pioneers in contributing to the empirical study of internal migration using sociological methods at a time when research in this field was almost unheard of. The work of the National Statistics Committee (NSC), furthermore, published in the book *Naselenie Kyrgyzstana* (2004), which analyzes the results of national censuses from a number of perspectives, including migration, is a remarkable source of information. Other notable works are the monographs of Zholbors Zhorobekov and Nur Omarov, who consider migration in the context of the Central Asian region. The World Bank's 2007 report on poverty in Kyrgyzstan is also used here as a resource for statistical data.

The last population census in Kyrgyzstan was conducted in 1999; the NSC is in the process of calculating the results of the new census carried out in spring 2009. In light of the active migration processes observed during the past ten years and the inability of official entities to register migrants, especially internal ones, this means that there is a lack of precise statistics for the last decade. Whereas the NSC provides some numbers in its annual publications, these statistics mainly include those people who officially registered when they moved place. Not all do so, however: students living in the city during their studies remain registered in their places of origin and labor migrants working in the city sometimes fail to change their registration. As a result, it is hard to calculate the precise number of migrants.

Development of Relations between the Urban and Rural Populations of Kyrgyzstan during the Pre-Soviet and Soviet Eras

Examining the process of Kyrgyzstan population development, and the changing proportion of urban and rural dwellers within it, is important in understanding contemporary internal migration. According to NCS figures in 2009, 35.1 percent of the population of 5.3 million was considered to be rural. This can be compared with the first census of 1897, which showed an urban population of only 9.5 percent, out of a population of 663,000, living on the territory of what is now Kyrgyzstan.[3]

There has thus been a rapid change in balance between the urban and rural over the course of a century. At the time of the first census of 1897, there were just a few urban areas in the south of the country and a near total absence in the northern part. Seventy years of Soviet rule dramatically changed the rural/urban balance.[4] Urban settlements and towns became administrative and cultural centers within the organizational structure of the country. Some of them, especially the capital, became the main recipient areas for internal migrants after the collapse of the Soviet Union. This was strengthened by the development during Soviet times of a common understanding that equated urbanity with modernity, and rural with being "traditional" and therefore backward.

The main drivers of population growth during the pre-Soviet and Soviet periods were immigration and rising birth rates. One can divide this population growth in Kyrgyzstan into three historic periods. The first took place at the beginning of the twentieth century, from 1897 to 1916, when the population grew by 30 percent. This growth was mainly driven by immigration from western and central Russia and Ukraine (1891 to 1916), due to famine in Russia and the prospects of better living and economic conditions in Central Asia. The second was from 1926 to 1939, which corresponds to the period of collectivization, the first stage of modernization, and active industrialization. As result of collectivization, almost all Kyrgyz nomadic pastoralists were made sedentary and new settlements appeared. The population grew from one million in 1926 to 1.46 million in 1939. Immigration from Kazakhstan (due to starvation) and other parts of the Soviet Union, in 1930 and 1931, also contributed to the increase in population. Immigration from Russia during this period saw the arrival of qualified engineers, workers, scholars, and representatives from the cultural sphere. They strongly contributed to the development of industry and culture in Kyrgyzstan. The third period, in the 1960s, and the one with the highest increase in the population with a growth of 3.2 percent, was

---

[3] Z. Kudabaev, M. Gyio, and M. Denisenko, eds., *Naselenie Kyrgyzstana* (Bishkek: National Statistic Committee 2004), 95.

[4] During the Soviet period, urban was understood to mean those areas with an urban administrative status. Read more on this criterion in *Ibid.*, 84–85.

attributable to rising birth rates along with immigration from other parts of the Soviet Union. It was also a time of industrial growth and deepening integration into the economic system of the Soviet Union.[5]

It should be noted that the period termed "pre-Soviet" here is considered to span from the end of the nineteenth century, because it is only from this time that statistics became available. People who lived on the territory of modern Kyrgyzstan, especially its northern part, were nomads, hence the reason there were no urban areas of note in the north and few in the south. According to the census of 1897, an overwhelming 91 percent of the population were employed in agricultural pursuits; another 5 percent worked in industry, transport, or communications; only 2 percent in trade; and a mere 26 individuals in public health.[6]

After being annexed to Czarist Russia, from the 1850s to 1870s the population of what is now Kyrgyzstan, as well as its urban proportion, started to grow. The majority of towns were founded in the second half of the nineteenth century. Pishpek (present-day Bishkek) was founded in 1878,[7] Przheval'sk (Karakol) in 1869, Tokmok in 1867, and Jalalabat in 1877. In the beginning, the populations of these towns predominantly consisted of Russians, Tatars, Uzbeks, and other peoples. Towns like Osh, Pishpek, Przheval'sk, and Tokmok were *uyezd*,[8] or towns with an agricultural population. Osh, a town with an ancient history, received the status of republican subordination equal to that of Bishkek in June 2003.[9] The growth of urban areas continued during the Soviet period. Small regional towns were established (for example, Suliukta in the Batken oblast) and so-called *poselki gorodskogo tipa* (PGT, or urban-type settlements between a town and a village) were built for factory workers. There were six towns

[5] A. Rovenskikh, "Osnovnye etapy migratsii v Kyrgyzskoi Respublike (1917–1991)," *Ekho nauki. Izvestiia NAN KR* (Bishkek: Ilim, 2006), no. 3: 59; Kudabaev, Gyio, and Denisenko, *Naselenie Kyrgyzstana*, 96–105.

[6] Rovenskikh, "Osnovnye etapy migratsii v Kyrgyzskoi Respublike (1917–1991)," 59.

[7] This was when the status of town, and then *uezdnyi*, was granted. Bishkek has an older history, as Joldoshbai Malabaev proves in his book *Bishkek—stolitsa Kyrgyzstana*. Bishkek is named after a historical person who established a fortress in the fifteenth century, after whose death the fortress fell into disrepair. The Khanate of Kokand restored it in 1825. He also gives information about the origin of other towns such as Tokmok and Kara-Balta, which were established as fortresses in the first half of the nineteenth century by the Khanate. See J. Malabaev, *Bishkek—stolitsa Kyrgyzstana* (Bishkek: Erkin-Too, 2002), 7–11.

[8] *Uyezd* was a political subdivision within the *gubernia* (province) administrative and territorial division in Czarist Russia. *Oblast* is the main political subdivision equal to gubernia in the administrative-territorial division of the Soviet Union and contemporary Kyrgyzstan. *Oblasts* are further divided into *rayons* (districts).

[9] Kudabaev, Gyio, and Denisenko, *Naselenie Kyrgyzstana*, 83–96.

and two PGTs in Kyrgyzstan in 1926; by 2003 there were 24 towns and 28 PGTs.[10] Each oblast displays differences in its urban versus rural composition (see Table 1).

Table 1. Population by Region in Kyrgyzstan (thousands of persons and percentages)[11]

	1959	1989	1999	2003	2005	2008	2009
Kyrgyzstan	2,065	4,257.8	4,822.9	5,012.1	5,120.5	5,252.0	5,362.7
Urban	691.5	1,624.5	1,678.6	1,765.3	1,826	1,849.6	1,827.1
	(33.5%)	(38.1%)	(34.8%)	(35.2%)	(35.7%)	(35.2%)	(34.1%)
Rural	1,373.5	2,633.2	3,144.3	3,246.8	3,294.5	3,402.4	3,535.7
	(66.5%)	(61.9%)	(65.2%)	(64.8%)	(64.3%)	(64.8%)	(65.9%)
Batken oblast	149.4	311.8	382.4	401.3	411.4	423.7	428.6
Urban	66.4	80.9	73.3	105.5	106.6	107.4	103.8
	(44.4%)	(26%)	(19.2%)	(26.3%)	(26%)	(26.4%)	(24.2%)
Rural	83.1	230.8	309.1	295.8	304.8	316.4	324.8
	(55.6%)	(74%)	(80.8%)	(73.7%)	(74%)	(74.6%)	(75.8%)
Jalalabat oblast	348.1	743.3	869.3	920.6	947.9	980.7	1,009.9
Urban	117.7	221.4	200.8	211.1	227.9	228.8	228.3
	(33.8%)	(29.8%)	(23%)	(23%)	(24%)	(23.3%)	(22.6%)
Rural	230.4	521.9	668.5	709.5	720.0	751.9	871.6
	(66.2%)	(70.2%)	(77%)	(77%)	(76%)	(76.7%)	(77.4%)
Issyk-Kul oblast	233.7	403.9	413.2	423.0	428.7	433.2	438.4
Urban	59.7	129.4	125.5	123.9	123.8	124	126
	(25.3%)	(32%)	(30.4%)	(29.3%)	(29%)	(28.6%)	(28.7%)
Rural	174.0	274.5	287.7	299.1	304.9	309.2	312
	(74.7%)	(68%)	(69.6%)	(70.7%)	(71%)	(71.4%)	(71.3%)
Naryn oblast	1,28.1	247.9	249.1	260.6	265.0	268.2	257.8
Urban	26.6	51.8	45.6	47.4	47.6	47.4	38.9
	(20.8%)	(21%)	(18.3%)	(18.2%)	(18%)	(17.7%)	(15.1%)
Rural	101.4	1,96.1	203.5	213.2	217.4	220.8	218.8
	(79.2%)	(79%)	(81.7%)	(81.8%)	(82%)	(82.3%)	(84.9%)
Osh oblast	379.1	941.8	1,176.0	1,000.3	1,030.5	1,062.1	1,104.2
Urban	93.6	268.0	272.5	70.3	88.9	91.1	87.8
	(24.7%)	(28.5%)	(23.2%)	(7%)	(8.6%)	(8.6%)	(8%)
Rural	285.6	673.8	903.5	930.0	941.6	971.0	1,106.4
	(75.3%)	(71.5%)	(76.8%)	(93%)	(91%)	(91.4%)	(92%)

[10] Read more on the criterion for defining urban areas in *Ibid.*, 84–89.

[11] Sources: *Itogi pervoi perepisi naseleniia KR 1999* (Bishkek: National Statistics Committee, 1999); *Demograficheskii ezhegodnik Kyrgyzstana*, 2008, 20–22; *Naselenie Kyrgyzstana, Perepis' naselenia KR 2009. Vol. II v tablitsakh (Part 1)* (Bishkek: National Statistics Committee, 2010), 19.

Table 2. (cont.)

	1959	1989	1999	2003	2005	2008	2009
Talas oblast	103.6	192.5	199.9	208.5	212.5	216.4	226.8
Urban	14.6 (14.1%)	31.5 (16.4%)	33.5 (16.8%)	35.6 (17%)	35.9 (17%)	35.9 (16.6%)	33.8 (14.9%)
Rural	89.1 (85.9%)	161.1 (83.6%)	166.4 (83.2%)	172.9 (83%)	176.6 (83%)	180.5 (83.4%)	193 (85.1%)
Chui oblast	459.0	796.7	770.811	752.8	754.3	758.2	803
Urban	97.6 (21.3%)	224.9 (28.2%)	169.2 (22%)	156.4 (20.8%)	155.6 (20.6%)	153.4 (20.2%)	144 (17.9%)
Rural	361.4 (78.7%)	571.8 (71.8%)	601.6 (78%)	596.4 (79.2%)	598.7 (79.9%)	604.8 (79.8%)	659 (82.1%)
Bishkek	263.9	619.9	762.3	797.4	816.1	831.7	835.7
Urban	215.4 (82%)	616.6 (99.5%)	758.2 (99.5%)	792.9 (99.4%)	811.6 (99.5%)	827.2 (99.5%)	831.6 (99.5%)
Rural	48.5 (18%)	3.3 (0.5%)	4.1 (0.5%)	4.5 (0.6%)	4.5 (0.5%)	4.5 (0.5%)	4.1 (0.5%)
Osh town				247.6	254.1	253.1	258.1
Urban				222.2 (89.7%)	228.1 (89.8%)	226.5 (89.5%)	232.8 (90.2%)
Rural				25.4 (10.3%)	26.0 (10.2%)	26.6 (10.5%)	25.3 (9.8%)

An important feature of rural-urban development during the Soviet era, as Baktygul Bekturganova notes, was the gradual and long-standing specialization of economies at the rural and urban levels. The urban area was oriented only to industry and concentrated on hired labor in enterprises, and later on individual enterprises. Collective and individual farms were the main specialization of rural areas.[12] The Soviet centralized economic system saw rural areas mainly as supportive resources for urban ones, where industrial, scientific, and cultural spaces were mainly situated. As a consequence, urban areas became the centers for the regions (*rayons*) in which they were located. The Soviets also introduced the concept that modernization and industrialization were emblematic of development, stating such with the slogan *my staryi mir razrushim* (we will destroy the old world). The traditional way of life contrasted sharply with modernity. Rural areas came to be understood as traditional, old, and underdevel-

12 B. Bekturganova, *Vnutrenniaia migratsionnaia orientatsia sel'skih kyrgyzov vo vtoroi polovine 90kh godov XX veka (Po materialam etnosotsiologicheskogo issledovaniia)*, PhD thesis (Bishkek, 2002), 99.

oped. This is an important factor in understanding migration flows in the country after the collapse of the Soviet system. Rural people moved to urban (central) parts of Kyrgyzstan, where they hoped to find better living and working conditions.

Ethnic Distribution

With north-south, center-periphery, valley-mountain, and urban-rural divisions, ethnic distribution is an important point in understanding migration in Kyrgyzstan. Furthermore, the emigration of the non-Kyrgyz population from the country, beginning at the end of the 1980s, was one of the main factors influencing internal migration. The ethnic distribution of the population of Kyrgyzstan is a result of many processes, but one of the main factors is immigration and emigration processes over a period of about 150 years. As a result of two large immigration flows, Russian, Ukrainian, Tatar, and other peoples came to Kyrgyzstan and settled in the northern part of the country, mainly in the Issyk-Kul and Chui valleys. The first movement was comprised mostly of peasants. In the second, the majority of the Russian-speaking migrants were workers, engineers, and other professionals and specialists needed for building the industrial sector of Kyrgyzstan. During the Second World War, around 30 industrial factories, scientific institutions, and cultural entities, along with two million people, were evacuated to Kyrgyzstan. For example, the Kyrgyz Academy of Sciences was established in 1943 as a branch of the Soviet Academy of Sciences. Almost all industries and institutions were located in the Chui valley and in Frunze (the name of Bishkek at that time).[13] Another growth in diversity was the deportation of ethnic groups from other parts of Soviet Union, such as the Germans who were moved to Kyrgyzstan in 1941–42 and Caucasian groups, like the Chechens, in 1944–45. They were also settled mainly in the northern parts of the country—Issyk-Kul, Chui, and Talas.[14]

---

[13] Kudabaev, Gyio, and Denisenko, *Naselenie Kyrgyzstana*, 100.

[14] Read more on the correlation between demography and ethnic relations in Kyrgyzstan in B. Haug, "Demograficheskie tendentsii, formirovanie natsii i mezhetnicheskie otnosheniia v Kirgizii," in Kudabaev, Gyio, and Denisenko, *Naselenie Kyrgyzstana*, 109–157.

Table 2. A Selection of Ethnic Groups in Kyrgyzstan and their Population Sizes[15]

	1926	1959	1999	2009
Total	989,971	2,065,009	4,822,938	5,107,700
Kyrgyz	661,171	836,831	3,128,147	3,804,788
Urban in %	1	11	27.7	29.7
Rural in %	99	89	72.3	70.3
Russian	116,436	623,562	603,201	419,583
Urban in %	39	57.8	65.5	65.4
Rural in %	61	42.2	34.5	34.6
Uzbek	109,776	218,640	664,950	768,405
Urban in %	47	37	34.4	36
Rural in %	53	63	65.6	64
Ukrainian	64,128	137,031	50,442	21,924
Urban in %	6	38.6	55.3	43.7
Rural in %	94	61.4	44.7	56.3
Tajik	2667	15,221	42,636	46,105
Urban in %	6	29.3	21.5	7556
Rural in %	94	70.7	78.5	12203
German	4291	39,915	21,471	9487
Urban in %	12	68.3	47.7	47.7
Rural in %	78	31.7	52.3	52.3

The correlation between urban and rural populations was conditional on the ethnic division of labor, industrial and agricultural growth, collectivization, the appearance of a wide range of new settlements, and the growth of urban areas (Table 2 gives the ratio of a number of ethnic groups and their urban/rural percentages between 1926 and 2009). The highest proportion of urban dwellers relative to the rural population was in the 1970s and 1980s, when it stood at 38.1 percent. From the 1960s until the second half of the 1980s, along with the growth of the population as a whole, the percentage of people who worked in industry, construction, and the cultural realm including science—rather than agriculture—increased.

---

15 Sources: *Vsesoiuznaia perepis' naselenia 1926 goda: Kirgizskaia ASSR, Otdel I: Narodnost', rodnoi iazyk, vozrast, gramotnost'* (Moscow: Central Statistical Administration of SSSR, 1928), 200–204; B. Haug, "Demograficheskie tendentsii, formirovanie natsii i mezhetnicheskie otnosheniia v Kirgizii," in Z.I. Kudabaev and M.B. Denisenko, ed., *Naselenie Kyrgyzstana*, 2004, 109–157; *Naselenie Kyrgyzstana, Perepis' naseleniia KR 2009, Vol. II v tablitsakh (Part 1)*, 91–94.

The period beginning in the 1960s witnessed the highest rates of immigration. Supporting this was the Soviet idea that migration, especially migration from the European part of the Soviet Union to Central Asia, and Kyrgyzstan in particular, was a sign of development and progress. The logic was that it would bring different peoples closer together and unite them. Broad immigration during this time led to a situation in which the Kyrgyz population became smaller than that of the Russian-speaking peoples in some northern regions. This also put constraints on the ability of Kyrgyz specialists to advance their careers.[16] Whereas this may have been the case early on, by the end of the 1970s and 1980s a comparatively larger number of Kyrgyz were being trained as specialists.

The "Titular" Nation as the Main Actor in Internal Migration

The majority of Kyrgyz people, especially in the northern regions, had been traditionally nomadic and thus migration was not actually a new phenomenon for them (of course, migration is not new for any culture). Saul Abramzon proved that the Kyrgyz had mixed pastoralist and husbandry activities already in the nineteenth century. Czarist Russian colonial policy considered Kyrgyzstan an agrarian area that could provide raw materials. The majority of the population was thus forced to move to the mountains and its arable land was confiscated.[17] The fact that the Kyrgyz people, especially in the north, had not developed an urban culture, allied with a common belief in a wholly nomadic Kyrgyz past, was used during Soviet times to confine the titulars to rural areas. Thus, Kyrgyz continued living in *aiyls*, nomadic and semi-nomadic hamlets consisting of *yurtas* (tents), in the summer and dugouts in the winter. Inhabitants of such hamlets were close relatives, or representatives of a lineage. During the first decades of the Soviet period, when the Kyrgyz were settled, especially during collectivization in the 1930s, approximately 50 to 100 households would live in such communities.[18] Thus the majority of settlements that appeared by that time were structured around one or more lineages.

The main activity of the Kyrgyz people during the Soviet period was cattle breeding, defined by the Soviet government as the main titular

---

16 Zh. Zhorobekov, *Etnodemograficheskie protsessy v Kyrgyzstane (vchera, segodnia, zavtra)* (Bishkek, 1997), 185–206.

17 S. Abramzon, *Kirgizy i ikh etnogeneticheskie i istoriko-kul'turnye sviazi* (Frunze: Kyrgyzstan, 1990), 182.

18 *Istoriia Kirgizskoi SSR* (Frunze: Izd. Akademii Nauk, 1986), 126.

specialty. The Kyrgyz population was therefore concentrated in rural areas and its movement between regions and to the city was controlled and limited. Officials explained this policy by citing Kyrgyz inexperience in intellectual, scientific, and technical activities, their tendency to maintain a patriarchal way of life, and historical modes of production. Providing control was the idea of communal life, such as that in a *kommunalka* (communal flat), where a few families shared facilities like a kitchen and toilet, and that the place of residence "is not a house, not a street, but the Soviet Union."[19] Along with the policy of constructing Soviet identity, these concepts formed the base for manipulating the population, including the controlled settlement of several ethnic groups (the Kyrgyz for example) in fixed places, the movement (deportation) of other groups to remote parts of the Soviet Union, and relocating Germans and Caucasian groups to Central Asia.

The Soviet period is thus remarkable for its control over the movement of people. The authorities were able to control internal migration along with outward migration. They maintained a centralized system of governance and pursued policies of bringing in specialists (especially for industry) from the outside to Kyrgyzstan, which lacked its own specialists as a consequence, and ensured that the Kyrgyz population worked primarily in the rural economy, which was justified based on the notion of a nomadic Kyrgyz past, the lack of urban culture, the problematic availability of accommodation in urban areas, and the lack of knowledge of the Russian language. These factors gradually caused a Kyrgyz ethnic dominance in the makeup of the rural population and unequal development between urban and rural areas, as well as central and peripheral areas of the country, which shaped the directions of internal migration in the post-Soviet period.

Administrative-Territorial Division of Kyrgyzstan: The Key to Understanding Migration

Key to understanding migration is the administrative-territorial division of Kyrgyzstan, where the center is not geographical but administrative (the location of the regional capitals). There are eight oblasts: Chui, Naryn, Issyk-Kul, Talas, Osh, Jalalabat, Batken, and the capital Bishkek, which is

[19] Zh. Zhorobekov, *Etnodemograficheskie protsessy v Kyrgyzstane*, 184–218.

an independent administrative unit. This administrative-territorial division into oblasts, inherited from the Soviet Union, was confirmed in the 1990s. The official division of all the settlements (*naselennye punkty*) into rural and urban ones was approved already in 1938.[20] The names given to oblasts were mostly attributed according to the names of the valleys where the oblasts are situated or by the name of the administrative center.

Kyrgyzstan is broadly divided into north and south. This division is based on the geographical isolation of the two parts, which are separated by a mountain range and by sub-cultural differences. The Bishkek, Chui, Naryn, Issyk-Kul, and Talas oblasts are considered northern. The Jalalabat, Batken, and Osh oblasts are considered southern, with Osh town as their center. Three macro-regions can therefore be identified: the south, including Osh, Jalalabat, and Batken oblasts, is the most populated region; the northern mountain areas, including Naryn, Issyk-Kul, and Talas oblasts, have a smaller population; and the Chui valley, including Bishkek and the Chui oblast, were the most attractive areas for immigrants during Soviet times and remain so for present-day internal migrants.[21]

The north and south of the country, and within them the urban centers and rural peripheries (which also exist within each oblast), display unequal social and economic levels of development. This inequality arose during Soviet rule and has been exacerbated since independence. Immigrants mainly settled in the north, starting with the influx of the first Russian-speaking peoples in the Chui valley and Issyk-Kul during the second half of the nineteenth century. These lands were more attractive in terms of water, soil, and climatic conditions. The administrative, economic, and political center was also established in the Chui valley at Bishkek. (This name was misrepresented as Pishpek in Czarist Russian documents and was changed to Frunze by the Soviets.) The Second World War, moreover, saw the evacuation from the western part of the Soviet Union of industrial, educational, and cultural organizations to the Chui valley, playing an important role in the formation of industry, education, and culture in Kyrgyzstan. During the Soviet period, therefore, the development of the country was mainly concentrated in the Chui valley. The geographical isolation of the two other regions played an additional and crucial role in the widening gap between the levels of development in the north and south.

---

20 Kudabaev, Gyio, and Denisenko, *Naselenie Kyrgyzstana*, 82.

21 *Ibid.*, 99, 105.

It was only between 1960 and 1965 that a highway was built connecting the two parts of the country.

Another factor in the growing regional gap was differing levels of education, with the Chui valley and the capital being ahead of the rest of the country. Schools in other regions were not even properly furnished. The system was supported by a policy in which the graduates of pedagogical and medical universities were obliged to go to regional and isolated settlements. The development of the educational system, however, was complicated by remoteness and difficulties in accessing the mountainous areas. The whole system unraveled with the collapse of the Soviet Union, the obligation policy of young graduates also coming to an end. Consequently, the level of education of the younger generations decreased. The difference in the levels of development between the three regions became one of the most important reasons for internal migration after independence. Additionally, the low level of education intensified the marginalization of migrants, along with the lack of employment opportunities in the cities.

Another important distinctiveness of this division is cultural relatedness based on ethnic distribution. The north, for historical reasons, has a Russian-language orientation, especially the Chui valley and the Issyk-Kul shore. Almost all immigrants from the western parts of the Russian empire, both during and prior to Soviet rule, settled in the northern part of Kyrgyzstan. In 1989, 77 percent of the capital Frunze and 71 percent of the Chui valley were comprised of non-Kyrgyz peoples.[22] Combined with the policy of Russification (*russifikatsiia*) during the 1970s, this Russian-speaking immigration had a deep influence on the culture of the northern region. Uzbek and Tajik, together with Kyrgyz peoples, primarily inhabited the south, especially the Ferghana valley. Cultural exchange between the three groups over between the three groups the centuries influenced primarily the Kyrgyz language, way of life, and traditions. It is common among Kyrgyz and other peoples in Kyrgyzstan to hold notions of a Russified north and an Uzbekified or, to a lesser extent, Tajikified south. This is one of the main arguments in discussing the cultural adaptation of internal migrants, especially in the capital.

It should also be mentioned that higher professional education and the greater availability of jobs was linked to knowledge of the Russian language, especially in the 1970s when a big push was made toward spreading

---

22 *Ibid.*, 92.

Russian. As a result, the Institute of Russian Language and Literature was opened and the majority of schools taught in Russian. The level of teaching at these schools was much higher than in Kyrgyz-language schools, where the level of training for teachers was lower. Being an inhabitant of an urban area was considered a privilege, but it was also connected to knowledge of the Soviet lingua franca. This resulted in a belief that the Russian language, and everything connected to it, was a sign of progress; Kyrgyz people, especially the youth in Chui and Bishkek, came to consider the Kyrgyz language and culture as representing backwardness. Notions of being *kul'turnyi* (civilized) started to be linked to an ability to speak Russian and ties to Russian cultural traits.[23] With the Russian language an indicator of being *gorodskoi* (urban), this widened the gap between urban and rural statuses. That is why the "old" inhabitants of a settlement (city, town, or PGT) consider "newcomers" moving to these places from remote areas as *ne kul'turnyi* (uncultured)—regardless that both areas are now Kyrgyz.[24]

Internal Migration since Independence

Reasons and Factors for Internal Migration

The collapse of the Soviet Union—with its centralized system of governance, economy, and culture—removed all controls and their propaganda tools. Control over the movement of people and the ideal of "my home is the Soviet Union" were weakened. The managed process of urbanization and the maintenance of the agrarian status of Kyrgyzstan within the Soviet economic system led to social problems such as the inability to provide employment opportunities, accommodation, medical services, and quality education, especially in rural areas. The system of collective farms

[23] See more on the Russification and other impacts of the Soviet period in J. Schoeberlein, "Shifting Ground: How the Soviet regime used resettlement to transform Central Asian society and the consequence of this policy today," in H. Komatsu, C. Obiya, and J. Schoeberlein, eds., *Population in Central Asia: Its History and Current Problems: Population Movements in the modern world from the JCAS Symposium Series 9* (Osaka: The Japan Center for Area Studies, National Museum of Ethnology, 2000), 41–64.

[24] Saulesh Yessenova makes an interesting analysis of the meaning of urban and rural for Kazakh people, and how this dichotomy affected relations between migrants and city inhabitants, in "Routes and Roots of Kazakh Identity: Urban Migration in Post-Socialist Kazakhstan," *The Russian Review* 64, no. 64 (2005): 661–679.

(*kolkhoz* and *sovkhoz*) had also been destructured; they were operating already at subsistence levels in the 1980s.[25]

In today Kyrgyzstan 52 percent of the labor force is employed in the agriculture. The liberalization of the economy[26] during the first years of independence, with a transition to new forms of property, led to a mass breakdown of the system of collective farms. The situation was at its worst in 1990–95, leading to an increased number of depressed regions releasing their populations. As result, there were many rural people who faced unemployment and who were unable to cultivate the land and obtain a decent income in rural areas. Economic reforms improved the situation from 1996, but there again followed a sharp depression in 2005. All of these changes influenced the size of internal migration flows, especially of rural dwellers.[27]

Ownership of land and the ability to cultivate it also factored into levels of rural migration. In its report, the World Bank noted the difference between the north and south in terms of land parcel sizes: land parcels in the less populated north were on average two hectares in size with 21 percent of people owning one; but in the more populated south, only 10 percent of people owned land parcels of this size.[28] Common cultivation problems for both regions are inequality between contributions to cultivation (money and physical labor) and the ability to sell harvests for profit. This problem eased somewhat during 1996–2004, especially in the northern areas, leading to a decrease in migration; however, the south encountered problems of water shortages, which, combined with smaller plot sizes, kept profits down. Ownership of livestock is also more widespread in the north. As the World Bank report showed, 53 percent of cattle and 47 percent of small ruminants in the country are concentrated in the north.[29] The above, together with the attraction of easier ways to earn money in urban areas, prompted large migratory movements from rural southern areas to Bishkek, starting from the second half of the 1990s, and to a lesser extent to Osh and Jalalabat.

Kyrgyzstan's industry was deeply embedded in the Soviet system, mainly as a source for raw materials and as an area for the preprocessing of goods. The crash of the centralized economy initially led to a crisis in the local industrial sector. The populations in urbanized areas, with

---

25 U. Asanov and A. Asankanov, eds., *Kyrgyz Tarykhy: Entsiklopediia* (Bishkek: 2003), 77.

26 *Ibid.*, 77–79.

27 *Kyrgyz Republic Poverty Assessment*, volume II: *Labor Market Dimensions of Poverty*, report No. 40864-KG, (Washington, D.C.: The World Bank, 2007), 23–25.

28 *Ibid.*, 32.

29 *Ibid.*, 33.

their small towns and PGTs, suffered from unemployment and a concomitant sharp drop in living standards. In 1998, the level of unemployment had reached 50 percent in urban areas and up to 80 percent in rural areas.[30] Another significant reason for Kyrgyzstan's rising poverty came in the period after the som replaced the ruble as the national monetary unit in 1993. Lacking strong support, the som rapidly became devalued, causing many to lose their savings. This can also be considered one of the factors driving increased migration in 1994–98. These processes led to widespread poverty, which became fused with unemployment as a reason for migration. In fact, Kyrgyzstan is the second poorest country after Tajikistan in the post-Soviet space. The World Bank determined the country's level of poverty at 43.1 percent of the population in 2005; rural poverty was 51 percent and urban poverty 30 percent. Poverty in the Naryn, Issyk-Kul, Jalalabat, Osh, and Batken oblasts was over 50 percent, but only 11 percent in Bishkek and 22 percent in the Chui oblast. The two poorest oblasts are Naryn and Talas with poverty rates in 2005 standing at 89 and 72 percent, respectively.[31] This disproves the commonly held idea that the "poor" south is *wholly* responsible for the large migratory flows at the end of 1990s and the first years of the twenty-first century. Nevertheless, in addition to unemployment, poverty, and regional inequality in economic development, there is a simple explanation for the notion of "the whole south moving north" (that is, to Bishkek): the higher population density in the south compared to the north, which made migration from the south seemingly more striking.

An important factor in internal migration is the inequality of rural and urban development. Bishkek and to a lesser extent the city of Osh became attractive as places with higher standards of living, where money could be earned more easily than in villages. In 2001, the average income per capita for an inhabitant of Bishkek was four times greater than in Naryn, 2.8 times that in Jalalabat, and twice as much as the Issyk-Kul and Osh oblasts.[32] After Bishkek, the Chui valley is the most attractive area because of its relatively higher living standards and the possibility of commuting or migrating seasonally to Bishkek. However, migrants' lack of

---

[30] N. Omarov, *Migratsionnye protsessy v Kyrgyzskoi Respublike v gody nezavisimosti. Itogi desiatiletiia* (Bishkek: 2001), 69.

[31] *Kyrgyz Republic Poverty Assessment*, 1–4.

[32] From the article "Labor migration in Kyrgyzstan," on the Omsk State University website, http://catalog.fmb.ru/kirghizia10.shtm (October 5, 2008).

professional education and of employment opportunities in the cities in turn caused unemployment and other social problems.

Social problems and hopes of escaping them in the city are other motivating factors. The statistics collected by Mendibaev at the end of the 1990s in the table below can be considered an illustration of the reasons why people decide to move. The survey is of 400 inhabitants of Bishkek's suburban settlements and 286 individuals from Osh's suburbs. Both regions cite unemployment as their main problem.

Table 3. The Main Regional Problems of the Osh and Chui Oblasts[33]

	Osh	Chui
Unemployment	70.6	52.6
Theft, crime	31.5	15.9
Worsening health or growth of diseases	21.3	6.4
Mafia, corruption	13.3	10.2
Alcoholism	12.6	4.2
Narcotics	12.2	2.2
Prostitution	10.8	4.4
Environment	9.4	2.4

Note: Numbers in right hand columns are given in percentages

This table also illustrates the social differences between the north and south. It should be mentioned that the author did not ask respondents to specify their place of origin. Besides the 286 respondents interviewed in Osh, it can be surmised that many southerners must have been among those 400 migrants interviewed around Bishkek, which makes the sample slightly more oriented to the south. Of course these statistics do not reflect the social problems of urban areas, which had also to face issues of unemployment. The social situation in urban areas even worsened in the 1990s as a result of the rising number of people arriving with hopes of earning money. It was further compounded by a lack of accommodation and the absence of social control from relatives (especially a problem among the youth).

From 1989 to 2003, approximately 860,000 people—of which 19.27 percent were foreign migrants, particularly refugees—moved within

33 N. Mendibaev, *Novye poselencheskie obshchnosti: Sotsial'nie problemy* (Turkestan: International Kazakh Turkish University, 2000), 154.

Kyrgyzstan.[34] Political instability, weak legal protection, interethnic tension, and armed conflicts resulting from the processes of gaining sovereignty led to large migration flows in the whole Central Asian region. The declared idea that "Kyrgyzstan is our shared home" attracted many Tajiks, Abkhaz, Afghans, and of course ethnic Kyrgyz returnees from neighboring countries, mainly Tajikistan. Some 15,000 people gained official refugee status in 1997, but as Omuraliev and Kokareva noted, the unofficial number of refugees and illegal migrants is much higher. These people are unregistered, unemployed, poor, possess no Russian or Kyrgyz language skills, and have no access to schools or medical services. As a result they have to take the most difficult jobs or turn to shadow economy.[35]

Emigration of non-Kyrgyz Peoples as a Factor in Internal Migration

Internal migration cannot be considered without looking at emigration from the country. The emigration of non-Kyrgyz people from Kyrgyzstan to their kin-states started already at the end of the 1970s. At that time indigenization policies were strongly promoted by the regime and a Kyrgyz professional community in industry and education had emerged. This led to fewer professional opportunities for potential incoming migrants.[36] However, the main outflow of migrants from the country came after the collapse of the Soviet Union as a reaction to, according to Kosmarskaya, the new independent status of the country, complete with economic crisis, rising tension between groups, and a more uncertain future. Peak immigration occurred between 1990 and 1995 when 326,600 Russians left the country for Russia, representing about 70 percent of all migrants.[37] In 1993 alone, 143,000 people departed Kyrgyzstan—the most of any year.[38] The numbers emigrating stabilized somewhat between 1994 and 1999, but rose again in 1999 and 2000, after the armed intrusion of the Islamic Movement of Uzbekistan in Batken oblast. This prompted a new

---

34 *Kyrgyz Republic Poverty Assessment*, 39.

35 N. Omuraliev and E. Kokareva, "Problemy bezhentsev i migrantov kak faktor obostreniia sotsial'noi napriazhennosti," *Etnicheskii mir. Informatsionno-analiticheskii biulleten'*, Bishkek, May 1997, 17.

36 N. Omarov, *Migratsionnye protsessy v Kyrgyzskoi Respublike v gody nezavisimosti: Itogi desiatiletiia* (Bishkek, 2001), 23–24.

37 N. Kosmarskaia, *"Deti imperii" v postsovetskoi Tsentral'noi Azii: adaptivnye praktiki i mental'nye sdvigi (russkie v Kirgizii)* (Moscow: Natalis, 2006), 53 and 59.

38 I. Babetskii, A. Kolev, and M. Maurel, "Kyrgyz Labor Market in the late 1990s: The Challenge of Formal Job Creation," *Comparative Economic Studies*, no. 45 (2003): 515.

flow along with more social, economic, and political problems. The last spike in emigration numbers was in 2005, after the so-called Tulip revolution of March 24. A major reason for those emigrating was the better economic situation of destination countries in comparison with Kyrgyzstan. The biggest percentage of emigrants came from Bishkek and the Chui valley, the main areas where almost 60 percent of non-Kyrgyz peoples live.

The main result of this emigration was a shift from a poly-ethnic to an increasing mono-ethnic composition. In 1959, Kyrgyz people accounted for 40.5 percent of the population of the republic, Uzbeks 10.6 percent, and Russians 30.2 percent. In 1989, Kyrgyz represented 52.4 percent, Uzbeks 12.9 percent, and Russians 21.5 percent of the population. But in 1999, the ethnic proportion had changed to Kyrgyz 64.9 percent, Uzbeks 13.8 percent, and Russians 12.5 percent.[39] During Soviet times, the Kyrgyz did not form an outright majority, but by 1999, the number of Kyrgyz had increased to over half the population as a result of high birth rates and the emigration of Russian and other non-Turkic peoples from the country.

Internal Migration from 1989 to 1994[40]

The start of the "great migration" in Kyrgyzstan was 1989. According to the World Bank, between 1989 and 1994 about 220,000 people moved; 77.3 percent were internal migrants while 22.7 percent immigrated.[41] A particular characteristic of this period was movement by migrants within the country seeking permanent relocation. Thus, this period mainly saw inter-oblast migration. With controls largely lifted, internal migration flowed from remote and mountainous areas, especially in the north, to the valleys and towns. The period 1990–94 saw the relocation of entire families—for example, from Chui settlements such as Kemin to Bishkek, or from the Naryn oblast[42] to Kemin. People from remote villages, *aiyls*, moved hoping for a better life in the face of harsh living conditions. The new inhabitants did not have enough money to buy houses in Bishkek, but

[39] *Naselenie Kyrgyzstana: Resul'taty pervoi natsional'noi perepisi naseleniia Kyrgyzstana 1999 goda v tablitsakh*, vol. II (Bishkek: National Statistical Committee, 2002), 70.

[40] The given period is relative while people's movement was and continues to be variable; these stages reflect the main changes in the political, economic, social, and environmental situations that influenced decisions to move.

[41] *Kyrgyz Republic Poverty Assessment*, 39.

[42] It should be mentioned that there was migration within oblasts. For example, D. Kalykov has written about the problems of migrants in Naryn oblast, when inhabitants of the villages moved to the town of Naryn in the beginning of the 1990s. See D. Kalykov, "Zaterialis' na sobstvennoi zemle," *Vechernii Bishkek*, August 11, 2000, 11.

they had enough to buy property in its surrounding regions, where Russians, Germans, and other Russian-speaking peoples (or Kyrgyz) had sold their houses for cheap prices. These houses were usually well-built with relatively good facilities. As transpires from interviews, the "native" inhabitants of these settlements—those who had lived there for more than two generations—perceived their new neighbors as "rude and uncivilized" and sometimes even as "aggressors."

Omarov differentiates between two categories of internal migrants. First are the economic migrants who mainly move voluntarily. The second are internally displaced people—in the case of Kyrgyzstan, ecological migrants of whom there were calculated to be 24,000 in 1994, mainly from the south. These people, as Omarov writes, had been forced to move due to natural disasters and other man-made ecological catastrophes. In 1993 and 1994, the phenomenon of so-called commuting or seasonal migration could also begin to be observed with people moving periodically after living three or four months in one place. The reason was stagnation of the industrial and agrarian sectors of the economy. From the early 1990s, Bishkek, and other northern and central parts of Kyrgyzstan became "seasonal" places to earn money—this together with the long-standing attraction of these areas as "contemporary" places of work.[43]

Internal Migration from 1994 to 1999

The second stage of internal migration, from 1994 to 1999, saw continuing albeit decreased movements between oblasts and more movement from rural to urban areas. According to the World Bank, there were around 100,000 migrants per year from 1994 to 1998. From 1999 to 2003, this declined to about 30,000 per year.[44] Economic reforms in the first half of 1990s led to a slight increase in living standards in 1996–97, but declined after the economic crisis in 1998 that hit Russia. In Babetskii's, Korlev's, and Maurel's analysis of the labor market in Kyrgyzstan, collected data confirming the low levels of economic development in the country and high levels of unemployment. Their figures show that privatization led to an increase in unemployment from 68 percent in 1995 to 78 percent in 2000. In rural areas, where collective farms were dissolved and people were occupied in agricultural cooperatives, unemployment increased from

---

[43] Omarov, *Migratsionnye protsessy v Kyrgyzskoi Respublike v gody nezavisimosti: Itogi desiatiletiia*, 58–61.

[44] *Kyrgyz Republic Poverty Assessment*, 39.

26 percent in 1995 to 38 percent in 2000. Transitions to self-employment after the dismantlement of collective farms provided slight relief: unemployment decreased from 37 percent in 1996 to 34 percent in 2000. The first decade of independence was thus the most active in terms of migration.[45] In spite of the increased poverty as a result of the Russian economic crisis in 1998, as the World Bank reports, there was nonetheless a substantive reduction in poverty levels between 1998 and 2001: from 60 to 47 percent in rural areas, and from 45 to 34 percent in urban areas.[46]

Internal migration during this period was a continuation of the trends that had started at the end of 1980s and which were intensified by the continuing crisis in industry and agriculture. After the reforms of 1993–95, when land was distributed among Kyrgyz citizens and people started to cultivate their lands, increased prices for agricultural goods and the resulting internal migration (especially from northern areas) eased.

M. Schuler and Z. Kudabaev give a fuller picture of this period.[47] They analyzed the demographic statistics and noted that from 1994 to 1999, three districts had the biggest population increases as a result of internal migration: Bishkek (17.8 percent) and its neighboring *rayons* of Alamudun (20.1 percent) and Sokuluk (10.6 percent). There were also a further 9 districts out of 54 where the population increased. The population of the cities of Karakol, Osh, Jalalabat, Kyzyl-Kyia, Mailuu-Suu, and Karakul increased 4.9 percent, 3.5 percent, 5.7 percent, 4.1 percent, 2.3 percent, and 1.4 percent respectively. The biggest flow of migrants came from the Naryn oblast to the valleys and towns, especially from the Jumgal district. Other "supply" areas were several districts of the Issyk-Kul and Talas oblasts, the Alay district of Osh oblast, and the Toktogul district of Jalalabat oblast. In general, Bishkek, Osh, and Jalalabat[48] were the main recipients of internal migrants.

Whereas the active emigration of Russian-speakers and the growth of labor migration led to some extent to the depopulation of some parts of the republic, internal migration to valleys (especially Chui) and urban areas from 1989 to 1999, according to Schuler and Kudabaev, compensated to some extent for the population decrease. In addition to some

[45] I. Babetskii, A. Kolev, and M. Maurel, "Kyrgyz Labor Market in the late 1990s: The Challenge of Formal Job Creation," 501–517.

[46] *Kyrgyz Republic Poverty Assessment*, 6.

[47] Kudabaev, Gyio, and Denisenko, *Naselenie Kyrgyzstana*, 281–302.

[48] For example, some 20,000 internal migrants were supposedly counted in the town of Jalalabat in 1999. See M. Khamidov, "Naplyv 'gostei' v Zhalalabade," *Vechernii Bishkek*, March 17, 1999, 7.

rural mountainous areas losing their populations, the small towns and urbanized settlements situated in sub-mountainous areas, which housed mainly factory and mine workers, such as Ak-Tiuz in Chui oblast, Min-Kush in Naryn oblast, as well as Khaidarkan, Suliukta, and other towns in the south, were almost totally depopulated. Another effect of internal migration was to contribute to the increasing urban sprawl of cities, especially Bishkek and Osh.

While migration was prompted in part by a desire for a better standard of living, the primary movement was that of labor migration, mainly from rural to urban areas, wherein migrants came to live temporarily in cities and their surrounding areas with the aim of earning money. These so-called sojourners[49] represented mainly seasonal migrants who came to the city to work in the informal sector, renting rooms or apartments in suburban areas, and then returning to their places of origin. However, in many cases such migrants also bought houses in the city or surrounding areas. From 1996 to 2000, 156,000 migrants moved from rural to urban areas—the Chui valley was the main recipient—while 54,000 migrated from one rural area to another.[50]

As Bekturganova noted in her survey of 1,668 respondents in 1996, the main reasons for migration during this period were as follows: 38.9 percent were looking for jobs; 18.6 percent because of family circumstances; 16.5 percent because their salaries were being regularly deferred; 11.4 percent of those who wanted to have better living conditions were categorized by the author under "cultural reasons"; 10 percent were young people who wanted to study in the city; and 4.5 percent disliked the climate where they were currently residing.[51]

There is also an interesting ethnic composition to internal migration. The least mobile group were the Uzbeks, of whom only 2 to 14.1 percent moved within the country during this period. The most active were the Kyrgyz who constituted 73 percent of migrants, Russians 15 percent,

---

[49] The concept of the sojourner was represented as a distinct type of migrant as opposed to the settler. See C.B. Brettell, "Theorizing Migration in Anthropology. The Social Construction of Networks, Identities, Communities, and Globalscapes," in C.B. Brettell and J.F. Hollifield, eds., *Migration Theory: Talking across Disciplines* (New York and London: Routledge, 2000), 97–136. In the context of Kyrgyzstan, sojourners constituted the majority of internal migrants, especially at the end of the 1990s and beginning of the 2000s.

[50] From the article "Labor migration in Kyrgyzstan," Omsk State University website, http://catalog.fmb.ru/kirghizia10.shtml.

[51] Bekturganova, *Vnutrenniaia migratsionnaia orientatsiia sel'skikh kyrgyzov vo vtoroi polovine 90kh godov XX veka*, 162.

Ukrainians 1 percent, and others 8 percent.[52] One peculiarity of Kyrgyzstan is the settlement of ethnic groups in particular areas; Uzbeks mainly live in the south, Russians and the majority of other Russian-speaking people live in the north.

Migration from 2000 to 2009[53]

The first five years of the new millennium were distinguished by the relative stability of the economy and social state of the country, which led, to a certain extent, to a stabilization of internal migration. This period was characterized more by seasonal labor migration within the country and also an increase in labor migrants going to foreign countries; about 500,000 people worked outside of Kyrgyzstan during these years.[54]

The World Bank report of 2007 illustrated the economic situation. The general economic improvement was seen in the rise in GDP growth—from minus 14.4 percent in 1994 to 4.8 percent in 2004. There was blip in 2005 when it decreased to minus 0.2 percent; but it grew again by 2.7 percent in 2006.[55] The decrease in 2005 can be explained by the Tulip revolution and its negative impact on trade. Continued agricultural development and decreased poverty levels—from 63 percent in 2000 to 43 percent in 2005—contributed to economic development. Urban poverty also dropped from 53 percent in 2000 (27% in extreme poverty) to 36 percent in 2005 (10% in extreme poverty); meanwhile, rural poverty fell from 69 percent in 2000 (36% in extreme poverty) to 51 percent in 2005 (18% in extreme poverty).[56]

Poverty and the lack of available jobs still persisted as reasons for internal migration. A larger number of higher institutions of education saw many young people pursue their studies, which provided another reason to migrate. According to research on childhood poverty done in 2004, in

[52] From article "Labor migration in Kyrgyzstan" on the Omsk State University website.

[53] Internal migration from 2000 to 2009 remains less studied. My analysis of this period is based mainly on material gathered from newspapers and the Internet. The main resource on statistics is the reports of the World Bank. Ruslan Rakhimov, working on land relations and internal migration, and Emil Nasritdinov, whose research focuses on the situation of internal migrants in the capital city, have both conducted recent studies at the American University of Central Asia. For some results of my research on issues of identity in urbanization and migration see, for example, A. Alymbaeva, "K voprosu ob urbanizatsii Kyrgyzstana," *Voprosy istorii Kyrgyzstana* (Bishkek: National Academy of Sciences, 2008), 65–77.

[54] *Kyrgyz Republic Poverty Assessment*, 39.

[55] *Ibid.*, 5.

[56] *Ibid.*

which 1,096 families in 22 urban and rural settlements were interviewed, the main reason given for migration was the search for a job (49.6% of respondents); 33.6 percent migrated for study, and only 5.5 percent migrated to be with their relatives. A further 5.2 percent represented young men serving in the military.[57]

The growth of the informal sector, which emerged in the 1990s as an alternative to the lack of employment in the formal sector, continued apace. Its main employees were primarily moving for seasonal work. Indeed, seasonal labor migration involved people from almost the entire country. A peculiarity was the increasing number of older people migrating, compared with mainly younger people during earlier periods.[58] In rural areas these people worked in the fields. In urban areas, especially in the capital city, many worked in markets, construction, and sewing. In total, 54 percent of people in rural areas and 39 percent in urban areas were employed in the informal sector in 2003.[59]

Inter-oblast migration involved more than 25,000 people each year between 2003 and 2007 (see Table 4). Four main directions persist: from rural to urban areas, from remote mountainous areas to valleys, from the periphery to administrative and economic centers, and more generally from the south to the north. Of course, these vectors are intertwined and cannot be considered separately. While urban areas are mainly situated in valleys or at lower sea levels, administrative and economic centers are mainly situated in urban areas.

In the south, the main recipient areas for migrants are the cities of Osh and Jalalabat; the latter is considered to be a transit step for further moves to Bishkek or outside of the country. As a whole, however, Table 5 shows that the Chui valley and Bishkek are the main recipients of internal migrants. Yet, the situation in Osh is interesting according to the statistics. For example, in 2007, fewer people left than new migrants arrived in the city. This can be explained on account of increased economic development in Osh concomitant with its status as the southern capital of Kyrgyzstan. Indeed, there have been major debates on moving the capital from Bishkek to Osh, which, or so it is argued, would improve the economic

---

[57] M. Ablezova and G. Botoeva, et al., *Pokolenie v opasnosti?! Detskaia bednost' v Kyrgyzstane, CHIP Report no. 15* (Bishkek: Research Center of Childhood Poverty and Policy Development, 2004), 27.

[58] N. Omarov, "Etnicheskaia situatsiia i migratsionnye protsessy v postsovetskom Kyrgyzstane," *Etnograficheskoe obozrenie*, no. 3 (2005): 78.

[59] *Kyrgyz Republic Poverty Assessment*, 20.

situation of the south and bring it a more equal status with the north. It could also be contended that this would decrease migration, both internal and external, from the south.

During this time, the tourism center of Issyk-Kul (its northern shore, where the majority of resorts are situated) emerged as a migration destination. One contact, D20, said his family was moving to one of Issyk-Kul's villages around Cholpon-Ata[60] to rent a yurt and open a café for tourists. His family was originally from the Chui valley and was living in one of Bishkek's suburban areas. They attempted this seasonal business for three summers at the beginning of the 2000s. He stated that this business was not as successful as they had hoped because it was dependent on tourism and had encountered major competition. Notwithstanding the challenges, more recently seasonal migrants from the south have actively sought to move to Issyk-Kul, the building boom along the northern shore of the lake attracting them.

According to the National Statistical Committee, there was a slight increase in inter-oblast migration in 2004, when more than 32,000 people officially changed their place of residence. Out of this number, 14,800 arrived in Bishkek from other areas, compared with an average of 10,000 for other years (see Table 5). One can assume that these statistics do not account for seasonal labor migrants. According to my observations in one of Bishkek's suburbs, Kelechek, in June 2004,[61] there was a greater proportion of seasonal migrants, while official statistics only shows those migrants who have a *propiska* (official residence registration). The majority of the observed labor migrants came from the south, especially from the Batken province. This is interesting, because according to the statistics, the north and south are almost equal as "supply" regions; even Naryn oblast "sent" more migrants than Batken (see Table 5). Because the population in the south is larger than in the north, the number of people from the south should be greater if taking into account unregistered migrants. Another assumption explaining the seemingly bigger flows from the south is the economic niches where migrants from different regions find work. Kelechek is situated near the biggest bazaar, Dordoy, and this attracts most of the migrants. In summer 2004, when my research started, I met dozens of migrants from the south who had rented rooms on streets close to Dordoy. Almost all came following their relatives. Well established in

---

60 Cholpon-Ata is a town on the northern shore of Lake Issyk-Kul. As an administrative and tourist center, it is where the majority of resorts are situated.

61 This study was part of a small pilot research project on the issue of migrant identities, in which my students were also involved.

Table 4. Internal Migration of Population between 2003 and 2009[62]

	2003	2005	2007	Jan–Feb, 2008	Jan–Feb, 2009
Internal migration in Kyrgyzstan:					
Arrived	40,200	38,100	36,500		
Left	39,100	38,300	36,400		
Inter-oblast migration:					
Arrived	26,400	28,800	27,400	5,670	5,180
Left	25,300	29,000	27,300	5,670	5,180
Internal-oblast migration:					
Arrived	13,800	9,300	9,100	4,090	3,670
Left	13,800	9,300	9,100	4,090	3,670
Out-migration:					
Arrived	4,500	3,700	4,000	605	669
Left	21,200	30,700	54,600	4,320	4,760

previous years, the family network had now became the main resource for migration. Those who came from the north were more widely distributed across the capital and thus not so conspicuous. Bishkek also served as a transit-point for international migration.

Extensive Urbanization as a Main Impact of Internal Migration

Each year Bishkek absorbs thousands of new arrivals who settle in the city for different periods of time; in the majority of cases for many years, if not permanently. The bulk of migrants stay in *novostroiki*, which are suburban areas of the capital and inhabited by migrants from every region of the country. There are more than 40 *novostroiki* situated around the capital.[63] Whereas the suburban areas of Bishkek are lined with a fair number of fashionable two-story houses in "prestigious" districts, the majority are small ramshackle homes, which usually contain one to three rooms and are covered with an asbestos slate roof. Each plot and the houses on them belong to a single family.

62 Sources: *Demograficheskii ezhegodnik Kyrgyzstana*, 2008, 352; *Sotsial'no-economicheskoe polozhenie KR* (Bishkek: National Statistics Committee, 2009), 117.

63 If one believes the words of former Bishkek mayor Arstanbek Nogoev (*Vechernii Bishkek*, no. 173, September 11, 2007), there are 47 *novostroiki* around the capital.

Novostroiki, which literally means new building in Russian, in this context means newly formed and still forming settlements around the capital. The history of Bishkek's *novostroiki* begins at the end of the 1980s and the beginning of the 1990s. According to my contacts at this time, factory workers occupied the first plots of land. This occupation took place without official permission. Those who occupy land without legal title to it are called squatters,[64] *samozakhvat* in Russian. In 1989, when the first wave of *samozahvat* occurred in Bishkek, most of the land claimed was connected to or situated close to the factories. Officials of the city were not able to control this process and finally legalized it through apportioning plots of land between workers according to existing property lines. *Novostroiki* are now occupying former fields and have contributed to the sprawl of the capital.

It is problematic to calculate the exact percentage of internal migrants who move to the capital because the relevant authorities that aim to control migration are unable to do so. For those who have a house in a suburban area, they first need to register their houses and plots of land, which is complicated by multiple bureaucratic offices with overlapping mandates. Others have difficulties in finding an address where one can be registered. Therefore it is hard for many migrants to obtain a *propiska*. Yet the overwhelming majority of migrants are not required to register in municipalities for work in the informal sector or for renting rooms in the suburbs. Several studies have indicated that there are 300,000 inhabitants in the *novostroiki*,[65] but this figure cannot reliably reflect the actual number of people who arrive and depart from the capital every season.

Michael P. Todaro and Stephen C. Smith point to two trajectories in the development of urban spaces in less developed countries. The first is the development of the modern formal sector, and the second one, which exists in parallel to the first, is the development of large informal urban sectors. This informal sector involves almost half of all urban labor. It is characterized by "low productivity, self-employment, a lack of complementary inputs, jobs in petty sales and services, and recent migrants."[66]

---

64 W.G. Flanagan, *Urban Sociology: Images and Structure* (Needham Heights: Allyn& Bacon, 1999, 3rd edition), 160.

65 See, for example, G. Sitnianskii, "Migratsionnyie protsessy i etnokul'turnye transformatsii v postsovetskoi Srednei Azii (na primere Kyrgyzstana)," in A. Derevianko, V. Molodin, V. Tishkov, eds., *Etnokul'turnoe vzaimodeistvie v Evrazii* (Moscow: Nauka, 2006, vol. 2), 263.

66 M.P. Todaro and S.C. Smith, *Urbanization and Rural-Urban Migration: Theory and Policy in Economic Development* (Washington, D.C.: The George Washington University and Prentice Hall, 2012), Chapter 8, http://wps.aw.com/aw_todarosmit_econdevelp_8/0,6111,284700-,00.html.

Todaro and Smith explain rural-to-urban migration as deriving from low incomes in rural areas, further pointing out that the informal sector often accounts for a third of the income of the entire city.

Present-day Bishkek with its suburban areas may serve as a model of migration and urbanization within globalizing economics. Permanent rural-to-urban internal migration has formed an informal labor sector consisting mostly of migrants. The majority of them are engaged in the bazaars, the biggest of which are Dordoy and Osh. These bazaars provide many small services like food outlets, salons, exchange counters, and telecommunications—all of which engage a large number of migrants. Another important kind of activity for male migrants is the transportation of goods for customers or sellers. Many women, on the other hand, work as cleaners in the bazaars. Some migrants are engaged in the expanding private construction sector. While some form teams of workers, others just seek day labor in low-skilled work. Sewing workshops are another essential sub-sector of informal labor involving a large number of women migrants. The next large segment is room rental, which is directly dependent on migration to the city. Depending on the income of a particular family owning a plot of land in one of the suburbs, especially those situated near a bazaar (like Kelechek), anywhere from one to a dozen rooms can be available for rent. Special but simple constructions consist of different numbers of rooms each with separate entrances. Finally, in *novostroiki* there are several small kinds of informal business: *bania* (bath-houses), *navoikana* or *tandyr* (a special oven for the round baked bread *lepyoshka*), small cafés, and shops of varying sizes commonly called *komok* (kiosk). A large number of komoks, navoikanas, and cafés can be observed along the main street of Kelechek.

Thus, urbanization in Kyrgyzstan sees the near absence of the growth of industrial entities that could be considered the main characterization of most urban areas. There has not been and still is almost no industrial sector growth in Bishkek, and industry remains almost in ruin after the collapse of the Soviet Union. Notwithstanding, Bishkek has become a center of trade and has gradually developed its own informal sewing sector. In the mid-2000s, construction also thrived. On a different note, the movement of rural, mainly Kyrgyz, populations to the city has contributed to Bishkek adopting a more "mono-ethnic face" and has led to its "ruralization," or at least that is the perception of those who call themselves *korennoi gorodskoi zhitel'* (original urban citizens).

Table 5. Inter-Regional Migration[67]

	2003	2005	2007
Kyrgyzstan			
Arrived	26,446	28,815	27,434
Left	25,334	28,994	27,252
Batken oblast			
Arrived	692	874	536
Left	1735	2169	2063
Jalalabat oblast			
Arrived	853	830	798
Left	2975	2416	2828
Issyk-Kul oblast			
Arrived	781	1133	1317
Left	2288	2856	2853
Naryn oblast			
Arrived	1456	1333	1103
Left	3105	4297	3454
Osh oblast			
Arrived	2014	1794	1367
Left	2756	2894	3329
Talas oblast			
Arrived	691	705	621
Left	1699	2025	1756
Chui oblast			
Arrived	9464	9642	10,555
Left	5710	4943	4549
Bishkek			
Arrived	10,495	10,234	9192
Left	5066	3728	4631
Osh town			
Arrived		2270	1945
Left		3666	1789

[67] Source: *Demograficheskii ezhegodnik Kyrgyzstana: Godovaia publikatsiia, 2001-2005* (Bishkek: National Statistics Committee, 2008), 389–390.

* * * * *

The current process of internal migration could be dubbed as an era of "great relocation" for Kyrgyzstan's population. Economic and social inequalities—that is, differences in access to quality education and living standards between urban and rural areas, central and peripheral areas, and northern and southern regions, along with higher unemployment and poverty levels in rural and peripheral areas—has defined the main direction of post-Soviet internal migration from rural to urban. A simple depiction of internal migration movements in contemporary Kyrgyzstan shows that the main pull for migrants is the capital city. And although in Soviet times the movement of people was strictly supervised, with independence this control weakened, leading to flows of internal migrants moving to the centers of each oblast, or from more remote oblasts to the comparatively more developed Chui valley in the north, to the city of Osh in the south, and then to Bishkek. As result of these flows, there has been a process of population concentration in and around the capital, where migrants hope to earn a better wage than in rural areas. Migration is thus a copying strategy for the population.

Another impact of migration and of high unemployment is the formation of the informal sector, which attracts and engages the majority of internal migrants, including youths who move to cities and towns to study. After graduation thousands of young people want to stay in the city but face unemployment. These two processes are interlinked: people are pulled by the city or big towns, with its promising informal sectors or education colleges, but the informal (or formal) sector is not able to engage every arriving migrant or new graduate. Employment opportunities cannot match demand, but migrants still stay on hoping to find work, resulting in myriad problems on all levels—social, economic, demographic.

The main actor in this internal migration is the Kyrgyz rural population, who is driven by unemployment and poverty from its homes to the valleys and urban areas. To finish on an optimistic note, however, we can hope that this process will have a positive influence on Kyrgyz culture and identity, precisely because meeting, working, or living near a person from another region or lineage helps to weaken engrained stereotypes. Perhaps in a generation or two it will be possible to see a more unified Kyrgyz national identity, free of tensions and cultural stereotypes based on region. Internal migration therefore plays an important role in achieving the birth of a civic nation.

SOCIO-ECONOMIC MIGRATIONS AND HEALTH ISSUES RESULTING FROM THE TAJIK CIVIL WAR

Sophie Hohmann

The consequences of the Soviet Union's collapse for society and the division of "One-People" into various independent territorial entities call for reflection on governance in a context where specific modes of functioning stemming from the Soviet system perpetuate themselves de facto, while other societal practices are rapidly evolving. Tajikistan, the poorest of the former Soviet Union's republics, is situated in an enclave between Uzbekistan, Kyrgyzstan, Afghanistan, and China. Three-quarters of it is rural and 95 percent mountainous, a situation that presents it with scarce economic resources. Beginning in the 1970s, the period 1989–2000 saw a trend of de-urbanization. A silent process of decolonization, the last to take place among the European colonial empires, also got underway in the 1970s[1] with the beginnings of a reversal in the migratory flow ledger between Russia and Central Asia.[2] It is in this context of Soviet and post-Soviet upheavals that labor migration ought to be analyzed, with this chapter consequently discussing the complexity of these socio-political and demographic phenomena and their repercussions on society in Tajikistan. It seeks to show that contemporary migrations—with a particular focus on the civil war legacy—are part of a long history of population displacements; it is especially interested in examining the health consequences resulting from the growth of these mobility flows. This study is based on available written data, namely the results of censuses, Tajik scholarly literature, reports from the International Organization for Migration (IOM) in the capital Dushanbe, as well as interviews with doctors from two hospitals in Dushanbe during the summer of 2007.

---

1 A. Blum, *Naître, vivre et mourir en URSS (1917–1991)* (Paris: Plon, 1994), 213–214.

2 Zh. Zaionchkovskaia, *Demograficheskaia situatsiia i rasselenie* (Moscow: Nauka, 1991); *Monografiia i atlas Respubliki Tadzhikistan po dannym Vseobshchei perepisi naseleniia 2000 g.* (Dushanbe: Goskomstat Respubliki Tadzhikistan—UNFPA, 2005); B.R. Rubin, "Russian Hegemony and State Breakdown in the Periphery," in B.R. Rubin and J. Snyder, eds., *Post-Soviet Political Order. Conflict and State Building* (London: Routledge, 1998), 153–155.

The Old Migratory Tradition

Before Tajikistan was created as an administrative and territorial entity in the 1920s, the corresponding regions of Eastern Bukhara and a part of the Khanate of Kokand had long been marked by a history of population movements that continued into the nineteenth century,[3] albeit in different forms. The various types of migration that emerged included student migration to the *madrasah* of Bukhara, as well as to other major Islamic religious centers, and temporary labor migration. Migratory trends at the end of the nineteenth century also included transhumance and merchant migration, especially to the region of Khudjand. The mountain dwellers had long practiced seasonal migration, which fluctuated between 25 and 75 percent of the male population in the Zeravshan mountains at the turn of the nineteenth and twentieth centuries. These migrants specialized not only in cleaning cotton for a growing industry that would rapidly dominate the Central Asian region, but also worked in construction and transport.[4]

The great national "demarcation" (*razmezhivanie*) of 1924–25, followed by the forced territorialization of the population and the collectivization that occurred at the end of the 1920s,[5] radically modified the migration habits. In line with the progressive industrialization of the Central Asian region, the Soviet political authorities displaced parts of the population living in the mountainous regions of the center and east of Tajikistan toward the plains of the south and north, where they worked in agriculture as well as in urban industries, led by Russian-born personnel.[6] In the 1950s and 1960s, migrants (*muhâdjir*) working in the low-altitude cotton valleys of the center and the south seeking to maximize the cotton yield, mostly came from the high valleys of the Gharm region, which was largely "forgotten" by the process of industrialization. Part of the Kuliabi population was also displaced in these years to work in fields recently exploited on the Afghan border and in the southern part of the Kurgan-Teppe province. Between the mid-1920s and the 1960s, it is possible that

[3] B.Kh. Karmysheva, *Ocherki etnicheskoi istorii iuzhnykh raionov Tadzhikistana i Uzbekistana* (Moscow: Nauka, 1976).

[4] S. Olimova and M. Olimov, *Migratsiia v gornykh regionakh stran Tsentral'noi Azii: Tadzhikistan, Kirgiziia* (Dushanbe: Sharq, 2005), 431.

[5] O. Roy, *La nouvelle Asie centrale ou la fabrication des nations* (Paris: Seuil, 1997), chapters 4 and 5.

[6] V. Bushkov, "Tadjikistan, quelques prémisses de la crise," in S. Dudoignon and G. Jahangiri, eds., *Le Tadjikistan existe-t-il? Destins politiques d'une nation imparfaite, Cahiers d'études de la Méditerranée turque et orientale (CEMOTI)*, no. 18, 1994, 20–22.

up to one-third of the population of Tajikistan was displaced—most under extremely harsh conditions.

Aside from internal migration, others left the republic for educational and other reasons. Starting in the 1930s, for instance, a minority of Tajiks were given the opportunity to receive an education in specialized universities and institutes, notably in Moscow and Leningrad.[7] Labor envoys to other republics were very rare, but some young Tajiks were occasionally able to participate in the great Soviet construction projects, for example in the construction of the Baikal-Amur railway (*magistral'*) or in the development of the gas and oil sectors in Siberia. The existing regime of obligatory military service also represented a form of emigration to an extent that, once finished, some conscripts employed in the army corps decided to remain in Russia.[8]

During the Soviet period, demographic growth remained very high. In fact, Tajikistan saw the strongest demographic growth in the whole of the Soviet Union, with a five-fold increase in 60 years, from just over one million in 1926 to more than five million people in 1989. Although labor migration from Tajikistan to Russia was largely negligible, flows from the opposite direction were significant. Faced with a lack of local specialists (engineers, technicians, and so on), Moscow called on the country's Russians and "Europeans" (natives of western Russia, Ukraine, Byelorussia, and the Baltic Republics) to assure Tajikistan's industrialization. Throughout the twentieth century, Tajikistan experienced many population flows, voluntary and involuntary, which helped forge the national identity of the country, but equally gave birth to strengthened local identities.

Displacements Caused by Civil War: Precursor to Labor Migrations

In Tajikistan, as in most Central Asian countries, living standards declined at the end of the 1970s, remaining well below those of other Soviet republics. This deterioration marked the beginning of a process that was to contribute to the dislocation of the Soviet Union. Russia's financial disengagement during the early 1970s intensified in the 1980s—investment in

---

[7] P. Mulladjanov, "Réflexions sur quelques effets du passage des générations dans l'intelligentsia contemporaine du Tadjikistan," in *Ibid.*, 32.

[8] S. Olimova and I. Bosc, *Trudovaia migratsiia iz Tadzhikistana* (Dushanbe: IOM—Sharq, 2003), 12.

Tajikistan was the lowest in the Soviet Union.[9] In 1985, investment in the Central Asian region fell to 1.5 percent, whereas it grew by 3 percent in the Soviet Union. It is worth noting that although agricultural and industrial production experienced a downward spiral, demographic growth in this period was very high. In the beginning of the 1980s, corruption scandals also broke out in Central Asia, including the Uzbekistan "cotton scandal,"[10] which tarnished the image of local authorities. The measures taken by Mikhail Gorbachev, exasperated with the local "mafia," were followed by the break-up of the Soviet Union just five years later—which proved to be disastrous for the national economies.

The fragile balance of Tajik society ever since its creation as a territorial entity was plunged into instability by the collapse of the Soviet Union. The ensuing institutional and political void led to a profound disorganization and armed struggle between two large power blocs (which concealed numerous other divisions) seeking to gain political and economic capital. Despite elections held at the end of 1991, the democratization process that started during perestroika did not succeed in regulating the conflicts, which became increasingly radical when faced with political impasse and increased repression. Less than one year after independence, Tajikistan found itself in the throes of a complex civil war, embodied by the conflict between the United Tajik Opposition, regrouping "Islamists" and "democrats" and the Dushanbe- and Khudjand-based "neo-communists."[11] Even if Russia and Uzbekistan made clear their will to intervene in the conflict, the civil war was firmly an intra-Tajik affair. Its origins could be traced back to the collectivization process launched by Stalin in 1929, which led to a complex territorial reshaping through the fabrication of solidarity groups based on territorial roots (*mahalgera'y*).

The causes of this political crisis were rooted in the past and were related to the distribution of economic resources and political responsibilities. From the start of the Soviet period, the Khudjandi had dominated

---

9 B.Z. Rumer, *Soviet Central Asia: 'a Tragic Experiment'* (Boston: Unwin Hyman, 1989), 31–40.

10 This was the biggest case of corruption in the history of the Soviet Union. During the Brezhnev era, Uzbek leaders developed a system for falsifying cotton production statistics to get around the impossible quotas imposed by the centralized plans. When this massive fraud was discovered, the Soviet central elites used the corruption claims to stigmatize the Uzbek authorities, and with it Uzbek society and its clan organization as a whole, by depicting it as a "mafia" (hence the expression, the Uzbek or cotton mafia).

11 For more on these issues, see O. Roy, "Tadjikistan: structures d'un conflit," in *Laïcité(s) en France et en Turquie, Cahiers d'études de la Méditerranée turque et orientale (CEMOTI)*, no. 19 (1994), http://cemoti.revues.org/document226.html.

the economic sector and provided the Tajik Communist Party with the majority of its leaders. The Pamiri, on the other hand, were represented not only in the security services, but also in some of the capital's academic milieus. The Samarkandi and Bukhariots, which both constituted the former intellectual elites of the Turkestani region in the nineteenth century, continued to retain control of the republic's intellectual circles. These three groups succeeded in divvying up the structures of the Communist Party and of the republican administration during the Soviet period. However in the 1970s, a new generation of elites emerged from the remote rural areas of the country, in particular from the mountainous areas of Karategin and Gharm. As they had little success in penetrating established networks, this new elite would rapidly become the leaders of the opposition. Some rallied to the Party of Islamic Rebirth while others endorsed democratic and nationalist slogans. Regardless of affiliation, the majority called for the toppling of the former Soviet elites. For the duration of the war, the central government in Dushanbe remained in the hands of a coalition, itself paradoxical, including the elites from the north (Khudjand) and the south (Kuliab).[12] Despite their internal rivalry, these two groups sought to thwart attacks from the Gharmi and the Pamiri, who had very little representation in the political organs. The imbalance between the more industrialized, richer north and the largely agricultural, poorer south gave rise to frustrations and bitterness in the southern regions of the republic, marked by the migratory flows of the mid-twentieth century, demographic pressures, and the deterioration in living standards from the 1970s and 80s onward.

The civil war officially ended with a peace agreement signed in Moscow on June 27, 1997, between the Tajik government and the United Tajik Opposition (UTO). The conflict had led to the destruction of the state apparatus as well as roads and infrastructure. The ruined transport, irrigation, and production networks further impeded the country's development. The unemployment rate rose from 0.6 percent in 1993 to 30 percent in 2001 (official data), and then to 46.7 percent in 2005.[13] The national economy was destabilized not only by the human losses, but also by the departure in droves of the "European minorities" in the country, namely Russians,

---

[12] S. Dudoignon, "Une segmentation peut en cacher une autre: régionalismes et clivages politico-économiques au Tadjikistan," in Dudoignon and Jahangiri, *Le Tadjikistan existe-t-il ?*, 73–130.

[13] "Republic of Tajikistan: Selected Issues and Statistical Appendix," International Monetary Fund, Country Report, No. 05/131, April 2005, 7.

Germans, Ukrainians, and Jews, who had held most of the important posts as technicians, engineers, and heads of industry. More than three-quarters of the Russian population had left the country by 1993. Other communities such as the Uzbeks, Tatars, and Jews also migrated in huge waves during this period. The Uzbeks, for example, went from constituting 23.5 percent of Tajikistan's population in 1989 to 15.3 percent in 2000. In their case, more so than the migrations headed for Uzbekistan, it seems that a tendency to declare oneself Tajik and no longer Uzbek constituted an important bias in the recording of their numbers. The 2000 census based on a "Tajik dictionary of nationalities" added nine nationalities to the list, diluting the Uzbek minority to the benefit of the titular nationality.[14]

Table 1. International Migrations of the Principal Nationalities of Tajikistan between 1989 and 1999[15]

Nationalities	Immigration	Emigration	Migratory balance
Tajiks	26,204	64,973	−38,769
Russians	35,483	268,755	−233,272
Germans	1372	41,152	−39,780
Ukrainians	4057	27,373	−23,316
Uzbeks	19,888	74,248	−54,360
Tatars	7374	56,521	−49,147
Jews	576	21,556	−20,980
Byelorussians	664	5150	−4486
Azeris	387	1582	−1195

In spite of the flood of people leaving the country, it was the social fabric of Tajikistan that underwent the greatest upheaval. The civil war resulted in nearly 100,000 victims. The number of displaced persons numbered 1 million—20 percent of the population of the country—including 500,000 as early as December 1992, representing 10 percent of the population.[16]

---

[14] O. Ferrando, "Manipulating the Census: Ethnic Minorities in the Nationalizing States of Central Asia," *Nationalities Papers* 36, no. 3 (2008): 489–520. See also D.I. Kertzer and D. Arel, eds., *Census and Identity: The Politics of Race, Ethnicity, and Language in National Censuses* (Cambridge: Cambridge University Press, 2002), 92–120; D. Arel, "Démographie et politique dans les premiers recensements post-soviétiques: méfiance envers l'Etat, identités en question," *Population-F* 57, no. 6 (2002): 791–820.

[15] *The Population of the Republic of Tajikistan 2000* (Dushanbe: State Committee for Statistics, 2002).

[16] "La protection des victimes de la violence à travers les activités du CICR," *Revue internationale de la Croix-Rouge*, no. 802 (1993): 328.

In addition, more than 250,000 people fled the country.[17] Between 60,000 and 75,000 Tajiks headed for Afghanistan, but the majority left for Russia or the neighboring Central Asian republics. Among the most affected southern regions of the conflict, Khatlon was particularly stricken: approximately 15 percent of its population was either displaced or fled the country. Meanwhile, the region of Leninabad, in the north of the country, constituted a "privileged" zone of reception for refugees. As Olivier Ferrando has shown, the refugees were in large part the descendants of the Ferghani who, during the Soviet period, had been displaced to work in the cotton fields of the south and center of the country. Civil war suddenly pushed them to walk the path of their parents, but in the opposition direction: homeward.[18]

Aside from the 700,000 internally displaced persons and the departure of some 200,000 Russians and other Slavs, the United Nations High Commissioner for Refugees (UNHCR) also counted (toward the end of the civil war in 1996) 30,000 refugees from Tajikistan still remaining in Uzbekistan, 20,000 in Turkmenistan, 18,900 in Afghanistan, 16,700 in Kyrgyzstan, and 6,000 in Kazakhstan.[19] Though the majority of Tajiks sought to migrate to Russia, members of the other Central Asian nationalities tended to return to their eponymous state. In 1996, more than 6,000 ethnic Kyrgyz from Tajikistan obtained Kyrgyz citizenship relatively quickly, thanks to an accord signed between the two states.[20] Out of the Tajik citizens who fled to Turkmenistan, the majority were reportedly of ethnic Turkmen origin. The majority of the Tajik refugees in Uzbekistan were apparently of Uzbek origin and were protected by a principle agreement between Tashkent and the UNHCR, until the latter was forced to leave Uzbekistan in 2006. However, many Uzbeks from Tajikistan settled with their families in Uzbekistan without notifying the authorities.

---

17 "Tajikistan: an Uncertain Peace," *International Crisis Group Asia Report*, no. 30 (2001): i.

18 O. Ferrando, "Déplacements de populations et identités dans la vallée du Ferghana: les limites du paradigme ethnique," *Cahiers d'Asie centrale*, no. 19–20 (2011): 177–212.

19 See the U.S. Committee for Refugees, "World Refugee survey 1997—Tajikistan," in *HCR Refworld 2006*, 15th edition, 2006.

20 A. Erlich, "Tajikistan: From Refugee Sender to Labor Exporter," *Country profiles, Migration Information Source*, July 2006, http://www.migrationinformation.org/Profiles/display.cfm?ID=411.

Table 2. Refugees and Asylum Seekers from Tajikistan between 1996 and 2005[21]

Destination Country	1996	1997	1998	1999	2000	2001	2002	2003	2004^	2005^
Uzbekistan	13	17	9	**	30,001	30,000	30,000	39,202	39,202	39,202
Turkmenistan	12,170	10,000	13,501	17,002	12,659	12,383	12,272	12,142	12,085	12,085
Kyrgyzstan	16,436	15,114	13,992	10,141	9,805	8,367	6,828	4,929	**	**
Kazakhstan	6,000	440	5,637	5,355	4,982	4,105	3,477	1,454	**	**
Russian Federation	54,031	50,192	22,952	12,299	2,061	759	698	593	**	**
Other	18,853	115	258	370	432	494	790	616	**	**
Total	107,503	75,878	56,349	45,167	59,940	56,108	54,065	58,936	**	**

*Note: ** signifies that data is not available*

After 1993, economic issues began to be responsible for migration more than fleeing the violence of the civil war. According to statistics from the Ministry of Labor and Employment, during the 1997 peace accords, more than 200,000 Tajiks were residing in different countries of the CIS.[22] Migration generated by the civil war rapidly transformed into migration for work. According to the IOM, cross-border migration has mostly been directed to the Russian Federation. Migrants choose Russia because most of them speak Russian and still have a shared feeling of belonging stemming from the Soviet period. More importantly, Tajik migrants do not need visas to go to Russia or Kazakhstan, which obviously influences the choice of destination. The IOM estimates that between 600,000 and 1.2 million[23] Tajikistanis (the terms covers all the country's ethnic groups) were living abroad in 2000 (there were 800,000 cumulated departures between 1991 and 2005, according to official data from the State Statistical Committee of the Republic of Tajikistan). Negative net migration since 1992 (93,400 in 1992 and 62,000 in 2005, according to their statistics) indicate that push factors are more important than pull ones (see tables and graphs).

[21] Source: *2003 UNHCR Statistical Yearbook: Tajikistan Fact Sheet, 2004 Statistical Yearbook, 2005 UNHCR provisional data.*

[22] *Tajikistan: Human development report 1998* (Washington, D.C.: UNDP, 1998).

[23] Olimova and Bosc, *Labour migration from Tajikistan*, 20.

The Professionalization of Migration

Between 2000 and 2002, 88 percent of all migrants left with the intention of finding work abroad. (Only 7 percent departed to improve their living conditions; 2 percent sought permanent relocation; 1 percent went to study; 1 percent left on vacation; and 1 percent went to visit family.) According to IOM data, which carried out a qualitative and quantitative survey in both Tajikistan and Russia, 93 percent of labor migrants from Tajikistan were men, unlike in Kyrgyzstan for example, where 40 percent of migrants were women.[24]

There are, however, variations that need to be taken into account, notably between the high and lower mountain regions and valleys. Mountain dwellers have different migratory patterns from the rest of the population. The proportion of migrants is particularly high in Gorno-Badakhshan Autonomous Oblast (GBAO), where 20 percent of all men have left, and in the district of Asht in the Sogd region where this figure is still higher—30 percent—while in the other regions of the country the average is less than 20 percent. The severe problems related to the remoteness and poverty of the high mountain regions, which lack any social, educational, or medical structures, combine with strong demographic pressure on an already restricted labor market. As a result, the migrations of mountain populations have a different character and can be likened more to definitive departures. According to a 2004 study carried out in Gorno-Badakhshan, only 2 percent of the GBAO migrants (out of 22 percent) had returned in the five years preceding the survey.[25] Female migration is higher than elsewhere in Tajikistan, and there is a greater proportion of young, single men in the 15–29 year age group (56.5 percent versus 25 percent for the rest of the country), as well as in the 30–45 year age group (36.7 percent versus 30 percent in all of Tajikistan).

---

[24] More in *Trudovaia migratsiia v stranakh Tsentral'noi Azii* (Almaty: IOM, 2005).

[25] I. Haknazar, *Migranty iz Badakhshana* (proekt Fonda Agakhana), 2004, quoted in S. Olimova, *Migratsiia v gornykh regionakh stran Tsentral'noi Azii (Tadzhikistan, Kirgiziia)* (Dushanbe: Sharq, 2005).

Table 3. Proportion of Migrants in GBAO[26]

	2002	2008	2009	2010
Darvoz District	2.4%	5.8%	7.1%	11.0%
Vanch District	3.0%	13.1%	12.2%	12.2%
Rushon District	4.5%	11.9%	19.2%	19.5%
Shugnon District	6.7%	16.8%	18.6%	21.7%
Rochkala District	15.0%	15.1%	21.2%	22.0%
Ishkoshim District	2.4%	6.1%	7.6%	7.4%
Murgab District	1.2%	3.5%	1.8%	6.1%
Khorog city	2.8%	5.2%	5.1%	5.2%
GBAO total	4.9%	10.3%	12.3%	13.2%

In addition, migrants from high mountain areas have not developed the same strategies as other migrants. Often unmarried, they rarely send back remittances compared with those from other regions who contribute more to the household income. They do not invest in agricultural technologies or cattle purchases, which would enable them to build up a local economic base (only 4.5 percent do so). The land is suffering from the impact of abandonment and is deteriorating as a result of not being cultivated for long periods. The lack of modernization and a labor force is, of course, aggravated by migration to Russia, but also by the lack of microcredit types of investment. One cannot attribute this deterioration to migration alone, however. The consequences of the collapse of the Soviet Union (reduced technological assistance and supplies of seeds) also fed into this process. It should be stressed that during the civil war, hundreds of thousands of people took refuge in the mountains, which also exacerbated the social and economic problems of these high, remote, and poverty-stricken regions. This particularly complex situation has only been partially ameliorated by development aid offered by the Aga Khan Foundation, which is firmly established in the Ismaili regions of Gorno-Badakhshan, and by the presence until 2005 of the Russian border guards, who mostly employed locals. Migration from the Pamir region increased again after 2001.[27]

According to Olimova and Olimov,[28] 36 percent of Tajik households sent one or several of their members to work abroad in 2006. They estimate labor migration in this year at between 600,000 and 800,000 people, which

---

26 Source: Khorog Committee for Statistics.

27 I. Haknazar, *Migranty iz Badakhshana* (proekt Fonda Agakhana), 2004, quoted in S. Olimova, *Migratsiia v gornykh regionakh stran Tsentral'noi Azii (Tadzhikistan, Kirgiziia).*

28 S. Olimova and M. Olimov, "Gender i migratsiia: chto zastavliaet muzhchin ekhat' na zarabotki?" *EARWARN Bulletin*, 2007, http://eawarn.ru/pub/Bull/BullFiles2007/74_49.htm.

would amount to 10 percent of the entire population, and more than 35 percent of the workforce. Generally speaking, the proportion of migrants per household is greater in rural areas (41.5 percent) than in urban ones (34.2 percent) or in the capital Dushanbe (25 percent). There are many reasons for this, including birth rates,[29] which are higher compared to urban areas. Another is poverty exacerbated by the civil war, which affected some areas more than others and which, after an initial urban phase in 1992, quickly moved to the countryside. The proportion of households with two migrant members is 10.5 percent in rural areas, 6 percent in urban ones, and 3 percent in Dushanbe. Furthermore, a 2006 study by the IOM showed that labor migrations from Tajikistan were intensifying. According to this survey, which was carried out among migrants in Russia and in Tajikistan, it was found that 74.2 percent of respondents from the Kuliab region and 64.2 percent from the Kurgan-Tiube region migrated for more than two years. Of these, 39.4 percent of labor migrants from the Kuliab region and 33.9 percent of those from the Kurgan-Tiube region left to work abroad for more than five years.[30]

Officially, remittances are estimated to account for about 25 percent of national GDP.[31] However, total remittances could in fact correspond to more than half of Tajikistan's GDP.[32] A precise figure is difficult to obtain because of the large volume of informal payments that are practically impossible to monitor. Informal channels were widely used until 2003, the year the banking system became a little more reliable and efficient, making it easier to transfer money.[33] However, the procedures for opening a bank account are not available to all, especially for people who do not have a work contract—most do not have such a contract. According to the results of a survey carried out by the IOM between 2000 and 2003, most of the male labor migrants are "fathers" and "eldest sons"—household members with economic responsibility for the rest of the family. Here one obviously sees the importance of solidarity ties and mutual family and community support that is typical of societies in Central Asia. Migrants

[29] One should emphasize here that the demographic transition occurred late in Tajikistan, around the end of the 1970s and the early 1980s, as in Iran.

[30] S. Olimova, "Trudovaia migratsiia i VICH/SPID," *EARWARN Bulletin*, 2006, http://eawarn.ru/pub/Bull/BullFiles2006/70_38.htm.

[31] In 2008, Tajikistan's GDP was estimated at US$4.7 billion, https://www.cia.gov/library/publications/the-world-factbook/geos/ti.html.

[32] "Republic of Tajikistan: Selected Issues and Statistical Appendix," *IMF Country Report*, International Monetary Fund, No. 05/131, April 2005, 7.

[33] Reportedly 54.8 percent of migrants used the banking system in 2005, for payments estimated at between $364–490 million.

mostly leave to finance the purchase of a home for their children, family events (weddings and circumcisions), work on their houses, or the acquisition of a small business. However, most fathers leave to earn money to feed their families. Younger unmarried men leave more rarely, although they may decide to migrate to save up for their wedding. That said, young single men (under the age of 24) also tend to spend more than save compared to other categories of migrants, since they have few if any family responsibilities, and they rarely send remittances home.

Labor migration has become a standard economic strategy for a large portion of Tajik society. However, although the decision to migrate is often considered at the household level, the migratory logic is underpinned by socio-economic, demographic, and cultural choices. Above all, one should not underestimate the importance of structures and ties of solidarity, such as the *avlod* (a patrilineal connection). These are prerequisite to understanding migratory phenomena, as well as the formation or reformation of a reliable community environment. Solid horizontal ties between the avlod that unite families within clans and clans within inter-regional groups also determine migratory motivation and the organization of departures.

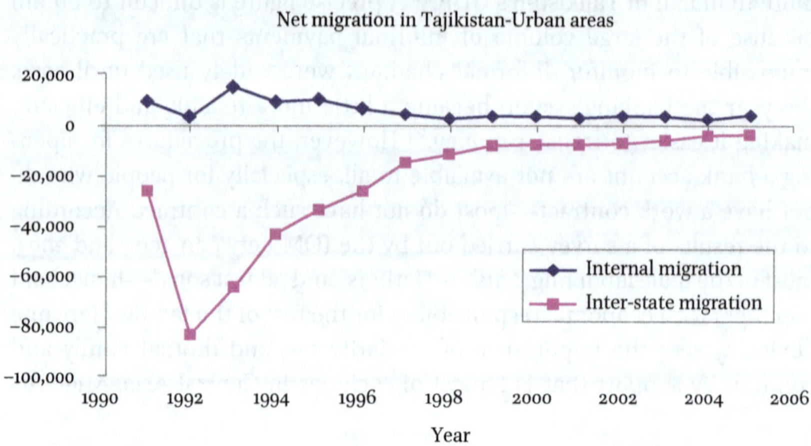

Figures 1 and 2. Net Migration Rate in Tajikistan: Rural and Urban Areas[34]

[34] Sources: *Tadzhikistan: 15 let gosudarstvennoi nezavisimosti. Statisticheskii sbornik* (Dushanbe: Goskomstat Respubliki Tadzhikistan, 2006); *Monografiia i atlas Respubliki Tadzhikistan po dannym Vseobshchei perepisi naseleniia 2000 goda* (Dushanbe: Goskomstat Respubliki Tadzhikistan- UNFPA, 2005), and www.demoscope.ru.

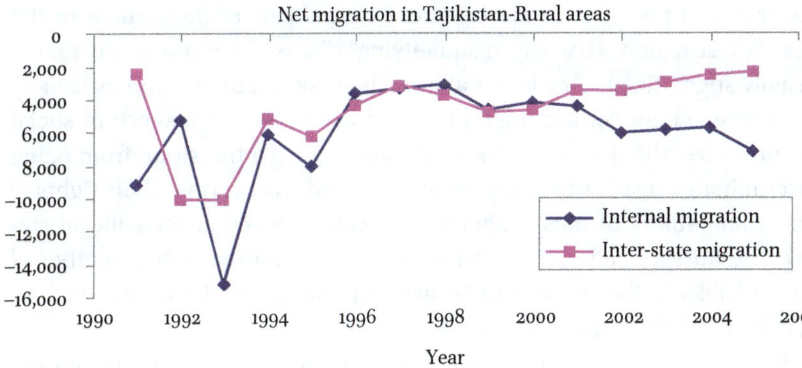

The Impact of Migration on Health and on Health Monitoring Policies

Young migrants are among the most vulnerable from the point of view of public health. The risk of HIV and sexually transmitted diseases (STDs) has increased largely because of drug use and unprotected sex with casual partners. Similarly, the "long term" (between two and five years) category of migrant is very susceptible to this kind of infection. They rarely send remittances home and spend far more on "going out" than seasonal migrants, including on the purchase of alcohol, drugs, and sexual services. These mostly single migrants are often from rural areas and from the high mountain regions previously mentioned (Sogd and Gorno-Badakhshan), where there is little health education or awareness about STDs and especially HIV infection. Rural migrants are thus less informed than the more "experienced" urban migrants and form a considerable high-risk group for HIV and STDs.[35]

The first sporadic cases of HIV in Tajikistan were recorded in 1991. As in the other former Soviet republics, there are considerable problems involved in measuring the extent of HIV infection among the population, and there are few means for promoting awareness and treating infected people with anti-retroviral therapy. Numerous risk factors are present for the development of an AIDS epidemic, including a high proportion of intravenous drug users, unprotected sex, an increase in incidences of STDs, tuberculosis,

[35] According to the 2006 IOM survey, 39.1 percent of migrants interviewed in Tajikistan had sexual relations with a prostitute and 27 percent had relationships outside of marriage.

poverty, and poor health management on the part of the state.[36] In the post-Soviet region, HIV is a "disqualifying" disease[37] for a migrant that is heavily stigmatized. This is not always the case in Europe, and especially in France, where certain migrants could even discover a sense of social raison d'être "thanks" to the disease,[38] undergoing a transition from being discriminated against to being recognized and "recovering" their rights.[39] The vulnerability of most migrants is a consequence of their illegal status. The Russian Federation's Migration Service estimates the number of illegal Tajiks in the country to be between 600,000 and 800,000 (or 10 to 15 percent of all illegal immigrants in Russia).

After independence in 1991, the deterioration of the health system occurred precisely at a time when the population required an efficient public health policy to tackle the problems arising from the collapse of the Soviet Union and the ensuing civil war. The public health system was hit by the emergencies generated by the population's growing impoverishment. The food crisis (86 percent of the population was unable to meet its needs) aggravated the already considerable nutritional problems in the country (stunting, for instance, affects 27 percent of children under five years of age, a rate that rises to nearly 50 percent in Gorno-Badakhshan). Carrying out vaccination campaigns comparable to those during the Soviet era was and remains impossible due both to the shortage of medical staff and the difficulties posed by a very mobile population. The number of qualified doctors per inhabitant fell dramatically (from 25.5 per 10,000 inhabitants in 1991 to 19 in 2005), as did the number of intermediary healthcare workers, who play an important role in the health system. Their numbers fell even further from 77.1 per 10,000 inhabitants in 1991 to

---

36 According to official data, in 2006 there were 27.51 cases of HIV for every 100,000 people in Russia and 3.08 per 100,000 in Tajikistan. In addition, sexually transmitted diseases such as syphilis and gonorrhoea affected 62.14 and 62.46 persons respectively per 100,000 people in Russia, and 8.4 and 13.32 respectively per 100,000 in Tajikistan. See the following website: http://data.euro.who.int/cisid/. Note that the prevalence of HIV is below 1 percent in both countries. According to the dispensary for venereal diseases in Tajikistan, in 2005 65 percent of people affected by these diseases were labor migrants (in 324 cases out of 420). For more about drug addicts and their risk of HIV infection in Central Asia, see S. Hohmann, "Le narcotrafic en Asie centrale: enjeux géopolitiques et répercussions sociales," *Revue internationale et stratégique*, no. 64 (2006): 110–119.

37 S. Paugam, *La Disqualification sociale : essai sur la nouvelle pauvreté* (Paris: PUF, 2000).

38 J. Pierret, *Vivre avec le VIH. Enquête de longue durée auprès des personnes infectées* (Paris: PUF, 2006).

39 D. Fassin, "Une double peine—La condition sociale des immigrés malades du sida," *L'Homme*, no. 160 (2001): 137–162.

42 in 2005; and from 131 per 10,000 inhabitants to 57 in Dushanbe alone.[40] Similarly, there was a reduction in the number of hospital beds, which dropped from 107 per 10,000 inhabitants in 1991 to 58 in 2005. Problems already inherent to the Soviet health system, which was unable to reform in time, were exacerbated by low salaries, inflation, the lack of any social security system, and migration, which further stymied the operation of the healthcare system and the population's medical coverage.

A newly introduced function, the family doctor (*semeinii vrach*) is responsible for between 1,200 and 1,500 patients on average, but often many more. The doctors interviewed in Dushanbe emphasized the work overload as well as the decline in staff since the Soviet period. Several interviews carried out in two hospitals in Dushanbe covering the local mahalla confirmed these difficulties.

Charlo, a young general practitioner[41] stressed early on in the interview the negative impact of the post-civil war migrations on the health of the population, and the breakdown of society and its operating modes: "After the civil war we saw a wave of migrations to Russia by Russians or European populations returning to there. But the internal migrations were also considerable, with populations from rural *kishlak* going to Dushanbe in search of work and settling with their families in the mahallas." Charlo explained that these were often very traditional rural people who did not function in the same way as those who had previously lived in the mahalla. "The new mentalities led to different behaviors, notably with regard to vaccinations, which were no longer carried out on children, leading to epidemics, as well as a lack of education and low literacy levels, which had a considerable impact on living conditions and health."

In Dushanbe No. 2 Medical Center, Bono, a trained cardiologist, explained the consequences of the migrations that began after the civil war and subsequently intensified: "The migrants who arrived from the villages do not operate in the same way as their predecessors, and the problem was aggravated by the fact that they are mobile and difficult to monitor. The doctors prepare medical records for them in which they try to write down as much as possible to help keep track of these people." Moreover, Charlo also mentioned her considerable workload, since she covers 378 households,

---

[40] *Tadzhikistan: 15 let gosudarstvennoi nezavisimosti, Statisticheskii sbornik* (Dushanbe: Goskomstat, 2006), 154–155.

[41] Interview with Charlo, a 35-year-old general practitioner and paediatrician by training, carried out at the Dushanbe No. 1 Medical Centre in the Borbad mahalla, June 23, 2007.

consisting of a total of 2,157 people, not to mention the administrative work she and all doctors are obliged to carry out. She mentioned, in particular, the problems in prenatal care: "Many women give birth prematurely, and it is often difficult to follow them since they move around a great deal because of internal migration. They move from an urban *kishlak* and return to their family one, and some disappear out of sight, and because they are not followed regularly—are not even aware of the importance of this—complications are becoming increasingly frequent."

Shakhzoda, the director of a gynecological surgery, also raised the issue of migration and gave an overview of its many consequences such as STDs, syphilis, and HIV, particularly in women. Shakhzoda said that she encouraged men and women to take free tests. She explained that it was a complicated and delicate process, but admitted that testing for AIDS was working better than in 2000. Nevertheless, it is difficult to keep tabs on people when it is not known how long they will stay in the area covered by their particular health center. When discussing migration and obstetric problems, Shakhzoda mentioned early religious marriages (*nikoh*), which are not registered with the State Office for the Registration of Civil Status, or ZAGS. In addition to factors such as poverty, war, and loss of family, migration also has repercussions on marriage in general, and particularly on that of young women less than 17 years of age. According to the State Statistical Committee, in the last census in 2000, the marriage rate stood at 13.4 percent for young women aged between 15 to 19. According to officials from this committee, early marriages are becoming increasingly widespread, but it was difficult to have a more accurate estimate since most are not registered. The proportion of married women (in registered marriages) aged between 15 and 17 out of the total number of married women in the 1979, 1989, and 2000 censuses, showed that it is on the rise: from 1 percent in 1979 and 1989 to 8 percent in 2000.

Officials from the State Statistical Committee produced a report[42] on the growing problem of registering marriages, as well as the difficulty in recording births. They believe that 30 percent of births are registered well after marriage in cases when the marriage itself has not been registered; 55 percent of births are registered within three days, 15 percent within a year, and 35 percent much later, perhaps only when the child reaches school age, which causes numerous problems with details in the birth

42 Interview with a head of the State Statistical Committee in June 2007 with a copy of the report provided but not published.

registration as well as in recording infant and child mortality, resulting in a considerable bias in demographic data.[43] The government has tried to pass laws on the registration of religious marriages and attempted to involve the religious clerics in the procedure, which would have religious weddings occur only after the civil marriage is registered.

Shakhzoda confirmed the difficulty in following-up on these young women, who are usually very mobile, marry in a religious ceremony, and possess virtually no rights, preventing them from receiving the necessary care. They frequently suffer from obstetrical problems and, in her experience, there is a high rate of death in childbirth. Furthermore, in rural areas (where the majority of the Tajik population resides) it is difficult to promote any awareness programs among the women and their families, resulting in a greater risk of epidemics and death, which she has also observed in other age groups. The entire system suffers from a lack of credibility, which also affects access to health and the relationship between the population and the state healthcare system. However, some malleability exists in social practice, even in societies perceived as having patriarchal traditions. The Soviet and post-Soviet upheavals obliged the populations and societies to adapt to change, as demonstrated by the migratory process and the strategies that lead to them.

An interview carried out in the Borbad mahalla[44] south of the capital provides a good individual illustration of the consequences of the war and how the people have coped with the end of the Soviet era and the dismantlement of the system. Ziârat was born in 1947 and has five children, four of which are girls. She is a doctor by training. In the course of the interview, her husband staggered into the courtyard looking distraught, lay on the *takhta* and said, trembling, that he needed psychiatric help. Ziârat told him to be quiet in an authoritative tone, but did not deny what he had said: "Yes, he does need help, and nobody takes care of those problems here." (It was clear he had spent money on alcohol; he was trembling, but appeared to be mentally composed. I did not ask further questions.) "And look at my daughter [her daughter arrived breast-feeding a baby], she gave birth four months ago and her husband has gone to Moscow to find work in the construction business, but who knows if he'll ever come back!" Ziârat was angry at her son-in-law for "abandoning" his wife after

---

[43] Officially the infant mortality rate was 23.4 per 1,000 in 1998, but according to the MICS survey, it was 89 per 1,000 in 2000, and 65 per 1,000 in 2005.

[44] Interview by the author in Dushanbe, June 2007.

the baby was born, angry at the authorities for "the poverty in this country and the state, which does nothing," and angry that health issues were not being tackled. "Look at what this country has become: there is more and more tuberculosis and cancer, and we don't understand why. My son died of lung cancer and suffered terribly. Typhoid too, and you know we had serious problems with reactions to vaccines in children, sometimes resulting in death. These vaccines are imported from who knows where, probably India, and they are of poor quality or counterfeit... All of that makes me so angry... The war was terrible, we all suffered and we will continue to suffer for a long time. We need psychological help, we need people who understand the burden of it all, and we need them to come to us [in our mahallas]. And the inertia on the part of the authorities is infuriating, we've got nothing left, our sons are dying or leaving to earn money elsewhere because there's no work here, and look at our old age pensions[45]—it's shameful!"

* * * * *

Migration in Tajikistan is an old and complex phenomenon. The characteristics of the various types of migration, and further still the impact of population displacements during the troubled period of the civil war, weakened the social fabric and de-structured the country's socio-economic organization. The considerable financial transfers stemming from migration certainly have had a positive effect, but one must wonder to what extent they will be maintained in the light of the global economic crisis and its impact on the economy, the social structure of the country, the familial insecurity inherited from the war, and migration processes. The Tajikistan government's health policies reveal the weakness of state management across all of its public policies.

[45] Retirement pensions range between 6 and 100 somoni. People who retired before 1991 get less than 30 somonis (or just under 10 dollars in 2007, when one dollar equaled 3.5 somoni), and pensions have not been re-evaluated since. A sack of flour cost 70 somoni in 2007 and one kilo of meat was 15 somoni.

AZERBAIJANIS IN RUSSIA: AN IMAGINED DIASPORA?[1]

Adeline Braux

The term diaspora[2] is one that has been widely used over the past 30 years. Complex transnational boundaries, human migration, and political changes have caused many groups with various destinies to be labeled "diasporas"—which include ethnic minorities, immigrant laborers, refugees, asylum seekers, and *gastarbeiter.* One can even come across groups calling themselves the film enthusiasts' diaspora, the Breton diaspora, or the virtual diaspora.[3] Indeed, the term has become so universal that some now regard diasporas as an obsolete phenomenon.[4] In Russia, the word diaspora bears a specific meaning related to the population displacements caused directly or indirectly by the collapse of the Soviet Union. Surprisingly enough, it now refers both to ethnic Russians who did not return to Russia after 1991,[5] as well as to the immigrant communities that settled in the Russian Federation after the end of the Soviet Union.

There are countless ways of naming immigrants in Russian. The word *migrant* is the most commonly used, by scholars, journalists, and the public alike; but the German version *gastarbeiter* is also quite popular to refer to temporary migrants. There are other specific Russian terms, too, the very semantic construction of which illustrates the ambivalent attitude of both the local population and Russian authorities toward immigrants. This is the case for the terms *priezzhaiushchie*, meaning literally "those who are coming" or en route,[6] and *priekhavshie*, "those who have arrived,"

[1] The expression "imagined community" is used by Benedict Anderson in *Imagined Communities: Reflections on the Origin and Spread of Nationalism* (London, New York: Verso, 2006).

[2] S. Dufoix, *Diasporas* (Berkeley: University of California Press, 2008), 1.

[3] S. Dufoix, "Voyage au centre de la diaspora," *Libération*, January 5, 2004, 35.

[4] R. Brubaker, "The 'Diaspora' Diaspora," *Ethnic and Racial Studies* 28, no. 1 (2005): 1–19.

[5] These ethnic Russians are more commonly referred to as *sootechestvenniki*, literally meaning compatriots, even if the word "diaspora" can also be used. See I. Zevelev, *Russia and its New Diasporas* (Washington, D.C.: United States Institute of Peace, 2001), 142.

[6] Present and past participles are very rich grammatical forms in Russian. They have been transformed into nouns to refer to a group of people.

as if distinguishing whether the migrants are staying in Russia on a temporary or permanent basis.[7]

Diaspora, in Russian discourse, is a flexible enough term to include immigrants bearing the same "nationality,"[8] regardless of their citizenship or the duration of their stay in Russia.[9] Yet, it has a rather disparaging connotation—when associated with an adjective referring to some nationalities, for instance the "Azerbaijani diaspora," it becomes nearly synonymous with "mafia."[10] This chapter intends to use the term diaspora in its widest possible sense, so as to properly address the transnational dynamics that affect Azerbaijani immigrants in Russia from an economic (namely money transfers), affective, and cultural point of view. It will also be stressed that whereas these immigrants do not share a "diasporic" self-consciousness, at least in the traditional sense of the term, their home country is actually making efforts to build what can be described as an "imagined diaspora."

Diaspora or Diasporas?

The word diaspora[11] has acquired a wider meaning than the one traditionally given to it, as a response to the failure of assimilation and integration theories, according to which immigrants were supposed to lose their identity and adopt local norms while maintaining a strong ethnic identity and feeling of community.

The term diaspora does not sound ambiguous when used to refer to the Jewish diaspora. Taking its source from the Greek language to qualify the Aeginetan people's exile,[12] it has been translated in Hebrew as *galut* to

---

[7] In a far less polished style, one can also hear, depending on the people met, the word *ponaekhavshie*, which could be translated very informally as "those who got their butts over here."

[8] This word is used in the present article according to its Soviet meaning, i.e. their ethnic belonging.

[9] The use of the word "diaspora" generally has an equalizing effect on the people to which it refers or is supposed to refer. See Dufoix, *Diasporas*, 60.

[10] The same negative meaning is sometimes applied to other people, but it does not originate from the majority group among the already settled population, like in Creole. See L. Green Basch, N. Glick Schiller, and C. Szanton-Blanc, *Nations Unbound: Transnational Projects, Post-Colonial Predicaments, and Deterritorialized Nation-States* (Amsterdam: Gordon and Breach Publ., 1994), 271.

[11] L. Antebi-Yemini, W. Berthomière, and G. Sheffer, eds., *Les diasporas : 2000 ans d'histoire* (Rennes: Presses universitaires de Rennes, 2005).

[12] This term is used by Thucydides in his *History of the Peloponnesian War*, II 27. See G. Chaliand and J.-P. Rageau, *Atlas des diasporas* (Paris: Odile Jacob, 1991), xi.

describe the exile of the Jewish people from Egypt in 586 B.C. Later on, this term was construed as meaning "dispersion." Diaspora finds its etymological origin in the verb *speiro* (to disperse), to which the prefix *dia* (further) has been appended. It also once designated Christian populations, who were dispersed all across the Roman Empire prior to the adoption of Christianity as the official religion.[13]

Traditional diasporas like the Armenian and the Greek aside, it is hard to distinguish between minorities and diasporas, or between migrants and diasporas. Indeed, the British people of the Commonwealth, Germans settled in Central and Eastern Europe as far as the Volga River, and Francophones in Canada are not called diasporas.

The evolution of diaspora as a concept is a reflection of the destiny of the populations to which it refers. In a book now regarded as a classic,[14] Robin Cohen asks where diasporas end. Conversely, one might also wonder where diasporas begin and what constitutes their defining characteristics. According to a basic, commonly accepted definition, it primarily implies a traumatic experience, often political in nature, resulting in the collective and forcible dispersion of a human group whose homogeneity lies in its common religion, ethnicity, or language.[15]

Next is the role that collective memory plays, whereby migrants recall the historical origin of the dispersion and pass their cultural, and often religious, heritage from one generation to the next. This is the case of peoples who have been victims of genocide, such as the Armenians. "The will to last as a minority group in order to pass on a heritage"[16] is itself dependent on three parameters: the culture of the host country, the numerical significance of the group, and the duration of the dispersion.

Gabriel Sheffer argues that three essential elements exist at the core of every diaspora: the maintenance and expansion of a specific identity among the "diasporised," the existence of an internal organization that differs from that of the home and host countries, and the existence of strong ties to the home country, be they direct contacts or mere symbolic references, such as a hypothetical "return to the homeland."[17]

13 *Ibid.*

14 R. Cohen, *Global Diasporas. An Introduction* (Seattle: University of Washington Press, 1997), 187.

15 *Ibid.*, 177; M. Bruneau, *Diasporas et espaces transnationaux* (Paris: Anthropos, 2004), 2.

16 Chaliand and Rageau, *Atlas des diasporas*, 11.

17 G. Sheffer, *Modern Diasporas in International Politics* (London: Croom Helm, 1986).

More flexible is the definition given by William Safran in a theoretical article published by the American review *Diaspora*.[18] In his opinion, diasporas are expatriated minorities whose primary characteristic is related to dispersal from an original center to at least two peripheral spaces. Safran also argues that members of a diaspora feel they are not or cannot be fully accepted by the country in which they are settled. The self-consciousness of one's otherness is indeed a strong indicator, which can be analyzed together with the policy, or lack thereof, of integration and nationality of the host country. Furthermore, by Safran's definition the relationship to the home country is multifaceted. The mother country is altogether the core of mythic memories, a place of return in proper times, and a cradle that the community intends to maintain and restore. It is also believed to be the primary and instrumental element of the self-consciousness and solidarity of the group, whose members maintain lasting and complex ties there.

These mainstream definitions tend to retain similar criteria and do not seem to be permeable to the disruptions that have affected human and migratory flows over the past 20 years. It is indeed only recently that population movements resulting from reasons of economics, politics, or occupation have been included in traditional definitions of diasporas.[19] Diasporic inflation cannot be analyzed without taking into account globalization[20] and related phenomena—economic globalization, fluidity, revolutions in transportation, the contingency of transnational migrations, the burgeoning of "global cities," the emergence of cosmopolitan and local cultures, deterritorialization of social identity, and, as a result, the transformation of nation-states.

Diasporas, paradoxically enough, have become a fashionable phenomenon. Long held in contempt, sometimes persecuted, and always suspected of disloyalty, they have today risen to become a symbol of cosmopolitan modernity. Hence the relevance of the hypothesis posed by Robin Cohen—that is, from a heuristic point of view, how legitimate is it to designate with a single word populations with heterogeneous trajectories, on the sole basis that they are geographically dispersed or that they bear an ethnic self-consciousness? Should the concept of diaspora not be

---

18 W. Safran, "Comparing Diasporas: A Review Essay," *Diaspora* 8, no. 3 (1999): 255–291.

19 C. Bordes-Benayoun and D. Schnapper, *Diasporas et nations* (Paris: Odile Jacob, 2006), 10.

20 *Ibid.*, 8; and Cohen, *Global Diasporas. An Introduction*, 157.

confined to particular historical communities, according to its more traditional definition?

Epistemological disputes aside, should one not consider these population movements "similar in that they concretize the existence of a transnational reality and a transnational solidarity in a globalized world where nations have become obsolete?"[21] From a Durkheimian perspective, would it not be preferable to shed diaspora as a concept and keep only the word?[22] Or, considering that the extensive use of the term in literature reveals mostly flexible identity constructions, employ it as a descriptive designation rather than a category? The above considerations constitute the main argument of this chapter, with a focus on the Azerbaijani diaspora[23] in Russia.

Methodology and Fieldwork

Prior to the dissolution of the Soviet Union and the establishment of new international borders, free circulation between Russia and Azerbaijan saw unchecked movements of populations. Even today, traveling between Russia and Azerbaijan remains fairly straightforward. Like nationals of all former Soviet republics, with the exception of the Baltic States, Georgia, and Turkmenistan, citizens of Azerbaijan can travel visa-free to Russia with just a passport. A thrice-weekly train service connects Moscow and Baku (58 hours), while Azal, the national Azerbaijani airline, and Aeroflot connect the capitals with four daily flights (3 hours).

Despite the establishment of borders in a formerly unified space, the number of Azerbaijanis in Russia, whether they possess Russian citizenship or not, is at an all-time high. Their precise number, however, is subject to widespread speculation. The media and some organizations representing the diaspora have a common tendency, though different motives, to overestimate them as a community of two million. Conversely most Russian

[21] Bordes-Benayoun and Schnapper, *Diasporas et nations*, 9.

[22] Dufoix, *Diasporas*, 2.

[23] The word "Azerbaijani" refers to the inhabitants of Azerbaijan after the collapse of the Soviet Union, whereas the word "Azeri" refers to the culture, language, or traditions of the Azeri people, wherever they are from.

scholars as well as the Federal Migration Service (FMS) agree on a number ranging from 600,000 to 1 million.[24]

Statistics should not obscure the fact that there are as manifold migrations as immigrants themselves, whose trajectories and reasons for moving are extremely diverse. To mention the obvious, a particular immigration can only be understood when taking into account the individual journey of an immigrant prior to his or her departure.[25] From this point of view, quantitative studies are insufficient to capture the subtlety of each peculiar migration history, be it that of an individual or that of a larger group.

The findings in this chapter are based on field studies conducted in October 2006, September 2007, and from October 2008 to March 2009,[26] as part of a doctoral thesis on South Caucasian immigrants in Russia.[27] Semi-directed interviews were carried out with these immigrants in Moscow and Toliatti.[28] The main motivation in selecting these two cities lies in their diversity. The Russian capital offers a wide range of migrant profiles—long-term residents, temporary immigrants, intelligentsia, and community organizations—while Toliatti offers privileged access to the "working class."

---

24 V. Mukomel, "Ekonomika nelegal'noi migratsii v Rossii," *Naselenie i obshchestvo*, no. 92 (2005): 2. The Federal Migration Service's data was provided by the Embassy of Azerbaijan in Moscow during an interview on November 20, 2008.

25 D. Schnapper, *La France de l'intégration, Sociologie de la nation en 1990* (Paris: Gallimard, 1991), 150.

26 The first two studies in the field were realized thanks to the funds provided by the French-Russian Centre for Research in Social Sciences of Moscow, and the third one thanks to a Lavoisier grant from the French Ministry of Foreign Affairs.

27 The expression "South Caucasian immigrants" refers here to people who have in common the following characteristics: they were born in Armenia (or the Soviet Republic of Armenia), Azerbaijan (or the Soviet Republic of Azerbaijan), or Georgia (or the Soviet Republic of Georgia); they have settled, temporarily or permanently, in the Russian Federation (or the Russian Soviet Federative Socialist Republic); and they share some cultural, linguistic, or religious features that distinguish them from the majority of the population in Russia. Incidentally, the children of people coming from these countries, and who were born in Russia, may also be included, even if the label "immigrant" does not apply to them.

28 Toliatti was constructed in the 1960s to provide accommodation for the staff of the Lada factory built there. It is located in the administrative division of Samara, in the Volga region, about 1,000 kilometers southeast of Moscow. The inclusion of this city in the study allowed the author to obtain a closer and more direct look at the "working masses" in the studied communities. Moscow, as the capital, is where most of the intelligentsia and organizations have settled.

Most migrants are men. With the exception of some women who belong to the "notable" class or the *babushkas* who commonly sell herbs at the market, most Azerbaijani women in Russia are the spouses of recent or long-settled immigrants. Although Moscow and St. Petersburg remain the most popular destinations, the Ural region and Siberia—particularly Yekaterinburg, and Tyumen,[29] where the workforce deficit is pronounced—has attracted and continues to attract large numbers of Azerbaijani immigrants.

Most Azerbaijani immigrants in Russia, regardless of how long they have been there, are involved in the trade sector, where they are believed to account for as much as 20 percent of those employed in the retail trade industry.[30] One only has to walk through any Russian market, especially in Moscow, to notice that Azerbaijanis run many of the stalls. Trade, predominantly through small shops, remains a convenient way for old and recent South Caucasian immigrants to achieve economic integration, although it is true this phenomenon is not limited to Russia.[31] The presence of the Azerbaijani diaspora in some "niche markets," such as the flower business, dates back to Soviet times.

Restaurants are another attractive economic sector for Azerbaijanis in Russia, especially for small investors. These vary from snack vendors at markets (intended mainly, but not only, for Azerbaijani customers) to restaurant complexes with several banquet rooms and hired singers, or even restaurants that offer European and Japanese food along with traditional Azeri cuisine. Overall, the range of activities undertaken by migrants is broad.

---

[29] From an historical perspective, Azerbaijanis have been present in this region since the end of the nineteenth century. Oil engineers, trained in Baku before the creation of the Soviet Union and during Soviet times, were sent to Tyumen in order to work in oil extraction. There is a direct train to Baku from this city, which is located in western Siberia. The trip lasts 50 hours and the train stops in the main cities of southeastern European Russia: Samara, Saratov, Volgograd, and Astrakhan.

[30] O.D. Vorob'eva, ed., *Migratsiia naseleniia. Trudovaia migratsiia v Rossii* (Moscow: RAN, 2001), 95.

[31] Research on small foreign entrepreneurs or entrepreneurs of foreign origin is involved in many studies on ethnicity, as the "ethnic business" is understood as a way to facilitate the employment of migrants, while providing them social mobility in a context of discrimination on the traditional labor market. See A.-S. Bruno and C. Zalc, eds., *Petites entreprises et petits entrepreneurs étrangers en France (XIXe–XXe siècles)* (Paris: Publibook Université Editions, 2003).

Ideal Types

Most interviews began with a simple question: "Why did you leave your country?" To make a living was the most common answer. Yet, it quickly appeared that this formulation was too narrow and did not leave enough room for variation. It could also sound like a reproach. It also became apparent that the details of *how* mattered more than the reasons *why*, especially when all the interviewees at some point came to explain their reasons for migrating. We therefore resorted to a semantic trick,[32] whereby the opening question was reformulated into a more efficient: "How did you end up in Russia?" (*Kak Vy popali v Rossiiu*?) Several ideal types have been identified from answers given by the interviewees: the pioneer immigrant, the short-term migrant, the adventurer, and the "notable."[33] A detailed analysis being impossible for the sake of brevity here, each of these categories will be presented only through their main characteristics.

The "pioneer migrant"[34] is an immigrant who arrived in Russia before the collapse of the Soviet Union[35] or who left his country in the early 1990s. The reasons for leaving are manifold and less frequently economic in nature, at least at first glance, when compared to more recent migrations. The pioneer migrant acts as a scout for immigrants following him: brothers at first, then cousins, and eventually even more distant relatives, friends, or acquaintances. Most of the time, the pioneer migrant runs a small business where he is the only employee, or sometimes works with a brother, a relative, or several people. He has accumulated financial and social capital, which gives him some legitimacy in the eyes of his family back home. Now a citizen of the Russian Federation, he is no longer subject to change and contingency, as his legal status allows for some stability. It is worth noting that the usual Russian word *migrant* does not apply to these long-time settlers. For the pioneer migrant, returning to his home country does not seem to be a presently feasible option, as it is dependent

---

[32] H. Becker, *Tricks of the Trade: How to Think About Your Research While You're Doing It* (Chicago: The University of Chicago Press, 1998).

[33] Alain Tarrius uses the expression "informal notables" as a reference to "circumstantial profiles." In the present study, the word notable is the author's choice, as these people enjoy, literally speaking, a real notoriety among immigrants, and are entrusted with symbolic, intellectual, and sometimes administrative power. See A. Tarrius, "Au-delà des Etats-nations: des sociétés de migrants," *Revue des migrations internationales* 17, no. 2 (2005): 14.

[34] Abdelmayek Sayad speaks of "precursors." See A. Sayad, *La double absence, des illusions de l'émigré aux souffrances de l'immigré* (Paris: Seuil, 1999).

[35] From this point of view, the word "immigrant" is somewhat problematic, as these individuals did not move from one state to another by "immigrating."

on economic improvement there, which he thinks will happen only in the distant future. Raising a family and taking care of elderly relatives seem to be the only factors that could turn the remote prospect of returning into a concrete reality. It is indeed unthinkable for many Azerbaijanis, even those who have been residing in Russia for many years, to raise a child in Russia; they often view Russian society as being too decadent and permissive, in particular as far as girls are concerned. Given the strong endogamy that characterizes this community, the easiest way to find suitable spouses for one's children is to send them back to Azerbaijan once they have completed secondary school, sometimes even a few years earlier in order to familiarize them with a country where they have barely lived, if at all.[36]

The "short-term" migrant, whose stay in Russia is only temporary, enjoys a generally advanced form of mobility. These immigrants are either single[37] or married, and in this latter case have often left their wives and children back at home (only one of the interviewees was living in Russia with his wife). Their legal status is almost always precarious. They appear to do with this situation, although details remained obscure to the outsider; some simply did not want to talk about it, while others avoided the question or seemed unaware of the legislation and lived on a day-to-day basis. The frequency of their trips to Azerbaijan varied: some declared they return for several months every six months, while others said they only go back once a year.

The "adventurer" is a sub-category of the previous type, especially regarding his legal status and the duration of his stay. He is a young bachelor immigrant, who feels the need to establish himself through this experience, and earn stature in his family or even his community. He is often indifferent to the possible consequences of his illegal status in Russia, as he intends to stay only for a short period of time before he returns to Azerbaijan and invests his earned capital and experience. To him, immigration

36 It could be interesting to later compare the situations of these families to, for instance, those of North African families living in France. North African immigration started exclusively as male immigration; this before the settlement of whole families who, at first, planned to return to North Africa, even if they eventually did not.

37 In this case, marriage becomes an issue in itself. As a part of one's life plan, it must be included in the migration project. Furthermore, the status of a single worker, apparently enjoying more freedom than his married compatriots, may vary according to his parents' or eventually his brothers' and sisters' situations back in Azerbaijan. If there is not a head of the family, or if he is not able to support his family, the unmarried migrant de facto becomes the main family provider. This is even more common when he is the only son, in particular when his sisters are single or about to marry.

is a digression whereby he will (or will not) earn, first of all, the esteem of his family, and possibly thereafter some respectability among the immigrant community or in Azerbaijan. In many cases, the "adventurer" is the second-born son in a family of at least three male children. He is sometimes the youngest, which can be a challenge to the family's structure, as Azerbaijani tradition dictates that the responsibility of staying and looking after the parents falls to the youngest son. Although less ritualized there than in other parts of the world,[38] this kind of migration remains a way for young men to demonstrate their virility, often leaving abroad immediately after finishing their military service in Azerbaijan.[39]

The "notable" category refers to two kinds of groups—businessmen and intellectuals. In the case of the former, their legitimacy as "notables" comes from the money they have accumulated in Russia, which in turn gives them the opportunity to engage in activities[40] that will gain them some social and symbolic capital. In Moscow, the most famous notables are courted by organizations representing the diaspora. Araz Agalarov and Vagit Alekperov, respectively the directors of Crocus International Holding and Lukoil, are members of the board of directors of one of the most important Azerbaijani organizations in Russia. But apart from businessmen, the "notable" category also includes Azerbaijanis whose occupations are deemed intellectual, as is especially the case for university professors or teachers with a high-ranking position within the educational system.[41] Considered a part of the Azerbaijani intelligentsia, they have been living in Russia since Soviet times for reasons of career or family.

One cannot help but acknowledge that opposing and sometimes conflicting trends are at play regarding the Azerbaijani diaspora in Russia. Nevertheless, what the aforementioned ideal types tell the observer is that departure involves three key factors, the combination of which may vary

---

[38] See, for instance, F. Adelkhah and Z. Olszewska, "Les Afghans iraniens," *Les études du CERI*, no. 125, April 2006.

[39] A. Sayad, *La double absence, des illusions de l'émigré aux souffrances de l'immigré*, 45. "May the one who wants to become a man go to France." This Algerian immigrant quotation could also feasibly be applied to the Russian context.

[40] This is particularly the case outside Moscow, where the organization's network is less dense and members of the intellectual elite are less present. Therefore, the notable role is generally played by small entrepreneurs or "self-made men" whose involvement in community interests is the result of their personal experience. Unlike his homologues in Moscow, the "countryside notable" seems to be more connected to reality.

[41] This is particularly the case for the school headmistress who launched an "ethnocultural" Azeri course and of the head of the Azeri teaching department of the Georgian school in Moscow.

from one group to another: economic, social, and affective. This chapter concentrates specifically on economic factors.

Remittances

Migrants' money transfers, however big or small, appear to be inseparable from migration itself. According to the International Organization for Migration (IOM), remittances worldwide attained a total of $337 billion in 2007, a 99 percent increase since 2002.[42] Yet only very recently have scholars started to take a closer look at this phenomenon, despite the enormity of the sums at stake and the considerable impact they have on the countries of origin. Standard-setting international organizations themselves, especially the International Monetary Fund (IMF), have established classifications that are relatively recent.

Evaluating remittances implies an agreed definition of the term itself. According to the IMF, remittances can be defined as "the sum of workers' remittances, compensation of employees, and migrants' transfers as recorded in the IMF Balance of Payments."[43] Each of these corresponds to a specific category in the balance of payments.[44] The "workers' remittances" are made by migrants whose duration of stay in the host country is less than one year, whereas the "compensation of employees" applies to longer-settled migrants. "Migrants' transfers" are understood as representing the net value of migrants' capital transferred from one country to another on the date of their emigration, being present in the host country for a year or more.[45]

Despite attempts to harmonize data, figures should be used with caution. Not only do many countries refuse to disclose their information, but the harmonized classification also contradicts long-established statistical

---

[42] *Managing Labour Mobility in the Evolving Global Economy* (Geneva: IOM, 2008).

[43] *Migration and Development Brief 2* (Washington, D.C.: The World Bank, 2006), http://siteresources.worldbank.org/INTPROSPECTS/Resources/334934–1110315015165/MigrationDevelopmentBriefingNov2006.pdf.

[44] "The balance of payments (BOP) is an accounting of a country's international transactions for a particular time period. Any transaction that causes money to flow into a country is a credit to its BOP account, and any transaction that causes money to flow out is a debit. The BOP includes the current account, which mainly measures the flows of goods and services; the capital account, which consists of capital transfers and the acquisition and disposal of non-produced, non-financial assets; and the financial account, which records investment flows," http://www.newyorkfed.org/aboutthefed/fedpoint/fed40.html.

[45] *Ibid.*, 2.

traditions in each country. Most importantly, the "workers' remittances" category used by the IMF appears problematic in two aspects. As of January 1, 2002, only banking transfers over 12,500 euros are declared as such, while lower amounts are subject to a statistical evaluation based on previous data.[46] This threshold seems quite high compared to the average income of most migrants. Of the interviewed Azerbaijani migrants, most told us they were sending at most one hundred dollars each month, and more often than not, on a much more irregular basis.[47]

Informal transfers often go unrecorded, whereas they regularly account for a non-negligible part of the overall transfers made by migrants. Only one in almost 30 interviewees said he resorted to a proper transaction agency to send money home. Regardless of age or date of arrival in Russia, the other respondents said they preferred to rely on their network of acquaintances. Transactions of this kind rely on a complete trust between the two main actors. Migrant X entrusts migrant Y, who is about to go to Azerbaijan, with the responsibility of handing over an amount of money to his relatives. Then migrant Y leaves Russia, hands the planned amount of money to X's family in Azerbaijan, and finally the money may be repaid to a third party Z (to whom Y is indebted) by X when he goes to Azerbaijan, so that the transaction stays within a small circle of people belonging to the same network. Some migrants also act this way to avoid being robbed on their long journey from Russia to Azerbaijan. According to World Bank data,[48] overall private transfers from foreign countries to Azerbaijan in 2006 amounted to $812 million, which accounted for approximately 4 percent of the country's GDP. Of this, $662 million were in workers' remittances, $128 million constituted employee compensation, and $22 million were migrants' transfers.

Obviously, not all Azerbaijani migrants function in the same way. A temporary bachelor migrant coming to Russia in order to sustain his family in Azerbaijan will likely send more money than an adventurer, to whom migration is not related to any family project. Conversely, a pioneer migrant settled with his family in Russia will primarily spend his money there, namely on housing expenses, children's education, or the expansion

46 Banque de France, http://www.banque-france.org/fr/stat_conjoncture/telechar/publi/not_info.pdf.

47 According to surveys done by Russian scholars, Azerbaijani citizens send an average of 133 dollars per month to their home country. See E. Turukanova, "Denezhnye perevody migrantov: beda ili blago?" *Naselenie i obshchestvo*, May 2006, p2, http://www.demoscope.ru/acrobat/ps98.pdf.

48 http://worldbank.org/prospects/migrationandremittances.

of a business. Transfers by such a migrant, if any, are only occasional and aimed at covering exceptional expenses: celebrations, a relative's illness, or an urgent repair to the family home. Notables turn out to be the least homogenous as far as money transfers are concerned. Small businessmen can send a few hundred dollars on occasion, whereas interviews suggested even less of a connection with the home country for those belonging to the intelligentsia.

On the whole, one is left to ponder whether the ties—objective, affective, or symbolic—that link Azerbaijani residents in Russia to their home country are significant enough to label them a "diasporic" group. That all evidence points to the contrary should not eliminate the questioning of Azerbaijanis in Russia as a diaspora, and more precisely as an "imagined diaspora" by their country of origin.

The Origins of the so-called Azerbaijani Diaspora

An "imagined diaspora," as this study sees it, consists of a symbolic construction existing in the country of origin. Authorities of this country consider their fellow nationals abroad, no matter how long ago they left, as being intrinsically linked to them in an effort to enhance the political and symbolic legitimacy of their country.

Most countries have set up some kind of structure—office, board, council, or ministry—that is in charge of what they either call their expatriated nationals or "diaspora" abroad.[49] Countries therefore try by various means to achieve a form of organization of their nationals settled in foreign countries, sometimes with the objective of controlling them, but more frequently to extend their economic, political, and socio-cultural reach.[50] This policy applies to both historical and modern diasporas, it being especially developed in those countries that have been subject to mass emigration.[51]

Whereas immigrants have long been accused of every possible evil—developing criminality in the host country, being traitors to their

---

[49] These words are relative, as the term "expatriate" is more frequent than the word "immigrant" when applied to Europeans.

[50] E. Ostergaard-Nielsen, *International Migration and Sending Countries, Perceptions, Policies and Transnational Relations* (Basingstoke: Palgrave MacMillan, 2003), 15.

[51] M.I. Choate, "Sending States' Transnational Interventions in Politics, Culture, and Economics: The Historical Example of Italy," *International Migration Review* 41, no. 3 (2007): 728–767.

motherland, or even causing prices to skyrocket during the seasons when they return home[52]—the economic boon they often represent has caused many countries not only to develop ambitious policies toward their expatriated nationals, but also to encourage more people to settle abroad.[53]

Azerbaijan has only recently developed a genuine policy towards its "diaspora," but this policy remains modest. In 2001, the Committee of the Expatriated Azerbaijanis was created and placed under direct presidential authority.[54] In addition, December 31 was declared "Azerbaijanis around the World Solidarity Day" by the late president Heydar Aliev. This celebration day is marked by a presidential speech that praises Azerbaijanis' spirit of dynamism and entrepreneurship.

A law entitled "the State Policy towards Expatriated Azerbaijanis"[55] defines the latter as "the citizens of Azerbaijan and their children who live outside the Republic, former citizens of the Soviet Republic of Azerbaijan or of the Republic of Azerbaijan living abroad and their children, and the individuals with links to the Republic of Azerbaijan for ethnic, linguistic, cultural, or historical reasons." Azerbaijani law is worded so as to encompass a wide understanding of the term diaspora, and the distinction it draws between "Azerbaijan" and "the Republic of Azerbaijan," subtle at first sight, may harbor some deliberate vagueness. Equivocal in itself, the term diaspora is made even more ambiguous in the case of Azerbaijan as the question arises of *who* should be counted, regardless of one's desire to be part of this group. Thus understanding Azerbaijan's tentative elaboration of a policy toward its diaspora requires a look back in history.

After the 1917 revolution, which brought the Russian Empire to an end, an ephemeral independent Republic of Azerbaijan was created in 1918 on the ruins of the eastern Transcaucasian principalities, which had been conquered by the Czars in the nineteenth century. This republic—the "first Muslim state based on secular principles and the rule of law, and providing civil and political rights to all citizens, whatever their ethnic,

---

52 A. Sayad, *La double absence, des illusions de l'émigré aux souffrances de l'immigré*, 331.

53 See J. Tyner, *Made in the Philippines: Gendered Discourses and the Making of Migrants* (London: Routledge, 2004).

54 In Azeri: *Xarici ölkelerde yaşayan Azerbaycanlilar iş üzre dövlet komitesi*, www.diaspora.gov.az. See also "Predsedatel' Goskomiteta po rabote s azerbaidzhantsami, prozhivaiushchim za rubezhom, Nazil Ibragimov," *Izvestiia*, December 28, 2006, http://www.izvestia.ru/azerbaijan/article3099898/?

55 In Azeri, they are called *Azərbaycanlılar*, that is to say "those from Azerbaijan," and not only ethnic Azeris.

social, or religious origin"[56]—did not last long. It faced insurmountable difficulties, most of which were military in nature. When Baku fell to the Bolsheviks in April 1920, numerous activists in this republic were forced to flee and take refuge in Istanbul, Paris, London, and Berlin, where they were met by those young people the republic had sent to study in prestigious Western universities. The fact that until 1991 residents of the Soviet Republic of Azerbaijan were not allowed to leave the territory of the Union, meant that the intellectuals, politicians, and their descendants who had fled their country formed what was only a very small diaspora outside of the Eastern Bloc.[57] Contemporary Azerbaijani authorities, their website reveals,[58] regard these emigrants as being the "first nucleus" of the diaspora or even its founding myth.

An Azeri World Congress was created at the initiative of Azerbaijan.[59] But so far it has not sparked much enthusiasm, because Azerbaijan remains unwilling to further embitter its relationship with the Islamic Republic of Iran[60] by appearing to sponsor separatists who advocate the reunification of the Azeri provinces of Iran with Azerbaijan.[61] Tensions also exist within the Congress itself, especially as to whether the envisioned common state for all Azeris should be secular or religious.[62]

On the contrary, the Committee of the Expatriated Azerbaijanis, an offspring of the Azerbaijani state apparatus, has acquired more legitimacy and capacity for action. It was recently renamed the State Committee for the Diaspora. Yet many major, obvious differences between host countries exist. With the exception of the modest website of a Turkey-based

---

[56] C. Çağla, "Les fondements historiques de l'Etat-nation en Azerbaïdjan," *Cahiers d'études de la Méditerranée turque et orientale (CEMOTI)*, no. 31 (2001): 103. To obtain a historical perspective, see S. Afanasyan, *L'Arménie, l'Azerbaïdjan et la Géorgie de l'indépendance à l'instauration du pouvoir soviétique, 1918–1921* (Paris: L'Harmattan, 1981).

[57] For an overview on Azerbaijan's history, see T. Swietochowski and B. Collins, *Historical Dictionary of Azerbaijan* (Lanham: Scarecrow Press, 1999).

[58] See http://www.prezident.az/browse.php?sec_id=54.

[59] See http://www.azerbaijanis-congress.com, which is only available in Azeri, perhaps indicating that there is only limited interest in this Congress.

[60] This is partly due to the disagreement between the states surrounding the Caspian Sea on the maritime borders of the latter, which hinge, among other factors, on whether it is legally defined as a lake or a sea. The distribution of offshore energy resources depends on the delineation of these borders.

[61] See B. Balci, "Azerbaïdjan/Iran: La mésentente persiste malgré le réchauffement en cours," *Caucaz.com*, April 23, 2006, http://www.caucaz.com/home/breve_contenu.php?id=338; and G. Riaux, "Les relations entre l'Azerbaïdjan et l'Iran : des représentations conflictuelles à l'apprentissage du réalisme," *Eurorient*, no. 28 (2008): 53–71.

[62] According to an interview conducted at the Embassy of Azerbaijan in Moscow, November 20, 2008.

organization, only the Azerbaijani diaspora in Russia is proving to be dynamic and making itself visible to its native country.

The Organization of the Azerbaijani Diaspora in Russia

In Moscow, the three most active organizations are the *Odjak* (fireplace) Cultural Association, the Federal National Cultural Autonomy of Azerbaijanis (FNCA, hereafter called "Automony"[63]), and the All-Russia Azerbaijani Congress (VAK).[64] There are also plenty of small organizations, many of which are inactive.[65]

Odjak was created in 1988, in the midst of the perestroika period, by representatives of the Azerbaijani intelligentsia in Moscow. Alarmed at seeing acculturation trends among children of the diaspora, especially from a linguistic point of view, a small group of enthusiasts, most of them teachers, launched a "Sunday school" for teaching Azeri language and culture.[66] Later events in Nagorno-Karabakh and Russian military intervention in Baku in 1990 fuelled anger among the diaspora and caused it to unite behind the motherland. Odjak's activities, however, never extended beyond the cultural realm.

VAK and Autonomy have a wider, mostly identical, range of activities. Both engage in cultural and charitable outreach, publish magazines of their own (*VAK* and *Azerros*[67]), provide legal counsel to their members, and collaborate with Russian authorities on immigration and diaspora-related issues. Some therefore question the usefulness of their separate existence which would appear to indicate a lack of unity. By comparison, the Union of Armenians in Russia offers a "single wicket"[68] to its constituents, and the main Georgian associations, too, have recently merged into the Organization of Georgians in Russia.

A difference in legal status is the primary cause of this situation. Contrary to VAK, Autonomy was formed pursuant to the 1996 Law on National and Cultural Autonomies, which allowed for organizations to be created with the purpose of defending the "national" (that is, communitarian)

63 www.fnkaa.ru, created on October 1, 1999.

64 Vserossiiskii Azerbaidzhanskii Kongress, www.vakmos.ru, which is not related to the Azeri World Congress.

65 Interview at the Azerbaijan Embassy in Moscow, November 20, 2008.

66 Interview with the founder and president of Odjak, December 2008.

67 Azerros is also a broadcasting firm, www.azerros.ru.

68 There is actually an Armenian Autonomy in Russia, but its activities are restricted to the cultural sphere.

interest of non-ethnic Russian citizens who were willing to choose "the ways and means of achieving their national and cultural development." Many of these exist today, such as those for Armenians, Jews, Latvians, Tatars, and Tajiks. They are the favorite interlocutors of Russian authorities on migratory and nationality-related issues. Autonomy stresses that its activities are primarily intended for Russian citizens of Azerbaijani origin, but remains reluctant on collaborating with the Azerbaijani authorities. Hence the fact that it was scarcely quoted by Azerbaijani officials interviewed for the purpose of this study, and only mentioned by them at the author's insistence.

In addition, the socio-professional profile of the leaders of Autonomy is quite homogeneous. With the exception of one university teacher, its board of directors consists of engineers and small- to medium-sized business owners, mostly graduates of economic institutes. Autonomy also has a council, whose members play a mostly honorific role and present a more variegated profile (artists, lawyers, and university professors), although the vast majority are still businessmen.

The first leaders of VAK, created in 2001, were actually founding members of Odjak. VAK's board of directors is full of renowned notables of the diaspora: executives of large Russian companies (Lukoil and Crocus International), university professors, entertainment personalities, and the dean of a Moscow school that offers an Azeri ethno-cultural program of study. Most of these individuals, whose settlement in Russia dates back to Soviet times, act as an intellectual and moral compass for the diaspora. As an organization, VAK is subject to Russian law. But politically speaking, its transnational Russian-Azeri dimension is far more developed than that of Autonomy. Its leaders maintain close ties with the government of Azerbaijan. While VAK portrays itself as a link between Russia and Azerbaijan, Autonomy claims to act as a mediator between the Russian authorities and their citizens of Azeri origin.

This latter aspect is worth stressing. Autonomy is intended for Azeris per se, in the same way that other such groups exist in Moscow for the Lesghian or Talych people.[69] VAK, by contrast, is willing to represent Azerbaijan's ethnic diversity, which comes as no surprise since many of its

[69] The Lesguians are a people from the Caucasus mountains, settled between north-eastern Azerbaijan and Dagestan, in the Russian Federation, where their population approximately numbers 200,000. According to the last census in 1999, there were 140,300 in Azerbaijan, making them the largest national minority accounting for 5.7 percent of the population. The Talych, who speak Persian and live primarily in southern Azerbaijan and northern Iran, represent roughly 1 percent of the Azerbaijani population.

members come from Baku, itself one of the most cosmopolitan capitals in the former Soviet Union. Its leaders often praise their fellow countrymen of Russian or Jewish origin for the success they may have achieved in business or politics; they scarcely do this, at least in public, for Azerbaijanis of Armenian origin, who used to be largely represented in Baku during Soviet times.

VAK is therefore the primary organization in terms of visibility. It is the main interlocutor of both the Russian and Azerbaijani governments, and it has a network of regional offices across the country, be they subsidiaries or local affiliate organizations. These include the League of Azerbaijanis of the Samara Region, which is headquartered in Toliatti. However, the lines between the two organizations can blur at times. Writer Chingiz Husseynov and drama author Rustam Ibrahimbekov, for instance, are members of the VAK central committee, while also belonging to the council of Autonomy, as both of them are popular enough not to be bound by a spirit of partisanship.

In addition to its task of promoting Azeri culture and the interests of Azerbaijan, the government in Baku sees the diaspora as a tool for political lobbying. This aspect is crucial for the Azerbaijani government, by reason of the conflict that pitted the country against its Armenian neighbor over Nagorno-Karabakh.[70] Conscious that the Armenians enjoy an edge over them with their ancient and widespread diaspora, Azerbaijanis nurture a feeling akin to an inferiority complex. On numerous occasions during the field study statements such as "Armenians, they know how to help each other" were voiced, although such declarations from people on the street should be viewed with caution.

VAK's publications[71] maintain a moderate tone on this sensitive issue, at least in comparison to the mainstream press in Azerbaijan. Articles pertaining to this issue are for the most part factual and never go any further than the official position of the government of Azerbaijan on preserving the nation's territorial integrity. This moderation probably reflects the

[70] Nagorno-Karabakh was mostly populated by Armenians when it was incorporated by the Soviet authorities into the Soviet Republic of Azerbaijan as an autonomous region in 1923. It proclaimed its independence in 1990, requesting to be incorporated into Armenia. As a result, an armed conflict started between Azerbaijan and Armenian Nagorno-Karabakh militias (officially), which were supported by Yerevan. For an overview of this conflict, according to a global geopolitical perspective, see F. Thual, *La crise du Haut-Karabakh: une citadelle assiégée?* (Paris: PUF, 2003). See also the International Crisis Group's periodic reports.

[71] In particular, *Azerbaidzhanskii Kongress*. Other publications, such as *SalamPress*, *Yeni Ses*, or *Azerbaycan Diasporu* are more virulent, but their origin could not be identified at the time of publication.

will to keep peaceful, if not cordial, relations with the Armenian diaspora in Russia. Moreover, as Moscow plays an important role in the ongoing negotiations aimed at solving the dispute, it is in Azerbaijan's best interest not to further embitter the situation.

This also demonstrates the limits to the influence that a state can exercise through its diaspora. In this respect, the Azerbaijani diaspora in Russia proves paradoxical in that, while enjoying numerical superiority and demonstrating unparalleled cultural and political dynamism, it is still very dependent on the state of the relationship between its home and host countries. The same could be said of other diasporas, such as that from Georgia. However well organized and integrated, Georgians in Russia could not help but keep the lowest possible profile during the conflict that broke out between the two countries in August 2008.[72]

* * * * *

As a concept, "diaspora" remains the subject of an ongoing dispute between those who advocate a narrow definition of it and those for whom such a definition ought to be discarded as elitist. For states and migrants alike, the question is not whether a specific group should be called a diaspora, but rather if this term correctly depicts the collective experience of human groups settled away from their country of origin, while maintaining strong but variegated ties with it. Transnational studies carried out since the beginning of the 1990s,[73] for all their flaws, have clearly challenged the unfavorable depiction of migrants as "forgotten populations" that play a marginal role in the economy, politics, and society of both their countries of origin and host countries. Diasporas are not a fact; like any other historical community, including those in the making, they build themselves through will and discourse.[74] In post-Soviet Azerbaijan, the diaspora remains largely imagined, as a result of its limited geographical distribution and the short time that has elapsed since independence. State-oriented as it may be, the Azerbaijani diaspora still retains a symbolic and political power that is critical to building legitimacy for a country that, while doubting its own identity, aspires to play a prominent role in the Southern Caucasus.

---

[72] Unlike Georgians settled in European countries, where they organized demonstrations and created support committees.

[73] A. Portes, L.E. Guarnizo, and P. Landolt, "The Study of Transnationalism: Pitfalls and Promise of an Emergent Research Field," *Ethnic and Racial Studies* 22, no. 2 (1999): 217–237.

[74] Bordes-Benayoun and Schnapper, *Diasporas et nations*, 176.

KYRGYZ MIGRANTS IN MOSCOW: PUBLIC POLICIES, MIGRATORY STRATEGIES, AND ASSOCIATIVE NETWORKS

Asel Dolotkeldieva

As in the other Central Asian republics, migration out of Kyrgyzstan, mainly to Russia, began with the disintegration of the Soviet Union. Between 1991 and 1994, it was characterized by the departure of the so-called European populations, mostly Russians, to their countries of origin. But beginning in the mid-1990s, emigration increasingly took on an economic dimension. Suffering from high rates of unemployment and declining standards of living, thousands of people including entire families emigrated in waves to Russia and, to a lesser degree, Kazakhstan.

Outward migration of the Kyrgyz population to Russia takes a number of forms. First are "trips" undertaken with the specific intention of earning enough money to finance, for example, the purchase of a car, the construction of a house, or payment for medical treatment. Geographical proximity to Russia facilitates this movement, which involves almost all social classes and age groups. Considering these trips abroad as "normal" economic activity, migrants may also do years or months of intensive work in Russia, followed by a well-deserved rest back home, in a regularly repeating cycle. Some may begin to see their home country, in this case Kyrgyzstan, not as a place of development and opportunities, but as a place to retire to once enough money has been earned abroad.

Besides these temporary and circular flows, there has been a noticeable increase in the number of individuals permanently moving to Russia. Some in this category of immigrants have chosen to settle down in small- to medium-sized regions and cities such as Astrakhan, Yekaterinburg, Samara, and even the island of Sakhalin. They come with their entire families, as their children have access to Russian public education. Most individuals, however, head to Moscow in search of higher wages and other opportunities.

Problems of Assessment

Such a range of movement makes it difficult to measure migration flows from the place of origin to the host country. In addition, census methodologies are outdated and inefficient. Today in Kyrgyzstan, the only source of information available is the household survey. The first, and so far the last, examination of this kind was conducted in 2006. This survey revealed that 18,700 households had members that had gone abroad for work, but according to its authors, the study does not reflect the actual scale of the phenomenon due to insufficient coverage.[1] Another type of documentation, conducted by the Ministry of Interior, consists of the departure notification application form; but it is not an alternative source of data, since notifying the authorities of one's departure is optional and therefore does not reflect the real size of emigration. Accordingly, the National Committee of Statistics, which uses such data, does not provide adequate information. Given these difficulties, the National Committee for Migration and Employment, which is in charge of migration policy, has attempted to quantify the number of migrants in Russia with the help of ethnic organizations active in almost all the regions where Kyrgyz citizens live. During her meeting with President Kurmanbek Bakiev on February 1, 2008, the head of the committee, Aigul Ryskulova, disclosed a figure of 253,000 migrants.[2] Although the census conducted by the aforementioned organizations is fairly accurate in small cities and regions, it might only be approximate in large cities, especially Moscow, where they do not have the same degree of access to all migrants.

Russia also does not have precise information on the number of foreigners working on its soil. Before the entry into effect of new legislation on migration policy on January 15, 2007, foreign workers were registered every time they entered the country. With the legal stay for professional activity limited to a maximum of three months, foreign workers were obliged to leave Russia. Since returning to Kyrgyzstan was too expensive—three months' work would not pay for a return ticket—migrants preferred to travel to neighboring Ukraine to save time and money, before going back to Russia again for three months. Each entry was then recorded as if a new person was arriving, creating an illusion of saturation of the Russian market by foreign labor. This also explains the very different estimates of the number of immigrants, especially illegal ones. According to researchers of the Russian Center for Migration Studies, this number amounted

[1] *Itogi edinovremennogo obsledovaniia naseleniia v iule 2006 g. Zaniatost', bezrabotitsa, trudovaia migratsiia* (Bishkek: National Committee of Statistics of the Kyrgyz Republic, Committee of Migration and Employment of the Kyrgyz Republic, 2007).

[2] "Aigul Ryskulova: v Rossii trudiatsia 253,000 migrantov is Kyrgyzstana," *Gazeta.kg*, February 1, 2008, http://www.gazeta.kg/news/2008-02-01/3742.

to between 3.5 and 4.5 million people in 2006,[3] while during the same year the Federal Migration Service (FMS) identified 11 million people.[4] Implementation of the new "very liberal"[5] migration policy in January 2007, including the expansion and possibility of renewed stays, would have regulated movement and allowed for the improved management of migration data. These recent improvements were nevertheless affected by the quota system, which was also introduced in January 2007.

Kyrgyz Migration Policy

Concerning the difficulty of evaluating and controlling migration in Kyrgyzstan, it should be noted that the inefficiency of the statistics system is not the only issue. More fundamentally, the Kyrgyz state did not employ any comprehensive migration policy and, until 2006, lacked concrete tools for its implementation. Up to that time, jurisdiction over migration was shared between several institutions, namely the Committee of Migration, the Ministry of Employment, the Ministry of Foreign Affairs, and to a lesser degree, the Ministry of Interior. A reform undertaken in 2005 sought to overhaul governmental bodies in order to delegate migration matters, which were becoming gradually more significant, to an independent and efficient institution. The merging of the Committee of Migration and the Ministry of Employment into a new structure, the Committee for Migration and Employment, reduced this superposition of institutional actors.[6] The urgency of reform was also a state response to growing social pressure inside Kyrgyz society, generated by repetitive violations of the rights of migrants abroad. An actual case of ill treatment of Kyrgyz workers during their work on a tobacco plantation in Kazakhstan during the summer of 2005 spurred the reform initiative.

It is interesting to note that the combination of what were previously viewed as separate issues, those of migration and employment, reflects the priority of the link the state has established between them. This is far from a coincidence. In 2006, the unemployment rate reached 16.8 percent

---

[3] For more information, see the Internet site of the Russian Research Centre for Migration, http://migrocenter.ru.

[4] Russian Federal Migration Service, 2006.

[5] Interviews with Zhanna Zayonchkovskaya and Elena Turukanova, Moscow, December 2008.

[6] Interview with the National Secretary of the Committee of Migration and Employment, Bishkek, March 2008.

of the active population,[7] while about 500,000 Kyrgyz migrants working in Russia and Kazakhstan represented approximately a quarter of the active population, excluding those working in Turkey, China, and the United States. The link between the lack of jobs in Kyrgyzstan and the exodus of the population thus seems clear.

However, beyond the migration-employment puzzle with which the Kyrgyz state is currently concerned, a considerable departure of the population inevitably raises questions of national sovereignty. Is emigration a threat or deliverance for Kyrgyzstan? Should the state facilitate its organization or hold it back? What is the impact on the integrity of the territory and population? The desertion by migrants of the southern regions and their occupation by Tajik and Uzbek families in need of land are an example of plausible long-term impacts. Some parliamentarians, such as Murat Juraev, speak of a "creeping migration" leading to the changing of state borders due to the settlement of foreign families—especially as these borders have still not been delineated with the neighboring countries—and describe the plausible risk of losing Kyrgyz territory.[8] These land occupations are considered to be a threat to national security, and in September 2008, the parliament passed a law on the protection of border areas. Specifically, it confers a special administrative status on a dozen villages along the border and provides social assistance to local populations in order to deter their departure. The law also prohibits foreigners from purchasing property in the border territories. This does not actually stop the activity; the law can be bypassed by buying a house in a Kyrgyzstani citizen's name.

In short, the question arises of how the state conception of Kyrgyz territory, its population, and borders changes under the pressure of migration processes? Conversely, how does the issue of migration, made public, influence the current political regime? In other words, does the free discussion of a mass exodus, which symbolizes basically the economic failure of the country, indicate the liberalization of the current political regime? Indeed, the migration agenda becomes more complex when one considers that it undeniably weakened the popularity and legitimacy of Kurmanbek Bakiev's government.

---

[7] National Committee of Statistics of the Kyrgyz Republic, 2002–6.

[8] "Murat Zhuraev: v sledstvii 'pol'zuchei migratsii' mi mozhem poteriat' tret' territorii strany," *Gazeta.kg*, March 6, 2008, http://www.gazeta.kg/interview/2008-03-06/4450.

One of the major attributes of the constitution of the official migration policy was to provide greater visibility and transparency to the issue. As stated by Aigul Ryskulova, "Under President Askar Akayev, discussion around the topic of migration was deliberately suppressed. And if it had a place, it was treated as a social phenomenon whose economic grounds were kept silent. Today, migration provokes not only debates, but a strong mobilization of public institutions."[9] When analyzing the action of the new committee and the rhetoric surrounding the topic within the government and the media, one can see that Kurmanbek Bakiev's government was more prepared to admit (compared to its predecessor) that socio-economic difficulties were the main driver of emigration. Did it do so in order to blame the Akayev regime for these problems and to gain new political capital? In fact, the government often dramatically portrays emigration as an unwanted event, expressed in terms of sacrifice. Frequent use of the term "forced emigration" in political discourse, a label usually applied in times of armed conflict, helps to reinforce the "compulsory" departure of individuals, even while increasing numbers of migrants are driven in their choice of departure by economic rationales, specifically the need to save and the desire to consume.

Most importantly, the acceptance or even facilitation of migration by the state of origin is linked to state efforts to avoid social tensions caused by the lack of employment. To limit or to prevent departures in a situation where economic stagnation hinders the creation of new jobs seems absurd. This concern is even stronger considering that the Bakiyev regime was brought to power in March 2005, in part thanks to young unemployed people on the outskirts of the capital, fuelled by alcohol. The lootings that took place in the days after the "Tulip Revolution" demonstrated how this category of society was easy to mobilize.

Unemployment particularly affects new graduates, who cannot find jobs at the end of their studies. In this context, the opening of borders seems to considerably alleviate pressures on the labor market. The message sent to the population is one of social autonomy. In the transitional period wherein the regime moves from socialist to liberal, emigration is presented as a means of adaptation and as a short- or medium-term response to the deterioration in the quality of life. If individuals feel able to migrate for employment, they should do so in order to solve their own

---

[9] Aigul Ryskulova's speech during the Intergovernmental Conference on Migration in Bishkek, March 2008.

financial problems, rather than wait for state assistance. To prevent a definite and massive outflow of labor and educated professionals, the government proposed a law on dual citizenship, aimed at facilitating seasonal and circular mobility between Russia and Kyrgyzstan.

However, the "retreat" of the state from private life, leading to greater freedom of movement, does not prevent it from seeking to control the financial transfers coming in from abroad. In 2008, migrants working in Russia sent $870 million using banking services, twice the amount of 2007.[10] In addition, this number does not account for the millions of dollars transferred through informal channels. Thus, official remittances represent about 43 percent of Kyrgyz GDP, an unprecedented figure in the history of the country. This high figure explains the desire of the state to better manage transfers and their circulation between the two countries; similar to Tajikistan, it seeks to tax remittances. Meanwhile, remittances have started to become a concrete form of development assistance. For instance, after the February 2008 earthquake in Naokat village, an association of migrants collected funds designed to help the families of victims recover.

At the Point of Arrival: A Sociological Portrait of Migrants

In Kyrgyzstan, as in the other republics of Central Asia, two groups seem to be particularly disposed to international mobility: young men who seek to gain financial independence from their parents, buy a house, and find a spouse; and mature men who face continued financial challenges related to events such as the marriage of their children and funerals. These two groups fall within a broader category of people whose ages range from 16 to 50. Women are also beginning to swell the ranks of migrants. Kyrgyz women appear to depart more frequently than women in Tajikistan and Uzbekistan, since traveling alone is less constrained by social norms.

Because of their education during the Soviet era, generations older than 30–35 years of age are more fluent in the Russian language than younger people, but this does not necessarily translate into gaining better positions of employment in Russia. The younger generation of migrants is less

10 "Migranty is Kyrgyzstana, rabotaiushchie v Rossii, v 2008 g. pereslali na rodinu bolee 870 millionov dollarov," *24.kg*, January 26, 2009, http://www.24.kg/community/2009/01/26/104271.html.

homogeneous, and divided between those who have completed higher or specialized education but could not find a job in Kyrgyzstan and those who migrated as soon as they obtained their first school certificate. The latter group is growing in number. Russia therefore hosts immigrants from a variety of social groups, ranging from highly skilled individuals, like medical personnel and teachers, to completely unskilled laborers. According to Shabolotov Tajimamat, 37 percent of Kyrgyz migrants are employed on construction sites, 13 percent in trade, 11 percent in industry, 5 percent in transport and communications, 3 percent in agriculture, and the remaining 31 percent in other sectors of the Russian economy.[11]

In Kyrgyzstan, the international migration of individuals is often preceded by an internal migration from rural to urban areas. A profound agricultural crisis, the decreasing quality of social services, and especially the lack of employment in rural areas encourages individuals, especially the young, to travel to large cities for seasonal or temporary jobs or to permanently settle there. Villages are thus deserted to the extent that it has become necessary to mobilize women and the elderly to plow fields and organize the harvest. At the social level, the abandonment of rural areas by men challenges traditional societal relations and customs, such as weddings and funerals. Consequently, in their absence it is impossible to carry out a funeral ceremony, a task normally performed by men according to the Muslim tradition.

According to official estimates of the National Committee of Statistics, between 1991 and 2005 the total volume of interregional displacement involved some 889,921 people, although this figure might not correspond to the actual reality.[12] The main destinations of internal migrants are the capital of Bishkek and the province of Chui. These localities are experiencing difficulties in adapting their infrastructures and are no longer able to absorb these massive inflows of people. Official statistics also point to reduced employment opportunities. Unemployment rates in Bishkek and Osh, the two largest cities of the country, stand at 14.6 percent and 22.9 percent, respectively, of those of working age.[13] The failure of the rural population to integrate in urban areas and sustainably earn a living there

[11] Interview with Shabolotov Tazhimamat, former head of the Overseas Bureau of the Committee of Migration and Employment in Moscow, March 2008.

[12] See the analytical report, "Uslovia i sostoianie sotsial'noi reabilitatsii trudovykh migrantov—grazhdan Kirgizskoi Respubliki, posle vozvrashcheniia na rodinu" (Bishkek: Social Research Center of the American University of Central Asia, PACT, 2007).

[13] National Statistics Committee of the Kyrgyz Republic, 2002–6.

is thus often followed by their departure to Russia, a trend that has been particularly pronounced in recent years.

Russian Migration Policy

Russia remains the primary destination for Kyrgyz migrants. Offering the possibility for migrants to save due to higher wages and the fact that no entry visa is required, thus obviating cumbersome administrative procedures and long waits before departure, makes it an attractive destination. Moreover, Moscow has not yet established a system of labor force selection, like in other countries such as France or Canada that receive a high number of immigrants, even though the idea is progressively spreading within Russian political circles. Finally, the common language of the post-Soviet space, Russian, eases the integration and work of migrants. These provisions did not, however, set up sufficient conditions for a regulated professional stay for the majority of migrants. In January 2007, when Russian migration policy was liberalized, only 10 percent of Kyrgyz workers were there legally.[14] With the new legislative changes, at least 30 percent of foreign workers of all nationalities were legalized and 85 percent gained the ability to register, compared to 54 percent prior to the reform.[15] However, inadequate management of the quota system, which was also introduced in January 2007, has hindered the final regularization of migrants.

The Russian government designed the quota system so that the number of migrant workers entering its territory would correspond to the real needs of the domestic labor market. It was then decided that the federal quota would be set annually using figures provided by regional administrations in charge of assessing labor needs, by centralizing the requests from the private and public sectors. In conformity with the law, these requests must be submitted to local administrations in May of each year in order to benefit from the quota the following year. However, many companies function on the basis of allocated credits and cannot therefore formulate and communicate their needs until the end of the year. Consequently, they do not submit applications, but may later acquire workers according

[14] Interview with Shabolotov Tazhimamat, former head of the Overseas Bureau of the Committee of Migration and Employment, Moscow, March 2008.

[15] Materials for the conference, "Forms of cooperation and mechanisms of labor migration management in the Russian Federation and Countries of Central Asia," Moscow, December 3–4, 2008. The conference is a part of a joint project with the International Organization for Migration and the International Labor Organization.

to a quota—there being no administrative control over quota requestors or the quantity of migrants requested.

This technical defect, in addition to the absence of an efficient mechanism to assess the real volume of migrants, has led to the establishment of insufficient quotas that do not correspond to actual demand. During the two years following the introduction of the quota system, all the working permits allocated for the entire year were distributed by June. Migrants arriving after this date were not able to receive one. To date, there is no mechanism for informing potential migration candidates of the status of the quota before they depart. Consequently, many foreign workers who do not receive a work permit upon arrival are obliged to enter the black market in order to find a job. The quota system therefore has not led to a better management of those working illegally. Also, quotas have not become an efficient control mechanism, as they do not prevent the entry of thousands of new migrants, who are not stopped at the border by a visa regime.

In addition to the quota, there is what can be termed a "reserve" that is supposed to allocate new permits in case the initial quota is insufficient, but which actually serves to dissimulate many failures of the system. In 2008, the reserve represented 50 percent of the total quota, confirming that the latter was so approximate that it was necessary to provide for a very large margin of error. For Zhanna Zayonchkovskaya, the existence of such a large reserve symbolizes the inefficiency of the quota system as a mechanism of migration policy. What is more, radical fluctuations can be observed in the quota and reserve levels. In 2007, the quota for immigrants from CIS countries that did not require an entry visa was equal to six million; it fell to 1.2 million in 2008, and increased to two million in 2009, rather than the planned four million. The magnitude of the global economic crisis prompted Russian political leaders to sharply reduce the quota by half. The question was whether Russian citizens would be willing to accept the economic niche occupied by foreign workers, which, in the eyes of decision-makers, seemed unlikely. The change therefore reflected a symbolic and populist objective to assuage the fears of the population—linked to the risk of unemployment—by turning migrants into scapegoats.

This measure seems to forestall any liberal trend in the new migration policy. The migration issue is particularly sensitive, closely related as it is to the problem of forming a multinational and multicultural nation-state in Russia. Beyond the economic advantages, immigration represents an opportunity to compensate for the demographic deficit caused by an ageing Russian society. The country lost 3.5 million people between 2002 and 2006, approximately 700,000 per year,[16] due to low birth and high mortality rates. To resolve this dilemma, the famous Russian demographer Anatoly Vichnevski has suggested hosting hundreds of thousands of migrants each year in an attempt to halt the decline of the Russian population. Even a positive forecast, based on the necessary increase of birth rates and the decline of mortality rates, stresses that the country needs an influx of between 500,000 and 600,000 migrants per year.[17] Another prominent Russian migration specialist Zhanna Zayonchkovskaya, a member of the National Academy of Sciences, supports this view and affirms that "Russia's future lies together with immigration."[18]

However, a massive influx of migrants from the South Caucasus and Central Asia would likely encounter stiff cultural and political resistance. The fact that the majority of the migrants are young, rural men, who after the collapse of the Soviet Union did not acquire the same level of Russian as those educated under the Soviet system, reinforces local concerns about their ability to integrate into the host society. Increased acts of xenophobia and pejorative terms—such as the widespread use of the expression *chernye*, literally, "the blacks"—directed against foreign workers reveals an undercurrent of hostility toward them. Indeed, the term chernye, with its racist connotations, has entered the everyday vocabulary of both law enforcement bodies and the Russian public. It refers not only to the color of the skin or hair, but also to "mud," highlighting in this context the pitiable work done by migrants. In addition, this generalizing term allows for all foreign workers to be grouped into a single socio-political group regardless of nationality. Vietnamese, Chinese, Tajik, Kazakh, Kyrgyz, or Afghan—it strengthens the sentiment that "security risks" emanate from the "south" of Russia. By equating drug traffickers from Central Asia with migrant laborers, the Russian media also contributes to the muddying of their already negative image.

At the political level, the immigration and permanent settlement of foreigners raises a profound discrepancy of views. On the one hand, nationalist xenophobic circles lobby the government to set up a visa regime with some CIS countries, wishing to reduce these "dangerous" inflows.

---

[16] See N. Eberstadt, "Russia's Peacetime Demographic Crisis: Dimensions, Causes, Implications," *NBR Report*, May 2010.

[17] A. Vichnevski, "Migrations et croissance démographique en Russie," *Migrations Société* 17, no. 101 (2005): 129–142.

[18] Interview with Zhanna Zayonchkovskaya, Moscow, December 2008.

On the other hand, trade unions with a direct interest in the professional integration of foreigners under Russian law call for the CIS to become a viable organization to liberalize human movement within it, as was the case during the Soviet Union.[19] Initially, the administration of President Vladimir Putin expressed its opposition to the opening up of the Russian labor market to foreigners.[20] In spite of this, in 2006 Putin promoted a number of laws to liberalize migration policy. Indeed, it is curious to note that migration policy is the prerogative neither of the government nor the Duma, but remains solely under the purview of the president.

Migrants vis-à-vis Representatives of the Russian State

The pre-2007 opacity of certain mechanisms of Russian migration policy deserves special attention. Before this date, for instance, nationals of CIS countries, except Turkmenistan and Georgia, had the right to enter Russia without a visa and stay for three consecutive months. A date of entry stamp affixed on the passport allowed law enforcement bodies to check the validity of a stay. People exceeding this period were thus considered to be in the country illegally.

However, a certificate of residence, or *propiska*, was requested for migrants and conditioned their right to reside temporarily in Russia. This certificate had to be submitted to police authorities[21] within a period of three days after arrival. The procedure was extremely burdensome due to the very short period of time allotted to complete administrative procedures, especially if coinciding with a weekend or a holiday. The consent of all individuals permanently occupying a residence was required as well. A simple certificate of consent was insufficient: the physical presence of each resident and the owner of the property was mandatory. Such regulations made it difficult or impossible to register foreign workers and led to an increase in illegal migration.

These control mechanisms engendered specific relations between migrants and various actors in the Russian state. As in all repressive

[19] Interview with O. Sokolov, Deputy Secretary of the Federation of Independent Trade Unions, Moscow, December 2008.

[20] Interview with an anonymous member of the scientific council of President Vladimir Putin on the issue of migration, Moscow, December 2008.

[21] Before the reform of the Ministry of Interior, the police were in charge of the registration of migrants. Today, the Federal Migration Service, created within the ministry, is tasked with its management; however, the three-day period has been maintained.

regimes, the regime of "documentation"[22] led to the growth of corrupt practices and false documents. The number of companies specializing in the falsification of propiska and *shtamps*, the entry stamp, gradually increased. Advertisements offering these services flooded the streets and subways of Moscow. Falsification, offered both by individual traders and private companies, took several forms, ranging from the petty sale of fake entry stamps at the Kazan train station in Moscow to the more significant, like fictitious naturalization or marriage.[23] Some providers of illegal services work closely with employees of the Federal Migration Service, which is in charge of Russian migration policy, and the police. But unlike private companies, state agents maintain individual relations with foreign workers and are involved in what one might call the "industry of migration papers."

By studying in depth this "industry," two distinct but interrelated areas of activity can be outlined. The first is the cycle of production and circulation of false documents. If the registration system is complex and encourages people to approach informal solutions, these actors contribute in turn to the continued illegality of many migrants. The second area of activity revolves around the disclosure and punishment of those holding fake papers. Through intimidation and pressure, the objective is to sow panic among migrants. Behind these two facets of the system are often representatives of the same bodies, namely the police and the FMS. Increasingly, fictive representatives of law enforcement bodies, easily imitating police checks, also take advantage of the system. Both activities are extremely lucrative and simple to implement because of the near absence of legal and social protection for foreign workers. The two cycles complement each other and form an integral "commerce" for migration papers.

In-depth interviews conducted with Kyrgyz migrants highlight some of the schemes. Production of a false certificate of residence serves as an example of the first type. In addition to taking money—an act considered now "normal" during paper checks at subway exits, on the street, and in workplaces—policemen have started producing fake home registrations. Unlike a propiska issued illegally by a company specializing in this sort of activity, a propiska created by the police is an "authentic counterfeit," or

---

22 In her ongoing research project "Unbecoming Citizens: Subjectivity and the Negotiation of 'Law' in a Moscow Migrant Community," Madeleine Reeves describes the Russian system of the control of migrants as a regime of "documentation."

23 See, for example, advertisements published on http://www.lesruk.ru, and http://www.delbraknarod.ru.

chistaia falshivka in Russian, and thus more desirable. The manufacture of a chistaia falshivka by local district policemen, *uchastkovy*, is the result of informal cooperation between migrants, a policeman, and the owner of a house[24] who is under the supervision of that law enforcement officer. At his request the house owner registers a number of foreigners in exchange for an amount of money. The "protection" (*krysha*) of local district policemen therefore allows migrants to obtain their right of residence. In the case of street controls, the police might make a phone call to a house owner in order to verify the authenticity of a registration, thus enabling the production of illegal papers to be traced, which is often initiated by law enforcement representatives exercising their powers of control.

Moreover, the introduction of several types of fictive documents, which allows for varying degrees of authenticity, is a sign of blurring boundaries between a genuine legal certificate and a "genuine" illegal certificate—in short, between legal and illegal, and formal and informal. Illegal police activities run the risk of coming into conflict with the general regime of the verification of migrants, but it seems that the existence of a "personalized" relationship between an uchastkovy and foreign workers in his district only contributes to better control. This explains the silence of the "surveillance" regime, to which Madeleine Reeves refers in her ongoing study based on the work of Michel Foucault, *Discipline and Punish: The Birth of the Prison*. She argues that documents related to the status of legality or illegality of labor migrants constitute real administrative technology, designed to render this group "visible" and thus controllable by the state.[25]

Each district police station acts according to its financial needs and issues control documents that sometimes might be valid only in its district. Some migrants say that after paying a "fine,"[26] they were escorted by police to the nearest subway station, seemingly in an act of sympathy, in order to avoid meeting with other officers, who might not be "colleagues" but a rival group of document providers/controllers. This observation leads to the suggestion that the implementation of migration policy is uneven and that district police stations enjoy a certain autonomy in the

[24] In general, they are elderly people, for whom false registration in exchange for money is a significant financial source to add to their meager pension.

[25] Reeves, "Unbecoming Citizens: Subjectivity and the Negotiation of 'Law' in a Moscow Migrant Community."

[26] During the field study, respondents were not able to distinguish whether they paid a legal fine or a bribe because the records were made on the basis of arbitrary or non-existent infractions.

management of their precincts and seek to preserve their control over migrants living or working there.

The reverse side of the industry in migration papers is designed to repair the damage caused by the production of fake documents. However, it does not penalize the providers, but the holders of the fictive papers. This task, at the basis of the law enforcement authorities' mission, is diverted in order to double the yield from immigration. Although the police used to limit its activity to checking the dates of entry and certificates of residence at subway exits and on the street, the new work permit inspections are carried out directly in workplaces, especially in the large companies that are likely to hire foreign labor. Such inspections usually occur unexpectedly, proving to be particularly successful as they allow for the collective punishment of foreign workers without any obligation to distinguish those with official papers. The "fines" collected in this manner are far greater than those accrued during individual checks on the street. In general, employers stay out of disputes, leaving workers at the arbitrary mercy of controllers. These inspections result in the vast majority of cases in a collective payment of "fines." Yet the ruthless character of these interventions leads one to believe that their objective is to intimidate workers, even those in compliance with the law.

The new legislation implemented on January 15, 2007, introduced a new certificate of residence. It can be obtained at the migrant's workplace and even be provided by the employer. However, acquisition of this certificate is only likely to be sought by large construction companies, which usually house employees directly on construction sites. Therefore, foreign workers employed in the trade and service sectors are excluded from this eased regime and are forced to approach private companies or the police to obtain a certificate of residence. Whether under the new or the old legislation, illegal operations by representatives of the Russian state do not seem to be decreasing.

The Kyrgyz State and its Migrants in Moscow

Given the conditions that its migrants face in Russia, there are a number of pertinent questions that can be asked of the Kyrgyz state. How, for instance, does it react to these developments and what policy does it implement to guarantee the rights of migrants? What is the level of efficiency of its delegated institutions? What is their image among migrant laborers in the host country?

The Kyrgyz embassy is charged with connecting Kyrgyz citizens permanently or temporarily living in Russia with their home country, mainly through cultural events, while the Moscow office of the Committee of Migration and Employment specifically deals with economic migrants. Its mission primarily consists of promoting the rights and interests of workers. The committee seeks to establish preferential relations between the Kyrgyz and Russian governments concerning the employment of Kyrgyz nationals, provides information on job vacancies, and supplies technical and judicial support to resolve any disputes between Russian employers and Kyrgyz migrants. The committee claims to have helped 9,000 people obtain employment in 2007.[27] In addition, negotiations have been conducted to obtain a specific quota for Kyrgyz workers in preparation for the Winter Olympics to be held in Sochi in 2014.

This complex field of activity requires cooperation with the Russian government, which is not always open to even the most fundamental of demands. An intergovernmental meeting of heads of institutions involved in migration processes and policy—bringing together representatives from Russia, Kyrgyzstan, Kazakhstan, Uzbekistan, and Tajikistan in March 2008 in Bishkek[28]—revealed a significant number of discrepancies between the countries of origin and destination. The Kyrgyz side claimed the necessity of officially recording the professional experience of migrants in Russia so that it could be recorded in the Kyrgyz register of employment. It was argued that such recognition would avoid workers having "gaps" in their professional histories as well as entitle them to receive a pension in Russia. Moreover, the claim of the right to retirement in Russia seems particularly reasonable considering what Kyrgyz citizens contribute to Russian GDP. In 2007, it was calculated that Central Asian labor contributed to 8 percent of Russia's GDP.[29]

Meanwhile, how does the Kyrgyz embassy manage massive and illegal flows of migrants seeking work? Does it aim to help them to legalize and thus control them? Extensive media coverage, the distribution of information leaflets, television debates, and a hotline, organized throughout

---

[27] Interview with Shabolotov Tazhimamat, former head of the Overseas Bureau of the Committee on Migration and Employment in Moscow, March 2008.

[28] Conference, "Forms of cooperation and mechanisms of labor migration management in Russian Federation and Countries of Central Asia."

[29] Speech of Nikolai Bailo, head of the Committee on Migration Issues within the Kyrgyz parliament, during the Intergovernmental Conference on Migration, Bishkek, March 2008.

Kyrgyzstan by the Committee of Migration and Employment,[30] were designed to raise awareness among the population on how to prepare for departure, find legal employment, and comply with Russian laws. However, this information would not seem to reach those intending to migrate, or those already living illegally in Moscow. For these individuals, the primary source of information remains personal contact with the host country. According to respondents, only a family member or a friend who actually lived in Russia could give a complete and real picture, while the information provided by the aforementioned committee was deemed not useful and "too official."[31] Emigration indeed requires a "specific know-how such as knowledge of informal circuits and codes of police officers, the FMS, train stations and airports, but also wily ways and strategies of survival,"[32] informal knowledge that the committee is unable to provide.

When workers were asked if they were aware of embassy activities in the regulation of migration and employment, nearly half of respondents answered in the affirmative. Although aware of the existence of a governmental structure for migration, they did not know its exact purpose and showed little interest in the missions of the committee, accusing it of inefficiency. The post-Soviet experience—where state institutions are cumbersome, inefficient, corrupt, and hypocritical—has always been present in the minds of those who avoid public institutions. Migrants have therefore chosen to rely on informal networks, such as family, clans, and networks of friends, which are perceived to be more efficient and reliable. With their distancing from state institutions and subsequent lack of legal and political protection, such groups slip out of the control of both the Russian and Kyrgyz governments.

Economic Strategies of Migrants in Moscow

How do migrants manage to migrate safely, make money, and send remittances to their families in spite of the Kyrgyz government's seemingly inefficient actions and the corrupt practices of Russian state officials and the private sector? Even when faced with bureaucratic obstacles at every

---

30 Because the committee's office is located inside the embassy, migrants usually confuse the two.

31 Interview with Ishen, driver and distributor in a private company in Moscow, March 2008.

32 *Ibid.*

turn, individuals manage to optimize revenue, rationalize their stay, and demonstrate a high capacity for resistance. In thus doing, it is possible to sketch a sociological study of their "entrepreneurial" choices.

Among the job opportunities existing in the service sector[33] in Moscow, migrants favor positions such as waiters in restaurants and hotels (which give access to free food, substantial tips, and contact with the host society, especially appreciated by young people) and manual labor (the employers may sometimes provide shelter, food, or free clothing, depending on the nature of the company). It is worth noting that the position of concierge has become particularly popular among Kyrgyz workers, since it offers many advantages like free housing, easy work, and physical security far from the reach of police officers and FMS controllers. In addition to a monthly fixed salary of 15,000 rubles, migrants are attracted by the multiple financial opportunities available to them. Residents living in the apartment blocks, for instance, often ask them to help with renovation projects or shopping. Furthermore, Kyrgyz concierges value direct "human" contact with the residents because it is the latter who decide on issues related to their payment and social benefits, often in opposition to established practices and Russian laws.

However, the initial establishment of contact with the Russian population is not always easy. Migrants who were interviewed recall, for instance, a great reluctance displayed on the part of certain residents. Among other names, they were curiously called "mujahedeen," as Central Asia is generally seen as an "obscure Islamic area." In spite of this, with the passage of time their dedicated work allowed migrants to establish a more trusting relationship. Direct protection from residents can help them not only to negotiate housing extensions, but also to better integrate in the local community through participation in construction, security, and community planning projects. Concierge work, a source of pride among migrants, therefore provides not only significant savings, but can also represent the means by which to achieve "successful" immigration. In view of these various survival strategies, one can suggest that some jobs exist that allow migrants to better adjust and achieve their individual economic objectives. The existence of such a typology weakens an analysis that portraits foreign workers only as victims and describes them as merely passive

[33] According to the Federal Migration Service, this economic sector hires the largest number of migrants in Moscow.

and oppressed actors, forced to comply with the conditions of the host country.

Social promotion of Kyrgyz workers can also be achieved through the acquisition of Russian citizenship. The "purchase" of citizenship, typically costing between 700 and 1,000 dollars depending on the "provider," is possible with the only restriction being financial. Although there is a provision in Russian legislation stipulating a simplified acquisition of Russian citizenship for nationals of the former Soviet Union, migrants often fail to obtain it through formal administrative procedures. They thus reach out to informal services and Kyrgyz community organizations. A Russian passport provides many advantages, such as exemption from police checks, the right to higher wages and better positions,[34] and greater freedom of movement. However, the upholding of the residence registration requirement remains a major obstacle to definitive or long-term settlement in large cities. Here the purchase of property is the only way to register, but it is also prohibitively expensive. Outside Moscow and St. Petersburg, this problem is eased due to more affordable housing prices. The acquisition of a Russian passport nevertheless remains the favorite tool of migrants. The number of Kyrgyz nationals who have become naturalized Russian citizens in recent years amounts to around 100,000.[35] The legal provision facilitating the acquisition of a Russian passport expired on January 1, 2009, however, and it is likely that the number of illegal immigrants increased since. In any case, facilitated naturalization of the first generation of immigrants will certainly leave room for further family reunifications and will contribute to the continuation of migration flows toward Russia. The remaining question is how this will affect the Neighborhood Policy of the European Union toward Russia, which runs the risk of becoming an area of migratory transit between Central Asia and Europe.

Kyrgyz Assistance Organizations in Moscow

In the conventional sense of the term, a diaspora is an ethnic community abroad. The Kyrgyz community in Russia seems to be far from this

---

[34] There is discrimination in hiring migrants. They are not authorized to teach, practice medicine, or to occupy high-level positions, even if they possess the necessary qualifications.

[35] "Okolo 100,000 kyrgyzstantsev za poslednie neskol'ko let stali grazhdanami Rossii," *Gazeta.kg*, March 25, 2008, http://www.gazeta.kg/news/2008-03-25/4767.

definition, however, particularly in terms of community organization. It is represented in Moscow by a dozen heterogeneous associations holding various objectives and employing ambiguous tactics. Their number is constantly changing; some split from their parent organizations, others become unpopular and disappear. In general, these are compact and mobile units because the majority of them do not have permanent offices, conducting business by phone or meeting in city cafes, and even if they claim hundreds or thousands of members, the actual number of activists is typically limited to a dozen or so individuals; some of them, even, are run only by one person. Moreover, the degree of institutionalization of these organizations is particularly low.

Concerning their legal status, they are registered with the Russian Ministry of Justice as "social organizations" and are regional, interregional, or federal depending on their geographical coverage. This status may have been justified at the time of their foundation because they met the goal of representing the immigrant community, but with the predominance of economic migration, cultural and social aspects have gradually given way to exploiting the financial opportunities on offer. Community associations have thus shifted their activities toward the production of migration documents, like private agencies, but continue, ostensibly at least, to draw their legitimacy from a purported ethnic unity with migrants. These paid services include the acquisition of work permits, entry stamps, certificates of residence, and naturalization papers. In order to maintain their community legitimacy, they hold regular cultural events, such as dinners on national holidays and sports tournaments. These events allow them to sustain a "connection" with migrants while ensuring the continuity of their financial activities, which often exist at the edge of legality. Russian legislation does not in itself hinder the activity of intermediaries; foreigners can apply for papers independently or through "professional" organizations, but the preferential relations established between Kyrgyz associations and Russian authorities involved in registering migrants are often murky.

The instrumentalization by community associations of ethnicity goes hand in hand with the commercialization of their activities. The fact that the associations do not perceive migrants as a vulnerable social group per se, but rather as clients and a source of income that should remain non-normalized, and that they compete among themselves to preserve their segment of the "migration market," precludes the establishment of a diaspora as an entity able to employ strategies of collective defense.

The degree of commercialization varies from one association to another. Some have seemingly already accumulated enough money and are now devoted to political objectives. These are the oldest associations, such as *Ala-Too* and *Eldik Birimdigi* (People's Unity). They provide concrete legal, social, and sometimes financial assistance to Kyrgyz workers for free. Aid includes finding missing persons, repatriating the bodies of deceased migrants, and claiming wages from recalcitrant employers. Businessmen who generally settled in Russia long ago and have the economic resources to support such activities typically run these groups. The objective is also political because they seek to lead the diaspora as a community of potential voters and/or to influence the political life of Kyrgyzstan through demonstrating the strength of support—real or not—among the community based in Russia.

The creation of a new political party called *Migrants*, which gathers under its auspices Kyrgyz workers in Russia, is an example of political aspirations influenced by the migration phenomenon. According to one of the founders of the party, it helped to organize in Moscow voting in the Kyrgyz presidential elections of July 2005, which saw migrants being literally bused in to vote for Kurmanbek Bakiev. Extensive propaganda and the organization of collective arrivals to the polling station on party-chartered buses ensured that virtually no one escaped. The political potential of these organizations is thus not negligible, especially as the number of workers is in the hundreds of thousands and continues to grow.

Another source of legitimacy was found by the newly created association Leilik, named after a village in Kyrgyzstan and located in Moscow. Its founder, a native of this village, established the organization with the intention of representing the natives of Leilik, although it is not a priori completely closed to others. The head of the organization explains that he alone knows the particulars of his village and can therefore best protect the rights of those from the village. It is important to note that it is usually through the community associations that financial transfers and contact with families are channeled. By targeting a specific population, small associations such as Leilik guarantee their small share of the market. The example of Leilik is by no means an exception. Several successful Kyrgyz businessmen in Russia have not attempted to conceal their assistance to migrants from their region, whether Naryn or Toktogul, which ensures that they receive popular support from what are in effect "captive" migrants. They derive their popularity by building houses, schools, mosques, and roads in the regions using money earned through successful business in

Russia. But unlike Leilik, and other village, town, or regional groupings, more national-based associations, as described above, aim to transform Kyrgyz workers into a united diaspora freed from regional divisions.

* * * * *

This chapter has sought to shed light on different features of the migration of Kyrgyz labor to Russia, and the living and working conditions of Kyrgyz migrants there. Different forms of migration to Russia, ranging from short trips to regular circulations and permanent settlement, have become a vital source for impoverished populations of the former Soviet Union. The Russian authorities experience difficulties in regulating these different forms of migration, however, lacking consensus not only over the nature of Russian citizenship and nationhood, but also control over their various bureaucracies. The lack of a proper migration policy, be it by design or an oversight, allows for the perpetration of serious human rights abuses and political blackmail. The dependence of the Central Asian republics on migrants' remittances, and thus on Russia's goodwill, causes some, even, to consider Moscow at the center of a policy of "neo-imperialism".

PART THREE

AN EVOLVING SOCIAL FABRIC: MOBILE NATIONAL AND INDIVIDUAL IDENTITIES

INTRODUCTION

Marlene Laruelle

The collapse of the Soviet Union and the Central Asian states' accession to independence inevitably had a decisive impact on the transformation of national and individual identities. The new states spared no effort in adapting their identities to the new political conditions—primarily by seeking to transform the social fabric, which they hoped was malleable, or in cases where developments were beyond their control, to adapt themselves to those conditions. Migration was at the heart of this dual phenomenon, partly shaped by state policies while being equally outside the purview of official bodies.

The Central Asian states are in the process of *nationalizing* and *ethnicizing*, intensifying the phenomenon of indigenization (*korenizatsiia*) that began in the Soviet era. The massive emigration of ethnic minorities in the 1990s, the considerable internal migration flows, as well as the relatively high birth-rate of the Central Asian peoples has led, over a period of 20 years, to the reinforcement of the titular group in each of the five republics. To accelerate this process, states such as Kazakhstan—and Kyrgyzstan to a lesser extent—encouraged the "return" of their co-ethnics from neighboring countries. The ethnic homogenization currently underway in the whole region consolidates the view of these countries as nation-states and is accompanied by a process of excluding minorities from public service, forcing them to move into specific professional niches in the private sector. Accordingly, Russians dominate the small-scale services sector, information technology and technical maintenance enterprises, cafes and restaurants, and sometimes private security services. Koreans, on the other hand, sell fresh produce at bazaars, just as they did in the Soviet period, while citizens of German, Polish, or Greek origin often become trade mediators between the kin-states and their Central Asian homeland.

Migration also profoundly transforms the identities of individuals. Even though some are exploited, dependent on their smugglers, or sold as human labor, many individuals enjoy relative autonomy and cannot be described exclusively as victims. They take advantage of the opportunities that the path of migration offers, which often has significant meanings in their life journeys. Migration is primarily a rite of passage and a sacrificial experience for the family unit, as much as it has meaning at an individual level. In Central Asian societies, where the group is traditionally considered paramount, the highly personal experience of migration and the emotional disconnection from one's family transforms individuals. Migrants also try to maximize their experience through strategies of upward mobility. Remittances are used to display wealth through the purchase of items regarded as luxury goods such as computers and cars. Funds are also spent to strengthen social bonds through material gifts to extended families as well as traditional celebrations involving the neighborhood community (mahalla), which allows the migrant-host to demonstrate his newly acquired wealth.

Since the money earned in migration is not reinvested in development strategies, the family of a migrant that promotes itself as *nouveau riche* and wants to maintain this acquired lifestyle must deal with further departures. These economic choices focused on strengthening social bonds cannot be interpreted as "irrational" gestures made at the expense of "rational" macroeconomic investments. Neighborhood solidarity is actually the most effective social safety net for responding to economic turmoil, as it guarantees each individual a place in the community. Having risen up the social ladder, a migrant can pursue more ambitious matrimonial strategies for his children, request community funds in the event of problems, and through his status gain greater access to decision-makers, be they political, legal, or social (for instance, to gain entry for his child into university or to guarantee better treatment at hospitals). The social impact of migration is thus a complex one. While the group seems to emerge stronger, the individual is hampered in taking initiative. The sense of "oppression" of individual autonomy—which may manifest itself in contradictory needs and ways of spending remittances—by the group is also growing.

These identity transformations at different levels form the core of the analysis in this section of the volume. In the 1990s, the massive migration of the so-called European minorities profoundly changed the Central Asian societies, which lost much of the ethnic diversity they acquired under the Soviet regime and during the Czarist era. In his chapter, Sebastien Peyrouse analyzes these population movements, which in their scale are unique for the region. In the last Soviet census of 1989, Central Asia had more than 12 million people "of European origin"; the figure is now around 7 million. The reasons ethnic minorities migrated were manifold.

They were driven mainly by economic motives (seeking employment or better living conditions) and also feelings of a certain "identity malaise" in the newly independent states (non-mastery of the national language, lack of prospects for their children), rather than by a desire to "return" to their ethnic homelands. This mass migration has reinforced the ethnic homogeneity of the Central Asian republics, even though Kazakhstan and Kyrgyzstan are still multinational states. The remaining European minorities in the region have had the label of "diaspora" conferred upon them. However, the question of their supposed "non-nativeness" is part of a political and identity construction. It serves the objectives of the host states, which consider that eponymous peoples must enjoy primacy over minorities, and it is also of use to the kin-state, which can create a symbolic link beyond its state borders with its co-ethnics, and sometimes propose repatriation strategies.

Each Central Asian state has also formed specific identity mechanisms and thus taken a stance on the question of its co-ethnics abroad, with their presence on the territories of neighboring states having significant ramifications. As Olivier Ferrando demonstrates, these co-ethnic minorities feel a dual affiliation. They enjoy the citizenship of their host-state, but at the same time they share common attributes with their eponymous kin-state. Associations of co-ethnics have tried to secure dual citizenship, free movement beyond borders, and schooling in their mother tongue, but their success has, to a large extent, depended on the goodwill of the authorities to cooperate with their neighbors. Becoming aware of the existence of a "diaspora" beyond one's borders has not necessarily given rise to policies of repatriation, which only Kazakhstan—and to a lesser extent Kyrgyzstan—has established on a large scale, having "repatriated" about 600,000 Kazakhs from Mongolia, Afghanistan, and China. These repatriation programs targeted mostly co-ethnics settled outside of the former Soviet Union, and avoided inviting potential returnees from other Central Asian countries. However, population movements have taken place that are not controlled by the state, and ethnic repatriations, whether or not state-organized, comprised the main form of inward migration in Central Asia in the first few years following independence.

Post-Soviet identity transformations have also affected individuals in their personal trajectories and their identity markers. Rural migrants headed for towns in search of a better life, as did those who left their countries to go abroad. This caused a profound evolution in their personal and community identities, both during the migration phase and upon their return to the town/country of origin. In the first of her two contributions to this work, Sophie Massot looks at rural Uzbek migrants who have settled in Samarkand. Once there, they discover that their "Uzbekness" is a new identity marker to dissociate themselves from other national groups like the Russians and the Tajiks, who symbolize urbanity. They learn to master urban behaviors, including the ethnic categorizations inherited from the Soviet era, and to partake in the most widespread phenotypical and psychological stereotypes. They also have to deal with the Russians, who allegedly embody Europeanness, as well as progressively internalize, sometimes at their own expense, the cross-references of symbolic hierarchy between rural and urban dwellers, and between Uzbeks and Tajiks. They are also obliged to rebuild their relationships with their home villages, often creating a distance with those who have remained behind. The migrants are simultaneously critical of the harshness of the living conditions found in the countryside, but respectful of the moral values when residing there. Eventually, they try to promote different bodily mannerisms and to flaunt the material symbols of their social success, thereby working to transform social codes even in the remote countryside.

Similar phenomena also emerge during migration for work abroad. In her second chapter, Sophie Massot delves into the lives of Uzbek migrants who have gone to work in Moscow, Seoul, and New York, and explores what happens when they return home. Here too, the experience of social and identity transformation is extremely strong, and shapes the views the migrants have on their place in society and of the "domestic sacrifice" they make in migrating. But their lived experience displays plenty of nuances. Although life during migration is presented as physically (working conditions) and morally (separation from their family) difficult, their return is no easier. Issues that seem to stand out are feelings of disconnection from social and familial realities, a loss of control over gender relations, and questions concerning the upbringing of their children. The resting period following migration can also create feelings of social uselessness, which retroactively revalorizes the hard times endured in migration. The acquisition of the status as a "New Uzbek" can suddenly lead to complications concerning the migrant's social place in his or her community web. All of these paradoxes of identity evolutions are therefore a driver of long-term social change in Central Asia.

FORMER COLONISTS ON THE MOVE: THE MIGRATION OF RUSSIAN-SPEAKING POPULATIONS

Sebastien Peyrouse

If looking for work abroad has become the determinant factor of demographic change in Central Asia in the 2000s, the ground was prepared by the emigration in the 1990s of the so-called European peoples. In the last Soviet census of 1989, Central Asia had more than 12 million people "of European origin," including some 9.5 million Russians. This figure is now around 7 million, including 5.5 million Russians. Having arrived during the imperial or Soviet periods, these populations are differentiated by extremely diverse historical paths. Some (Russians, Ukrainians, and Belarusians) came to take up the professional opportunities offered by the Czarist conquest and the modernization of the region under Soviet leadership. Others were deported to Central Asia as "punished peoples" (Germans), or exiled due to their suspected collusion with the enemy during the Second World War or on account of their post-war "bourgeois nationalism" (Poles, Ukrainians, Balts, and Greeks). Despite this historical diversity, these populations are perceived as a unified group vis-à-vis the titular or eponymous nationalities. Using an old Soviet classification scheme, they are also distinguished from third entities, peoples of "non-European" origin, such as Koreans, or those of "Muslim background" such as Tatars.

All of these ethnic categories are reified, constructed by political representatives, and shared by the actors involved. Within these schematic divisions, several elements must be questioned. First is the issue of non-nativeness of people of "European origin". The Central Asian authorities' emphasize their exogenous nature in order to denounce the essentially imperial nature of their arrival, signs of a bygone era, and to highlight, by a mirror play, the autochthonous nature of the eponymous people, and therefore its political legitimacy in the independent country. However, in reality, the vast majority of European immigrants had been born or lived for several decades on the Central Asian territory. Only with rare exceptions did they have any personal history in the kin-state to which they are emigrating in the post-Soviet period. The idea that the population of "European origin" is leaving in the name of its ethnicity, rather than for economic reasons, which would distinguish it from ethnic Central Asian migrants, is also questionable. The few sociological surveys that do exist confirm that the decision to migrate is rarely made with the idea of "going home," but rather in order to pursue opportunities for a better life. Integration in the new country, even if seen as a kin-state, is difficult, and countries of origin are often left with regret and considered as the "real" homeland. People decreed to be "national minorities" then find themselves enmeshed in a complex triangular web between their representatives or those who claim to speak on their behalf, the state in which they reside, and the external homeland that often claims a competing (at least symbolically) authority over them.[1]

Furthermore, the strict ethnic divisions are not valid and reveal logics common in the post-Soviet space. Rather than talking about "European" peoples, a geographical reference without much consistency, it is probably more appropriate to talk of "Russian-speakers" in the sense that they all share a common Soviet culture, often but not exclusively urban, a past history of having been "settlers," voluntary or forced, and broad cultural and linguistic Russification. It should be recognized, though, that the term is not fully satisfactory because it suggests that the eponymous Central Asians neither speak Russian nor share the common Soviet culture, which distorts the analysis. However, lacking more appropriate concepts—the absence of which confirms the tangle of identity referents and symbolic attributes—the term "Russian speaking" is used here to describe populations who in the Soviet censuses declared themselves to be of Russian, Ukrainian, Belarusian, Polish, German, Jewish, or Greek nationality.

The Course of Colonization: Migratory Movements toward Central Asia

The presence of Russian colonists in Central Asia was a dominating factor in the subsequent military and political conquest of the region. The first Russian population settled in Central Asia in the eighteenth century. As was also the case with Russian expansion into Siberia, Cossacks—soldier-peasants integrated into the Czarist army—established the first fortifications that gave rise to the establishment of colonial power in the region. Peasants fleeing serfdom and the central authorities followed, along with

[1] R. Brubaker, *Nationalism Reframed: Nationhood and the National Question in the New Europe* (Cambridge: Cambridge University Press, 1996).

persecuted religious communities, in particular Old Believers and Protestants. Tightly controlled by the Commission of the Steppes, colonization accelerated in the latter half of the nineteenth century in tandem with the pace of political and social events in Russia. In 1896, the number of Russian colonists that had settled legally in the governorate of Turkestan was estimated to be 400,000. This number had grown to 1.5 million by 1916, representing a third of the registered departures headed toward the Asian part of the Russian Empire (the remaining two-thirds headed to Siberia).[2]

Other populations joined the Russians. The Ukrainians and Belarusians came mainly from the eastern region of what is now Ukraine and Belarus, which were then incorporated into the Russian Empire.[3] The Poles were exiled after the rebellions of 1830–31, 1848, and 1863 to western Siberia, including territory that belongs to present-day Kazakhstan.[4] Others were exiled to what is now Turkmenistan. Half of the soldiers and one-fifth of the officers of the Russian army stationed in Turkmen territory before the First World War were Polish. In 1908, the Poles made up 8 percent of the population of Ashgabat, the number continuing to increase in subsequent years to over 10,000 people.[5] Besides the Slavs, the Germans were the largest nationality of "European origin" present in Central Asia. Settled in the Volga region since the eighteenth century at the invitation of Catherine II, they began to head out to the most remote lands in Central Asia after the repeal of their privileges in 1871, in thus doing seeking to escape new military obligations and increasing persecution of their religious practices (Protestant and Catholic). Initially settling on the Kazakh steppes close to Karaganda, from the 1880s some Germans relocated further south in the area of the Syr Darya. At the end of the century, almost 9,000 Germans lived on Central Asian territory, including a third in the major urban centers of Tashkent, Akmolinsk, Uralsk, and Semipalatinsk. New waves of German migration followed the agrarian reforms of Peter Stolypin,

---

[2] A majority of the information presented here on the emigration of Russians is taken from S. Peyrouse, "Les flux migratoires des Russes d'Asie centrale vers la Russie," *Espace, Populations, Sociétés*, no. 1 (2007): 47–57.

[3] A. Finko, "Ukraine, the Turkic World, and Central Asia," *Central Asia and the Caucasus* 56 no. 2 (2009): 104.

[4] C. Poujol, "Les Polonais du Kazakhstan entre l'intégration et la Patrie rêvée," *Espace, Populations, Sociétés*, no. 1 (2007): 93.

[5] W. Tyszkiewicz, "Polish Diaspora in Turkmenistan. A Colonial Narrative," *The Sarmatian Review*, 2000, http://www.ruf.rice.edu/~sarmatia/400/tyszkiewicz.html.

between 1906 and 1910. In addition, the first Ashkenazi Jews arrived with Russian settlers at the turn of the century.[6]

After this first pre-revolutionary migratory flow, several others followed throughout the 1950s. In 1926, the Soviet census listed 1.28 million Russians in Kazakhstan, representing 20 percent of the population, and 241,000 in Uzbekistan, 5.4 percent of the population.[7] A vast majority of them settled in urban areas, particularly in Tashkent, where they accounted for 13 percent of the inhabitants. This trend continued in subsequent decades, thanks to the Soviet economic programs, industrialization, and the extensive development of cotton farming. Many petroleum engineers and semi-skilled workers also arrived and contributed to the socialist economy in the 1930s. Between 1926 and 1939, 1.7 million people left European Russia to live in Central Asia. On the eve of the Second World War, Russians in Kazakhstan numbered 2.5 million, representing 40 percent of the population of the republic.[8] In Uzbekistan, the number of Russians grew to 727,000 in 1939, or 13 percent of the population. The Ukrainian and Belarusian peoples settled according to similar patterns of economic modernization. In 1926, there were more than 860,000 Ukrainians in Central Asia, particularly in Kazakhstan.[9] Under the Soviet administration's first five-year plans, new Ashkenazi communities also arrived.[10] The first wave of Greek immigration dates back to the 1930s, lured by regional enterprises, especially tobacco cultivation.

However, migration to Central Asia was not all voluntary. As in the Czarist period, the region was thought of by the central authorities as an area of exile for regime opponents and dissidents of all kinds. During the campaigns of collectivization at the turn of the 1920s and 1930s, thousands of Russians, Ukrainians, and Germans were deported as landowners (*kulaks*), followed by more than 70,000 Poles living in the border areas of Ukraine and Belarus.[11] In June 1941, during the invasion of the Soviet Union by Nazi armies, 180,000 Ashkenazi Jews were evacuated, mainly

[6] They joined the Bukharan Jews, who had been living in Central Asia at least since the time of persecution against them in the Persian Empire, or the fifth century A.D.

[7] Statistics from the 1926 Soviet census are available at: http://demoscope.ru/weekly/ssp/sng_nac_26.php?reg=2275.

[8] N.M. Lebedeva, *Novaia russkaia diaspora. Sotsial'no-psikhologicheskii analiz* (Moscow: RAN, 1997), 54.

[9] For a history of Ukrainians in Kazakhstan, see A.F. Makarenko, *Ukraintsy* (Almaty: Bilim, 1998).

[10] M. Shterenshis, "Jews in Central Asia: The Past for the Present," *Central Asia and the Caucasus*, no. 1 (2001): 189–200.

[11] Poujol, "Les Polonais du Kazakhstan entre l'intégration et la Patrie rêvée," 94.

to Uzbekistan, to avoid extermination. In 1959, there were more than 50,000 Jews in Tashkent.[12] Among the deported "punished peoples," one million Germans—or 80 percent of the entire German population of the Soviet Union—were exiled to Central Asia, of which half were in Kazakhstan. Over 25,000 Greeks originally from the Black Sea were also deported. Those exiled on the grounds of "bourgeois nationalism" were also numerous: over 30,000 Ukrainians and about 5,000 Lithuanians, Latvians, and Estonians. The first Ukrainian deportees were joined during and after the war by at least 100,000 others, this time from the eastern regions of Poland annexed by the Soviet army.[13] Although Kazakhstan continued to be a destination of exile for minorities deemed refractory, Uzbekistan was also home to 35,000 Poles, a majority of whom came from the Perm region and the Mari autonomous republic.[14]

The growing number of people arriving from the European regions of the Soviet Union in Central Asia continued after the war. In 1949, a new wave of Greeks arrived from Abkhazia to Alma-Ata and its surrounding area. In the same year, Central Asia also hosted communist refugees from the Greek Civil War. In 1959, Kazakhstan alone hosted more than 55,000 Greeks. This "European" presence intensified during the Virgin Lands Campaign: from 1954, Nikita Khrushchev launched a gigantic program of land development that saw a surge of two million people, mainly Russians, Ukrainians, and Belarusians who had volunteered to go to Kazakhstan.[15] The proportion of Russians in the total population of Kazakhstan jumped from 20.6 percent in 1926 to 42.7 percent in 1959.[16] The campaign also saw the arrival of more than 100,000 Ukrainians. In the late 1950s, Kazakhs represented only 30 percent of the population, numbering less than three million compared to four million Russians.

While pre-Revolutionary emigration to Central Asia primarily consisted of peasants—it also included soldiers and civil servants—the Russian-speaking populations that settled in the Soviet era were predominantly urbanites. As all the southern republics were in need of professional specialties related to the industrial and service sectors, they attracted young people and graduates from the upper and middle classes: teachers,

---

12 Shterenshis, "Jews in Central Asia: The Past for the Present," 198.

13 A. Kiiash, "Nakazannyi narod," in *W stepie dalekim: Polacy w Kazachstanie, V stepi dalekoi: Poliaki v Kazakhstane* (Poznań, Almaty: Wystawa, 1997), 57.

14 Poujol, "Les Polonais du Kazakhstan entre l'intégration et la Patrie rêvée," 95.

15 M.B. Olcott, *The Kazakhs* (Stanford: Hoover Institution Press, 1987), 225–236.

16 I.V. Erofeeva, N.E. Masanov, Z.B. Abylkhozhin, et al., *Istoriia Kazakhstana: narody i kul'tury* (Almaty: Daik-Press, 2001), 396.

engineers, technicians, and doctors.[17] In the Kazakh and Kyrgyz republics, the Russian-speaking population was also important in rural areas: numerous Russians, Ukrainians, and Belarusians stayed in the Virgin Land areas and on the shores of Lake Issyk-Kul. Germans and Poles, who were not permitted to settle in cities until the late 1950s, worked in the farms of central Kazakhstan. In 1955, following the visit of Chancellor Konrad Adenauer, relations between West Germany and the Soviet Union were normalized and this helped to ease the living conditions of the German population. They were allowed to move to cities, but were banned from returning to their region of origin on the Volga. In the late 1980s, of the more than two million Germans living in the Soviet Union, 957,500 were settled in Kazakhstan and 101,300 in Kyrgyzstan.[18]

Despite the November 1956 Soviet-Polish friendship treaty, the Soviet Poles did not regain their civil rights until 1959. And although the Soviet authorities promoted an assimilation policy, the Poles of Central Asia gradually recovered some cultural rights in the regions where they were concentrated. For example in Karaganda, the Polish language gained official status at the local universities. Whereas some Poles had returned to Ukraine, many preferred to stay in Kazakhstan. There were still 60,000 Poles resident in the country at the collapse of the Soviet Union. The 1989 census also reported just under 46,000 Greeks in Kazakhstan (located in Alma-Ata, the southern cities of Shymkent and Dzhambul, and the northern cities of Pavlodar and Kokchetau) and just over 10,000 in Uzbekistan, a significant decrease compared with the 1970 census, which had counted 32,400 Greeks living in this republic.[19] Greek presence remained very low in the three other republics. There were also about 17,000 Balts residing in Kazakhstan.

The Hemorrhage of the 1990s: Great Waves of Emigration

Despite the influx of "European" populations to the whole Central Asian region in the Soviet era, the demographic balance began to tilt in favor of the titular peoples by the time of the 1959 census, mainly due to their

---

[17] H. Carrère d'Encausse, *L'Empire éclaté : la révolte des nations en URSS* (Paris: Flammarion, 1978), 109–146.

[18] V.I. Mukomel and E.A. Pain, "Deported People in Central Asia (a Socio-Demographic Analysis)," in V.V. Naumkin, ed., *State, Religion and Society in Central Asia: a Post-Soviet Critique* (Reading: Ithaca Press, 1993), 150.

[19] *Ibid.*, 146.

high birth rates. In the 1960s and 1970s, because of significant emigration flows, the proportion of the Russian-speaking population began to decline. Central Asia was no longer a priority for development, and the Virgin Lands Campaign was abandoned. The Soviet authorities focused on the Russian Far East instead, which saw the launch of important projects, in particular the new railroad between Baikal and Amur (the BAM), which required a labor force of several hundred thousand people. Leonid Brezhnev's policy of indigenization (*korenizatsiia*) made it possible for the titular populations to attain positions of power in the administrative, cultural, and political republican structures, and reduced the need for the presence of Russians. Additionally, it accelerated the urbanization of the titular populations, who were invited to leave rural areas. This led to a surge in the urban population in Uzbekistan, which saw a 70 percent increase between 1970 and 1979.[20]

As a result of those evolutions, migratory flows toward Central Asia—and the South Caucasus—slowed down. Although some 117,000 individuals from Russia arrived in Central Asia in 1971, the figure dropped to 80,200 in 1977, and declined further to 75,900 in 1980.[21] During the 1970s, Kazakhstan experienced a net loss of almost half a million people through migration, while Kyrgyzstan lost approximately 100,000. On average, the other three republics also experienced a net loss of 200,000 people between 1976 and 1980.[22] These early signs of an involuntary "decolonization" accelerated in the 1980s: Kazakhstan lost an additional 784,000 people (about 60,000 to 85,000 each year), and 850,000 people left the other four republics.[23] Russians dominated these outward flows. In 1980, for every 1,000 Russians who settled in Central Asia, 1,256 left.[24] But their overall representation relative to the total population declined not only because of these negative migratory balances, but also due to the high birth rate of the titular population. Ukrainians and Belarusians experienced a trend of statistical

---

[20] L.L. Rybakovskii, "Tsentral'naia Aziia i Rossiia: mezhgosudarstvennyi migratsionnyi obmen," in G. Vitkovskaia, ed., *Migratsiia russkoiazychnogo naseleniia iz Tsentral'noi Azii: prichiny, posledstviia, perspektivy* (Moscow: Carnegie Endowment for International Peace, 1996), 70.

[21] V.A. Tishkov, "Russkie v Srednei Azii i Kazakhstane," *Issledovaniia po prikladnoi i neotlozhnoi etnologii*, no. 51 (Moscow: RAN, 1993).

[22] Rybakovskii, "Tsentral'naia Aziia i Rossiia: mezhgosudarstvennyi migratsionnyi obmen," 69.

[23] M. Suzhikov, ed., *Mezhnatsional'nye otnosheniia v Kazakhstane* (Almaty: Gylym, 1993), 139.

[24] Rybakovskii, "Tsentral'naia Aziia i Rossiia: mezhgosudarstvennyi migratsionnyi obmen," 70.

increase but proportional decrease. In Kazakhstan, Ukrainians numbered 760,000 in 1959, representing 8.1 percent of the population, while in 1989 they were 896,000, but this represented only 5.4 percent of the total population of the republic. Similarly, Belarusians numbered 107,000 in 1959, and as many as 183,000 in 1989, but their percentage in terms of the total population remained stable at around 1.1 percent.[25]

The Slavic-speaking peoples were not the only ones who wanted to emigrate. As a result of pressure from West Germany and the international community, Leonid Brezhnev was forced to abolish the emigration ban on Soviet Germans. From 1971, several thousand of them became returnees.[26] From 1986 onward, those in Central Asia started to be granted exit visas; over 1,000 Germans from Kazakhstan were allowed to leave the Soviet Union each year, the number soon increasing to 13,000.[27] Soviet Jews also gained the right to leave, albeit with difficulties, in the late 1970s. In Uzbekistan, the numbers of Ashkenazi and Bukharan Jews decreased from 93,000 in 1970 to 73,000 in 1979, and eventually to 65,000 in 1989. A similar downward trend was also seen in Kazakhstan where the numbers of Ashkenazi fell from 27,000 in 1979 to 18,500 in 1989.[28]

While the mass departure of the Russian-speaking population is often attributed to the collapse of the Soviet Union, statistical data suggests that the reversal of migration flows actually became prominent much earlier. The disintegration of the Soviet Union thus served to accelerate these migration flows not only to Russia, but also Germany, Israel, the United States, and Canada. By the early 1990s, Russia was receiving migrants from all over the former Soviet Union—but it was the flows from Central Asia that were the most striking. The five Central Asian republics collectively accounted for over half of all the migrants in Russia—this compared with only 17 percent from the Caucasus, 20 percent from Ukraine, and 3 percent from the Baltic States.[29] In 2000, migration from Kazakhstan alone constituted more than 28 percent of migration in the post-Soviet space.[30]

---

[25] More figures are available in N.B. Alekseenko and A.N. Alekseenko, *Naselenie Kazakhstana za 100 let (1897–1997 gg.)* (Ust'-Kamenogorsk: Vostochno-Kazakhstanskii tekhnicheskii universitet, 2000).

[26] Carrère d'Encausse, *L'Empire éclaté*, 206.

[27] G. Wettig, ed., "No Future for the Ethnic Germans in Kazakhstan?" *Aussenpolitik* 44, no. 2 (1993): 153–162.

[28] Soviet census figures for 1970, 1979, and 1989 for the republics of Kazakhstan and Uzbekistan, http://demoscope.ru/weekly/pril.php.

[29] O.D. Borob'eva, *Migratsiia naseleniia*, vyp. 6 (Moscow: Migratsiia v Rossii, 2001), 25.

[30] Zh. Zaionchkovskaia, "Migratsionnye trendy v SNG: itogi desiatiletiia," in *Migratsiia SNG i Baltii: cherez razlichiia problem k obshchemu informatsionnomu prostranstvu* (Moscow: Adamant, 2001), 181–82.

Along with the war zones of the South Caucasus, the region of Central Asia saw the highest number of people departing.[31]

The first to leave were the Germans, followed by the Jews. Over 200,000 Ashkenazi and Bukharan Jews left Central Asia in the first years of the 1990s,[32] and in Tajikistan, 99 percent of the Jewish population left.[33] Nearly three-quarters of Germans left Central Asia in the first decade of independence; in 1992 alone, 115,000 left Kazakhstan, followed by 195,000 in 1993. A total of over 700,000 Germans departed during the 1990s.[34] This hemorrhage was also significant among other groups. From 1989 to 1999, the Ukrainian population of Kazakhstan fell from approximately 900,000 to fewer than 550,000; Belarusians from 182,000 to 119,000; Poles from 60,000 to 47,000; and Greeks from 46,000 to 12,000. During the same period, Kyrgyzstan lost more than half of its Ukrainians, two-thirds of its Belarusians, and nearly four-fifths of its German population, from 100,000 to just over 20,000 people. This decline continued in the next decade. In 2007, there were no more than 27,000 Ukrainians and 12,000 Germans left in Kyrgyzstan, less than half of what this figure had been in 1999.[35]

In absolute terms, Russians made up the largest number of emigrants since they also made up the largest part of the "European" population.[36] Kazakhstan recorded the highest number of emigrants.[37] Between 1989 and 1999, Russians decreased there in number from 6 million to 4.5 million, or from 40 percent to 30 percent of the population of the republic, with an average departure per year of 150,000 individuals. In the first half of the 1990s, departing Russians came primarily from the southern and western areas of the country, where residents are mainly ethnic Kazakhs and Uzbeks. Some of the migration flows were internal, as Russians from the south, as well as those from nearby republics such as Uzbekistan, relocated

---

[31] "Stenogramma ekspertnogo soveshchanie po itogam monitoringa, provedennogo v stranakh SNG i Pribaltiki," *Materik*, no. 106, September 15, 2004, http://www.materick.ru/index.php?section=analitics&bulid=89&bulsectionid=7899.

[32] Shterenshis, "Jews in Central Asia: The Past for the Present." See also M. Degtiar, "The Jews of Uzbekistan—The end of the epoch," *Central Asia and the Caucasus*, no. 4 (2001): 176–181.

[33] J. Thorez, "*Khorosho gde nas net.* L'émigration des 'Russophones' d'Asie centrale," *ÉcoGéo*, no. 9 (2009), http://echogeo.revues.org/index11212.html.

[34] Wettig, "No Future for the Ethnic Germans in Kazakhstan?" 160.

[35] *Naselenie Kyrgyzstana. Itogi pervoi natsional'noi perepisi naseleniia Kyrgyzskoi Respubliki 1999 goda v tablitsakh*, vol. II (1) (Bishkek: National Committee of Statistics, 2000).

[36] *Kratkie itogi perepisi naseleniia 1999 goda v respublike Kazakhstan* (Almaty: Agentstvo respubliki Kazakhstan po statistike, 1999), 11.

[37] T. Klimova, "Tendentsii migratsionnykh protsessov v respublike Kazakhstan," *Tsentral'naia Aziia i Kavkaz*, no. 3 (2001): 206.

to the Slavic-dominated areas in northern Kazakhstan.[38] In the second half of the decade, the northern and eastern regions of Kazakhstan also began to lose their Russian, Ukrainian, Polish, and German populations.[39] Over a ten-year period, the Akmolinsk region lost 122,000 people, or 24 percent of its population; the North Kazakhstan region lost 186,000 people (20 percent); and the Karaganda region 335,000 (19 percent).

In Kyrgyzstan, the number of Russians fell by 34 percent during the period from 1989 to 1999: they numbered 916,500 in 1989, but this figure dropped to around 603,000 in 1999.[40] Uzbekistan experienced its first massive wave of departures in 1989. The country counted 1.6 million Russians, representing 8 percent of the population at the 1989 census. According to some researchers, more than 500,000 Russians left between 1990 and 1997, equivalent to 23 percent of the total Russian population, or 44 percent of emigrants from the country.[41] According to other estimates, approximately 5 percent (about 70,000 people) of the Russian population left Uzbekistan each year in the 1990s.[42] Both sources agree that since independence, about half of the Russian community in Uzbekistan has migrated. Although migration has slowed down, the daily queues in front of the Russian consulate in Tashkent testify to the fact that this flow has continued in the 2000s.[43] Although no census has been conducted since 1989, it appears that the Russian community of Uzbekistan still consists of about 800,000 people today, which is less than 4 percent of the country's population.[44]

In Turkmenistan, the census of 1989 counted 334,000 Russians, constituting about 9.5 percent of the total population of the republic. Six years

[38] A.N. Alekseenko, "Etnodemograficheskie protsessy i emigratsiia iz suverennogo Kazakhstana: prichiny i perspektivy," in G. Vitkovskaia, ed., *Sovremennye etnopoliticheskie protsessy i migratsionnaia situatsiia v Tsentral'noi Azii* (Moscow: Carnegie Endowment for International Peace, 1998).

[39] A.N. Alekseenko, "Pervaia perepis' naseleniia v Kazakhstane: nekotorye itogi i otsenki," in *Migratsiia SNG i Baltii*, 90.

[40] G. Piadukhov, "Kirgiziia: politicheskii faktor kak prichina vynuzhdennoi migratsii," in Vitkovskaia, *Migratsiia russkoiazychnogo naseleniia iz Tsentral'noi Azii*, 141; S.S. Savoskul, *Russkie novogo zarubezh'ia. Vybor sud'by* (Moscow: Nauka, 2001), 395.

[41] L.P. Maksakova, "Osnovnye cherty migratsionnoi situatsii v Uzbekistane," in Zh. Zaionchkovskaia ed., *Migratsionnaia situatsiia v stranakh SNG* (Moscow: Kompleks-Progress, 1999), 238.

[42] P. Kolstoe, *Russians in the Former Soviet Republics* (London: Hurst, 1995), 224.

[43] Observations on the ground and interviews conducted between 1998 and 2000, and between 2002 and 2005.

[44] Because Uzbekistan and Turkmenistan did not carry out censuses in 1999–2000, figures remain uneven.

later, this figure fell to 6.7 percent; it is now at a low of just 2 percent. With the authorities in Ashgabat allowing dual citizenship with Russia in 1993, migratory flows were limited in the first half of the 1990s. However, they began to accelerate in 2003 following the country's increasing authoritarianism and the harsh suppression of the right to dual citizenship. Currently, the population of Turkmenistan is believed to include 150,000 Russians, a figure that remains difficult to confirm.[45]

Finally, Tajikistan is the Central Asian republic that has been most severely affected by emigration: 82 percent of Russians, 90 percent of Ukrainians, and 96 percent of Germans left the country.[46] The July 1989 law that made Tajik the official state language led to an initial departure of approximately 10,000 Russians. New emigration flows followed the violent confrontations in Dushanbe in February 1990. Before the onset of civil war in the country in 1992, some 380,000 Russians were still living in Tajikistan, accounting for about 7.6 percent of the population.[47] The outbreak of hostilities, however, further accelerated their emigration. In 1993 alone, more than 200,000 Russians—half the community—left.[48] This figure represents the highest proportion of departures of a Russian minority from a post-Soviet republic, alongside Armenia. In 1989, Russians made up 32.4 percent of the population in the capital city, but the number fell to 17 percent in 1996. According to the 2000 census, Russians represented a mere 1 percent of the total population of the republic, or just 68,000 people,[49] a figure that continues to fall; it was estimated at fewer than 50,000 people in 2010.[50] Today, more than half of Tajikistan's Russians are pensioners who predominantly reside in Dushanbe.

The number of people who emigrated from the republics of Central Asia was particularly high in the first half of the 1990s. As previously mentioned, the number of emigrants from Tajikistan reached a peak in 1993. In 1994, meanwhile, about 500,000 people left Kazakhstan, including some

---

[45] S. Peyrouse, *Turkmenistan. Strategies of Power, Dilemmas of Development* (Armonk: M.E. Sharpe, 2011), 91–93.

[46] R.H. Rowland, "National and Regional Population Trends in Tajikistan: Results from the Recent Census," *Eurasian Geography and Economics* 46, no. 3 (2005): 202.

[47] S.K. Olimova, "Migratsionnye protsessy v sovremennom Tadzhikistane," *Demoskop Weekly*, nos. 223–24, November 21–December 4, 2005, http://demoscope.ru/weekly/2006/0245/index.php.

[48] Kolstoe, *Russians in the Former Soviet Republics*, 211.

[49] S.K. Olimova, "Protsess suverenizatsii strany i migratsionnye protsessy v Tadzhikistane," in Zaionchkovskaia, *Migratsionnaia situatsiia v stranakh SNG*, 222.

[50] Rowland, "National and Regional Population Trends in Tajikistan: Results from the Recent Census," 219.

300,000 Russians and 100,000 Germans.[51] The same applies to Kyrgyzstan where, in 1993 alone, 100,000 Russians left. In Uzbekistan, the main outflow of Russians occurred between 1992–93 and 1993–94, with 170,000 and 200,000 departures, respectively. Although statistically migration was still significant, the pace of migration actually subsided in the second half of the 1990s, and then declined further in the 2000s, particularly from Kazakhstan. The vast majority of people who wished to emigrate had already succeeded in leaving during the first years following independence. Those who remained in Central Asia out of choice were mixed couples, people with well-integrated local networks, and individuals benefiting from privileged social or economic circumstances. Some of them, however, could not leave for a number of reasons: people without any income to finance emigration, those without professional opportunities or a personal network in their ethnic homeland or elsewhere, and elderly people. The ageing of the Russian-speaking population that remained in Central Asia further accelerated their proportional decline.

Sociology of Departure and Complexity of Identity Referents

There are a number of factors that explain the over-representation of Russian-speaking people among emigrants from Central Asia: the low levels of mixing with titular populations, lack of knowledge of national languages, an "everyday nationalism" (*bytovoi natsionalizm*) directed against them in the first years after the Soviet collapse, a particularly difficult economic situation, and widespread pessimism about the future of the newly independent states. Regardless of republic and the year, all sociological studies conducted in Central Asia demonstrate that only a minority of Russians declared their firm intention to stay on irrespective of the country's trajectory. However, not all succeeded in migrating. Potential migrants also remained either because the material conditions necessary to realize their departure were not met or they ended up finding professional or familial niches that were sufficient to make them feel integrated. Moreover, the stated desire to emigrate is sometimes only a declaration of intent—part of a personal narrative to express discomfort regarding a new situation, but not necessarily a future intended to materialize.

---

[51] E.Iu. Sadovskaia, "Migratsionnye protsessy i migratsionnaia politika v Kazakhstane," in Zaionchkovskaia, *Migratsionnaia situatsiia v stranakh SNG*, 120–22.

The motivations for departure are manifold, reflecting above all economic, social, and cultural concerns. The decline in the standard of living following the disintegration of the Soviet Union was clearly a main driving force behind migration, especially because the Russian population was working in the industrial sector that was most affected. In the mid-1990s, the proportion of individuals who desired to emigrate was much higher (43 percent in Uzbekistan, 36 percent in Kyrgyzstan, 66 percent in Tajikistan) than that of individuals who wished to stay (18 percent in Uzbekistan, 25 percent in Kyrgyzstan, 6 percent in Tajikistan).[52] In Tajikistan, more than 75 percent of the Russians who stayed after the civil war claimed to live in difficult or very difficult conditions. In this republic, the desire to leave appeared to transcend generations: 88 percent of Russians under 24 years of age, and 77 percent of elderly Russians wished to emigrate.[53]

A 1998–99 study found that 60 percent of Central Asia's Russians said they wanted to leave, but only 10 percent considered their departure certain. Large proportions of Russians in Kyrgyzstan (38 percent) and Uzbekistan (34 percent) expressed a hope to leave, but only 8 percent and 4 percent, respectively, had made the final decision to depart.[54] According to a 2004 study completed in Kazakhstan, 9 percent of Russians surveyed were on the verge of leaving the republic and 31 percent desired to leave. In republics with particularly difficult social conditions, such as Uzbekistan and Tajikistan, Russians' stated requirements before emigration were fewer than in Kazakhstan or Kyrgyzstan, where they were more unwilling to leave if they had not first secured housing and work in Russia.[55] The other "Europeans" also see themselves emigrating en masse; but again, this does not always correspond to the actual definitive act of departure. At the beginning of the 2000s, half of the Germans still living in Kazakhstan declared that they would leave the country if they had the opportunity to do so.[56]

---

52 Rybakovskii, "Tsentral'naia Aziia i Rossiia: mezhgosudarstvennyi migratsionnyi obmen," 79.

53 Olimova, "Protsess suverenizatsii strany i migratsionnye protsessy v Tadzhikistane," 225.

54 G.S. Vitkovskaia, "Vynuzhdennaia migratsiia v Rossiiu: itogi desiatiletiia," in Zaionchkovskaia, *Migratsionnaia situatsiia v stranakh SNG*, 191.

55 G.S. Vitkovskaia, "Migratsionnoe povedenie netitul'nogo naseleniia v stranakh Tsentral'noi Azii," in G.S. Vitkovskaia, ed., *Migratsiia russkoiazychnogo naseleniia iz Tsentral'noi Azii: prichiny, posledstviia, perspektivy* (Moscow: Carnegie Center, 1996), 90.

56 A.C. Diener, "Homeland as Social Construct: Territorialization among Kazakhstan's Germans and Koreans," *Nationalities Papers* 34, no. 2 (2006): 219.

Besides economic reasons, migration has also been a response to policies of nationalization on the part of the Central Asian governments. Whereas these started well before independence, they intensified after 1991. Although Russians were primarily affected, the other Russian-speaking populations were similarly disadvantaged: 42 percent of Germans believed they were discriminated against because of their nationality, and 61 percent said that inter-ethnic relations had deteriorated since the collapse of the Soviet Union.[57] Indeed, in all Central Asian states, despite the proclaimed equality of citizens irrespective of their ethnic identity, segregation of economic activity by ethnicity actually increased. Non-titular peoples were largely excluded from government services and access to resources, forcing them to retreat into the private business sector or into small trade niches and services. Although it was never formalized in legislation, except in Turkmenistan, the ethnic criterion is nonetheless present in the whole region. In Kazakhstan, for instance, a Russian who does not speak Kazakh is not allowed to enter public service, but a Kazakh who does not speak his titular language does not face such discrimination. The government administration, the cultural domain, and key economic sectors such as oil and cotton are some of the main areas where policies of ethnic preference are openly pursued.

Linguistic nationalization is another strong and long-term motivation for emigration. In Soviet times, Russians and other Russian-speakers very rarely mastered the titular language of their republic of residence.[58] The situation, however, has improved somewhat over the past ten years. Today, children are systematically introduced to the titular language under the present educational system, but in schools where Russian is the language of instruction, these initiatives still have a limited impact. Moreover, virtually no state programs have been developed to support adults learning the titular language. The absence of state support, coupled with a strong sense of disdain for Central Asian languages, is a demotivating factor for Russian-speakers to learn the titular languages.

One of the main reasons for emigration is the lack of—or the perceived lack of—a future for the young generations. In studies carried out in the 1990s on the motivations for emigration, the lack of prospects for children, language policies, and poor living standards emerged as the main

---

[57] *Ibid.*, 210.

[58] Carrère d'Encausse, *L'Empire éclaté*, 179–186.

reasons.[59] The drop in educational standards and the breakdown of preferential ethnic systems encouraged members of ethnic minorities to send their children abroad to study, mainly to Russia. Parents who were either unwilling or lacked the ability to leave sent their children away with the intention of joining them in retirement.

Despite the lack of statistical data, one can sketch a rough portrait of Russian-speaking migrants: they occupied administrative or technical positions; and many of them have an educational level higher than the average population in their home republic. Furthermore, departures tend to be a trait of those with professional qualifications—the more skills they have, the more likely they are to have left. Exceptions are found in certain key sectors in which the new Central Asian states have maintained their specialists, such as the nuclear and space industries in Kazakhstan, and gold mining in Uzbekistan. In the second half of the 1990s, close to half of the Russian migrants who left Kazakhstan had completed a higher or specialized education.[60] Most of the individuals who left the country, whatever their ethnic background, were of working age (64 percent) or younger (22 percent). This resulted in a significant ageing in the minority population in each republic, since the youngest and most educated Russians, and those of childbearing age, had left in huge numbers. In Kazakhstan for instance, the average age of Russians is now 45–47, while that of Kazakhs is 23–25.[61]

Those Russians who arrived during the Virgin Lands Campaign or in the final years of the Soviet regime tended to leave first. Since their roots in the republics were only a few decades old, they still maintained close familial ties to Russia. Those who had opportunities to resettle in Russia's large cities, particularly Moscow, or take up professional positions that were in demand, also left quickly. Russians who stayed in Central Asia were either from the lower social strata or elderly. The situation is particularly difficult for those Russians whose families had been settled in Central Asia for many generations, specifically the descendants of peasants who arrived at the beginning of the twentieth century, as they no longer have family links with Russia.

Despite the present Central Asian authorities insisting on the "non-nativeness" of Russians and other European populations in the name of

---

59 Vitkovskaia, "Vynuzhdennaia migratsiia v Rossiiu: itogi desiatiletiia," 164.

60 Klimova, "Tendentsii migratsionnykh protsessov v respublike Kazakhstan," 209.

61 A.N. Alekseenko, "Pervaia perepis' naseleniia v Kazakhstane: nekotorye itogi i otsenki," 96.

their nation-building projects, the issue of nativeness is complex. Nearly half of all Russians living in Central Asia at the collapse of the Soviet Union were born there (ranging from 43 percent to 48 percent in the five republics), and could therefore claim to be "native." Furthermore, a significant share of those not born in Central Asia had lived in the region for more than 20 years: 37 percent in Kazakhstan, and 41 percent, on average, in the other republics.[62] Overall, of the 9.5 million Russians counted in the five republics of Central Asia in 1989, more than 8 million had built their lives in the region and were not temporary migrants. In addition, the feeling that the Russians of Central Asia are "different" from those of Russia is widespread among the concerned populations. In Uzbekistan, 80 percent of Russians in a 1997 survey said they worked harder, were friendlier, studied more, and drank less than their counterparts in Russia.[63] The idea of having "orientalized" oneself through contact with local people is common; paradoxically it often exists hand in hand with a contempt for the culture of the titular population.

A parallel can be found among other populations of "European origin" for whom the link with the ethnic homeland was also often just a construct. The Germans deported to Central Asia did not come from Germany, but from the Volga autonomous republic, where they had been settled since the eighteenth century. The Poles deported to Central Asia came mainly from the Belarusian, Ukrainian, and Lithuanian areas of the Soviet Union, not from Poland, and the Greeks, from around the Black Sea, were not from Greece per se. The ethnic homeland to which they migrated was therefore a foreign world, albeit one with the advantage of being economically developed.

The nebulous feeling of not being at "home" in Central Asia did not mean that the ethnic homeland suddenly appeared as an obvious destination for emigration. The difficult economic situation in Russia in the 1990s and the many stories of failing to integrate dampened the desire of some Russians in Central Asia to emigrate there. Although the Russians who emigrated were largely urban, few were able to obtain a permit to live in the capital city or in the large cities of the Russian Federation. They thus had to settle in small towns, the countryside, or in the depopulated zones of Siberia. Loss of social status is the main consequence of their

62 Rybakovskii, "Migratsionnyi obmen naseleniem mezhdu Tsentral'noi Aziei i Rossiei," *Sotsiologicheskie issledovaniia*, no. 9 (1995): 92.

63 Lebedeva, *Novaia russkaia diaspora. Sotsial'no-psikhologicheskii analiz*, 98.

emigration, as the occupations available in rural areas do not correspond to the education they received in Central Asia. For many, emigration was therefore synonymous with "a return to the land." In their pre-departure discourse, Russians from Central Asia present Russia as a depopulated country in need of agricultural labor. This return to the land is thus, from their point of view, regeneration, making it possible to build a new life after the failures of their integration into the newly independent Central Asian states.[64] But this myth of the pioneer, exalted in the speeches of potential migrants, very often runs up against reality: not all former engineers and teachers have succeeded in living off the land. In addition, they settle in regions already in a deep social crisis, face hostility from villagers, and find themselves ghettoized in villages full of other Russians from Central Asia.[65] Such difficulties explain the boomerang phenomenon of Russians returning to Central Asia, mainly to Kazakhstan. Supporting figures and sociological analyses are lacking, however. Other migrants have also experienced difficulties in integrating. German emigrants, for instance, found integration in Germany difficult because of their lack of knowledge of the German language and the differences in culture and social habits. They also tended to concentrate in certain cities or districts, which slowed their integration. The former Soviet Jews form an even more distinct group within Israeli society.

Therefore the motivation to emigrate rarely correlates to a desire to return to an ethnic "motherland." In the first years following the disappearance of the Soviet Union, numerous Russians in the "Near Abroad"—between 52 percent and 78 percent—identified themselves as Soviet citizens. In 1997, only 35 percent of Russians in Kyrgyzstan, 28 percent in Uzbekistan, and 20 percent in Kazakhstan identified with the new post-Soviet states. In Kazakhstan, according to data from the Moscow-based institute INDEM, a quarter of Russians surveyed in 1998 continued to regard themselves as citizens of the Soviet Union,[66] a figure similar

---

64 M. Laruelle and S. Peyrouse, *Les Russes du Kazakhstan. Identités nationales et nouveaux États dans l'espace post-soviétique* (Paris: Maisonneuve & Larose—IFEAC, 2004), 249–253.

65 H. Pilkington, *Migration, Displacement and Identity in Post-Soviet Russia* (London, New York: Routledge, 1998); M. Flynn, *Migrant Resettlement in the Russian Federation: Reconstructing "Homes" and "Homelands"* (London: Anthem, 2004). Many Russians expressed the same feeling during interviews conducted across Central Asia between 1999 and 2005.

66 *Analiticheskii otchet o sotsiologicheskom issledovanii "Politicheskie vzgliady naseleniia Kazakhstana"* (Almaty, Moscow: Institut Giller, 1998).

to that in Uzbekistan.[67] For the majority of Russians from Central Asia, being Russian does not necessarily mean living in Russia to affirm that identity; the language and culture are considered to be more important criteria.[68] Many of them affirmed Russia as the land of their ancestors (*otechestvo*), but only a quarter defined it as their motherland (*rodina*).[69] To them, Russia represents the symbolic country of reference, but they still regard Central Asia as the real homeland, with which they retain emotional bonds and memories of their life there. The situation is sometimes, but not always, different for Germans and Poles, whose memories of deportation and discrimination may mean they have less sentimental ties with the Soviet Union. However, according to Alexander Diener's study on Germans residing in Kazakhstan in the early 2000s, only 29 percent considered themselves citizens of Kazakhstan, while 55 percent felt that it was difficult to answer the question.[70]

Repatriation Programs Launched by Ethnic Homelands

Germany and Israel were the first countries to organize the repatriation of their Soviet co-ethnics after decades of diplomatic negotiations. Even before the collapse of the Soviet Union, repatriated Germans, *spätaussiedler*, benefited from an institutional and legal framework adopted after the Second World War, and were recognized according to the terms of the 1953 German federal law on the expelled and refugees.[71] After 1991, new legal measures were adopted to invite the "returnees," but the German government quickly became aware of the financial cost of such measures, particularly in light of the country's reunification. It was also concerned by the integration problems faced by those former Soviet citizens who had arrived earlier, the majority of whom had headed to former East Germany. The number of Germans from the former Soviet Union allowed to "return" was therefore limited to just over 200,000 people per year.

---

67 O.I. Vendina, "Russkie v stranakh byvshevo SSSR," http://geo.1september.ru/2001/11/6.htm.

68 N. Kosmarskaia, *"Deti imperii" v postsovetskoi Tsentral'noi Azii: adaptivnye praktiki i mental'nye sdvigi (russkie v Kirgizii)* (Moscow: Natalis, 2006).

69 Lebedeva, *Novaia russkaia diaspora. Sotsial'no-psikhologicheskii analiz*, 60–61.

70 Diener, "Homeland as Social Construct: Territorialization among Kazakhstan's Germans and Koreans," 208.

71 T. Darieva, "Recruiting for the Nation: Post-Soviet Transnational Migrants in Germany and Kazakhstan," in E. Kasten, ed., *Rebuilding Identities. Pathways to Reform in Post-Soviet Siberia* (Berlin: Dietrich Reimer Verlag, 2005), 153–172.

In 1996, a new system of repatriation was adopted, which required immigrants to take a German-language test; nearly half of candidates failed.[72] Meanwhile, the German government encouraged German minorities to remain in the republic in which they were residing by offering a wide range of cultural assistance, including subsidies to schools and the establishment of German cultural centers, and support to new business ventures as well as capital investment for German-Central Asian joint ventures. In 1997, for instance, nearly $100 million was invested in Kazakhstan for the benefit of the German minority.[73] This strategy contributed to the "re-ethnification" of minorities, who have an interest in developing identities bonded to their kin-state. For instance, those who can claim to have German ancestors now have the opportunity to take German-language courses offered by the Goethe Institute, partly to better prepare them for emigration, but also to get easier starting capital to begin a business.

Other groups have also benefited from the support provided by their ethnic homeland. Since 1986, Greece has granted Greek citizenship to those Greeks arriving from the former Soviet Union. According to a census conducted by the General Secretariat of Greeks Abroad (GSGA) in 2000, over 152,000 Greeks from the Black Sea have "returned" to Greece, including 31,000 from Kazakhstan.[74] Many of them settled in Western Thrace. Although government programs have encouraged them to stay in this relatively remote region, many have preferred to go to Athens, Thessaloniki, or more economically prosperous regions.

The Poles from the former Soviet Union did not have access to repatriation programs until much later, due to Warsaw's lack of financial resources to support such programs in the 1990s. Following the disintegration of the Soviet Union, Wspólnota Polska in Warsaw and the Polish House in Krakow set up the first repatriation programs.[75] Although other funds were subsequently created, the limited financial resources made it difficult for

---

[72] W. Stölting, "Staatliche Sprachenpolitik und politische Gegenwehr—der Fall des Sprachtests für Spätaussiedler," in I. Gogolin and U. Neumann, eds., *Migration und sprachliche Bildung* (Münster: Waxmann Verlag, 2005), 263–273, quoted in B. Alicheva-Himy, "Les Allemands du Kazakhstan: retour dans la *Urheimat* ou 'Patrie historique'," *Regard sur l'Est*, April 1, 2008, http://www.regard-est.com/home/breve_contenu.php?id=831.

[73] Wettig, "No Future for the Ethnic Germans in Kazakhstan?" 161.

[74] A. Triandafyllidou and R. Gropas, eds., *European Immigration. A Sourcebook* (Aldershot: Ashgate, 2007), 144.

[75] Poujol, "Les Polonais du Kazakhstan entre l'intégration et la Patrie rêvée," 98.

any concrete action to be carried out.[76] It was not until the early 2000s that the Polish government began to put increased focus on the issue. Yet in 2000, although a new law carved out a special status for returnees so that they would not be considered foreigners, there was still little financial assistance offered to them.[77] In 2003–4, only 256 Poles returned to Poland under the framework of this law.[78] Of all the Poles who were granted official repatriation status, the majority of them had come from the Ukraine (1,670), 447 from Russia, and 80 from Kazakhstan.[79] Returnees almost automatically receive Polish citizenship and financial benefits, professional training, and tax relief, to facilitate their move. Despite these measures, many returnees were uninformed of their rights, and as a result, experienced difficulty in accessing employment.[80] While some municipalities have established their own support systems, they remain few and far between: for instance, between 1999 and 2007, only 19 families received an official repatriation invitation from the City Council of Krakow. Because Polish aid for co-ethnic repatriation is extremely modest, the Poles of Central Asia who decided to settle in their ethnic homeland have done so mainly on their own initiative. Some have instead preferred to settle in Ukraine, Belarus, or Lithuania, in those cases where they could still benefit from family support.

For the Russians, state-level policies of repatriation have also been very limited and far from efficient. In the 1990s, Russian nationalist movements called for the massive repatriation of Russians from the "Near Abroad" and the implementation of financial aid and political support for the Russian minorities who wanted to stay in the former Soviet republics. The Russian state did not act upon such demands, however. The Russian associations in Central Asia openly criticized Moscow, accusing it of preferring to coddle local regimes, rather than defending their rights or helping their co-ethnics to return. In the 1990s, only 23 percent of the Russians in Tajikistan and 4 percent of those in Kazakhstan expressed hope that they would receive Russian state support to surmount their daily difficulties.[81] The

[76] K. Iglicka, "The Migration of Ethnic Poles from Kazakhstan to Poland," *International Migration Review* 32, no. 4 (1998): 995–1015.

[77] K. Iglicka, "Poland," in Triandafyllidou, and Gropas, *European Immigration. A Sourcebook*, 264.

[78] Poujol, "Les Polonais du Kazakhstan entre l'intégration et la Patrie rêvée," 99.

[79] Iglicka, "Poland," 267.

[80] *Ibid.*, 273.

[81] "Stenogramma ekspertnogo soveshchanie po itogam monitoringa, provedennogo v stranakh SNG i Pribaltiki."

first laws stipulating the existence of "compatriots" (*sootechestvenniki*)—an ambiguous term encompassing everything from Russian expatriates to Russian-speaking populations that are citizens of other states with no legal ties to the Russian Federation—were voted on in 1996. Compatriots, in theory, are granted specific rights including that of "return," but such rights do not exist in practice. Moscow barely protested Turkmenistan's abolition of dual citizenship in 2003, or the subsequent expulsion of Russians who refused to take Turkmen passports. This served to confirm the feeling of abandonment by Moscow on the part of the different Russian "diasporas."

In more recent years, however, the Kremlin has become more interested in the idea of an ethnic homeland. Vladimir Putin's discourse on the demographic crisis and the need for a Russian-speaking workforce from neighboring states gave rise to a lot of public debates. In 2006, Moscow launched a "Program of State Assistance for Voluntary Travel of Compatriots to Russia,"[82] which provides a framework for "returnees" to be implemented by 2012. It defined "returned compatriots" as "those who were educated in the traditions of Russian culture (*rossiiskaia kul'tura*), speak Russian, and who do not wish to lose their relationship with Russia."[83] The state agencies in charge of the program seek primarily to bring back expatriate citizens as well as those with dual nationality, whether they live in the so-called Near Abroad (former Soviet Union) or Far Abroad (the rest of the world). In reality, the program raised interest only among Russians or Russian-speakers from Central Asia and the South Caucasus who have so far failed to emigrate on their own.[84] In theory, six million "compatriots" would be eligible to return,[85] a figure not envisaged by the program, which forecasted a more modest return of people—about 450,000.

It was planned that the returning migrants be sent to selected areas, mainly Siberia, the central Chernozem (Black Hearth) region, and the enclave of Kaliningrad. Compared to the federal budget, subsides for the repatriation program were very modest—only $635 million. The central state was responsible for the transport of selected migrants and their families, providing them with Russian citizenship within six months, and

[82] *Gosudarstvennaia programma po okazaniiu sodeistviia dobrovol'nomu pereseleniiu v Rossiiskuiu Federatsiiu sootechestvennikov prozhivaiushchikh za rubezhom.*

[83] See http://www.perekrestok.de/?mn=2#programma2.

[84] M. Laruelle, "Les 'Russes de l'étranger proche': le thème diasporique et ses lobbies en Russie," *Revue d'études comparatives Est-Ouest*, no. 4 (2008): 5–28.

[85] See http://www.russkie.org/index.php?module=fullitem&id=10317.

guaranteeing their social rights (such as pensions for the elderly, education for minors, and access to minimum social welfare), while the regions were responsible for creating public and private employment opportunities, as well as providing migrants with housing. However, this repatriation program has, by and large, come too late. The majority of Russians who wished to settle in Russia had already arrived there before the program, and those remaining in the Near Abroad are now relatively well integrated. Moreover, the efficiency of the program, especially the job and housing opportunities to be provided by the regions, is very reduced, and Russians continued to emigrate by themselves, without being connected to the program. In 2008, only 10,000 people were officially repatriated and 43,000 were awaiting "return" through the program. However, the financial crisis of 2008 led to a drastic cut in the budget, and support is now provided to about 20,000 returnees a year.[86] Since its inception in 2006, about 80,000 people have been repatriated under the program, far from the planned 450,000, and federal funding has fallen to $6.5 million for 2012. While in the same year President Vladimir Putin revised the state program, simplifying the process for former compatriots to move back to Russia and bringing relatives with them, there are still huge doubts that these changes will significantly alter migration flows.[87]

* * * * *

The emigration flows of Russians and "European" populations from Central Asia have been unprecedented in the history of the region and have important implications for the current Central Asian societies. Within a decade, the population of Kazakhstan declined by more than 1.5 million people, and Kyrgyzstan lost 500,000 people, or about 10 percent of its population. This mass migration has accentuated the process of nationalization of the republics and reinforced ethnic homogeneity, even though Kazakhstan and Kyrgyzstan remain multinational states. With the exception of the larger cities of Almaty, Bishkek, and Tashkent, urban culture has widely and swiftly become mono-ethnic. These flows have also facilitated the creation of a ladder for social mobility among the titular populations, who have filled job vacancies left by those departing and overtaken the state administration. Russian-speaking communities are now defined as "diasporas" by the Central Asian states, a definition which valorizes in

---

[86] See http://www.russedina.ru/frontend/heading/fellow?id=14158.

[87] N. Krainova, "Russia Puts Renewed Hope in Repatriation Program," *The Moscow Times*, September 18, 2012, http://www.themoscowtimes.com/mobile/article/468389.html.

contrast the legitimacy of a new, ethnically-based nationhood, but which also allows kin-states (mostly Russia, Ukraine, Germany, Poland, Greece) to create a new kind of interaction with their "co-ethnics" in this region.

The departure en masse of Russian-speakers has a long-term impact that is as important, if not more so, than the political disengagement of Moscow from Central Asia. The ethnic diversity of this region, the symbol of a bygone colonial era, seems destined to disappear with the advancing age of those Russian-speakers still remaining. However, some elements of cultural proximity are still widely spread and valorized: knowledge of the Russian language, references to Russian culture are omnipresent, and world politics continues largely to be seen through Moscow's prism. The emigration of Russians from Central Asia to Russia, however, should not mask other equally essential population movements. Although the departure of Russian-speakers took center stage during the migration of the 1990s, it is now surpassed by flows of Central Asians to Russia. Central Asia seems therefore destined to remain one of the main sources of emigration in the Eurasian space for years to come. The participation of Central Asians in this geopolitical and social re-composition and the subsequent demographic changes prove that the relationship between Russia and Central Asia will not disappear as quickly as some observers had predicted following the disintegration of the Soviet Union.

THE CENTRAL ASIAN STATES AND THEIR CO-ETHNICS FROM ABROAD: DIASPORA POLICIES AND REPATRIATION PROGRAMS

Olivier Ferrando

The collapse of the Soviet Union in 1991 led to a major upheaval in international relations. The opening up of the external borders of the Soviet Union—previously sealed—allowed the Soviet peoples to escape from their isolation and (re)discover a historical and territorial continuity beyond the Iron Curtain. This was the case particularly in Central Asia where Kazakhs, Uzbeks, Turkmens, Kyrgyz, and Tajiks had their own national republics within the Soviet Union, but also where they had significant populations in neighboring countries such as Iran, Afghanistan, China, and Mongolia. On the one hand, the opening of external borders contributed significantly toward restoring relations between the Central Asian states and their co-ethnic[1] minorities abroad; on the other, the break-up of the Soviet Union into 15 independent states also led to the internationalization of their borders. All of a sudden, former internal administrative limits were transformed into international frontiers dividing the newly formed sovereign states.

The millions of Russians who were stranded outside their historic homeland have received widespread scholarly attention.[2] In Central Asia, the indigenous population experienced a less widely explored dispersal that was not a result of past migrations—as was the case for the Russians—but rather the consequence of the drawing of borders across settlements. The territorial division of Central Asia by the Soviet authorities led to the creation of five fully-fledged national republics, but it could not avoid creating major mismatches between borders and populations. As long as all

[1] This neologism refers to people who share a common ethnic identity, whether this identity is officially recognized by the state (China, Mongolia, Afghanistan), or is the expression of personal belonging with no legal framework (Iran, Turkey).

[2] See, for example, V. Shlapentokh, M. Sendich, and E. Payin, eds., *The New Russian Diaspora: Russian Minorities in the Former Soviet Republics* (Armonk: M.E. Sharpe, 1994); P. Kolstoe, *Russians in the Former Soviet Republics* (London: Hurst, 1995); G. Smith, "Transnational Politics and the Politics of the Russian Diaspora," *Ethnic and Racial Studies* 22, no. 3 (1999): 500–523; N. Kosmarskaia, *"Deti imperii" v postsovetskoi Tsentral'noi Azii* (Moscow: Natalis, 2006); M. Laruelle, ed., "Les Russes de l'étranger proche et la question de la 'diaspora'," *Revue d'Études Comparatives Est-Ouest* 39, no. 1 (2008).

Central Asians were Soviet citizens, residence was just an administrative issue. However, when the republics gained independence, over five million Central Asians remained on the "wrong side" of the border. Rather than being part of their eponymous kin-state, they became kin-minorities "hosted" by neighboring states across the border.

This chapter explores this intertwined population issue in Central Asia and particularly the triadic nexus between kin-states, their kin-minorities abroad, and the host-states where they reside. Using the concept of diaspora as an analytical frame, it proposes to analyze how Central Asian states develop diasporic politics that may or may not lead to the implementation of repatriation programs. This research focuses on the five post-Soviet Central Asian republics and is supported by existing literature, particularly the work of Sally Cummings and Alexander Diener on Kazakhstan, as well as documents and official data from statistical committees and migration agencies. It is also grounded in comprehensive empirical research, carried out during several field visits to the region between 1999 and 2008, where interviews were conducted with state policy makers, local authorities, and ethnic community leaders.

Background: The Formation of Kin-Minorities

The History of the Dispersal of Central Asian Nations

One of the most captivating features of Central Asia is undoubtedly its multi-ethnic population. This mosaic of peoples, cultures, religions, and languages displays a rich history. Pre-colonial Central Asia was a borderless region stretching from western China to Persia and from Russia to British India. Its population was typical of oasis societies, where sedentary farmers, artisans, and traders lived side by side with nomadic herders.

In the nineteenth century, the Russian conquest of Central Asia had two major consequences for the local populations. First, the establishment of interstate borders with China, Afghanistan, and Iran created an artificial separation between those living under Russian rule and their fellow tribal, clan, or even family members who were left stranded on the other side of the border. This was the case for numerous Turkic- and Persian-speaking communities in Afghanistan and Iran, as well as Kazakh and Kyrgyz groups in China and Mongolia. The extension of Russian rule to Central Asia, the 1916 revolt, and the period of civil war following the 1917 Bolshevik revolution caused the flight of many Central Asians over the border into neighboring countries; and even further as far as the

Ottoman Empire. The consolidation of Soviet power in Central Asia was a second force behind the dispersal of native peoples. From an economic perspective, Soviet rule aimed to modernize traditional indigenous societies through an ambitious program of industrialization and collectivization. For the nomads, this process was backed up through their forced sedentarization, entailing a brutal change in their way of life. Some two million people, totaling 42 percent of the Kazakh population at the time, reportedly died in the early years of Soviet power. A third of the remaining Kazakhs fled abroad, mainly to China, Afghanistan, Iran, and Turkey.[3]

In administrative terms, the region's boundaries were determined during the national-territorial demarcation of 1924–1936. In accordance with communist rationale, five native peoples—the Kazakhs, Uzbeks, Kyrgyz, Turkmens, and Tajiks—were promoted to the rank of "nationalities" and granted national republics. The Soviet federation was a political system in which ethnic affiliation was both reified and valorized: reified in that it was actively constructed by Soviet ethnographers, linguists, and historians; valorized in the sense that the promotion of these nationalities and the creation of republics along ethno-national lines privileged ethnicity and underscored ethnic identity as a focus of group solidarity.[4]

However, the intertwined settlement of newly created Central Asian nations made the initial plan of establishing five ethnically homogeneous republics clearly unattainable. The result was that although each Central Asian republic comprised the largest number of the nationality it was named for, the other four other nationalities constituted significant populations, there also existing myriad non-native groups. In 1989, out of a total of 49 million inhabitants in Central Asia, 33.4 million belonged to one of the five Central Asian nationalities; the rest were descended from non-native families who had settled in the region under Russian or Soviet rule, either voluntarily (most of the Slavs and Uralian Tatars) or by forced deportation during the Second World War (Germans, Koreans, Caucasians, Crimean Tatars, and so on) (see Table 1). Among the Central Asians, 5.7 million—one in six—lived outside the administrative boundaries of their eponymous republic, albeit still within the Soviet Union, while more than 7.7 million lived outside Soviet borders (see Table 2).

---

[3] S. Cummings, "The Kazakhs: Demographics, Diasporas, and 'Return,'" in C. King and N.J. Melvin, eds., *Nations abroad. Diaspora Politics and International Relations in the Former Soviet Union* (Oxford: Westview Press, 1999), 136.

[4] A. Haugen, *The Establishment of National Republics in Soviet Central Asia* (New York: Palgrave MacMillan, 2003), 109–137.

Table 1. Ethnic Composition of the Republics of Central Asia in 1989[5]

	Uzbekistan	Kazakhstan	Kyrgyzstan	Turkmenistan	Tajikistan	Total
Uzbeks	**14,142,475**	332,017	550,096	317,333	1,197,841	16,539,762
Kazakhs	808,227	**6,534,616**	37,318	87,802	11,376	7,479,339
Kyrgyz	174,907	14,112	**2,229,663**	634	63,832	2,483,148
Turkmens	121,578	3,846	899	**2,536,606**	20,487	2,683,416
Tajiks	933,560	25,514	33,518	3,149	**3,172,420**	4,168,161
Sub-total Ethnic groups of Central Asia	*16,180,747*	*6,910,105*	*2,851,494*	*2,945,524*	*4,465,956*	*33,353,826*
Russians	1,653,478	6,227,549	916,558	333,892	388,481	9,519,958
Ukrainians	153,197	896,240	108,027	35,578	41,375	1,234,417
Belarusians	29,427	182,601	9,187	9,220	7,247	237,682
Koreans	183,140	103,315	18,355	2,848	13,431	321,089
Tatars	467,829	327,982	70,038	39,245	72,228	977,322
Germans	39,809	957,518	101,309	4,434	32,671	1,135,741
Others	1,102,450	859,154	182,787	151,976	71,214	2,367,581
Sub-total other ethnic groups	*3,629,330*	*9,554,359*	*1,406,261*	*577,193*	*626,647*	*15,793,790*
Total	*19,810,077*	*16,464,464*	*4,257,755*	*3,522,717*	*5,092,603*	*49,147,616*

From Nationalities to Minority Status: The New Central Asian Ethnic Homelands

In Soviet Central Asia, all citizens enjoyed the same Soviet citizenship and were consequently granted equal rights regardless of their nationality and their country of residence. In 1991, the Soviet republics became independent states and sought new national identities for the titular group after which they were named. Dominant elites endeavored to legitimate state sovereignty by promoting the characteristics of the titular group to the rank of state attributes—language, cultural traditions, demographic position, history, and literature. Each nation-state had a multi-ethnic population comprising of a titular nation as well as hosting many other nationalities, which did not share its state attributes and were therefore reduced to the status of ethnic minorities. This geopolitical upheaval challenged the population of the region to reformulate basic notions of "home" and "abroad." As a result, each state had to develop new political relations

[5] Source: 1989 Soviet census, http://demoscope.ru/weekly/ssp/sng_nac_89.php.

Table 2. Distribution of Central Asian Ethnic Groups within and outside the Post-Soviet Space[6]

	Within the post-Soviet space[a]			Outside the post-Soviet space	
	Kin-republic (percentage of the country's population)	Other republics			
Uzbeks	14,142,475 (71.4 percent)	2,555,350		1,000,000	
		Central Asia:	2,397,287	Afghanistan[b]:	1,000,000
		Russia:	126,899	China[c]:	14,763
Kazakhs	6,534,616 (39.7 percent)	1,601,202		1,330,000	
				China[c]:	1,110,758
		Central Asia:	944,723	Mongolia[d]:	177,000
		Russia:	635,865	Turkey[d]:	25,000
				Afghanistan[d]:	3–21,000
				Iran[d]:	3–5,000
Kyrgyz	2,229,663 (52.4 percent)	299,283		146,000	
		Central Asia:	253,485	China[c]:	143,537
		Russia:	41,734	Afghanistan[b]:	2,000
Turkmens	2,536,606 (72.0 percent)	192,359		1,500,000	
		Central Asia:	146,810	Afghanistan[b]:	400,000
		Russia:	39,739	Iran[b]:	1,055,000
Tajiks	3,172,420 (62.3 percent)	1,042,952		3,600,000	
		Central Asia:	995,741	Afghanistan[b]:	3,500,000
		Russia:	38,206	China[c]:	33,223
Total	28,615,780	5,691,146		7,576,000	

not only with its own multi-ethnic population, but also with neighboring states that hosted co-ethnic minorities.

These co-ethnic minorities experience a double affiliation: they enjoy the citizenship of their host-state while simultaneously sharing common attributes with their eponymous kin-state, which I shall term "ethnic homeland."[7] Therefore this understanding of the diasporic fact in Central

[6] Sources: (a) 1989 Soviet census, http://demoscope.ru/weekly/ssp/sng_nac_89.php; (b) *Encyclopaedia Iranica*, http://www.iranica.com/newsite/; (c) 1990 Chinese census, http://www.stats.gov.cn/english/statisticaldata/yearlydata/YB2000e/B09E.htm; (d) Cummings, "The Kazakhs: Demographics, Diasporas, and 'Return,'" 137.

[7] This expression is borrowed from Rogers Brubaker. The kin-state should be understood as a putative homeland, not in historic terms, since many co-ethnics abroad have no genealogical links with their eponymous state, but in ethnic terms in the sense that

Asia does not aim to designate kin-minorities that have been cut off from their ethnic homeland in a static way. Instead it qualifies the dynamic interactions between a state, its kin-minorities abroad, and the host-states where these minorities reside. The diasporic fact arises from an active triadic nexus between, first, the ethnic homeland in the way it engages in the construction of diaspora politics toward its co-ethnics abroad (a top-down process); second, the kin-minority abroad in how it influences state policies (a bottom-up process); and finally, the host-state in the way it allows or limits the expression of diasporic identities within its citizenry. This triadic nexus actually frames the development—or not—of diaspora policies, repatriation programs, and potential migration flows.

A Diasporic Rhetoric toward Co-Ethnics Abroad

In their attempt to define the nation, all five Central Asian states encouraged a diasporic narrative encompassing all co-ethnics irrespective of their country of residence. Through this appeal to their kin-minorities abroad, the states made the choice of an ethnic definition of their national identity. But at the same time, they paid special attention to maintain the cohesion of their own multi-ethnic societies. Therefore each state coupled its diasporic discourse toward co-ethnics abroad with a rhetoric of tolerance and cultural diversity. This was intended primarily for domestic audiences in order to promote a shared sense of civic belonging to the nation within its territorial borders and regardless of the ethnic identity of its citizens.

Tajikistan provides a revealing illustration of such diasporic rhetoric. The creation of the Tajik Soviet Socialist Republic (Tajik SSR) in 1929 was a turning point in the history of Persian-speaking Central Asia, classified as Tajiks by Soviet ethnographers. From this date, Tajikistan became the only tangible homeland for all Tajiks of the Soviet Union and as such became the proper locus of a Tajik national identity.

Even though a large part of the Tajik population and most Persian historical cities were located outside the Tajik SSR, the very existence of this political entity shifted the center of Tajik national consciousness to

---

it embodies the identity features of an ethnic group and offers a privileged ethnic affiliation to its members, both the inner titular group and kin-minorities abroad. R. Brubaker, "Nationhood and the National Question in the Soviet Union and Post-Soviet Eurasia: An Institutionalist Account," *Theory and Society* 23, no. 1 (1994): 47–78.

a new kin-state and a new capital, Dushanbe.[8] Following independence, Tajik nationalists faced a paradoxical situation. On the one hand, they presented Tajikistan as a modern state with internationally recognized borders. But on the other, they were in search of a new legitimacy, and that search involved tracing a direct genealogy between independent Tajikistan and the Emirate of the Samanids, known as the first and last Persian dynasty to have ever ruled Central Asia (in the tenth century), and is now considered the first historical Tajik state. According to the official line, Tajikistan is the only repository of a historical region stretching beyond its current borders and whose dynastic shrine lies in Bukhara in present-day Uzbekistan. Such a discourse can be qualified as diasporic in that it promotes a Tajik identity rooted in a mythicized national history transcending state boundaries and seeking to encompass all of Central Asia's Persian-speaking communities. However, this diasporic rhetoric was articulated primarily with a domestic objective: to strengthen the national consciousness of inner Tajiks. It did not find expression in actual foreign policy toward countries hosting Tajik kin-minorities abroad.

In Kazakhstan, the discourse toward co-ethnics abroad arose under Gorbachev's perestroika, a period of political and economic liberalization starting in 1985, which permitted ethnic associations to denounce the state-led Russification of the Kazakhs and the threats that this posed to Kazakh national identity. These associations placed their demands for ethnic regeneration on the political agenda and regarded co-ethnics from outside the Soviet Union as a powerful weapon in their armory, since Kazakh communities abroad had been spared the experience of Soviet assimilation and managed to preserve their knowledge of both written and spoken Kazakh. From 1991, independent Kazakh authorities developed a diasporic rhetoric toward distant Kazakhs, who were viewed as living repositories of Kazakh national traditions and whose repatriation would help inculcate traditions long lost by Soviet Kazakhs in the homeland.[9]

The First Degree of Institutionalization of Diaspora Politics: Worldwide Pan-Ethnic Congresses

Besides diasporic rhetoric toward their kin-minorities abroad, Central Asian states quickly developed a more structured approach. The first

[8] Haugen, *The Establishment of National Republics in Soviet Central Asia*, 159–164.

[9] Cummings, "The Kazakhs: Demographics, Diasporas, and 'Return,'" 140.

degree of institutionalization of diaspora politics was the creation in the early 1990s of pan-ethnic congresses that were intended to embrace all co-ethnics residing outside their ethnic homeland and to promote cross-border links between kin-states and their kin-minorities abroad. Such gatherings were made possible because of the existence of kin-minority associations in their various countries of residence. Most of them were set up during perestroika in the former Soviet republics, and to some extent outside the Soviet Union (China, Mongolia, Iran, Afghanistan, and Turkey). The very existence of worldwide pan-ethnic congresses endorsed the central role of the ethnic homeland and acknowledged its symbolic function as cross-border guardian of all co-ethnic minorities abroad.

In 1991, Uzbekistan called its first *kurultai*[10] and created the World Association of Uzbeks in Tashkent to encourage language and cultural exchange. Representatives of Uzbek communities from the Middle East, Afghanistan, China, and from the four Central Asian republics met with Uzbeks who came from Russia, Ukraine, and several Western countries. A U.S. citizen of Uzbek origin was subsequently elected president of the association. The same year Turkmenistan convened its kin-minorities at its first World Congress of Turkmens, with President Saparmurat Niyazov appointing himself as general-secretary of the Congress. In 1992, the first World Congress of Kazakhs was organized with government sponsorship in Almaty to regroup Kazakhs from around the world. Kyrgyzstan followed suit and organized its World Congress of Kyrgyz in Bishkek. Apart from Uzbekistan, which stopped the activities of its association at the second congress in 1993,[11] pan-ethnic gatherings were held periodically. The eleventh congress of Turkmens took place in October 2008,[12] while Kazakhstan and Kyrgyzstan organized their third congresses in 2005 and 2008, respectively.

---

[10] This word of Turkic-Mongolian origin means a traditional gathering of tribal leaders in nomadic societies. Central Asian states use it to designate various types of political gatherings, including pan-ethnic meetings.

[11] At this second and last congress, the representatives of the Uzbek minorities of neighboring Central Asian states refused to support the Uzbek government's project to switch from the Cyrillic to the Latin alphabet. They feared that such a reform would create a language barrier between latinized Uzbekistan and its Uzbek minorities, who were fully dependent on their host-state's language policy and had no other choice but to keep using the Cyrillic script. The Uzbek government played down criticisms and requested Uzbek representatives from abroad "not to interfere in the state's domestic affairs." Reported by N. Fahriddinov, founding member of the Uzbeks' association of Tajikistan, Dushanbe, Tajikistan, September 11, 2008.

[12] "V Ashkhabade proshel forum gumanitarnoi assotsiatsii turkmen mira," *Central Asia News*, October 25, 2008 http://www.ferghana.ru/news.php?id=10496.

In Tajikistan, the civil war delayed the planning of such gatherings. It was not until September 1994 that Tajik communities met for the first time in Dushanbe at the so-called first World Congress of Tajiks and Persian Speakers (WCTPS). The Tajik initiative seems to differ from the other Central Asian congresses in three respects. Firstly, in terms of structure, while all the gatherings have clearly been promoted with a top-down approach, the WCTPS is the only Central Asian pan-ethnic congress to have a permanent executive committee sponsored by the state, as well as to publish a yearly magazine—*Pajvand* (Liaison)—in the Tajik and Persian languages. This organizational frame helps to foster close links between its members across the kin-state borders and to maintain a regular schedule, with congresses taking place every other year.[13]

Second, the late establishment of the WCTPS in comparison to the other Central Asian congresses led to major discrepancies between the WCTPS objectives and the mandate of its member associations. In Uzbekistan, Turkmenistan, Kazakhstan, and Kyrgyzstan, each pan-ethnic organization developed at the same time as associations of kin-minorities in the neighboring host-states, enabling them to formulate common objectives. But in Tajikistan in 1994, the WCTPS gathered ethnic associations that had already been functioning for several years and were initially founded according to their host-state agenda. This put the Tajik associations in an awkward position since they had to manage their primary task of representing and promoting the rights of their community within their host-state, and at the same time play a role in the diaspora politics of their kin-state. Last but not least, the name of the congress can lead to confusion in the sense that its identity is defined in terms of both ethnicity (Tajiks) and language (Persian-speakers), the latter being much wider and blurring the ethnic border between Tajiks, Afghans, and Iranians. Therefore, the WCTPS comprises leaders of Tajik minority associations from Central Asia and other former Soviet republics, as well as representatives of Persian-speaking communities from Iran, Afghanistan, India, and Western countries such as the United States, Canada, France, and Germany. Interestingly, these latter members do not lead an ethnic association nor represent Tajiks from abroad. Instead, they play the emblematic role of delegates of the WCTPS abroad. In most cases they are not of Tajik but rather Iranian origin.[14]

---

[13] The last congress took place in August 2008 on the occasion of the 1,150th anniversary of the birth of the poet Rudaki, considered to be the father of Persian literature in the time of the Samanids.

[14] Interview with Masud Mirshahi, WCTPS delegate in France, Paris, March 17, 2009.

Co-Ethnic Minorities Abroad at the Heart of Interstate Negotiations

More symbolic than anything else, worldwide pan-ethnic gatherings have only a limited capacity and are barely able to carry out diaspora politics vis-à-vis kin-minorities abroad. Since in Central Asia kin-states and kin-minorities are frequently contiguous, host-states maintain strong control over a whole spectrum of cross-border activities. For this reason, any state program overtly supporting co-ethnics abroad necessitates prior negotiation with the host-state—which often takes the form of bilateral agreements.

Securing Education in the Mother Tongue

In Soviet times, all children had the right to "an education in [their] mother tongue."[15] Education was delivered in seven languages in Uzbekistan, six in Tajikistan, five in Kazakhstan, and four each in Kyrgyzstan and Turkmenistan.[16] Such a school system was managed through a double chain of command that was based on the territory and the language of education. For instance, an Uzbek-language school in Tajikistan was under the administrative supervision of the Ministry of Education of the Tajik SSR, but at the same time the school was supplied with Uzbek-language textbooks and pedagogical material from the Ministry of Education of its kin-Uzbek SSR. However, this integrated regional system did not outlast the collapse of the Soviet Union. Instead, each independent state endeavors to manage on its own this Soviet legacy of multilingual schooling.

In post-Soviet Central Asia, there are very few examples of interstate cooperation in the sector of education. Education plays a key role in the process of state-building, in particular by inculcating the new national ideology to young generations. One example, however, is an agreement between Tajikistan and Kyrgyzstan that addresses the education needs of their respective kin-minority in bilateral terms. Kyrgyzstan's Tajiks represent 0.9 percent of the country's population (42,636 in 1999).[17] They are schooled in Tajik-language schools, and, in 1992, founded an ethnic

[15] Article 45 of the 1977 Soviet constitution.

[16] J.M. Landau and B. Kellner-Heinkele, *Politics of Language in the ex-Soviet Muslim States* (London: Hurst, 2001), 166–203.

[17] *Naselenie Kyrgyzstana. Itogi pervoi natsional'noi perepisi naseleniia Kyrgyzskoi Respubliki 1999 goda v tablitsakh*, vol. 2, no. 1 (Bishkek: National Committee of Statistics, 2000), 70.

association to defend their rights. Similarly, Tajikistan's Kyrgyz population amount to 1.1 percent of the country's population (65,515 in 2000),[18] their children attend Kyrgyz-language schools, and, in 1995, an association was launched with the same objective of protecting their cultural rights.

As these minority-language schools were isolated from their kin-state and from the support of their kin-Ministries of Education, the leaders of the two associations joined forces to support their children. On the one hand, they endeavored to make their ethnic homeland aware of the issue of education, in particular at the worldwide pan-ethnic congresses that they were attending. On the other hand, they made repeated claims to their host-state on the right to be educated in their mother tongue.[19] The two Ministries of Education agreed to open bilateral negotiations, and, in 2001, they signed a win-win inter-governmental agreement consisting of the mutual provision of materials and services. The agreement represented a mere restoring of the former dual chain of command that had existed in Soviet times. Both minority-language schools remained under the administrative and financial supervision of their host-state's Ministry of Education, but they depended on their ethnic homeland to order textbooks, train teachers, and provide further education for students in their mother tongue. It is clear that both the active mobilization of kin-minorities and the willingness of state authorities led to the actual materialization of an interstate agreement and, therefore, made effective the expression of diaspora politics.

Securing Freedom of Movement

As a result of the artificial delimitation of Central Asia, most families living in border areas had relatives in a neighboring republic. After independence, administrative boundaries suddenly became international frontiers. In 1992, however, the Central Asian states signed a regional agreement in Bishkek that guaranteed their citizens the freedom to move within the Commonwealth of Independent States (CIS). Accordingly, inhabitants of Central Asia could continue to move without restriction across their interstate borders.

---

[18] *The Population of the Republic of Tajikistan in 2000* (Dushanbe: State Committee on Statistics, 2002), 155.

[19] Interview with A. Raimzhanov, head of the Association of Kyrgyzstan's Tajiks, Bishkek, Kyrgyzstan, May 4, 2007, and with Z. Davlatlieva, head of the Society of Tajikistan's Kyrgyz, Dushanbe, Tajikistan, November 15, 2006.

But in 1999, following a series of bombings in Tashkent which were officially ascribed to transnational Islamic movements, Uzbekistan decided to take firmer control of its borders. It denounced the Bishkek agreement and introduced a very strict visa regime for its neighbors. Suddenly, citizens of Kazakhstan, Turkmenistan, Tajikistan, and Kyrgyzstan—including 2.5 million ethnic Uzbeks living outside of Uzbekistan—could not enter their ethnic homeland and visit their relatives without a visa. In return, neighboring countries imposed more or less successfully a converse visa regime on Uzbekistan. Consequently, their co-ethnics living in Uzbekistan were cut off. The administrative and financial burden dramatically affected the relationship between kin-states and their kin-minorities.

As the Uzbek authorities continued to refuse to enter into regional agreements, each country undertook bilateral negotiations with Uzbekistan in order to cancel the visa regime and restore freedom of movement to their kin-minorities. In 2002, Kyrgyzstan and Uzbekistan signed a mutual agreement that granted all citizens three-day transit without the need for a visa. In addition, residents of bordering districts were permitted to stay for up to 60 days in the neighboring state as long as they did not go beyond 40 kilometers from the border. This latter provision was obviously intended for Kyrgyzstan's Uzbek minority (664,950 people in 1999)[20] and Uzbekistan's Kyrgyz minority (estimated at 370,000 people in 2005),[21] both of whom were living in compact areas just over the border from their respective kin-states, and as such, were negatively affected by the visa regime. In 2006, further bilateral negotiations extended the visa-free 60-day stay to all citizens and removed the 40-kilometer limitation.[22] In spring 2007, Uzbekistan and Kyrgyzstan eventually ratified a bilateral accord permitting their citizens visa-free travel for up to two months. This bilateral agreement notwithstanding, the Central Asian countries have not yet reached a regional framework to replace the 1992 Bishkek agreement that has virtually ceased to operate. For instance, Kazakhstan had

20 *Naselenie Kyrgyzstana*, 70.

21 As there are no official updated statistics on the ethnic composition of Uzbekistan, this figure comes from the report that Uzbekistan submitted to the United Nations Committee on the Elimination of Racial Discrimination (CERD), *Fifth Periodic Reports of State Parties due in 2004. Uzbekistan*, CERD/C/463/Add.2, September 2, 2005, http://www.unhchr.ch/tbs/doc.nsf.

22 "Visa-free regime accord for citizens of Kyrgyzstan and Uzbekistan comes into effect," *Central Asia News*, February 16, 2007, http://enews.ferghana.ru/article.php?id=1839.

no visa regime for its neighbors, but in 2003, it introduced migration cards in order to monitor entries into the country.[23]

Securing Dual Citizenship

Dual citizenship is a central tool of diaspora politics in that it establishes formal relations between a state, its kin-minority abroad, and the host-state. The conferral of dual citizenship allows minority members to retain the citizenship of their host-state and carry out their rights and duties there, as well as adopt the citizenship of their kin-state as a symbolic attachment to their putative ethnic homeland.[24] During Soviet times, all Central Asians enjoyed the same Soviet citizenship irrespective of their ethnicity or place of residence. After becoming independent, each state introduced a new citizenship that applied to all former Soviet citizens residing within the border of the state in question. Central Asian governments immediately denied dual citizenship because they feared that the multi-ethnic nature of the population would lead to weak civic awareness among minorities and therefore erode the very legitimacy of the state. Consequently, any person choosing the citizenship of his kin-state was required to first abandon the citizenship of his host-state.

In accordance with this rule, the first Kyrgyz constitution of 1993 banned dual citizenship,[25] and the 1995 presidential decree on measures to regulate citizenship in Kyrgyzstan also stipulated the need for any applicant to Kyrgyz citizenship to provide a certificate of relinquishment of past citizenship. These legal provisions made it difficult for Kyrgyz co-ethnics abroad to move to Kyrgyzstan and become Kyrgyz citizens. To facilitate the shift in citizenship, the Kyrgyz government decided to add to the general framework exceptional arrangements that would be applied on a case-by-case basis through bilateral negotiations.

The first case concerned Kyrgyz refugees from Tajikistan. The Tajik civil war (1992–97) caused the displacement of civilians from Tajikistan to neighboring countries.[26] Among the 16,700 people who found refuge

---

23 V. Tishkov, Z. Zayinchovskaya, and G. Vitkovskaya, *Migration in the Countries of the Former Soviet Union* (Global Commission on International Migration, 2005), 35.

24 A.C. Diener, "Kazakhstan's Kin-State Diaspora: Settlement Planning and the *Oralman* Dilemma," *Europe-Asia Studies* 57, no. 2 (2005): 347.

25 Article 13 (2): "Citizens of the Kyrgyz republic shall not be recognized as citizens of other states."

26 The fighting led to the displacement of more than a million people—one in five inhabitants. Besides the 700,000 internally displaced persons and the exile of 200,000 ethnic Russians and other Slavs, the United Nations High Commissioner for Refugees (HCR)

in Kyrgyzstan, most were actually ethnic Kyrgyz who moved back to their region of origin.[27] Following the ratification by the Kyrgyz government of the Geneva Convention relating to the status of refugees in 1996, these exiles were granted the status of refugees and could take advantage of assistance programs under the supervision of the High Commissioner for Refugees to settle in their homeland and obtain Kyrgyz citizenship. However, this status did not apply to Kyrgyz migrants moving to Kyrgyzstan from other countries or from Tajikistan after the civil war. They had no choice but to conform with the legal framework and provide a certificate to show that they had discarded their former citizenship. Problematically, however, the authorities of their country of origin were reluctant to provide them with such documents. The increasing number of ethnic Kyrgyz who were left stranded without citizenship urged the Kyrgyz government to enter into bilateral negotiations with neighboring countries from which these migrants had left. A first interstate agreement was signed with Tajikistan in 2004 to simplify the procedure for relinquishing citizenship. Since then, 14,540 Kyrgyz, who moved from Tajikistan after 1997, and who were therefore not eligible for refugee status, have reportedly been granted Kyrgyz citizenship in a simplified procedure.[28]

Kyrgyzstan developed a similar approach toward Uzbekistan in 2005, in order to regularize the status of some 2,000 ethnic Kyrgyz families who had arrived from Uzbekistan since independence.[29] However, the Uzbek Ministry of the Interior has, so far, refused to take any action. The lack of a bilateral agreement made it impossible for ethnic Kyrgyz from Uzbeki-

---

registered 30,000 refugees from Tajikistan in Uzbekistan in 1996, 20,000 in Turkmenistan, 18,900 in Afghanistan, 16,700 in Kyrgyzstan, and 6,000 in Kazakhstan. U.S. Committee for Refugees, "World Refugee Survey 1997—Tajikistan," in *HCR Refworld 2006*, 15th edition (Geneva, 2006).

[27] In many cases, ethnic Kyrgyz who fled the Tajik civil war did not originally come from Tajikistan. The virgin lands of southern Tajikistan were brought under cultivation in the twentieth century after the development of irrigation and the settlement of thousands of families from all over Central Asia and the Soviet Union: Tajiks of course, but also Uzbeks, Turkmens, Kyrgyz, and Kazakhs, as well as Russians, Ukrainians, and Tatars, among many other ethnic groups. Kyrgyz moved down from the Dara mountainous area in southern Kyrgyzstan. Their exile from Tajikistan then took the form of a return to the land of their ancestors. O. Ferrando, "Déplacements de populations et identités dans la vallée du Ferghana: les limites du paradigme ethnique," *Cahiers d'Asie Centrale*, no. 19–20 (2011): 179–182.

[28] "Okolo 14 tysiach etnicheskikh kyrgyzov iz Tadzhikistana poluchili kyrgyzskoe grazhdanstvo," *Kginfo.ru*, April 8, 2009, http://kginfo.ru/diasporas/tj/news/.

[29] As reported by the State Committee on Migrations of Kyrgyzstan. "V Kyrgyzstane 257 semei etnicheskikh kyrgyzov iz Uzbekistana poluchili kyrgyzskoe grazhdanstvo," *Central Asian News*, June 5, 2008, http://www.ca-news.org/news/28497.

stan to discard their Uzbek citizenship. However, public pressure encouraged Kyrgyzstan to amend unilaterally its provision on dual citizenship. The constitutional reform of December 30, 2006, adopted by referendum on October 21, 2007, simply removed the ban on dual citizenship and introduced a new clause for Kyrgyz co-ethnics abroad: "Kyrgyz residing abroad have the right to obtain the citizenship of the Kyrgyz republic with a simplified procedure, regardless of the existence of another state's citizenship."[30] For the time being, Kyrgyzstan is the only Central Asian state to recognize dual citizenship and to provide constitutional guarantees to foreign citizens on an exclusive ethnic basis. By doing so, the Kyrgyz government overtly proclaimed its diaspora politics vis-à-vis co-ethnics abroad, in particular the Kyrgyz minority living in Uzbekistan, as well as the recent, albeit large, community of Kyrgyz migrant workers in Russia.

Repatriation Policies and Special Status Granted to "Ethnic Repatriates"

The adoption and effective implementation of repatriation programs is the logical outcome of the process of institutionalization of diaspora politics. Such programs postulate that an ethnic group can only flourish within the boundaries of its ethnic homeland, that is, a state where it constitutes the titular group. They are a prime example of the existing tension between two distinct conceptions of the nation—either ethnic or civic. In domestic terms, Central Asian states promote the image of a tolerant multi-ethnic society, where all citizens have the same rights irrespective of their ethnic affiliation. This civic conception of the nation finds institutional expression in the People's Assembly (*Assambleia naroda*) in Kazakhstan and Kyrgyzstan, or the Civic Council (*Obshchestvennyi sovet*) in Tajikistan. These advisory bodies were initiated by each state as a forum for ethnic minorities and civil society. They consider all ethnic groups as constituents of the nation and offer them the opportunity to enter into dialogue with state authorities and assert their rights. Besides promoting common civic values internally, Central Asian states also developed an ethnic conception of the nation through diasporic rhetoric and pan-ethnic gatherings

---

30 Article 20 (4) of the amended constitution, available at: http://www.sras.org/constitution_of_the_kyrgyz_republic.

of their kin-minorities abroad. Repatriation programs conceived on an exclusive ethnic basis partake of this essentialist approach.

To date two countries, Kazakhstan and Kyrgyzstan, have developed active repatriation policies. In both cases, the interest in co-ethnics abroad was actually couched in terms of two interlinked domestic policy imperatives. First the authorities sought to legitimize the territorial boundaries of the new state and overcome the disadvantageous demographic position of the titular nation. Unsurprisingly the two states that made the choice to pursue an overt repatriation policy were precisely those with a less favorable ethnic structure. In 1989, Kazakhs represented only 39.7 percent of Kazakhstan's total population.[31] The government invited Kazakhs from abroad to move to their ethnic homeland with the clear objective of increasing the proportion of the titular Kazakh group. In addition, repatriates were sent primarily to those regions where Kazakhs were less numerous—to northern provinces dominated by Russians, and southern ones with compact Uyghur and Uzbek settlements.[32] In Kazakhstan, this relocation actually dovetailed with a separate policy of internal migration, initiated in 1992 and designed to encourage ethnic Kazakhs already residing within the republic to move to regions dominated by non-Kazakhs.[33] In Kyrgyzstan, the titular group enjoyed a small absolute majority in the country as a whole (52.4 percent in 1989) but was seriously challenged in the northern province of Chui (38.2 percent Kyrgyz and 35.5 percent Russian), in the capital Bishkek (55.7 percent Russian and 22.9 percent Kyrgyz), and in several southern districts, where the Uzbeks dominated.[34] To counterbalance these ethnic statistics, priority was given to these areas in the settlement of co-ethnic Kyrgyz moving from abroad.

The second domestic imperative of repatriation was historical. Kazakhs and Kyrgyz are descendants of nomadic tribes that were dramatically affected by Russian colonization and the politics of modernization forcibly implemented by the Soviet regime. The eradication of traditional societies had either caused the death or exile of the majority of Central

[31] By comparison, Tajiks constituted 62.3 percent of the population of their eponymous state, Uzbeks 71.4 percent, and Turkmens 72 percent. *Natsional'nyi sostav naseleniia SSSR po dannym vsesoiuznoi perepisi naseleniia 1989 g.* (Moscow: Goskomstat SSSR, 1991), 92, 102, 130, and 136, http://demoscope.ru/weekly/ssp/sng_nac_89.php.

[32] D. Arel, "Démographie et politique dans les premiers recensements post-soviétiques: Méfiance envers l'État, identités en question," *Population-F* 57, no. 6 (2002): 805–6.

[33] Cummings, "The Kazakhs: Demographics, Diasporas, and 'Return,'" 140–43.

[34] *Natsional'nyi sostav naseleniia SSSR po dannym vsesoiuznoi perepisi naseleniia 1989 g.*, 126.

Asian nomads. In 1991, both Kazakhstan and Kyrgyzstan could address the legacies of the past in an official rewriting of national history, where the creation of their own independent states was portrayed as the culmination of a traumatic history of dispersion and struggle. The restoration of relations with kin-minorities abroad drew on this re-examination of the past. Repatriation was thus perceived as the imperious duty of a kin-state toward its co-ethnic exiles.

Who are the Recipients of Repatriation Policies?

Given the multi-ethnic nature of Kazakhstan's and Kyrgyzstan's societies, the development of repatriation policies raises the question of who is entitled to state assistance. Repatriates could be defined either ethnically, as ethnic Kazakhs or ethnic Kyrgyz respectively, or on a territorial basis and that would, therefore, comprise all groups considering Kazakhstan or Kyrgyzstan to be their homeland, regardless of ethnicity. This would apply to the Uzbek and Uyghur communities who were living on the territory of present-day Kazakhstan and Kyrgyzstan in pre-colonial times, and were incorporated into these Soviet republics during the ethno-territorial division of Central Asia. In other words, a territorial definition of the repatriate would consider autochthony the prime criterion for claiming right to repatriation.[35]

However, Kazakhstan and Kyrgyzstan failed to capture the multi-ethnic essence of their indigenous population. In November 1992, at the opening of the First World Congress of Kazakhs, President Nazarbayev appealed

[35] Debates that took place in Russia in the early 1990s about the definition of the Russian diaspora and the related right to repatriation give an interesting perspective on this issue. There were conflicting conceptions, with many nationalists supporting a narrow ethnic definition of the "Russian diaspora" (*russkaia diaspora*); others preferred the linguistic criteria of "Russian-speakers" (*russkoiazychnye*), the oxymoron "ethnic citizens of Russia" (*etnicheskie rossiiane*), or the term "compatriots" (*sootechestvenniki*). On December 9, 1995, a declaration was passed in support of the Russian diaspora and Russian compatriots, with the following definition: the Russian (*rossiiskaia*) diaspora consists of "all those who (1) have issued from (*vykhodets*) the Russian empire, Russia, the RSFSR, and the Soviet Union, and their direct descendants irrespective of their national or ethnic affiliation, their occupation, place of residence, or citizenship, and (2) recognize a spiritual or cultural-ethnic link with the Russian Federation or any of its subject territories." The Duma clearly opted for a territorial definition of its diaspora in which any ethnic group having an administrative entity in Russia is in theory eligible for the status of compatriots. N.J. Melvin, "The Russians: Diaspora and the End of Empire," in King and Melvin, *Nations Abroad. Diaspora Politics and International Relations in the Former Soviet Union*, 27–57.

to "all Kazakhs to unite under a single flag on the soil of Kazakhstan."[36] The following year a first repatriation program was signed with the Iranian government, but it applied only to Kazakh co-ethnics from Iran.[37] In Kyrgyzstan, the legislation defined repatriates as ethnic Kyrgyz "returning to their historical homeland (*vozvrashchaiushchiesia na istoricheskuiu rodinu*)."[38] Authorities targeted only ethnic Kyrgyz who were residing abroad on the grounds of their ancestors' resettlement. Such a definition clearly ignored the fact that many Kyrgyz who were living abroad, particularly in Afghanistan and China, had actually no ancestry from the territory of modern Kyrgyzstan. The concept of "return" to the historic homeland was therefore purely mythical.

Besides this issue of defining repatriates, it should be noted that their treatment was unequal and highly dependent on the relationship between their kin-state and their country of residence. Repatriation programs developed by Kazakhstan actually targeted only co-ethnic Kazakhs from outside the former Soviet territory (Mongolia, Turkey, Afghanistan, and Iran). They did not concern Kazakh minorities from other Central Asian states, or those from Russia or China, although these constituted the largest communities. This reluctance to claim overtly the repatriation of co-ethnics living in neighboring countries can be explained by the intertwined ethnic composition of Central Asia. The Kazakh government is well aware of the fact that the extension of its diaspora policies over the border with Uzbekistan, where nearly one million Kazakhs live, would be perceived as interference in Uzbekistan's internal affairs and, in turn, would probably prompt Tashkent to take a more active stance on co-ethnic Uzbeks from Kazakhstan (400,000 people).

Similarly, Uzbekistan also hosts the largest Kyrgyz minority, but Kyrgyzstan has never pursued an overt repatriation policy in regard to this minority for fear that Uzbekistan would mobilize the 750,000 ethnic Uzbeks in Kyrgyzstan, who represent the latter's largest minority (14.3 percent in 2006).[39] In 1989, China and Russia hosted sizeable Kazakh (1,110,758 and

---

36 Diener, "Kazakhstan's Kin-State Diaspora: Settlement Planning and the *Oralman* Dilemma," 339.

37 Presidential decree no. 1184 on "Immigration quotas and the organization of immigration of co-ethnics from Iran and other states," April 15, 1993; Cummings, "The Kazakhs: Demographics, Diasporas, and 'Return,'" 142.

38 Presidential decree on "Support to ethnic Kyrgyz returning to their homeland," August 29, 2001.

39 *Demograficheskii ezhegodnik Kyrgyzskoi Respubliki 2001–2005 gg.* (Bishkek: National Committee of Statistics, 2006), 102.

635,865 people, respectively) and Kyrgyz communities (143,737 and 41,734, respectively). Neither Kazakhstan nor Kyrgyzstan seems ready to sacrifice their strategic partnership with these two powerful neighbors. Economic and political concerns—in other words *realpolitik*—took precedence over the interest that Kazakhstan and Kyrgyzstan may have developed toward their kin-minorities in both countries.

The Content of Repatriation Policies

Whereas Kazakhstan's and Kyrgyzstan's repatriation policies were curtailed in some countries, as outlined above, they developed progressively elsewhere. The first provisions for repatriation to Kazakhstan were formulated in bilateral agreements with Iran (1992) and Mongolia (1994). In 1995, President Nazarbayev launched a program to fix annual quotas of repatriates and support their resettlement in Kazakhstan. However, this first decree had no budget and very limited legal provisions.[40] During the period from 1991 to 2000, there were reportedly 180,000 Kazakh repatriates, mostly originating from Mongolia.[41] Because of the inconsistency of the national legislation and the general confusion in which repatriates were managed, the Kazakh parliament in 1997 adopted a law on the migration of population, which introduced the legal status of *Oralman* (repatriate in Kazakh) and provided a clearer legal framework to implement repatriation policies. The law defines the Oralman on exclusively ethnic grounds as "any foreigner or stateless person with Kazakh ethnicity who resided outside the boundaries of Kazakhstan on the day of independence and who entered Kazakhstan in order to settle on a permanent basis."[42]

The law also delegates tasks and duties to various law enforcement institutions. The Ministry of Labor and Social Protection coordinates the repatriation process by organizing quotas, managing the state repatriation fund, supervising housing, employment, and training programs. The Ministry of Foreign Affairs oversees departure procedures from the host-states, while the Ministry of Transport and Communications provides logistical

---

40 Presidential decree no. 2366 on "Implementation of presidential directives on repatriation," July 18, 1995.

41 Diener, "Kazakhstan's Kin-State Diaspora: Settlement Planning and the *Oralman* Dilemma," 339.

42 Article 1(11) of the law on the "Migration of the population," December 13, 1997. The text is available in Russian on the web site of the Kazakh mission to the International Organization for Migration, http://www.iom.kz/index.php?lang=rus&podmenu_id=4&menu_id=3.

support, for instance free flights on the state airline. The Customs Committee ensures the smooth passage of repatriates and their property such as belongings and livestock, and the Ministry of Interior is in charge of processing residency and citizenship documents.[43] Kazakh legislation therefore provides the Oralman with a large range of services to support the repatriation process, from their residence of origin to their final place of destination in Kazakhstan.

Unlike its neighbor, Kyrgyzstan took a longer time to develop a comprehensive legal framework to manage its repatriates. The 2001 presidential decree on support to ethnic Kyrgyz returning to their homeland was a first step toward an official recognition of repatriates, but with no legal status. In 2007, the media reported that 22,800 ethnic Kyrgyz who arrived from Uzbekistan were facing difficulties obtaining Kyrgyz citizenship.[44] Faced with public pressure, the Kyrgyz government finally addressed this gap in the law and developed a legal framework based on the Oralman model. The law on state guarantees to ethnic Kyrgyz returning to their historical homeland was adopted in 2007, with the status of *Kajrylman* (repatriate in Kyrgyz) granted to all "ethnic Kyrgyz migrants (*pereselentsev-etnicheskikh kyrgyzov*) and stateless people of Kyrgyz ethnicity." This status provided all Kajrylman with rights to temporary shelter, free medical care, access to real estate, and Kyrgyzstani citizenship. The law was accompanied by a program that fixed the tasks of the state for the period 2006–8. It consisted of completing the existing legislation on migration, fixing annual quotas of Kajrylman, and conducting information campaigns directed at Kyrgyz communities abroad to explain the legal conditions and their eligibility for repatriation.[45]

Limits and Shortcomings of Repatriation Policies

Despite their willingness to attract co-ethnics from abroad, and the development of legal and institutional frameworks to implement repatriation programs, the diaspora policies of Kazakhstan and Kyrgyzstan remained largely ineffective. The overall figures prove to be limited in comparison

---

43 Cummings, "The Kazakhs: Demographics, Diasporas, and 'Return,'" 142–43.

44 D. Verkhoturov, "Oralman i kairylman," *Zakon.kz*, 2006, http://www.zakon.kz/our/news/news.asp?id=30074316.

45 "Kyrgyzstan: Uzakoneny garantii etnicheskim kirgizam, vozvrashchaiushchimsia na istoricheskuiu rodinu," *Central Asia News*, November 28, 2007, http://www.ferghana.ru/news.php?id=7792; Internet portal of the Kyrgyz government, http://www.gov.kg/modules.php?op=modload&name=News&file=article&sid=2449.

to the repatriation potential. Out of an estimated population of 3.1 million Kazakhs living outside their kin-state, only 430,000 co-ethnics (14 percent) actually moved to Kazakhstan in the period 1991 to 2005.[46] As for Kyrgyzstan, out of a potential of 500,000 co-ethnics abroad, less than 50,000 people (10 percent) left for Kyrgyzstan in the same period, including 16,000 Kyrgyz exiles from Tajikistan. This shortcoming can easily be explained by the fact that both kin-states decided not to extend their diaspora politics to China, Russia, and Uzbekistan, all of which hosted large co-ethnic communities. The Kazakh government, however, launched the new *Nurly Kosh* program ("blessed migration") in 2009, with an ambitious budget of $1.3 billion to accelerate and expand inward migration. The program increases the annual quota of Oralman by a third to 20,000 families over the three-year program, and offers a large range of subsidized services to those who settle in target areas where Kazakhs are in the minority.[47]

A second shortcoming is the lack of equality in the treatment of co-ethnic migrants. Those who enter the country within the limit of annual quotas are automatically granted the status of Oralman in Kazakhstan and Kajrylman in Kyrgyzstan, and they benefit from various state services. However, those who enter their kin-state outside the quota system are not granted this status and cannot therefore enjoy the same rights. In Kazakhstan, some ethnic Kazakhs originating from China even found themselves counted as stateless if they had given up their previous citizenship without being extended Kazakhstani citizenship.[48] Such inequality is even more blatant in Kyrgyzstan between the Kyrgyz refugees from Tajikistan and Kyrgyz migrants coming from other countries of the region, particularly those from Uzbekistan. The former were provided with social programs under the auspices of the international community (food distribution, allocation of land plots, building of houses, schools, health centers, agricultural programs, and so on),[49] while the latter received no assistance. In addition, due to the administrative burden inherited from Soviet rule, most Oralman and Kajrylman did not benefit from the

---

[46] Diener, "Kazakhstan's Kin-State Diaspora: Settlement Planning and the *Oralman* Dilemma," 339.

[47] "Kazakhstan: Astana lures ethnic Kazakh migrants with financial incentives," *Eurasia Insight*, February 27, 2009, http://www.eurasianet.org/departments/insightb/articles/eav022709.shtml.

[48] A. Cerny, "Going where the Grass is Greener: China Kazaks and the *Oralman* Immigration Policy in Kazakhstan," *Pastoralism* 1, no. 2 (2010): 218–247.

[49] Interview with V. Makeev, office for refugee protection, HCR, Osh, Kyrgyzstan, December 13, 2006.

simplified procedures that the law granted them. A large number of repatriates were refused access to real estate and the acquisition of their kin-state's citizenship.[50]

Finally, despite active rhetoric from the Kazakh government on the "ethnic purity" of distant Kazakhs, the anticipated "regeneration" of Kazakh society proved to be simply utopian. The meeting of Kazakhs from Kazakhstan, many of whom were urbanized and largely Russified,[51] with repatriates who spoke Kazakh and were used to living in remote rural areas of Mongolia or Iran, led to mutual cultural misunderstandings. The locals (*mestnye*) regarded the repatriates as backward Kazakhs tied to anachronistic traditions, and referred to them as "those from abroad" (*iz-za rubezha*).[52] Similarly, refugees from Tajikistan to southern Kyrgyzstan encountered Kyrgyz who had been molded by the same Soviet history. Despite the shared Soviet Kyrgyz identity, the two groups had little in common. The refugees from Tajikistan came from multi-ethnic cotton *kolkhozes*, where their language as well as religious and cultural practices had changed. In the meantime, the local population of southern Kyrgyzstan was living in an ethnically homogenous environment. Their unexpected encounter in the context of political transition and economic reform led to competition over scarce natural resources, in particular over access to agricultural land and water. These tensions eventually took the form of cultural intolerance, with the local Kyrgyz refusing to acknowledge that the refugees were descendants of the same ancestors, instead preferring to call them "the Tajiks."[53]

* * * * *

This chapter shows that the triadic nexus between a state, its kin-minority abroad, and the host-state of this minority greatly conditions the development of migration flows. In post-Soviet Central Asia, both the perception of co-ethnic communities abroad and the diaspora politics pursued in relation to these co-ethnics follow three patterns. In Uzbekistan, after a first attempt in the early 1990s to diasporize its kin-minorities abroad, the Uzbek government sought to downplay the significance of its co-ethnics

---

50 "Pomozhet li 'Kairylman,'" *Development and Cooperation in Central Asia*, May 28, 2008, http://www.dcca.kg/?p=60.

51 In 1989, 64 percent of Kazakhstan's Kazakhs declared Russian as their mother tongue or their second language of communication. *Natsional'nyi sostav naseleniia SSSR po dannym vsesoiuznoi perepisi naseleniia 1989 g.*, 102–3.

52 Cummings, "The Kazakhs: Demographics, Diasporas, and 'Return,'" 143–47.

53 Personal observation in the province of Batken, Kyrgyzstan, October 1999.

abroad in public opinion and decided to break all official links with them. This attitude actually conforms with the process of nation-building that Tashkent has developed since independence. Uzbekistan opted for a civic and territorial conception of the state, based on the values of Uzbekness (*O'zbekčilik*), and intended to regroup all those who embraced Uzbek customs and traditions regardless of ethnic belonging.[54] The unity of the Uzbek nation within its territorial boundaries prevailed over diaspora politics that many considered hazardous for state stability. Tajikistan represents a second pattern, based on diasporic rhetoric and institutions aimed at reinforcing the state. However, this half-hearted diaspora politics lacks a clear strategy and the means to encourage actual migration flows. The last pattern is the one developed by Kazakhstan and Kyrgyzstan. It consists of the enforcement of comprehensive repatriation policies, albeit with shortcomings, providing clear legal provisions and the needed funding to implement assistance programs to repatriates.

Repatriation constituted the main form of inward migration in Central Asia during the first years after independence.[55] But this phenomenon is becoming marginal in comparison with the dramatic rise in recent years of the emigration of *gastarbeiter* to Russia. Official statistics reveal a negative migration balance for all Central Asian states, except Kazakhstan since 2004.[56] In Kyrgyzstan, the repatriation of co-ethnics could explain the positive balance of ethnic Kyrgyz in the 1990s (plus 17,219 in 1990–99), but the outflow of migrant workers resulted in a negative balance in the 2000s (minus 46,467 in 2000–7).[57] Therefore, the Kyrgyz population abroad consists of historical minorities, long established in their host-states, and émigré communities who have recently moved in. For instance, in Russia, the two groups coexist but have limited contact. In addition to existing repatriation programs, the Kyrgyz government is trying to cope with this new migration picture. In 2008, the State Committee on Migrations,

---

[54] M. Fumagalli, "Ethnicity, State Formation and Foreign Policy: Uzbekistan and 'Uzbeks abroad,'" *Central Asian Survey* 26, no. 1 (2007): 105–122.

[55] It should be noted, however, that the main form of migration at that time was the outflow of the European ethnic groups (Russians, Ukrainians, Belarusians, Germans, Poles, Jews).

[56] Kazakhstan had a negative migration balance in 2003 (minus 8,306). But the economic boom that the country is experiencing has limited the outflow of Russians and attracted workers from neighboring countries. The balance was plus 69,460 for the period 2004–7. See, Agency of Statistics of the Republic of Kazakhstan, http://www.stat.kz/digital/naselsenie/Pages/default.aspx.

[57] State Committee on Statistics of the Kyrgyz Republic, http://www.stat.kg/rus/part/census.htm.

which was already responsible for the repatriation process of Kajrylman, required all diplomatic missions located in destination regions for Kyrgyz gastarbeiter to appoint an attaché (*trudovoi attashe*) in charge of assisting these migrant workers.[58] It would appear that repatriation programs are now of secondary importance to labor emigration, both in terms of official statistics and the degree of attention that state authorities pay to these social trends.

58 "Svyshe dvukh tysiach etnicheskikh kirgizov-pereselentsev ne imeiut pravovogo statusa," *Central Asia News*, June 5, 2008, http://www.ferghana.ru/news.php?id=9344&mode=snews.

FROM UZBEK *QISHLOK* TO TAJIK SAMARKAND: RURAL DEPOPULATION AS A MIGRATION OF IDENTITY

Sophie Massot

Rural depopulation is characterized as a process that is both historical and political. Since the early 1990s, with the collapse of the Soviet Union, low wages have been insufficient to sustain family needs, and rural infrastructure has crumbled—which has resulted in impassable roads, regular power cuts (in those villages that even have electricity), and no gas or running water in many places. At the same time, Russian and the other so-called European populations migrated on a massive scale, leaving their urban jobs and dwellings vacant. This dual situation accelerated rural depopulation. As A. Le Borgne-David states, "the aim of migration is the search for better living conditions and that improvement is the result of the differences between the conditions of origin and the conditions of destination."[1] However, she adds: "the exchanges of information, the myths vehiculated through migrations, and perceptions are all elements interfering with migratory behaviors."[2] Therefore, this chapter attempts to analyze the transformations of identity achieved by rural Uzbek migrants[3] settling in Samarkand, a town with a strong Tajik identity.[4] These evolutions are principally of two kinds: migrants discovering their "Uzbekness" when coming face to face with other national groups such as Russians and Tajiks; second, in encountering symbols of urbanity, they urbanize their lifestyles and habits in a complex process of distancing themselves from their village customs.

---

[1] A. Le Borgne-David, *Les Migrations paysannes du Sud-Brésil vers l'Amazonie. Le salariat plutôt que la malaria* (Paris: L'Harmattan, 1998), 17.

[2] *Ibid.*

[3] The author studied only the movements of people who declared Uzbek nationality, were born and raised in the countryside, and then moved to Samarkand, where they still live. Therefore, they did not cross state boundaries during their migration. None of the migrants interviewed stopped to reside in another town for any period. Their moving to Samarkand was a long-term settlement. One cannot say that it is permanent, however, not knowing the future wanderings of interviewees, but most of them considered it as such.

[4] O. Roy, *La Nouvelle Asie centrale ou la fabrication des nations* (Paris: Seuil, 1997), 116.

Individual Departures as Family Choices

The vast majority of the male and female migrants interviewed in this study were the youngest in their families. In Uzbekistan, it is customary that the youngest son should remain with his parents to care for them in old age, and inherit their real estate. This can be a problem for families that only have daughters. As B.M. Pétric explains, "The son, *o'gil*, is the one who will ensure descendants and the permanence of the family group."[5] However, in many cases, the youngest son is the one who migrates, leaves his parents, and goes to live in Samarkand, usually permanently. Tradition can therefore be adapted to the post-independence social and economic changes.

Such deviation from social norms may be explained by economic reasons. In villages, families have many children, on average between four and eight. Having numerous children is very costly for parents, particularly when they have to pay for events such as circumcisions and weddings, in addition to hosting hundreds of guests at large festive events. Weddings are thus often celebrated only when the necessary amount of money has been accumulated, which does not always coincide with when the children want to get married. It seems that once the eldest child has married and gained financial autonomy, parents feel freer, knowing that they now need only to organize the wedding of their youngest son or to find a husband for their youngest daughter. They therefore indulge in extra expenses, such as those linked to the departure of the youngest son or daughter to Samarkand to study.

The decision to select the future migrant among siblings is never explicit; the migrant-to-be is rather introduced as "the best pupil" or the one who "always did his homework properly." In many stories, the allegorical figure of a teacher appears, someone who detected exceptional intellectual qualities in the future migrant and encouraged him in his decision to continue his studies. Such codified talk, heard on numerous occasions, obscures the driving force behind the migration—families. The decision to continue one's studies[6] seems indeed to be made, or at least handled,

---

[5] B.M. Pétric, *Pouvoir, don et réseaux en Ouzbékistan post-soviétique* (Paris: PUF, 2002), 62.

[6] Most of the migrants the author met came to Samarkand to study and *not* to find a job. At the end of the eleventh class, young people wishing to continue their studies must take a test on the subjects of history, Russian, or Uzbek, as well as a specialized subject for which they choose to enter university or an institute. The best students are granted a

by the parents as marriages are. Norbek, the head of the Foreign Languages Department at Samarkand Medical Institute, and the eighth and last child of a family from a village in the Koson district (Qarshi region), explained his departure as follows:

> I was eager to go to the Institute and my mother urged me to continue studying French by going to Samarkand. But we knew no one there, and my father was already absent at this time. So, my mother forced my brothers to help me to pay for my studies, for the rent and food expenses, etc. That is how I managed to become a student in Samarkand.

For families, it is a significant investment to have to pay rent, buy food, pay an institute's admission fees, and sometimes even bribe teachers for good grades. Can one then refer to a long-term family investment strategy? When migrants find a job in Samarkand at the end of their studies, it is expected that significant sums of money be remitted back to the families. It would thus appear that this constitutes a collective strategy for social promotion aimed at having at least one family member in a well-paid job. This may explain, among other things, why migrants desire to learn foreign languages, which may give them access to positions that enable interaction with foreigners. However, this investment for the future does not always bear fruit and can be risky. One of the respondents, Alisher, claimed that he had used the money "for nothing," since the son he sent to Samarkand to pursue his studies came back only two years later and was now a farm worker.

The motivations for departure to a city may also take root in a certain social and cultural conception of social promotion. For example, this is what motivated Sobir to leave:

> At first, I was thinking of having the same job as my mother [an Uzbek literature teacher in a village school]. But one day I met a man from the village. Everybody envied him because he behaved properly, was well dressed, etc. So, I asked him why he had changed so much and he answered that he was a student at the Foreign Languages Institute [in Samarkand].

The change of status, from being a pupil in a village to a student in a city, could be enough to induce a conscious change in one's appearance. Moreover, it is interesting to note that when villagers go to Samarkand, they do not dress as they usually do. It was quite surprising to discover

biudzhet (scholarship) so waiving tuition fees; the others are allowed in on *kontrakt*, which means that they have to pay for their studies.

that Ulugbek, when visiting his brother, Istam, in Samarkand, went bareheaded with his hair carefully combed and was dressed in trousers and a jumper that looked brand-new. In his village, he always wears a *duppi* (a sort of cap)[7] and dresses in work clothes that are often torn and splattered with mud. This demonstrates that clothing commonly accepted in the village is not acceptable in the city. Most of the migrants' family members have gone to Samarkand at least once. The Uzbekistanis I met had never travelled as tourists through their own country. They would travel either for trading reasons or to visit acquaintances. As a matter of fact, except for Nodira, who was driven to Samarkand when she was a child once a year to spend a day in a park and have a ride on a merry-go-round, the rest of the migrants' parents had only been to the city to carry out practical tasks or to visit relatives. Migrants arrive in Samarkand filled with assumptions, but discover the city's numerous other aspects.

As R. Descloîtres states in reference to the Ivory Coast, "rural depopulation … underlines, should we need to be reminded, the deep differences between town and countryside. The objective conflicts analyzed by observers and the distinctions experienced by migrants that motivate them make up a body of incentives to leave. It would be vain and surely false to dissociate the economic causes from the social causes. They act together and combine in the migrants' minds … For research convenience, the economic and the social factors can no doubt be separated, even though it must always be taken into consideration that they are interdependent."[8] After the event, many migrants explain their departure in terms of cultural not economic reasons, even though such a discourse is only expressed in Samarkand or during the journey there, never in the village. They list the faults of the village compared to the city: lack of infrastructure, withdrawal of the state, difficult living conditions, the harshness of work in the fields, "villagers' bad habits," and unhealthy lifestyles.

---

[7] In Russian, *tiubeteika*. C. Poujol describes the cap worn by many Uzbeks as "traditional male headgear … often black with white-peppered embroidery to keep the evil eye away," in C. Poujol, ed., *Dictionnaire de l'Asie centrale* (Paris: Ellipses, 2001), 95.

[8] Preface by R. Descloitres in R. Deniel, *De la savane à la ville* (Paris: Aubier-Montaigne, 1968), 10–11.

First Steps toward Ethnic Categorization

The novelty of arriving in the city typically induces feelings of amazement. In particular, one of the most striking elements is the revelation to the migrants of their Uzbek identity. In fact, their arrival in Samarkand puts them face to face with Uzbekistanis expressing different identities, which serve to challenge or reinforce their own. "Uzbekness" was of no importance in their village of origin, since that notion was unanimously shared. Fredrik Barth, in his book *Ethnic Groups and Boundaries*, declares: "Ethnic groups only exist in relation to others... They are defined in relation to the others through a set of cultural differences and similarities."[9]

Uzbekistan has retained Soviet notions of citizenship (*grazhdanstvo*) and nationality (*natsional'nost'*), which are currently listed on Uzbekistani passports. The adjective "Uzbekistani" makes a distinction between citizenship (Uzbekistani) and nationality (Uzbek). Yet as E. Chanudet-Lentz rightly mentions, Uzbekistan since independence, unlike Kazakhstan, has refused to call its citizens "Uzbekistanis." This neologism would enable the state to account for all of its citizens, without any reference to their nationalities and would illustrate the multinational nature of the republic. President Karimov's regime instead chose a middle way, whereby any citizen in Uzbekistan is "Uzbek" in accordance with the name of the country, including non-titular nationalities.[10] Moreover, to the great displeasure of the Russian government and despite the insistence of Andrey Kozyrev, the then foreign affairs minister of the Russian Federation,[11] Karimov refused to allow dual citizenship arguing, "one cannot have two native lands."[12] Although the regulations to obtain citizenship are complex, the regulations to define nationality are particularly flexible—or at least that is what Sobir suggests:

> For instance, if you [the author] were to become an Uzbek, it would be mentioned on your passport that you are of "French nationality." It is the same for Tajiks, Koreans, etc. They are Uzbek citizens but not Uzbeks in their nationality... This declaration is based on people's sincerity. Anyway,

---

9 F.F. Barth, "Les groupes ethniques et leurs frontières," in P. Poutignat and J. Streiff-Fenart, *Théories de l'ethnicité* (Paris: PUF, 1999), 211–212.

10 E. Chanudet-Lentz, *Du plov et des blinis. Les Slaves d'Ouzbékistan : de minorité dominante à minorité dominée* (Paris: Institute of Political Studies, Thesis, 1998), 87.

11 R. Yakemtchouk, *Ouzbékistan : puissance émergente en Asie centrale* (Paris: L'Harmattan, 2003), 97.

12 Islam Karimov cited by Chanudet-Lentz, *Du plov et des blinis*, 87.

> nobody lies because everyone is proud of his nationality. Besides, you can see their nationality on their faces.

The pride mentioned by Sobir suggests that nationality is a stronger identity than citizenship. The statement that nationality "can be seen on people's faces" is also a remark to which one should pay attention. A genuine classification grid does exist, enabling city-dwellers, of whom the migrants are not yet a part upon their arrival in Samarkand, to "recognize" or identify people according to several criteria.

F. Barth expounds on such when he writes: "The features taken into account are not the sum of objective 'differences,' but only the ones considered significant by the protagonists themselves ... The agents use some cultural characteristics as signals and emblems of difference while they do not mention others, and in some relations, radical differences are minimized or denied. The cultural content of ethnic dichotomies can be analyzed within two ranges: 1) obvious signals or signs—the diacritic marks that individuals look for and display to show their identities, such as clothing, language, habitat, or lifestyle as a whole; and 2) trends toward fundamental values: the morality by which acts are judged. Since belonging to an ethnic category infers that one should be a certain type of person, with that fundamental identity, it also suggests that one should accept the right of being judged and to judge others following criteria that are pertinent, as far as that identity is concerned."[13]

Migrants, therefore, learn how to recognize the features of nationality. A set of phenotypic features are used to classify encountered individuals, as my contacts explained to me many times, and they were surprised by the fact that I could not distinguish a Tajik from an Uzbek. "True" Tajiks can be distinguished, it was said, from their dark (black) skin, round eyes, and bushy (particularly thick) eyebrows joining right above the bridge of the nose. One of the students in the Foreign Languages Institute pointed at her eyebrows to show me how "Tajik eyebrows" look, but was offended at my wondering if she was Tajik. In fact, what are presented as typical Tajik features can also be found on the face of an Uzbek girl. Even if one was only to take into account the features considered significant by the actors themselves, national categories are porous, though all are constantly put forward as criteria of distinction. Along with the fact that the Uzbeks recognize Tajiks through these physical features, several Tajik people showed me their faces, and particularly their eyebrows, as a sign

---

13 F.F. Barth, "Les groupes ethniques et leurs frontières," 211–12.

of their nationality. In regard to the other nationalities, pale eyes and fair hair are attributed to Russians and other "Europeans," or to be of short stature means someone is Korean. These phenotypes, however, are not monolithic and variations do appear.

In addition to these phenotypic characteristics used to identify unknown people, other signs help to clarify classification. Some diacritic features are maintained. Accents and spoken language enable one to distinguish Tajiks, Russians, and Koreans. Clothing is also used as an identifier, mainly for Russians who, according to contacts, dress like "Westerners." Distinguishing between nationalities in terms of housing is more difficult. In discussions, "Russian apartments" did exist, but people of all nationalities, not only Russians, live in them. It is common to hear that the Tajiks in Samarkand live in houses overlooking a courtyard, but that this is not necessarily a Tajik specificity. Nodira claimed in fact, "it is our Uzbek tradition to live in houses overlooking courtyards." The argument could thus be put forward that it is only because Tajiks are richer than the Uzbeks that they are able to buy such houses, of which others can only dream.

This whole set of markers, constituting the boundaries between various nationalities, would appear to be particularly important in the city; in villages, on the other hand, migrants had hitherto only been in close contact with other Uzbeks. As J.F. Gossiaux states, "the object to be examined is society and possibly the ethnic groups existing in that society... Ethnic groups only exist in relation to one another."[14] It is insofar as people recognize themselves as belonging to an ethnic group, or are recognized by it, that ethnicity reveals itself through distinctive features, not only phenotypic and diacritic ones, but also those dealing with features of personality attributed to specified identities.

Once in the city, migrants have to learn these codes in order to self-identify as Uzbeks and to be recognized as such, and to be able to identify their interlocutors. In Samarkand, two nationalities have been symbolically dominant in city life, Tajiks and Russians.[15] These two groups are distinguished as being urban: their members are not supposed to live in the countryside; that would be against their "true nature." Even if the two

---

[14] J.F. Gossiaux, *Pouvoirs ethniques dans les Balkans* (Paris: PUF, 2002), 12.

[15] To obtain the 1989 figures on the population of the Samarkand region, cf. chart 1 "La popolazione urbana della regione di Samarkand (1989)," in M. Buttino, "I confini che cambiano: Stato, città, quartiere, casa nell' Asia centrale post-sovietica" (Bolzano: Confini—Grenzen, September 23–25, 2004, Società Italiana per lo Studio della Storia Contemporanea), http://www.sissco.it/ariadne/loader.php/it/www/sissco/attivita/convegni/sem-set-04/buttino/.

groups share the same characteristic of being urban, they maintain great differences. Whereas Russians are supposed to have "different habits" and are largely accepted as not being a part of Uzbek culture, Tajiks are supposed to share a common culture with Uzbeks. The presented differences are aimed at distancing them from one another.

In Samarkand, it is still considered "normal" to speak Russian. Whereas some young non-Russian Uzbekistanis continue to learn Russian, it is extremely rare for Russian children or adults to know the official language of the country where they live. According to E. Chanudet-Lentz, "[their] ignorance of the Uzbek language leads Russians to be excluded from the national life of the republic and reinforces their suspicion of the Uzbeks. Many Slavs are often ill at ease in Uzbek social life, whose traditions they do not understand, and they show some 'irritation' when the local people use their native language."[16] There are apparently very few Uzbek-Russian marriages in comparison to other mixed unions: Uzbek-Tajik, Uzbek-Kyrgyz, and Uzbek-Korean. However, their cultural differences are admitted and are not considered by the Uzbeks as defects. This is what Sobir illustrates so well when he told me:

> Any [non-Russian] woman dressed like that, so scantily clad and with so much make-up, would be thought of badly and have many problems. But with the Russian women, it is different. We do not mind. They do as they like.

Even behavior judged to be shameful is accepted when it concerns Russians, as Nodira stated:

> You know when someone is dead in a Russian family of the neighborhood, they go and talk to the 'head of the house' [appointed by the head of the mahalla to take care of several buildings] so that he can collect money from the neighbors. I always give something. Uzbeks would be ashamed of doing so, because the children of the deceased have to manage to pay for everything by themselves if they do not want to become ridiculed! But the Russians do not have the same traditions as we do.

These differences in customs, accepted in the city, are still viewed as too great to contemplate any union such as marriage. Especially in villages, mixed couples are not viewed favorably. Born in a village but married to Katia, an ethnic Russian, Murad experienced this non-acceptance firsthand:

---

[16] Chanudet-Lentz, *Du plov et des blinis*, 22.

> Villagers are stupid. When they see someone of a different nationality [non-Uzbek], they don't want to accept him or her.

This fact was confirmed to me when Istam confided:

> Alisher told me to be careful about Katia. He advised me not to hire her and to distrust her. The villagers do not like her very much and do not trust her. I am afraid they do not like her because she is Russian.

And so, in the very rare cases when a Russian settles in a village, he or she is regarded with suspicion or even rejected by the inhabitants. In the city, however, migrants discover that relations between Russians and Uzbeks can be more cordial. Nodira, for instance, appreciates the presence of her next-door neighbor, a *babushka* (grandmother), to whom she sometimes leaves the keys of the house when her husband has forgotten them. Even if Uzbeks and Russians live side by side without specific problems within Samarkand, this is not the case in the villages. Moreover, Russians, as Tamara makes clear below, typically have a negative view of Uzbeks coming from the countryside to settle in Samarkand:

> The *qihslok* [village] ... Living there is horrible. I sometimes go there in summer to visit my cousin, who lives there with her parents. The contact with nature is very pleasant. But the living conditions are awful ... I think that the Uzbeks who leave their village to go to Samarkand are mainly young people who come here to study. They are not normal people. They often live on the top floor of the buildings. Many people live in the same room, sometimes ten of them, boys and girls together. Some of them live above my grandmother's flat. She always has to knock on the wall to make them be quiet, because they keep having parties, dancing and singing. That's how it is. They come to town and there's no longer anyone to keep an eye on them, so they do stupid things. And they are often very aggressive because they don't know how to behave in the city, they don't know the rules.

That statement may leave one perplexed, particularly as far as the allusion to the mixing of the sexes in flats is concerned, which is unthinkable for Uzbeks outside the family network. Migrants seem to be aware of this contempt toward them on the part of others, but Istam was dismissive of it, retorting as follows:

> You know, one of our Russian neighbors behaves outrageously. She is a prostitute and she takes people back to her home. I called the police, but they came and I heard them laugh together ... So, in the end, it did not work. I knew that she was afraid of me in the beginning, because I am from a village, so I threatened her with a knife and since then she has been careful. We had Russian neighbors who were complaining about the noise made by Otabek and Gulnoza when they were small children. Then I went downstairs

> to meet them and I pretended I was mad, and I spoke my mind. They think I know nothing about city customs… They're mistaken!

Migrants gradually learn how to master the urban rules and negotiate relations between the inhabitants of Samarkand of various nationalities. Whereas interactions with Russians are based on a boundary that both sides recognize and that cannot be crossed, it would seem that relations between Uzbeks and Tajiks are much more commonplace and fraught with tension, because the barrier between the two groups is more porous.

According to official figures, Tajiks make up 5 percent of the population in Uzbekistan, with most of them concentrated in Bukhara and Samarkand. These figures should be viewed with caution, not only because the identity boundaries between Uzbeks and Tajiks in these two cities are vague, but also because authorities have led a virulent Uzbekization policy toward Tajiks by inviting them to declare themselves as Uzbeks.[17] The fact that President Karimov was born in Samarkand incites fierce debate between inhabitants, who often discuss whether the head of state in fact conceals his Tajik origin. The cohabitation and relationship of the two nationalities is strained. An Uzbek saying illustrates the nature of these relations well: "If your friend is Tajik, buy an axe." This saying has a variant: "If your friend is Tatar, buy an axe." After relating these two versions to me, Sobir explained:

> The Russians, we don't mind them. We are indifferent to their behavior; we've got nothing to say about that. Nevertheless, they are very different from us. On the contrary, with Tatars and Tajiks, who are Muslims as we are and who have almost the same customs, things don't always go well!

During the Soviet period, the Uzbeks from the villages seemed to be reluctant to go to the city, in particular to Samarkand, among other reasons because of the large-scale presence of Tajiks, as Sobir recounted:

> When I still lived in the village, I happened to go to Samarkand two or three times to make some purchases. At the markets, there were only Tajik shopkeepers. With them, it is always the same thing: I wanted to get information on the price of an item, but the shopkeeper pretended he could not hear properly. So I spoke louder and in the end he managed to answer, announcing an outrageous price that he knew I could not pay! So I learned how to ask for prices in Tajik, but anyway I couldn't go on talking, and in the end it

---

[17] Figures for 1999–2000 mentioned by M.R. Djalili and T. Kellner, *Géopolitique de la nouvelle Asie centrale* (Paris: PUF, 2003), 35.

> changed nothing. They despised us, and it was like this for all Uzbek villagers, because they didn't want us to come to Samarkand.

The situation has changed, however. Since 1991, the tendency toward "nationalization" has emboldened Uzbeks to regard it as their right to live in Samarkand. As B.M. Pétric explains, "in Uzbekistan ... a few groups that would like to be referred to as 'Uzbeks' have to cope with some resistance from the new social forces embodied by the 'Uzbekization' policy of society. It is particularly true in Samarkand and Bukhara, for example, where, in recent years, a massive migration of the Uzbek population coming from the villages has occurred. These newcomers find themselves in social competition with the Tajik-speaking population traditionally settled in the city."[18] Thus, the collapse of the Soviet Union enabled the Uzbeks to put the Tajiks, now obliged to cohabit with the Uzbeks coming from the countryside, "back in their place." This spurred a historical and political dispute, something which my contacts were keen to debate. For instance, Istam explained:

> The Tajiks believe that they were the first inhabitants of Samarkand, since they settled there during the Sogdian period [populations settled in Sogdian during the pre-Islamic period]. But we [Uzbeks] like to joke at that and say that if they were there, it was as the Persian slaves of Tamerlane. More seriously, they were better settled in Samarkand because they were sedentary traders whereas the Uzbeks were semi-nomadic.

Nodira claimed: "now, we [Uzbeks] are more numerous than they are. They can no longer do what they want." It is impossible to get figures as far as conflicts between the groups are concerned, but it is clear that some male Uzbeks are fond of recounting and boasting about their feats in street fights with Tajiks. Istam, who at the end of festive family meals enjoyed reminiscing about these "beautiful fights," justified his actions to me as follows: "It's not my fault, they get on my nerves. When I have drunk a little and I meet one of them, I can't help hitting him." After a fight with some Tajiks that nearly went badly, Nodira took away the knife he always kept on him to avoid worse outcomes. "Anyway, he is racist," she told me in French so that he could not hear.

This racism, should we quote Nodira, does not convey a belief in a link between typical physical features (round eyes or thick eyebrows) and a specific nationality, for the use of phenotypes for identification purposes

---

[18] B.M. Pétric, "Uzbekistan ne iavliaetsia obshchestvom, osnovannym na printsipe etnichnosti. No mozhet takovym stat'," *Etnograficheskoe obozrenie*, no. 1 (2005): 88.

is not viewed as racist in Uzbekistan. Racism consists of hating people because of their nationality. In spite of the tensions, it cannot be said that any deep racism is at play in Uzbek-Tajik relations in Samarkand. Mixed marriages are not rare and are only denigrated in the case of divorce, as another interviewee Lobar explained:

> I married a Tajik soldier. My mother-in-law was a monster. She was always behind me checking if the housework was done well and all that. One day I went to the market with a friend. And there, I saw my husband with his lover…He was buying her a dress. We divorced. I was granted alimony. I live at my mother's with my son and my sister. It's a bit hard, but with my mother's retirement pension and our two salaries, my sister's and mine, we make do. But I shouldn't have married a Tajik, they are too unfaithful.

In fact, the unfaithfulness of Tajik men is a recurring theme. Lobar's ex-husband has the double "disadvantage" of being both Tajik and a soldier; soldiers as well as policemen are seen as being unfaithful. This double "negative" means that the behavior of the wife is not called into question because her fate of being abandoned was inevitable. Nevertheless, some Uzbek women are happy to be married to a Tajik man. Khilola, the wife of a Tajik, explained as follows:

> My husband [a Tajik] fell in love with me when I was a student because he was a shopkeeper next to the [Foreign Languages] Institute. Every day he saw me passing by and found me to be pretty. He sent his ambassadors [people from the suitor's family who come to ask for the young woman's hand] to my parents and we married. My in-laws are Tajik and live here [in the building adjoining hers, both overlooking a common yard]. My mother-in-law is kind to me; I have no problems. Since I came here, they have been speaking Uzbek together. But the rest of the family does not agree with that. When they are around, they want to speak Tajik.

The good relationship between Khilola and her mother-in-law is notable. Conflicts between mothers-in-law and their *kelin* (daughters-in-law) are the cause of many divorces, as the new brides experience difficulty putting up with the authority of their mothers-in-law. The fact that Khilola's parents got in to the habit of speaking Uzbek is rather amazing. Even though all Tajiks living in Samarkand understand and often speak Russian and Uzbek, with an apparently typical and easily recognizable accent, it is surprising that Khilola's in-laws have adopted the use of the Uzbek language in the domestic realm. It is also interesting to note that Khilola is said to look like her father, because he has "Tajik eyes," as if nationality were passed on more by the father than by the mother in mixed marriages between Uzbeks and people of other nationalities.

I heard of several mixed marriages with Tajiks and they were all between female Uzbeks and male Tajiks. However, they only concerned Uzbek girls who had been born in Samarkand, not migrants. Conversely, in the villages I visited, I met just one example of such a mixed marriage (between an Uzbek man and Tajik woman), which was commented on at length during alcohol-fueled evening parties:

> Murad: Look how black he is, Sophie! [He points to one of the men sitting by him, who is throwing the dice to play *narda*, equivalent of the Turkish "tric-trac."] We call him black dog [*chernaia sobaka*], don't we? [Laughs. The designated man shows his fist, smiling, obviously amused.] You must take him back to France, because you've got plenty of Blacks over there!
>
> Ulugbek: Moreover, you know, his wife is Tajik! From Tajikistan! She is almost as black as he is! [Laughs.]
>
> Man in Question: Yes, it's true. She comes from over there, in the mountains [he points in a certain direction]. Over there, they wear feathers on their heads and dance shouting "Wahoo! Wahoo!" [At this point he mimics Indians, patting his mouth while shouting at the same time, and then he laughs with the other guests.]

It is interesting to note that the woman mentioned above is Tajik and from Tajikistan, meaning that she is or was a Tajikistani citizen. Uzbek stereotypes are such that all Tajiks from Tajikistan are "black-skinned because they are used to living in the mountains. Only those living in Dushanbe look like the Tajiks here [from Samarkand]," according to Nodira's fellow workers. And thus, as I traveled with some other local students, they would hide from the sun, explaining that they did not want to "become black." The typical features of the Tajiks in Samarkand are thus very different from those of the Tajiks in Tajikistan, according to Uzbek migrants. Whereas the latter are viewed as rustic, black-skinned mountain-dwellers of savage appearance, the former are seen as merchants who have always been involved in trade, have a passion for gold, harbor ambitions to grow richer, and hold contempt for the poor.

There is a hierarchy in nationalities and citizenships, which can be seen in the "hypogamic"[19] marriages of men. Thus, Tajik men of Samarkand can marry Uzbek women born in Samarkand, and Uzbek men in villages can marry Tajik women from Tajikistan. However, it is unlikely that a Tajik man from Samarkand could marry a rural Uzbek girl, or that

---

[19] A union is called "hypogamic" when it involves a partner considered to be of a higher social rank. Here, the wife has a lower social status than her husband.

an Uzbek man could marry a Tajik girl from the city. There is an implicit hierarchy from the most urban to the most rural, or from the most to the least "civilized": Tajiks of Samarkand, Uzbeks of Samarkand, migrants, rural Uzbeks, and finally Tajiks from Tajikistan. This classification, tacitly shared and admitted to by everyone, enables men to marry a woman from a different nationality who is from a social rank immediately below his, and living in the same area (urban or rural).

None of the migrants that I met had married a Tajik (male or female). It is left to question whether the identity of migrants lies at the boundary between the urban and rural, between Samarkand and the village, belonging to neither. When arriving to the city from their villages, they are considered, or rather derogatorily viewed to be, backward "villagers." But while the Tajiks of Samarkand would look down on recently arrived migrants (and their incomprehension of the Tajik language), they seem to fear the Uzbeks remaining in the villages. Two migrants, Rasul and Norbek, said to me:

> Most of the taxi drivers working in Samarkand are Ironis [Bukharan and Samarkandi Shiite minority] or Tajiks. But those driving to villages or other regions are only Uzbeks, because Tajiks fear the villagers, they feel threatened because they think that villagers are brutes!

The hierarchy between Uzbek and Tajik nationalities, and between life in Samarkand and the villages, is not as inflexible as it seems. In fact, the migrants do have access to urban attributes and integrate them as their identities evolve. Nodira claimed that Tajik shopkeepers sometimes think she is Tajik and that she goes along with it so as to get better prices. Several times when I was with her, shopkeepers asked her if she was from Tashkent, even more of an urban center than Samarkand. On another occasion, when she had bought clothes at Siob Market and quickly put them on to go to work, her colleagues wondered whether they were presents she had received from France to which she replied yes. Thus, it would seem that she has acquired the look of a city woman—either Tajik, or from Tashkent or France—that in any case differs from her former identity—that of an Uzbek woman from a village.

Breaking Free from the Village and Realizing Urbanity

Migrants are proud of the fact that they no longer have to work in the fields. During the interviews, a keen awareness emerged of "being lucky" not to have remained in the village and become a farmer, judged as an exhausting and unrewarding occupation. Expressions like "being broken" or "tired out" were used to describe their ageing parents, physically marked by years of work in the fields. However, it is necessary to distinguish between what Marcel Mauss calls "body techniques"[20] and the physical marks due to a repetitive activity. On this topic, Mauss wrote: "I believe that the fundamental training regarding these (body) techniques consists in making one's body adapt to that use."[21] Both enable us to distinguish the migrants from their families of origin.

Body techniques have adapted to the migrants' new ways of life, for example sleep and rest.[22] Consequently, migrants have got used to sleeping in a bed with a mattress and no longer on the floor on a blanket (*kurpocha*), as they used to do in the villages. When Alisher visited his brother in Samarkand and inadvertently fell asleep on the sofa while watching television, he complained of a sore back after waking, claiming to have "not slept well." If Istam happens to lie on the floor with a cushion under his elbow to watch television after dinner and falls asleep, he quickly wakes up and then lies on his son's bed or sofa, as he is no longer used to sleeping on the floor. In the same way, Istam and Nodira always sit at a table for meals, either in the kitchen or in the living room when they have guests. When villagers are around, they do not feel at ease and sit on wooden chairs. Nodira often whispered in my ear when we had dinner in the village sitting on cushions on the floor: "I'll soon have to get up. I can't stand sitting like this for hours! My knees get really too painful." Old habits are thus forgotten and have given way to new body techniques deemed better suited to urban life.

Moreover, bodily attributes enable the identification of a certain person, as mentioned previously when referring to phenotypes. They are not only used to distinguish one nationality from another; in villages, they are used to recognize a rural worker from a city-dweller. Hands can tell a lot about someone—in particular, the way they are placed on the body is open to deciphering. Thus, when he is walking in his village, Alisher joins his hands together at his back. On one occasion, Ulugbek pointed at him, and laughingly told me, "He is a *bobo*!" (grandfather, or a respected

20 See "Les techniques du corps," in M. Mauss, *Sociologie et anthropologie* (Paris: puf, 2001), 365–386.

21 *Ibid.*, 385.

22 *Ibid.*, 378–379.

man). (Actually, as one of the eldest brothers in his family he *was* a bobo[23] and was head of a mahalla.) The hands themselves also reveal the activities they practice. A Russian proverb has it that "white hands love other people's work" and this is what Nodira's sisters certainly thought when she and Istam were away studying for which their families had to pay. Nodira explained to me that farm work makes hands rough, dry, and sunburned. On the contrary, city women, who supposedly do not have arduous jobs and have fewer household tasks to carry out, maintain their physical appearance more in accordance with the beauty standards currently accepted in Samarkand. They also have the opportunity to take greater care of their appearance, with creams, especially hand creams, being considered very trendy in town.

A body "shaped" to become more beautiful is a source of pride for migrant women. One of their concerns is remaining slim, which is contrary to Uzbek notions of beauty, which instead dictate that women should be plump. Nodira, led by an Uzbek neighbor, went regularly to a gym, in the beginning without telling her husband, Istam. When she announced her decision to practice a sport, he responded that it was a waste of money: "just keep walking quickly and walk to work, that will be sport." But behind the financial argument, there was a reluctance of another type, as I discovered during a meal in a restaurant:

> Istam: Come on Sophie! Slim women are not so pretty. You should get fatter! You know, in Uzbekistan we like good healthy girls who eat a lot!
>
> Abdukodir: That's your opinion! I prefer slim girls to the stout ones in the village. [Laughs.]
>
> Istam: It's true that girls here [in Samarkand] look prettier, anyway!

Female bodies are not viewed and taken care of in the same way in cities as they are in villages: instead of "instruments" for work, they become objects to which they pay attention. Women in the city also have more access to medicines and treatment. Residents of Samarkand have better access, compared to the surrounding villages, to specialists (dentists and gynecologists) and enjoy superior facilities (clinics and hospitals). And

23 Alisher was the second oldest brother in the family; he had an elder brother Bahtier. However, the latter was actually a half-brother, since he was from the first marriage of his mother, who, on the advice of her parents-in-law, divorced her first husband because of Bahtier's paralysis. Remarrying, the mother's second husband accepted the child and brought him up "like his son." The villagers apparently do not remember the adoption or the secret was well kept, since everyone considers him to be the eldest brother.

though such a matter is difficult to discuss during interviews, it emerged out of Nodira's confidences that the notion of female sexual pleasure is unthinkable in the villages whereas, even though this remains a taboo subject, city women secretly allude that there are some postures that could be more favorable to sexual pleasure than others. As a matter of fact, the woman appointed by Nodira's mother to teach her how to prepare for the wedding night (by removing unwanted hair "from the place you know where") gave her no other details, assuming that as she had been living in Samarkand she certainly "knew these sorts of things." In sum, bodies, especially those of women, are loaded with new symbolic weight in the city; their external transformations enable identification and differentiation between people from the city and those from the villages.

As Descloîtres remarks in regard to migration to the city in the Ivory Coast, there is an "aspiration for improved conditions on the one hand, and for a new way of being as well. The interdependence between economic needs and social motives can be found again here. As a matter of fact, the city means, first of all, for a good many people, and at the most superficial level of social life, new food and dress ... techniques associated with new attitudes that will involve individuals much more. Moreover, the relative uniformity of the habits and customs in town will consolidate the integration of new city dwellers in a group that exceeds ethnic specificities."[24] As far as migration toward Samarkand is concerned, these ethnic specificities are actually preserved and even deliberately emphasized. But such uniformity of habits and customs in the city is effectively relative, since each person's behavior reveals their identities. However, there are more specific urban traits, though not all people living in the city possess them, which embody a form of attractive modernity that cannot be found in villages and to which many inhabitants of Samarkand—whether Russian, Uzbek, Tajik, or other—aspire.

Clothes, explored below, further add to the attraction of physical appearance. What is more, possessing an array of accessories seems necessary if one is to be viewed as the "perfect" city dweller. Sobir's decision to come and study in Samarkand was, among other factors, motivated by meeting a well-dressed migrant. To be well dressed means the possession of new and trendy clothing. What is considered to be such is mainly defined by what people wear in the streets and what is sold in shops. Russian television channels that broadcast Western films are sometimes

---

24 Preface by R. Descloitres in Deniel, *De la savane à la ville*, 15–16.

sources of inspiration. Whereas men's fashion seems rather constant, the textures, patterns, and colors of the fabrics that are used by Uzbek women to make their dresses change very rapidly. It is interesting to notice that when they go back to their villages of origin, young female migrants dress "like the village girls," or in the so-called traditional Uzbek dress and with their hair tied back. One of them, Ozoda, told me that she does this so that the neighborhood is unable to claim that she is disrespectful of Uzbek customs. On the other hand, when she goes to a village that is not hers, like when she went to Kholida's engagement party, she dresses "like a boy" in trousers as she does in Samarkand.

In Samarkand, competition to be at the forefront of fashion is not optional. Nodira told me several times that she had to put some make-up on if she did not want to be criticized by her colleagues at work. She carefully chooses the clothes she wears before going out. She told me she liked to feel pretty and to regularly buy new clothes. If her husband disapproves of the expenses, she either says it is a present from a friend of hers or that a friend lent her the clothes, expressing her desire that she would like to buy the same thing herself. Sometimes these purchases prove unusable. This was the case with a pair of high-heeled shoes she had bought a year previously, which she had never dared to take out of the closet for fear of "being ashamed to go out with them on"; this was partly based on Istam's possible reaction—he might be resentful that his wife, already a tall woman, would stand a head taller than him. Whereas women migrants dress in a very different way from their parents in the village, or at least consider themselves to be fashionable women, their freedom in this realm is not complete. They cannot not allow themselves to dress "like Russians," for instance, for fear of being harassed.

Clothing is an important marker for migrants that allows them to identify both villagers and other non-Uzbek inhabitants of Samarkand. Other material indicators of having changed location and way of life also exist; these are not only a distinguishing feature of migrants but of city dwellers as a whole. For example, migrants' belongings serve as symbols of modernity and of social success. The most obvious are mobile phones. Even if not ringing, they are always exposed to view, often attached to a belt. Possessing a mobile phone is unquestionably a sign of prestige. Another such indicator of social status is having a lot of keys. While in the villages keys are separated (when there are several keys) and hidden in a place known only to family members (like under a carpet or above a door), migrants' keys are most often grouped together on a key ring, including keys to the migrants' flats, most often "Russian apartments," and also car keys. Indeed, this latter purchase bears the advantage of being highly visible to all, particularly the neighborhood, which is the main vehicle of information to the mahalla and carves out reputations. Arriving in one's home village in one's own car is a major source of pride for migrants like Istam, who loved repeating to me: "I care a lot about [my car] because it's my second wife."

These various possessions—mobile phones, Russian apartments, and cars—are the ceremonial outfits of the migrants and the tokens of their social rise; they enjoy exhibiting them when they come back to their villages of origin in order to showcase their success. Nevertheless, these indicators of social ascent seem also to bear the stamp of individualism. As H. Fathi underlines, it is usually the case in Uzbekistan that "at the social or the moral level, individuals do not exist as such. They depend not only on the neighborhood, but above all on their own families."[25] The migrants, however, are undermining and overturning this tradition. They no longer possess family objects, just personal ones; they no longer share their flats with their relatives; and by owning cars they can also avoid public transport. By climbing up the social ladder, which sees them leave their villages to live in the city, migrants discover they are singular beings and no longer just the members of a line of descendants. This, obviously, does not much please their parents who adhere more to tradition.

Acquiring the whole array of accessories undoubtedly gives migrants real prestige when they are back in their villages of origin. However, as R. Deniel specifies, "on the whole, although being rich and powerful enables a rise above the ordinary and is a coveted position, it is risky as well. In that position, one attracts to oneself the resentment not only of one's enemies, but those favored as well."[26] Indeed, showing off one's wealth does not assure only the bestowal of blessings on the migrant. If they want to avoid villagers' opprobrium, they must not be too overbearing in flaunting themselves to their relatives. The migrants' visits, though apparently welcomed with pleasure by their families, are also the root of jealousy. Incessant, envious looks at their prestigious set of accessories can occasionally prove harmful. By coming back to their villages, the migrants undergo the risk of being looked at too much and attracting the evil eye.

---

[25] H. Fathi, *Femmes d'autorité dans l'Asie centrale contemporaine. Quête des ancêtres et recompositions identitaires dans l'islam postsoviétique* (Paris: Maisonneuve & Larose—IFEAC, 2004), 204.

[26] Deniel, *De la savane à la ville*, 84–85.

* * * * *

Pressed by their families to leave their native villages, the migrants find themselves in a world with new social codes. They discover that they are Uzbek through the glances of other Uzbekistani city dwellers, and through this discovery find "externality." They learn how to categorize the people they meet in Samarkand according to their "ethnic types." For migrants, becoming a Samarkandi means both learning how to move in non-homogeneous (in terms of nationality) circles that differ from the *qishloq* and obtaining the necessary indicators to prove their own urban credentials. Nevertheless, migrants still attach the greatest importance to their rural origin, which is the primordial facet of their identity. In Samarkand that identity is negatively perceived by some who feel that migrants are uncouth people who do not know city customs, but it is well received by others who seek to integrate groups for the promotion of regional solidarity. These groups are particular in that they gather only people originating from certain districts (who were previously unknown to one another), owing their acquaintance to the fact that they came to Samarkand.

Migrants' identities are constructed both by references to their native places of origin and also by the hallmarks of newly acquired urbanity. Visits to the villages allow one to understand this second dimension, because it is during family reunions that the changes in the migrants' attitudes are most evident and when migrants direct their own roles. The traditional family hierarchy and household organization is subsequently undermined, caused by this change in the status of migrants. In sum, their social and economic rise leads to visible consequences both in the city of Samarkand and in the surrounding villages.

ECONOMIC MIGRATIONS FROM UZBEKISTAN TO MOSCOW, SEOUL, AND NEW YORK: SACRIFICE OR RITE OF PASSAGE?

Sophie Massot

"Going abroad for a better life in Uzbekistan." This paradoxical phrase from an Uzbek migrant interviewed in New York sums up perfectly what is at stake in emigration flows from Uzbekistan. For migrants, the main rationale for leaving their families behind is to temporarily work abroad, where they expect to take advantage of significantly higher salaries than those available in their country of origin, before then returning to Uzbekistan. This leads to a migratory loop, each step of which is essential for understanding the present cultural, social, economic, and political issues of the country.

Population movements from contemporary Uzbekistan to Moscow, Seoul, and New York form part of a complex set of issues, which stem from historical and recent events. As part of Turkistan during the Czarist Empire and the Soviet Union during the twentieth century, before declaring independence in 1991, Uzbekistan has experienced many political, economic, social, and cultural changes, of which migration has been one result. This challenges the demographic balance of a republic in continuous transformation.

The migratory phenomenon—which cannot be comprehended through a statistical approach since the flows escape official censuses—redefines the identity of the migrants, the social organization of the family, district, and town, as well as the political links between Uzbekistan and the destination countries for migrants. All are interwoven to create an amorphous web that constitutes a real challenge for researchers.

This chapter focuses on the contemporary labor migration of Uzbeks to Moscow, Seoul, and New York. It employs a political science approach as well as utilizes the fields of sociology and ethnology in the methods used.[1] The objective is to elaborate what the migration phase represents for its participants. Some view it as a "familial sacrifice"; in other words,

[1] Preliminary fieldwork conducted in Uzbekistan in July–August 2005, in Moscow in April–May 2006, in Seoul in July–August 2006, in New York in February–March 2007, and in Uzbekistan in April–May 2007.

migration bears the characteristics of a rite of passage, which can be divided into three phases according to the model of Arnold Van Gennep.[2] To carry out this study, field research consisted primarily of interviews with would-be migrants in Uzbekistan, migrants in the three host cities above, and migrants who had returned to their country of origin.

The Causes of Emigration

The year 1991 is an obviously pivotal date in the history of the former Soviet republics in general, and in the study of international migration from Uzbekistan in particular. Prior to its dissolution, the 15 republics of the Soviet Union represented a single territory in which any bearer of a Soviet passport could move with relative freedom. The borders between the republics did not represent a major administrative obstacle. A popular song of this period encapsulated this: "My address is the USSR."[3] The fall of the Soviet Union, however, transformed the status of the internal borders into international borders of new states. In thus doing, the territorial limits established by Stalin were maintained, as was true of the entire post-Soviet space, in creating the republics of Kazakhstan, Kyrgyzstan, Tajikistan, Uzbekistan, and Turkmenistan. The border issue inherited from the Soviet period proves particularly problematic in this part of the world, as the territories of the five states are closely interwoven with the existence of a number of enclaves.[4]

In addition, 1991 signaled an opening up beyond the former Soviet bloc.[5] The gates of an up-to-then inaccessible world opened and migratory strategies could begin to take shape. Although it is now officially possible to travel overseas, reaching some countries is harder than others, due to the costs of transport and the administrative barriers established in order to regulate the number of migrants. Many Uzbekistanis actually feel that

---

[2] A. Van Gennep, *Les rites de passage. Etude systématique des rites* (Paris: A.J. Picard, 1981).

[3] "Moi adres—Sovetskii soiuz" is a popular song from the Brezhnev era by the Russian pop group *Samosvety*.

[4] Cf. E. Gonon and F. Lasserre, "Une critique de la notion de frontières artificielles à travers le cas de l'Asie centrale," *Cahiers de Géographie du Québec* 47, no. 132 (2003): 433–461; J. Thorez, "Enclaves et enclavement dans le Ferghana post-soviétique," *Cahiers d'Etudes sur la Méditerranée et le Monde Turco-Iranien (CEMOTI)*, no. 35 (2003): 28–39.

[5] Cf. A. de Tinguy, *La Grande Migration. La Russie et les Russes depuis l'ouverture du rideau de fer* (Paris: Plon, 2004), 23–147.

their freedom of movement has been reduced compared to the Soviet era. Whereas they could previously travel almost throughout the entire Soviet Union, they now feel under "house arrest" as a result of financial and visa-related barriers. They are also overwhelmed by the deterioration in their living conditions and the rapid impoverishment that the government of Islam Karimov, in power since 1989, has seemed unable to tackle.

President Karimov has had to face the same dilemma as the other leaders of former Soviet republics—that is, how to manage the transition to a free market economy.[6] The intensive cultivation of cotton established during the Soviet era has continued and, together with gold, constitutes one of the main resources of the country. As L. Bazin[7] emphasizes, "the term 'gradual transition' toward a free market economy is put forward to justify the economic politics carried out... Actually, the economy is still submitted to the punctilious control of the public authorities or their officials." Thus, this gradualism obscures a certain inertia as far as reforms are concerned.

Many Uzbekistanis hold a certain nostalgia for the Soviet period when, according to them, there was enough work for everyone, efficient and accessible schools and medical equipment existed, salaries ensured an acceptable standard of living, water, gas, and electricity were provided without frequent outages, and roads were well maintained. Since 1991, if the contacts for this study are to be believed, and on which point they were fairly unanimous, citizens have witnessed their progressive impoverishment and a significant decline in their purchasing power.[8] Unemployment affects 35 percent of the "working-age population."[9] Although an August 2007 decree[10] allowed for a 25 percent rise in salaries, it has not

[6] Cf. S. Peyrouse, "Les années d'indépendance (1991–2007)," Chapter 6, in P. Chuvin, R. Létolle, and S. Peyrouse, *Histoire de l'Asie centrale contemporaine* (Paris: Fayard, 2008), 175–195.

[7] L. Bazin, "Travail, État et dépendances: Quelques aperçus ethnologiques de la circulation monétaire en Ouzbékistan," http://halshs.archives-ouvertes.fr/docs/00/11/12/07/PDF/Bazin_2006_Travail_dep_Uzb.pdf.

[8] The cost of living in Uzbekistan was calculated at 291.34 soums per person per month (including food, social services, and urban transport) in 2007. Clothes, leisure, and travel were not included in this figure. Estimates proposed by *UzMetronom.com*, translated and presented in French by the Internet site of the French Embassy of Uzbekistan, http://www.ambafrance-uz.org/article.php3?id_article=357.

[9] Figure given by the representative of the European Union in Uzbekistan. Cf. H. Rousselot, *Deutsche Welle*, cited in "Le taux de chômage en Ouzbékistan serait de 35 percent," April 27, 2006, http://www.regard-est.com/home/breves.php?idp=487&PHPSESSID=eaa.

[10] "Salaries in Uzbekistan set to increase 25 percent on average from August 1," Uzbek government web site, July 13, 2007, http://www.gov.uz/en/content.scm?contentId=28401.

been sufficient to keep pace with rapid inflation. The rise in prices has been particularly noticeable in the last decade and the real-estate sector has experienced inflation that makes it difficult for many Uzbekistanis to purchase or rent accommodation. Daily purchases made at markets cruelly reveal to consumers the meaning of inflation; the prices of some products may double from one day to the next, and the cost of meat has become out of reach for many households.

Emigration, then, appears as a means of obtaining better living conditions. It is a strategy that is most often familial in nature, enabling a brighter future for the family member that moves abroad and also, through the money earned, hopefully improving the lot of the family left behind. Thus, to reiterate, the push factors in Uzbekistan are mainly due to the economic difficulties rampant in the country since independence.

Characteristics of Migrants and their Migratory Destinations

Most migrants are male, which induces an important demographic disparity, since some rural regions are now short of men. Many Uzbekistanis mention this depopulation in certain places, like in Samarkand, where Nodir[11] lamented, "Only women, children, and old aged people are left." This mostly male migration can be explained through cultural factors. Women stay at home to take care of housework and children while their husbands are supposed to support their families by bringing back wages. It would be out of place for a young woman to break social convention by going abroad where her "honor" could be tainted, affecting the reputation of her family. The large-scale migratory phenomenon—up to 30 percent of the working-age population could be involved—does not encompass only one generation but the entire active population; migrants I met were between 17 and 57 years of age. However, it affects neither the richest, who do not feel the need to leave their country for economic reasons, nor the poorest, who cannot afford the costs associated with emigrating. Another characteristic of migrations is that the migrants view them as temporary; their aim is just to save enough money to allow their families to have a "better life." They are for the most part former villagers—but also city dwellers wishing to improve their standard of living—who wish to earn

[11] The names used in this chapter are pseudonyms in order to respect the anonymity of my contacts.

and save money abroad that will allow them to live in the city once they return to Uzbekistan.

In order to carry out this research, I chose to consider three cities of immigration that, along with Kazakhstan, are among the main destinations for labor migration: Moscow, Seoul, and New York. Russia has very close links with the former Soviet republics and is in need of foreign labor since its own population, undergoing radical demographic decline, does not have the capacity to meet demand. No visa is required for Uzbek nationals but, like all foreigners, they are required to register with the authorities within three days of arrival. However, due to administrative harassment and rampant xenophobia, it is quite often difficult for them to meet this regulation.

Since its startling industrial boom, South Korea has signed bilateral agreements with various states, including Uzbekistan, to obtain cheap labor. At present, many ethnic Koreans live in Uzbekistan; formerly settled in the Russian Far East, many were deported to Uzbekistan under Stalin's rule. South Korea represents a kind of Eldorado for Uzbek migrants, who consider it is easy to find a well-paid job in the capital, Seoul. Many, furthermore, do not hesitate to stay and work in the country illegally.

Migrants to the United States, meanwhile, exemplify the American dream. It is particularly difficult to enter the country from Uzbekistan: usual demands for visas are very often refused. As a result, a real traffic in invitations is currently underway in Uzbekistan, where candidates for migration shell out very significant sums of money with the hope of entering the country. Once they have obtained the precious "open sesame," some of them stay illegally in the United States, even though their visas have expired.

A Family Decision

Before examining the above in more detail, it is worth considering the decision-making processes that drive migrants to leave their countries of origin. As a social group, the family is governed by tacit regulations and organized into a coded hierarchy of roles. Some members defer in authority and obedience to others, following a social logic that seems inflexible. Generally in Uzbekistan, younger family members are required to show respect to elders, which is moreover expressed in forms of address.

Article 66 of Uzbekistan's constitution, in a section entitled "Family," sheds light on the importance of the family unit in Uzbekistan, by stating that "Children who are of age and apt to work must take care of their parents"[12] and secure for them sufficient material comfort. A perpetuation of the tradition of the youngest child providing assistance to his parents can be observed, albeit in new forms. The youngest child no longer gives assistance by being present at their side, but sends money from abroad to secure them a decent income.

The final "blessing" to leave lies with the migrant's parents. However, this does not signify the passivity of the migrant-to-be, but rather his ability to participate in the decision, "emphasiz[ing] the relative autonomy of the actors who are never the passive objects of the situations that they are facing, even though these situations are characterized by relationships of power and domination."[13] Is it possible, then, to go as far as observing a family strategy of long-term investment? The question is a pertinent one because when a migrant finds a job abroad, a significant part of the money accrued is intended to be remitted back to his family. While there appears to be no apparent connection between the heads of the mahalla and migratory strategies, it is nonetheless clear that the society as a whole applies pressure on families. For instance, every family is obliged to celebrate the wedding of their child. As weddings are mass participatory occasions and therefore costly, money needs to be raised, with migration constituting a means to achieve this.

The three destination countries mentioned above are expected to provide migrants with a better salary than in their country of origin, and the migrants' families often choose between these destinations in accordance with their financial capacity. It is, therefore, difficult to speak about a true "choice" of destination, it depending instead on the sum of money the family is able to accumulate. The more loans they receive, the higher the migrants will be able to rise on the destination scale: Moscow for the least funded, Seoul for those who have managed to rally a social network, and New York for the richest. These degrees of investment are related to a wage hierarchy. It is often heard that, among the three destinations, the lowest wages are in Moscow (200 to 400 dollars per month), intermediate wages in Seoul (800 to 1,000 dollars), and the highest in New York (1,000 to

---

[12] *The Constitution of the Republic of Uzbekistan: Adopted December 8, 1992, at the eleventh session of the Supreme Soviet of the Republic of Uzbekistan of the Twelfth Legislature* (Tashkent, 1992), 19.

[13] V. de Rudder, I. Taboada-Leonetti, and F. Vourch, *Stratégies d'insertion et migration* (Paris: CNRS-IRESCO, 1989), 3.

2,000 dollars). Thus, the larger the initial investment, the more significant the expected economic gains. On the contrary, the more extended a social network is in stumping up the money to dispatch a migrant, the more his premature return (for instance, being deported for working illegally) will be considered a tragedy. Those who do not stay long enough to earn the amount equivalent to the debts they have incurred in Uzbekistan will be obliged to return abroad to repay them, but will have more difficulties in being lent money again because of their perceived "failure."

It would appear that the more difficult access is to the destination country, the more migrants attempt to enter, under the assumption that countries well protected also harbor more wealth. To understand the migrants' strategies, it is important to know the administrative obstacles they have to overcome. Each of the concerned (including Uzbekistan) countries tries, in its own way, to stem the immigration of populations on its territory, notwithstanding that these policies are often circumvented rendering them ineffectual.

Exhausting Jobs: A "Domestic Sacrifice"?

In Uzbekistan, talking about emigration is not without its dangers. People are wary of foreigners showing interest in these issues, as is the government, suspicious that academic research on the subject conceals other intentions. For various reasons, interviews also prove complex in the three destination countries—in particular, winning migrants' trust, especially when they are in breach of the regulations of the host countries, is no easy matter. However, fieldwork in ethnological observation enabled me to approach the migratory issue from the "inside," and in a roundabout manner understand the stakes involved for migrants. Therefore, extracts of interviews presented here are used to shed light on some aspects of the lives of Uzbek migrants abroad.

The jobs held by migrants, at least initially upon their arrival in the host country, are most often those that nationals of the country do not want. Quite frequently they are low-skilled jobs, physically exhausting and sometimes dangerous. Most of the jobs are illegal or unregistered, occupied by workers in breach of regulations. The main sites of employment for the Uzbek migrants I met were concentrated in factories, construction sites, services, and catering.

In terms of factory work, South Korea is particularly relevant. The salaries of workers with a *kontrakt* seem to be fixed; contacts in this field were paid 650,000 won per month (650 dollars at the time of research), supplemented by doing overtime. This was the case with Murat, who worked at a company making doors. The interview took place in Seoul, where Murat came to spend his Sunday off:

> Now, I took one day off because I'm a bit tired. I like to come to Dongdaemun, just like that, to relax. To go back to the factory where I live, I must go to Incheon City Hall and then ride a bus. I work every day but I'm allowed to take days off when I want. I usually take them on Sundays. It's better to come to Seoul and it's livelier. Otherwise, I work seven days a week, eight hours a day, to which I voluntarily work four extra hours to earn more. It's exhausting, of course, but it's worth doing it. I make a lot of money now.

Murat had an official kontrakt and had legally migrated for work. However, I noticed that in the case of another migrant, Sardor, the notion of working extra hours for better pay also existed among illegal workers, too.

> We are eight Uzbeks here. We form teams of four, and each week, we change our working shifts. This week, for example, it's day work. We work from 8 am to 5 pm, or to 8 pm if we want extra hours. The night shift takes over from 8 pm to 8 am the next morning. Most of us work overtime during the day shift. It's exhausting, but we are here to make money. All of us are illegal. We are paid 650,000 won a month. The first year, we work to repay the travel expenses and then it's essentially savings since we don't spend much here, and above all, we don't pay any rent. We don't work on Sundays.

Work hours are particularly demanding: from 9 to 12 hours a day, totaling 54 to 72 hours a week for six working days, significantly exceeding the legal working week of 44 hours. International organizations, such as Amnesty International, have protested against these practices, stating that "immigrant workers have overly long working hours for salaries inferior to those of Korean workers. They are the recipients of much physical and verbal violence in their working places and work in dangerous conditions."[14] Among my contacts, it appeared that no-one was paid under the monthly legal minimum salary (514,150 won at the time).

Meanwhile, in the catering sector, working hours in Seoul's restaurants would also appear to be long and demanding. Ozoda, who had been working for a short time in the restaurant Ala-too in Seoul, admitted that:

> I'm really exhausted. The atmosphere in the restaurant is very friendly and my colleagues are adorable, they keep telling me to sit down when there are no clients, but still, I feel very tired. In Samarkand, I didn't work, I just

[14] See http://archive.amnesty.org/library/Index/FRAASA250092006?open&of=FRA-KOR.

> looked after my children and I'm not used to such [work] patterns. We work every day from morning to night. I came to Seoul three months ago, but I've worked here as a waitress for only four days. That job was found for me by my husband's friends (he is an Uzbek businessperson in Seoul). We are entitled to two vacation days per month. I have already asked for one, to get some rest.

In New York, Muzaffar's salary as a waiter in a Central Asian restaurant is 100 dollars a day, which, based on a five-day week, translates as 2,100 dollars per month. Even in jobs that would require less movement and physical exertion, the hours are so long that the work becomes exhausting. Typically working 12 hours a day, seven days a week, another migrant in New York, Nasiba, was working about 84 hours a week (the legal working week is 40 hours). Married to a computer technician, she described their situation as follows:

> I was born near the border, in Leninabad. I'm an Uzbek from Tajikistan... But my husband is from Tashkent and our four children live there. We got green cards [permanent residency], but it doesn't apply to them, because they're over 18... First, we worked in the Queens area, doing odd jobs. Then we came to Brighton Beach. I look after an old lady from Leningrad who's got Alzheimer's disease [Nasiba, like many Russian-speaking people, does not use the current name, St. Petersburg]. I take care of her from 9 am to 9 pm. After that, she goes to sleep. I make 2,500 dollars a month and I work seven days out of seven. If I want a day off, I've got to make arrangements with the lady's son. He lives in New York, too, but he works and can't look after her. Unfortunately, I won't be able to introduce my husband to you. He's a computer technician. He works day and night to make as much money as he can. What else can we do?

In Russia, the situation is different still and the wages lower than in the United States or South Korea. An article about the products sold at Cherkizoy market in Moscow mentioned that "all the sweaters, jeans, and boots that crowded the stalls were brand-new, made by Chinese or Turkish dressmakers, and most of them fraudulently imported."[15] According to many testimonies, a great deal of these clothes are sewn in sweatshops in the suburbs of Moscow, where Tajik and Uzbek women work day and night for only a cup of *kasha*. It is difficult, however, to provide supporting evidence for this information. In Moscow, salaries differ widely depending on the job, but a vast majority of those I interviewed were working for wages ranging from 200 to 300 dollars a month as street cleaners,

[15] See http://www.ruvr.ru/main.php?lng=fre&q=1355&cid=78&p=23.10.2007.

workers on construction sites, or waiters in restaurants. This can be compared to the average salary in Moscow (as of March 2008) of 6,100 rubles (220 dollars). Thus, these migrants earn approximately the equivalent of the average minimum wage. Even Komil, whose job was (working alone) to manufacture fake immigration cards, made only 200 to 300 dollars a month on average. It was uncertain, however, if this sum represented the amount left once he had paid off police officers. The better-off migrants are apparently those who work in trade. A more atypical example was Mahmud, a warden at the Uzbek embassy in Moscow, who told me that he was paid up to 1,500 dollars a month and got his accommodation paid by the embassy.

In general, migrants embark on their lives abroad working in unattractive, badly paid, and physically and symbolically degrading jobs. Some of them, after a little time and a better knowledge of the host country, succeed in more rewarding forms of employment. Yet the predominance of hard jobs echoes the opinion of Farhod, a night guard in New York, that migrating is a "domestic sacrifice" shouldered to improve the family's living conditions in Uzbekistan.

Risks Taken by Illegal Workers

In a book called *Moonlighting, A Sometimes Vital Fraud?*, Florence Weber emphasizes how the terms "moonlighting" or "clandestine" carry negative connotations. If one were to use her definitions, it could be said that Uzbek migrants are mostly "concealed workers."[16] In South Korea and the United States, there are specific visas for immigrant workers; working without the appropriate papers constitutes a breach of the law. The majority of the migrants I questioned in these two countries had come with visas that did not allow them to work (many also stayed beyond the expiration of their visas). In Russia, too, they are required to obtain a work permit, but employers very seldom take the necessary steps to do this for illegal workers coming from Central Asia.

The risks taken in case of a breach of the law differ from one host country to the next. In the United States, very few identity controls are carried out without a specific reason, such as if the apprehended person is suspected of having committed crimes other than just illegally residing

[16] F. Weber, *Le travail au noir: une fraude parfois vitale?* (Paris: Ed. Rue d'Ulm, 2008).

on U.S. territory. The Uzbek migrants I met in New York did not seem to fear deportation at all, though this is the sanction they risk if they are discovered. The real penalty they feared was being banned from reentering the United States; upon leaving the country, they would have to show their passports and expired visas. According to them, they are not subject to risk of capture while staying in the country because no one checks the validity of their visas. They expressed the opinion that although they thought labor inspections existed, only the employers would be sanctioned for having employed illegal migrants without declaring them. It is necessary to make a distinction between an absence of authorization to employ foreign migrants and concealing their employment, even if both go hand in hand; hence, moonlighting results in employers' concealing employment in order to avoid paying taxes and to obscure the fact they are employing non-authorized persons.

In South Korea, fear of the police is particularly striking. Passport controls to check visa validity, and therefore the right to stay in the country, were dreaded by the migrants I met. This concern leads them to hide whenever they see policemen.[17] Migrants also fear the frequent controls at their places of work, which are conducted in order to check whether employees are legal and if their employers have declared them. The risk of arrest for many migrants is twofold: as illegal immigrants and as illegal workers. The illegal Uzbek workers I met in Seoul feared the *zelenyi koridor* (literally the green corridor), an expression for deportation back to Uzbekistan. Previously, in addition to being deported, a fine was paid to the police, except in cases where "arrangements" had been made, for example in return for "cooperation" such as the denunciation of employers. Migrants now only have to pay for their flights back and are banned from South Korea for a period of five years. An example of a deportee was Bahtior, who was residing with his family again in Bukhara. I had previously encountered him in Seoul, but following a passport check in Ansan, he had been arrested and subsequently deported.

In Russia, migrants unanimously denounce the "hunt" of which they are the victims and fear police controls. Russian militia often perform "face control," arresting almost systematically anybody with a non-Slavic appearance, particularly those referred to pejoratively as *chernye* (literally,

[17] The author had an appointment with Bahtior in Ansan, a Seoul suburb. He was one hour late and apologetic that I had had to wait for him. He had in fact been very near our meeting point and was delayed because he had chosen to stay hidden as long as he could still see police officers. He feared being asked for his papers.

blacks), mainly people who originate from Africa, the Caucasus, and Central Asia. Officially, the arrested foreigners risk a fine and deportation. However, in the end, these penalties are rarely imposed. Russian police officers usually prefer to receive a payment than initiate tiresome proceedings that will not be lucrative for them. A new law was also passed in 2006 that makes it easier for migrants to obtain a work permit.[18]

As demonstrated above, the three states do not invest in the hunt for illegal migrants on their territories in the same way, and Uzbek migrants do not have the same fears about their administrative statuses in each destination. While the concerned countries have established strict legislation in order to punish breaches of national regulations, they do not necessarily rigorously implement them—there existing a discrepancy between the text of the laws and their actual enforcement. Corruption aside, this may also be explained by the impossibility of entirely stemming population flows and keeping watch on every immigrant.

The inherent difficulties of the jobs that migrants take, combined with the often unenviable accommodation conditions and fears of being arrested on account of their illegal status, enables one to better understand the respondent Farhod's depiction of migration as a "domestic sacrifice." Nevertheless, it seems that once they are back in Uzbekistan, migrants not only make the most of the economic benefits of their migration, but above all, of the consequences that this has on their social statuses. Notwithstanding, they also face challenges upon their return.

Changes in Uzbekistan Regarding Migrations

Returning migrants are at first often surprised at the changes in their families and places of origin. Many report feeling overwhelmed by the reunion with their children or other relatives: time spent abroad has accentuated the differences between them. Renovations and new building works carried out in their towns or villages of origin also stun them. Some also

[18] Since 2006, the Russian authorities have become aware of the importance of regulating migratory flows, and accordingly, passed legislation which aims to select immigrants. The new law on migrants was voted on July 18, 2006, and entered into effect on January 15, 2007. It reduces the requirements for registration and obtaining a work permit for those migrants who cross, or crossed, the border legally. It does not, however, normalize those already present on Russian territory without formal status. More in M. Laruelle, "Central Asian Labor Migrants in Russia: The 'Diasporization' of the Central Asian States?" *The China and Eurasia Forum Quarterly* 5, no. 3 (2007): 113.

notice, to their utter amazement, the growing shortage of men in Uzbekistan; "all gone abroad," they remark. Other changes mark the passage of time, as Mamat noticed when he introduced a physics and chemistry teacher to me at Namangan University:

> When I left, she was my student. Now, I've returned and she's my colleague! [Laughs] It is stupid, but it sounded very strange to me at the beginning of the academic year to discuss the lectures with her. I told myself, "What a long way we've come." And all that time I was in Korea. C'est la vie! [in French.]

"The long way we've come" refers both to the migrant in Seoul and his former student in Namangan. Their two paths had diverged, and when they crossed again five years later, one had acquired the status of teacher, which the other, Mamat, had just regained. Most significant, albeit often just hinted at or expressed through humor, is the feeling of a loss of values in their family and a concomitant decline in their authority. Migrants may even sense changes afoot before they return. Eldor, a migrant in New York, complained that:

> I don't really understand how things evolve. I can realize that my children attach great value to having fashionable designer clothes. It's never enough for them! I don't know how many trousers are necessary to be fashionable, but we'll soon have to buy a new house just to keep their clothes, I'm afraid! [Laughs] Each time I call, I learn that they have been shopping. But me, in my village I had only one set of clothes and I did not worry about that. Today for youngsters, it's different. My wife told me it was out of the question for my daughter to wear an Uzbek dress [here he refers to dresses custom-tailored from a spare piece of fabric]. It's a necessity for her to go and buy some Chinese or Turkish clothes, or I don't know what. But, still, our traditions are important and we ought to keep them.

This seeming need of children to acquire products that their parents could not find when they were young is recurrent in migrants' statements, both when abroad or when they have returned. Fashionable clothes and electronic devices have become the prerogative of the children of migrants, who want to show that they are clearly distinct from the previous generations by becoming Westernized, for example by seeking to imitate Russian and American culture through the adoption of clothes and listening to music.

This can be compared to Catherine Poujol's observation concerning the appearance "of spoiled child behaviors in the urban privileged classes of Kazakhstan, akin somewhat to the child king [phenomenon] developing in Chinese society." Poujol goes on to argue that "improving living conditions of a small part of the population, the dramatic opening of the media to the external world (Internet access, satellite receivers, and broadcasting of foreign films) may have had psychological consequences, detected in the form of well-known pathologies in the Western world (addiction to video games and delirious fits). The brutal casualization of an increasing part of the population also has an inescapable psychiatric affect."[19]

There may also be other unexpected demands on migrants. For example, events in the family may have occurred in their absence which lead to the demand for extended and more regular financial contributions, the family expenses now deemed to be larger than when they first left. The migrants come back to a family in which their children have grown up, their wives have taken on new public roles in the absence of their husbands, and parents have assumed new domestic duties. These changes occur gradually, without the migrants necessarily becoming aware of them while abroad. They are now confronted with a changed situation that may serve to isolate them from their families. Bekzod, a migrant to Seoul, related such a story to me in Kokand:

> I was really in a hurry to be back in Uzbekistan. I kept thinking about it for many long hours in Seoul. I dreamt of how it would be to be back home. But in the end, it's not as simple as I imagined. I'm happy to be here [home], of course, that's not the issue. Things have slightly changed for me. I no longer accept that, as before, my parents should run my life and tell me to do this or that with my own money. And I realize that they, though they say nothing, think that I have changed. They call me "the Korean" as a joke. I don't know really what's happening, but I don't want to work as I did over there, and at the same time, I miss it a little. Because over there, I did what I had to do; that's all.

Several components ought to be underlined in the story above. First is the feeling of loss after his return. Migrants do not necessarily have jobs waiting upon their return to Uzbekistan and many initially allow themselves a resting period before they search for work. While this period of inactivity is impatiently awaited in the host country, the migrants do not always view it the same way once at home. Work schedules that were considered exhausting in the host country are remembered with a tinge of nostalgia by some migrants, who now feel useless and without aim. When migrants their goals had been clear: work hard, make money, and come

[19] C. Poujol, "Santé mentale et société en Asie centrale post-soviétique ou comment tenter de diagnostiquer un mal-être social?" *Outre-Terre* no. 16 (2006): 12, http://echosdegrozny.free.fr/wp-content/sante-mentale-en-asie-centrale.pdf.

back to their country of origin. Once they have reached this point, the incentives to work are less strong. Second, Bezod refers to his own changing attitude in regard to his parents. He no longer accepts their remarks; the lack of freedom he feels is new to him. Being far away made him forget the omnipresent and all-powerful nature of parental authority, which he is now reluctant to respect. As Poujol observes, "[t]he end of the Soviet system led to a breakdown in ethics and behaviors due to the sudden loss of points of reference in previously highly structured societies. That breakdown was not backed up with explanations or inter-generational dialogues [that were needed] mainly between parents and children. The rule was to leave matters unsaid." The retired generations, meanwhile, nostalgic for the past, are quick to point out that "in the past, things didn't happen like that."[20]

Some parents fear the potential changes in behavior resulting from migration and are reluctant to let their children go abroad for fear that this experience will cause negative shifts in the family dynamics. This was Mardjona's case:

> All of my children speak English and my second daughter had the opportunity to go to the United States. But I didn't want her to. She is resentful of me because of that. But, first of all, I didn't want her to go by plane, it's too dangerous. Anyway, I trust my daughter, but you never know what may happen over there; she might change her manners. I want my children to keep being brought up nicely, to bow and obey their parents, even though they're grown-ups. And to look their father in the eyes. Those who have been abroad, you can't recognize them when they come back; they've become cheeky, disrespectful.

To the generation gap between migrants and their parents can be added that between the migrant and his own children. The latter no longer defer to their migrant parent's authority, calling into question the place of the migrant in his own family.

The Emergence of the "New Uzbeks"

Migration appears to constitute an intervening period when migrants find themselves in a transitional phase toward a new status. They no longer belong to their former status—Uzbeks in search of a better life—but neither have they yet acquired the one they seek to become: that is, newly

[20] *Ibid.*, 12.

rich Uzbeks in Uzbekistan. Indiscreet in their consumption patterns and habits, the term "New Uzbeks," derived from the Russian expression *novyi russkii* (New Russian), itself taken from *novorich*, which is derived from the French *nouveau riche*, has come to be bestowed on the newly wealthy. (In Russia, these two terms refer primarily to the businessmen and oligarchs who suddenly grew rich from the collapse of the Soviet Union, mostly through illegal activities related to mafia networks.) The term is especially directed at those Uzbeks who have become rich quickly; and although many envy the status, it is not necessarily complimentary. One woman I interviewed, Mirkomil, remarked with some irony that

> Our neighbor, I've known him since he was very young. He would play with my children. He would call me "auntie." We were very close. He liked staying at home to have dinner, he was a simple man. But since he came back from Korea, he fancies himself as an emir. [Laughs] He can't walk out without his mobile phone and when he turns up at his parents, he hoots his horn for them to open the gate, but I rather think it is for everyone to see his brand-new Nexia [a car built by Daewoo and a symbol of social success in Uzbekistan].

While the financial change in status of the newly rich is duly noted, this also goes hand in hand with severe criticism of what is perceived to be ostentatious behavior. In fact, it has been claimed that Uzbekistan has become a "huge laundry in the region for illegal benefits. Only a very small part of the laundered money is invested in the region, but it feeds imports of luxury products: French perfumes, luxury clothes, and foodstuffs out of reach for a large part of the population. The . . . system, besides favoring the emergence of a relatively well-off class employed in the nebulous groups involved in mafia dealings . . . takes deep root in the social structure of the country."[21] The New Uzbeks are thus the agents of this phenomenon. Representative of this "need" to purchase luxury goods was Boriboi, another of my interviewees, who was prepared to spend the equivalent of several monthly salaries of the average Uzbek worker to buy European-made clothes. The main driver for such behavior is to make money and, above all, to let it be known to all and sundry. Hence, according to a similar logic, matrimonial strategies are also formed, with many taking advantage of the money they have earned abroad in order to marry off their child to the heir of a prominent citizen.

---

[21] See http://www.voltairenet.org/article7396.html.

* * * * *

In conclusion, the "domestic sacrifice" shouldered by migrants in working abroad quite often represents a painful period that could be seen as the preliminary phase of a rite of passage. After the separation from their group of origin, migrants find themselves on their own, or in any case, far from the social control exerted by the mahalla. For most of them, it is a step tinged with nostalgia for the country they have left, and many experience pain at being far from their families. This period of exclusion is, moreover, not without its dangers. Its outcome may be even fatal, especially in Russia, where human trafficking, the mafia, xenophobic groups, and other threats weigh heavily on them. Nevertheless, if this phase is to succeed (that is, if the migrants manage to accumulate enough money) their return to the country of origin will be celebrated and they will reap the benefits of their success. This does not mean to say that they do not face new challenges of reintegration, as this chapter has explored. Furthermore, the richest of the returnees acquire the non-official status of being New Uzbeks, which although sometimes ironically implied, nevertheless aptly encapsulates their newfound wealth and status, as well as their habits of conspicuous consumption and propensity to flaunt them.

PART FOUR

IMPACT ON GENDER RELATIONS: MASCULINITY AND FEMININITY IN FLUX

INTRODUCTION

Marlene Laruelle

As with all large-scale social changes, the phenomenon of migration has had an impact on gender relations. Central Asian societies are conventionally described as conservative and patriarchal. However, gender identity, presented as a permanent given of nature, is in fact subject to continual readjustments. Historically, the weight of the Soviet regime on modifying gender relations, as well as the presence of many so-called European minorities, has meant that gender identity is less marked by a strict male/female divide than in other regions of the Muslim world. Today, conventional divisions are also being challenged by migration. While traditionally more male than female, a growing number of women are also migrating, notably in Kyrgyzstan, where women migrate either in a family unit or alone, and where their move is socially more acceptable. In Tajikistan and Uzbekistan, where the distribution of social roles assigned to genders is much more rigid, feminine migration has also become an emerging trend, although it has developed at a much slower pace since its social costs are seen as hard to bear. Three types of specifically female migration can be observed in the whole region: shuttle trade, a highly female specialty throughout the post-Soviet space ever since Gorbachev's perestroika; unskilled labor sent to work in markets or in domestic services; and migration for marriage, which is almost exclusively the preserve of women.

Gender relations in Central Asia changed dramatically during the course of the 1990s and the first decade of the twenty-first century. These changes occurred both within the migratory movements themselves, and in the daily lives of those who remained behind. Increasingly, local patriarchal societies have had to learn to live with the absence of men. Rites of passage typically take place during the winter months, when the men return, to ensure that social relations within the community web are not overly transformed by their absence. In families where men have migrated, women can gain independence by becoming the head of the household and being the sole breadwinner. However, this also means they have to deal with the multitude of everyday problems alone: working in the cotton fields, managing domestic life (including care of children and elderly dependents from both sides of the family), and, if possible, selling products at markets. Cases of men disappearing following migration, whether due to accidents, crimes, or because they sever ties with their families, has a major impact on the future of the spouse and children left behind. Migrants' spouses thus live in constant fear of being abandoned, jettisoned because of a second wife found in the host country or of being subject to polygamy should the husband return to the village with the second wife. They also have to face the possible scenario of remarriage either to a brother-in-law or cousin should the husband disappear. Those migrants who depart immediately after getting married leave their wives behind, so delaying their entry into motherhood and keeping them longer in a kind of domestic servitude to their in-laws. Finally, the long-term impact of a father's absence on the upbringing of children in societies that are highly structured around paternal authority remains unknown.

Although gender studies traditionally concentrate on the evolution of the status of women, Madeleine Reeves' chapter focuses on the impact of migration on masculinity. Masculine performance is validated by the rite of passage of migration—a symbol of a young man's coming of age and of his ability to provide for the needs not only of his own family, but also of his parents and, if possible, his extended family. Moreover, it involves enduring what may sometimes prove to be dangerous conditions at his workplace and/or living conditions deemed degrading. On the flip side of the coin, however, those men who cannot or do not want to migrate are also forced to confront an evolution in their masculinity. Indeed, those who "stay behind" suffer from a weakened status of not being able to offer substantive revenues that are able to compete with those sent by migrants. The evolution of masculinity in migration also presumes that men are able to manage contradictory desires: does one spend the income on one's well-being and that of one's spouse or does one reserve it for one's social standing within the neighborhood community? Does one take a lover or a second wife in the destination country without abandoning the one who has remained behind in the country of origin? How does one deal with changes in gender and sexual relations following contact with foreign women?

The status of women is also being deeply transformed by these migration processes. As Luisa Piart shows in her studies of female Uzbek petty traders in Istanbul, the shuttle trade carries with it many stereotypes about gender identity. While men are allegedly incapable of saving money, women are supposedly gifted in "doing good business" and in managing their expenses prudently. Moreover, Central Asian shuttle trade essentially concerns goods considered germane to women—clothing, household furnishings, and handicrafts—while the masculine identity of the men who engage in the trade is denigrated. Uzbek women working in the shuttle trade in Istanbul have different profiles: young women follow family strategies controlled by their father or husband; while, on the other hand, older women, particularly grandmothers and those who are divorced, have a higher status because they are no longer "required" for domestic duties. They often, however, feel socially downgraded or stigmatized. Moreover, the shuttle trade is risky since making a profit is not guaranteed; the goods may be stolen or corrupt custom officers may confiscate the revenues. This helps to spread the image of women as victims of "popular capitalism" and largely informal market economies.

The Tajik women at the Moscow bazaars, studied by Nafisa Khusenova, find themselves in much more precarious situations. Selling their labor services for subordinate positions, such as a market trader, dishwasher, waitress, or cook in a restaurant, yields less income, less prestige, and less autonomy compared to the shuttle trade. In their cases migration is not a result of capital accumulation strategies, as it is with petty trade, but is necessary for the economic survival of their household. Nonetheless, most of the Tajik women in Moscow's bazaars have professional qualifications unrelated to their current job; many are secondary school teachers, nurses, or university graduates. Their earnings serve to support their children, who they may have entrusted to grandparents, and to invest in housing, which they consider a safe investment. Migrant women usually continue to value their traditional roles and internalize the negative stereotypes attached to those who migrate. They hope their daughters will adhere to the social norms of early marriage and a large family, rather than seek emancipation through migration. The economic transformation driven by migration and the emergence of new sources of income are not, therefore, signs of the "Westernization" of gender roles and moral values.

Migration also affects professional urban women, who, above all, seek to leave the post-Soviet space to move to a more developed country, preferably a European state or, less commonly, a Gulf country. As shown by Stéphanie Bélouin, these women possess valuable cultural capital that allows them to implement diverse strategies. They may study abroad, become an au pair, work for international recruitment agencies, or try to marry a foreigner. However, it would be wrong to simplify their motives as merely opportunistic. Indeed, there are many other factors that motivate such women to migrate: feelings of being ill-at-ease in their society of origin; refusal to adopt the gender norms imposed on them; the desire to "Westernize" culturally; already established international networks with female friends from their university years; and the frequenting of places which they feel more comfortable in than other more "native" haunts. Their aim is therefore to increase the value of their cultural capital through migration. Mobility, social ascension, and personal happiness are seen as going hand in hand. These migration strategies, therefore, highlight all the complexity of the human character and its capability of building an individualized rationale from externally imposed social and economic situations.

MIGRATION, MASCULINITY, AND TRANSFORMATIONS OF SOCIAL SPACE IN THE SOKH VALLEY, UZBEKISTAN

Madeleine Reeves

This chapter explores the relationship between gendered migration and transformations of social space in several kin-related villages in the Sokh district (*tuman*) of Uzbekistan's Ferghana *oblast'*. Like many other rural regions of Central Asia, Sokh is characterized by high rates of seasonal migration to Russia's urban centers, here principally to markets and informal construction sites across southern Siberia. Migration from Sokh is also gender-marked: although there are rare instances of "family migration" in which a husband and wife travel together, typically accompanied by children, seasonal long-distance migration from the district is overwhelmingly undertaken by men.

This gendered nature of work abroad is the subject of considerable local debate. Some within Sokh speak of male-dominated migration from Sokh as a sign of the region's distinctive "culturedness" (since women are not expected to live or work far from home); others as a mark of the region's "backwardness" and the persistence of patriarchal domestic arrangements. The long-term absence of large numbers of young men is also spoken of as having a considerable impact upon family structures and dynamics, incorporating women in new ways into communal labor projects locally, and often leading to open tensions between young wives and their husbands' families over the disbursement of remittances and the distribution of domestic responsibilities.

The aim of this study is to foreground an exploration of Central Asian labor migration as a gendered field, with particular attention paid to the significance of migration on Sokh masculinities. Different rates of male and female migration have been widely documented in the growing scholarly literature on labor migration from Central Asia.[1] However, little

[1] S. Olimova and I. Bosc, *Labour Migration from Tajikistan* (Dushanbe: International Organization for Migration, 2003); I. Röhner, "National and International Labour Migration. A Case Study in the Province of Batken, Kyrgyzstan," *NCCR North-South Dialogue Working Paper* no. 8 (Berne: NCCR North-South, 2007); C. Bichsel, S. Hostettler, and S. Balzer, "*Should I Buy a Cow or a TV?* Reflections on the conceptual framework of the NCCR North-South Based on a comparative study of international labour migration in Mexico, India and Kyrgyzstan," *NCCR North-South Dialogue Working Paper* (Berne: NCCR North-

explicit attention has been paid to its gendered dimensions, that is, to the way in which migration decisions are shaped by situated understandings of appropriate male and female behavior on the one hand and, on the other, how migration itself becomes constitutive of normative ideas about masculinity and femininity.[2] Men, the implicit "actors" in many scholarly and popular accounts of migration from the region, nonetheless typically remain rather one-dimensional figures: bread-winners or patriarchs; laborers or victims. In the analysis presented here, I follow Osella and Osella's call for us to attend to the ways in which migration may "feed into local frameworks of self and subjectivity."[3] How, I ask, do understandings of what it is to be a "good" father, son, or husband inflect decisions of whether to remain or depart for work abroad? How are male identities shaped by precarious and often exploitative work on the margins of the law? And how are competing domestic and community pressures balanced in the investment or performative distribution of remittances? I argue that migration and masculinity are co-constitutive, in ways that reveal much about the complexities of gender and generational dynamics in contemporary Sokh. A period of work in Russia has the potential to confirm a young man's status and identity *as* a man, but it is also fraught with existential and emotional risks. Meanwhile, widespread male absence is raising the stakes of "staying behind" for those men who are unable, or unwilling, to leave to work "in town" in ways that are likely to be important for future migration dynamics.

Theorizing Central Asian Masculinities

The complex interplay of migration and masculinity can best be illuminated by an approach that understands gender to be socially emergent

---

South, 2005); E. Isabaeva, "Leaving to Enable Others to Remain: Remittances and New Moral Economies of Migration in Southern Kyrgyzstan," *Central Asian Survey* 30, nos. 3–4 (2011): 541–554; V. Ruget and B. Usmanalieva, "Citizenship, migration and loyalty towards the state: a case study of the Kyrgyzstani migrants working in Russia and Kazakhstan," *Central Asian Survey* 27, no. 2 (2008): 129–141; J. Thorez, "Itinéraires du déracinement—L'essor des migrations de travail entre l'Asie centrale et la Russie," *Espaces, Populations, Sociétés*, no. 1 (2007): 59–71; and the contributions to this volume by Khusenova, Piart, and Belouin.

[2] Though see M. Reeves, "Staying Put? Towards a Relational Politics of Mobility at a time of Migration," *Central Asian Survey* 30, nos. 3–4 (2008): 555–576 and S. Thieme, "Living in Transition: How Kyrgyz Women Juggle their Different Roles in a Multi-local Setting," in *Gender, Technology and Development* 12, no. 3 (2008): 325–345, on the need to bring a gendered perspective to the analysis of labor migration from Central Asia.

[3] F. Osella and C. Osella, "Migration, Money and Masculinity in Kerala," *The Journal of the Royal Anthropological Institute* 6, no. 1 (2000): 117.

and mutable. As Lindisfarne notes, "anthropological descriptions have often emphasized idealized, hegemonic versions of gendered identities and ignored the shifting reality of people's experience as gendered beings."[4] This is perhaps especially true in analyses of masculinities in Muslim-majority settings where, as Marsden has noted in an insightful recent analysis of male-only musical gatherings in northern Pakistan, the tendency is to treat manhood in rural Muslim societies as "rigid, inflexible, and defined within unchanging codes of honor and systems of 'patriarchy.' "[5] The analysis that follows approaches masculinity not as a stable characteristic that is biologically "given," nor simply as a normative set of practices and dispositions, but as emergent within a particular set of gender relations, or what Connell calls a "structure of social practice."[6] This social practice has biological referents—"gender . . . constantly refers to bodies and what bodies do," but it is not determined by biology, nor is it reducible to sexual dimorphism. Indeed, in this reading, gender exists "precisely to the extent that biology does *not* determine the social."[7]

This framing is helpful for the analysis that follows, firstly, in that it allows us to challenge essentialist readings of masculinity, while also recognizing that bodies matter. When gender is problematized in this way, as Lindisfarne argues, "it becomes possible to ask how people make gender known to themselves and how gendered identities may be reified to express apparently absolute differences between men and women."[8] Secondly, and significantly in considering the gendered dimensions of labor migration, it allows us to explore masculinity and femininity as relational configurations of identity. Those configurations emerge in practice and they are socially organized—that is, for any given society at any historical moment, there are repertoires of "male" and "female" that are learned and embodied from our earliest days of life. Nor are these repertoires immutable: they change through the life-course and from one historical epoch to another; and, as studies of migration elsewhere attest, new regimes of

---

[4] N. Lindisfarne, "Variant masculinities, variant virginities: rethinking honour and shame," in A. Cornwall and N. Lindisfarne, eds., *Dislocating Masculinities: Comparative Ethnographies* (London: Routledge, 1994), 82.

[5] M. Marsden, "All-male sonic gatherings, Islamic reform, and masculinity in northern Pakistan," *American Ethnologist* 34, no. 3 (2007): 475.

[6] R.W. Connell, *Masculinities* (Cambridge: Polity Press, 1995), 71.

[7] *Ibid.*

[8] Lindisfarne, "Variant masculinities, variant virginities: rethinking honour and shame," 82.

(im)mobility can lead to the re-articulation of gender roles, and cause gender regimes previously taken for granted to enter discourse in new ways.[9]

In thinking about shifting gender regimes in Central Asia, this approach can help us to bring masculinities more fully into the theoretical frame. Studies of Central Asian women have proliferated in recent years, including nuanced and insightful accounts of the meanings of veiling and the negotiation of "multiple modernities" by women in southern Kyrgyzstan, the dilemmas of "coming of age" for teenage women in contexts of dramatic social rupture, the use of "sexual strategies" by young women as a resource for survival in urban Kazakhstan, and the mobilization of "shame" to elicit social and sexual conformity among young women.[10]

By contrast, while men have often been the actors in ethnographic accounts of change in this region, there has been correspondingly little attention paid to masculinities and their social production.[11] This situation is far from unique to scholarship on Central Asia. As Chopra, Osella and Osella note in a collection of South Asian ethnographies, while masculinity is no longer a "muted field" within gender studies, theoretical work has concentrated overwhelmingly on Europe, North America, and

---

[9] See, indicatively, Osella and Osella, "Migration, Money and Masculinity in Kerala"; M. Ruth Gimbaud, *The Kitchen Spoon's Handle: Transnationalism and Sri Lanka's Migrant Housemaids* (Ithaca: Cornell University Press, 2000); P. Levitt, *The Transnational villagers* (Berkeley: University of California Press, 2001), 97–106; L. Keough, "Globalizing postsocialism: Mobile mothers and Neoliberalism on the margins of Europe," *Anthropological Quarterly* 79, no. 3 (2006): 431–461.

[10] On veiling and "multiple modernities," see J. McBrien, "On Push-up Bras and Headscarves: Experiencing Multiple Modernities in Kyrgyzstan," paper presented to the Central Eurasian Studies Society Conference, 2007; on the dilemmas of "coming of age," see K. Kuenhast, *Let the stone lie where it has fallen: Dilemmas of gender and generation in Post-Soviet Kyrgyzstan* (PhD dissertation, Department of Anthropology, University of Minnesota, 1997) and the insightful documentary by S. Andrea Helminen, "Love and Broken Glass" (Denmark, Norlys films, 2006). On the use of sexual strategies, see J. Nazpary, *Post-Soviet Chaos: Violence and Dispossession in Kazakhstan* (London: Pluto Press, 2001); and on the mobilization of "shame," see G. Tett, "Guardians of the faith? Gender and religion in an (ex) Soviet Tajik village," in C. Fawzi El-Solh and J. Mabro, eds., *Muslim Women's Choices: Religious Belief and Social Reality* (Oxford: Berg, 1995); C. Harris, *Control and Subversion: Gender Relations in Tajikistan* (London: Pluto Press, 2004); C. Werner, "Bride abduction in post-Soviet Central Asia: marking a shift towards patriarchy through local discourses of shame and tradition," *The Journal of the Royal Anthropological Institute* 15, no. 2 (2009): 314–331; and N. Borbieva, *Development in the Kyrgyz Republic: Exchange, Communal Networks, and the Foreign Presence* (PhD Dissertation, Harvard University, 2007), 119–152.

[11] A valuable exception is Nick Megoran's recent analysis of the mobilization of hegemonic Uzbek masculinity in President Karimov's rhetorical responses to the Andijan events of May 2005. N. Megoran, "Framing Andijan, Narrating the Nation: Islam Karimov's Account of the Events of 13th May 2005," *Central Asian Survey* 27, no. 1 (2008): 15–31.

Australia.[12] Similar arguments about the "translatability" of accounts of masculinity and the theoretical apparatuses that have been developed to study them in non-Western contexts have been made by scholars exploring masculinities in the modern Middle East, the broader Islamic world, and post-Soviet Russia.[13] In the case of Central Asia this relative silence has created the paradoxical coupling of rich, nuanced accounts of female identity with rather "thin" readings of male subjectivities. In certain instances, this approach leads to the characterization of men as irreducibly aggressive and violent, drawing on essentialist readings of male identity that decades of feminist scholarship have worked to challenge in relation to women.[14] As Cornwall and Lindisfarne note in the introduction to one of the few comparative volumes on masculinities, it is "ironic that the logic of feminism as a political position has often required the notion of 'men' as a single, oppositional category."[15] It is with the hope of expanding that category in our study of Central Asian migrations that this analysis is framed.

Research in a "Valley of Traders"

The research that I draw upon to do so forms part of a larger period of ethnographic fieldwork in the borderlands of the Ferghana valley that I conducted between March 2004 and September 2005.[16] My concern was with transformations in "lived geographies" in an area of new international boundaries, and in the work of border guards, customs officers, herders,

---

[12] R. Chopra, C. Osella, and F. Osella, eds., *South Asian Masculinities: Context of Change, Sites of Continuity* (New Delhi: Women Unlimited, 2004), 1.

[13] See M. Ghoussoub and E. Sinclair-Webb, eds., "Preface," to *Imagined Masculinities: Male Identity and Culture in the Modern Middle East* (London: Saqi Books, 2006), 4; L. Ouzgane, "Introduction," in L. Ouzgane, *Islamic Masculinities* (London: Zed Books, 2006), 1; R. Kay, *Men in Contemporary Russia: The Fallen Heroes of Post-Soviet Change?* (Aldershot: Ashgate, 2006); S. Ushakin, "Chelovek roda on: futliary muzhestvennosti," *Voprosy filosofii*, no. 7 (2005): 34–56.

[14] In a study of motivations for bride "kidnap" in Kyrgyzstan titled, indicatively, "hunting for women," Lori Handrahan depicts kidnap for marriage as "a method for Kyrgyz men to mark their ethnic coming-of-age—hunting, capturing and physically forcing Kyrgyz women to marry them." L. Handrahan, "Hunting for Women: Bride-Kidnapping in Kyrgyzstan," *International Feminist Journal of Politics* 6, no. 2 (2004): 208.

[15] Cornwall and Lindisfarne, "Introduction," in *Dislocating Masculinity: Comparative Ethnography*, 1.

[16] M. Reeves, *Border Work: An Ethnography of the State at its Limits in the Ferghana Valley* (PhD dissertation, Department of Social Anthropology, University of Cambridge, 2008).

traders, and international organizations in rendering new administrative boundaries meaningful in everyday life. As fieldwork progressed, I became increasingly aware that the everyday experiences of space and distance in which I was interested were profoundly mediated by recent, wide-scale labor migration of young men to Russia. I was often told that the young men had, as during war time, left "for town" and that women and children were increasingly responsible for finding sources of livelihood that would previously have been undertaken by men.

In the absence of reliable village, or regional-level, statistics on who was leaving and for what kinds of work, I decided to couple the ethnographic interviews that I had been conducting during the previous year with a more systematic household survey to gauge changing rates and patterns of migration from the Sokh and Isfara valleys. The material here draws on both the interview and survey data that I came to gather in the Sokh valley, drawing from each of the district's four informal "zones."[17] With the help of several returned migrants and former schoolteachers, I conducted 361 survey interviews, each lasting on average 70 minutes, in the spring of 2005. Households were chosen randomly for inclusion from the selected mahallas, with migrant and non-migrant households having an equal chance of being surveyed.

The resultant patterns can thus be considered "representative" for the district as a whole, and indicative of broader trends from the southern Ferghana valley. However, they should be extrapolated from only with caution. What emerges from an intensive analysis of migration from any particular village or town is the considerable localization of migration patterns and strategies. A city in Russia that is a "popular" destination for migrants from one mahalla, for instance, may barely figure in the data for a neighboring mahalla. Rates of migration vary considerably, between different parts of the country, and even between different districts in the same oblast', for reasons that cannot be reduced to economic differentials alone.[18]

Moreover, Sokh is in several respects a quite distinctive region within Uzbekistan, and this should be borne in mind in any attempt to interpret

[17] These zones are spatially distinct, but also mark the typical boundaries within which marriage partners are chosen and within which ritual visits are maintained. I have changed the names of the mahallas and all interview and survey participants here to protect the confidentiality of my informants.

[18] This is a theme that I explore in more detail in M. Rivs [Madeleine Reeves], "Po tu storonu ekonomicheskogo determinizma: mikrodinamika migratsii iz sel'skogo Kyrgyzstana," *Neprikosnovennyi zapas* 66, no. 4 (2009) http://magazines.russ.ru/nz/2009/4/ri24.html.

broader trends from the data. An administrative and geographical exclave, Sokh is at once anomalous within the Uzbekistani nation-state and paradigmatic of the complex legacies bequeathed to the Ferghana valley by the national-territorial delimitation of the 1920s. The district, with a population of 54,000 living in 23 mahallas, takes its name from the Sokh river, which begins high in the Alay Mountains to the south (in Kyrgyzstan) and opens into the plains of the Ferghana valley, creating a fertile ribbon of land on which wheat, corn, and rice are sown, alongside apricot and apple orchards. Like several other tributary valleys that water the rich and economically critical Ferghana basin, Sokh was initially connected to the Uzbek SSR by a thin strip of land. As the area under cultivation grew in the post-war era, however, land was leased between one Union republic and another, and canals and roads were constructed with little regard for where the formal administrative boundaries of the republics lay. The result, at both geographical ends of the Sokh valley, is a "chessboard" formation, with competing claims over authentic ownership of land, and a border that criss-crosses back the single road connecting the enclave to the nearest sizeable town of Rishton.

This administrative complexity is compounded by the fact that the vast majority of the district's population are Tajik-speaking and Tajik-identifying, creating, as one of my informants put it, a "double box" of separation from their broader ethno-linguistic group.[19] The sense of cultural isolation is particularly acute for that cohort of middle-aged Sokh men—those who now constitute the district's intelligentsia, working as school and college teachers, as musicians for weddings, as doctors and chemists, or in the local administrative structures—who studied in Tajikistan during the life of the Soviet Union. The district's brightest and best, I was often told, had been sent to receive higher education in Khudjand or Dushanbe—cities reachable today only with great difficulty. Some lived through Tajikistan's civil war and have been profoundly shaped by that experience. Many more have kin who are today citizens of Tajikistan, with whom practical and personal contacts in the form of telephone

[19] There are several Kyrgyz-identifying families in some of the outlying mahallas, where Kyrgyz-Tajik intermarriage has historically been common, but most "Kyrgyz" families living within the Sokh district today speak Tajik and give their children Persian names. This is in marked contrast to the villages higher up the Sokh valley, administratively part of Kyrgyzstan, where Kyrgyz-identifying and Kyrgyz-speaking villagers scorned the idea of Kyrgyz-Tajik inter-marriage and emphasized the cultural, linguistic, and economic differences between the two ethnic groups.

connections, letters, and ritual visiting have been rendered perilous by the vagaries of bilateral visa regimes and the rising costs of travel.[20]

Even those who rarely travelled beyond Sokh during the life of the Soviet Union would have experienced "home" as firmly embedded within a "Tajik" cultural space. Soviet school textbooks here, for instance, were distributed from Dushanbe rather than Tashkent; wedding singers would be more likely to travel from Khudjand in Tajikistan to perform than from the regional center of Ferghana; and the republican system of information distribution meant that newspapers were easily available from Dushanbe. For most women in Sokh who went through their schooling before 1991, Uzbek is spoken and heard as a foreign language, and despite the increasing presence of Uzbek in the public sphere, Tajik remains the dominant language of public and domestic life.

Histories of Migration

Yet if Sokh identity, *so'xchilik*, is often spoken of as characterized by a social conservatism that is the product of isolation (as Omid, a 45-year-old car-mechanic once explained it to me: "Look at us: we've got mountains on four sides. Things change slowly here."), the district is also marked by what Gidwani and Sivaramakrishnan call "invisible histories of movement."[21] Practices of commemoration, stories of exploration and of famine, artifacts, and genealogies link Sokh historically to sites in Tajikistan, both in the Ferghana valley and "over the peaks," on the other side of the Alay range. Places that were "far away" on my own mental map of Central Asia, such as Jirgatol in Tajikistan's Karategin district, were often imaginatively "close" to my informants—measured in the number of days, on foot or by donkey, it would take to reach them over summer mountain passes.

These memories of movement are coupled with more recent experiences of mobility. The region's relative isolation and land poverty meant that migration became firmly embedded within domestic livelihood strategies rather earlier than in other parts of the Ferghana basin. Even during Soviet times, many Sokh families would supplement their incomes

---

[20] M. Reeves, "Travels in the Margins of the State: Everyday Geography in the Ferghana Valley Borderlands," in J. Sahadeo and R. Zanca, eds., *Everyday Life in Central Asia: Past and present* (Bloomington: Indiana University Press, 2007), 281–300.

[21] V. Gidwani and K. Sivaramakrishnan, "Circular Migration and Rural Cosmopolitanism in India," *Contributions to Indian Sociology* 37, no. 1–2 (2003): 339.

through seasonal trade in Russia. Sokh is renowned for its apricot orchards, and older men, particularly those who had previously worked as teachers within the Soviet state, would reminisce about travelling during the summer months to sell apricots in Ufa and Simbirsk (today's Ulyanovsk), Lenin's birthplace.[22] In a subtle reversal of the usual spatialization of "modernity" and "tradition," Valijon, one of my most outspoken and insightful interlocutors in Sokh, joked that when American cosmonauts first landed on the moon they found that Sokh men had arrived there first, and were ready with their trading stalls to sell their dried apricots (*kuraga*) to anyone who cared to purchase them.

Small-scale trade of Sokh apricots continues to this day in Russia, though restrictions upon foreigners' rights to trade in Russia may severely limit its future viability. Survey data indicate that among those who travelled to Russia for work in the mid-2000s, 10 percent had first travelled there in search of work before 1991. It is precisely this older generation who predominate today among those involved in market and wholesale trade.[23] However, as many informants reminded me, labor migration has come to take on qualitatively new dimensions in the post-Soviet period, with construction work—particularly unskilled "black work" (*chernaia rabota*)—now much more common among Sokh migrants than market trade.

Survey data confirm the scope of the new, post-Soviet dimensions of this migration. Of all respondents whose household member(s) had worked in Russia, 13.7 percent first began to work there between 1997–99, 37.3 percent first migrated in 2000–2, while 30.4 percent had made their first trip specifically for the purposes of work since 2003. At the time the survey was conducted, early in 2005—before the major seasonal departure of young men to Russia that occurs between mid-March and May—a striking 44.3 percent of all household heads responded that at least one person from their household was *currently* working in Russia. Moreover, of the 361 households surveyed, 78.1 percent indicated that one or more household members[24] had travelled to Russia for the purposes of work at

---

22 Nor is the depiction of Sokh as a "valley of traders" confined to Sokh men alone. In the upstream Kyrgyz villages of Sogment and Gaz, where labor migration, while common, is less pervasively a livelihood strategy, the Tajiks' skills at trade were the topic of frequent and often acerbic commentary. "They'd sell the air we breathe, if only they could find a way to bottle it," one elder from Sogment told me.

23 This figure excludes those travelling for the purposes of study or military service.

24 Households were taken as the unit of analysis rather than "family" because of the difficulties of delineating the contours of the latter in the Uzbekistani context. A household, as the wording of the first question sought to emphasize, was taken to include all of

least once in the preceding five years. When one factors in the number of people whose livelihood depends directly upon the migrant economy—by organizing transport, facilitating money transfers, or acting as intermediaries (*mienarav*) in finding work—a conservative estimate in 2005 suggests that four-fifths of Sokh households depend directly upon seasonal migration as a significant or primary source of domestic income.

The reasons for this new economic dependence can be situated, in part, within a well-rehearsed narrative of post-Soviet rural decline. With a population of a medium-sized Central Asian town, Sokh has no industry to speak of, and relatively few administrative or commercial jobs. The technical college where I taught occupies the grounds of a former shoe factory, which even Uzbekistan's protectionist economic policy could not save from closure. The other main source of industrial employment—the mercury mine across the border in Khaidarkan—was operating at just a third of its previous capacity in the early 2000s, and many of its employees from Sokh had been laid off in recent years.

Such decline is far from unique to this region, of course. But, as I was often told, Sokh's unusual administrative status had meant people had "left for town" (*ba shakhr*) rather earlier than in other parts of the Ferghana valley. The reasons are not difficult to find: although arable land here is relatively fertile, at least in those areas directly watered by the Sokh river, it is in extremely short supply. Many mahallas have no remaining plots of land to distribute to new couples, such that several generations continue to live together as one domestic unit around a single courtyard (*hovla*). This places great pressure on young men to find the resources to buy a land plot commercially, and often to finance their wedding themselves.[25]

Secondly, and in contrast to contiguous districts of Kyrgyzstan, land here has not been privatized. Farmers who sow and harvest cooperatively owned land thus have little control over which crops they can grow, and at what price they can sell. Given its spatial proximity to Kyrgyzstan, comparisons concerning economic well-being are common in Sokh, and during my fieldwork there in 2004–5 there was widespread (if publicly muted) feeling that families would be better off if they could grow and

---

those currently residing together under one roof and typically constituting one economic unit. It might include more than one nuclear family, and several generations. The mean household size was 6.55, with the lowest consisting of one person, and the highest consisting of 18.

[25] In contrast with Tajiks in other parts of the Ferghana valley, it is usual for men in Sokh to pay bride-price (*qalym*) in the form of cash (typically 300,000 Uzbek sum or about $300) and clothing, as well as providing a bull calf for the wedding feast.

harvest privately. Thirdly, market-traded goods tend to be considerably more expensive than in other parts of Ferghana oblast' due to the high import costs. Friends and acquaintances would often complain that meat, the index of Sokh hospitality, was more expensive even than in Ferghana city, and many imported goods, such as clothes, fertilizer, and cooking oil, were sold at a mark-up price because of the difficulties of getting them past the customs officers posted on each side of the enclave.

Gendered Mobility

Seasonal work at a distance has historically been, and remains, gender-marked in Sokh. Despite the efforts of the Soviet state to incorporate women into paid work, few Sokh women had the opportunity to gain a higher education, and relatively few were therefore incorporated into the district's formal economy. In part this is the result of the practical difficulties of obtaining a higher education in Tajik, and the perceived "risks" for future marriageability of a daughter having studied far from home.[26] Historically, the departure for Samarkand, Khudjand, or Dushanbe where higher-level instruction was offered in Tajik, was spoken of as acceptable—indeed, prestigious—for sons but was seen to expose daughters to the potential indignity of long years awaiting a suitor in marriage. To this day, it is rare for a female school leaver from Sokh to enter more than a two-year medical training course at technical college following the ninth grade of school, and the economics of higher education have tended, in recent years, to privilege sons over daughters in access to university.

This has a direct impact on women's prospects for formal employment, but it is also much more likely to mean that women are married early (typically before the age of 19 and often before they leave school), bear children young, and their mobility away from their in-laws' households concomitantly constrained. Parviz who, at 24, was making preparations to marry the 17-year-old daughter of his mother's sister,[27] responded to my question concerning the young age of his bride with the comment "we have a *hadith* that says, 'why delay a good deed?' " Girls of school-leaving age often spoke of their anxiety at being a "burden" to their parents if

---

[26] On this theme see Harris, *Control and Subversion: Gender Relations in Tajikistan*, and G. Tett, "Guardians of the faith? Gender and religion in an (ex) Soviet Tajik village."

[27] First-cousin marriage is common in Sokh, and economic pressures seem, anecdotally, to be increasing its frequency.

they lived too long at home unable to contribute to the household budget, while for the mothers of unmarried daughters, questions, jokes, and speculation regarding who would ask for the daughter's hand and when she would be able to "give" her daughter were some of the most persistent and emotive topics of evening conversation.[28]

Once married, a young bride is expected to demonstrate "service" (*xizmat*) toward her in-laws, living in their home and attending to the daily running of the household under the instruction of her mother-in-law (*kain-ona*). The regional literature has documented well the practical and emotional obstacles with which such relationships can be fraught. What is less-often noted is that *xizmat* is as much a spatial as it is a social practice, and that relations of authority are marked and elaborated precisely through regulation of women's mobility. In Sokh, for instance, the daughter-in-law (*kelin*) is expected to request permission from her in-laws before leaving the household compound. Visits to her natal home are regulated by her husband's family, and within the mahalla certain spaces are codified as exclusively male (notably the mosque, the tea-house, and the billiard room).[29] Domestic space is also gendered: when her husband arrived from work, Sayora, in whose home I lived, would typically remove herself and her infant son to a space closer to the door, laying out mattresses and pillows to enable her husband to stretch out along the warm back wall furthest from the door. If her husband's male friends came to visit she would retreat altogether to the (unheated) outdoor kitchen, entering the main house only to bring food and clear away food bowls once her husband and his friends had eaten.

Such gendered domestic relations often figured, albeit indirectly, in explanations concerning the lack of "family" migration to Russia, in which husband and wife travelled together, with or without children. "Who would look after the children if she were to come too?" I was often asked in response to questions about possible family migrations. Mahalla men would often comment that Russia was "no place to bring our women." Life in Russia was "harsh," I was told; there was little respect for modesty, and "our women don't know Russian," making them vulnerable to abuse. Moreover, the conditions in which men worked and lived—on building

---

[28] Compare Harris, *Control and Subversion: Gender Relations in Tajikistan*, 99.

[29] On the mahalla as a space of gendered "distinct manners," see M. Liu, *Recognizing the Khan: Authority, Space and Political Imagination among Uzbek Men in Post-Soviet Osh, Kyrgyzstan* (PhD Dissertation, Department of Anthropology, University of Michigan, 2002), 94–146.

sites, in railway wagons, or packed several to a room in a rented apartment—would prevent the kinds of gendered comportment and spatial segregation that were a central feature of Sokh sociality. At an evening gathering to celebrate the breaking of the Ramadan fast in the mahalla where I lived, Tolibjon, a minibus-driver in Sokh when he was not working in Russia, elaborated on the claim that the Russian building site was no place for women "from here." Contrasting the situation in Sokh with the "relaxed" gender roles that existed in Uzbekistan's cities, he remarked: "If I want to call round on Parviz, for instance, but he is not there and only Sayora is home, I should wait outside, or come back later. If I go inside she'll be embarrassed. So just think how it would be if we were all living in a [railway] wagon together. [Laughing] 'Can I come in?!' No, that wouldn't work. I have to show him respect."

Migration patterns are shaped, then, by expectations concerning adequate female expressions of care, respect, and modesty, a fact reflected in survey data if we compare rates of migration for men and women from Sokh. Of the 437 work-related journeys to Russia on which information was collected for the period 2000–5, just 8 were undertaken by women, giving a migration rate for women over the five-year period of less than 2 percent.[30] By comparison, in Kyrgyz-majority villages in the neighboring Isfara valley, the proportion of journeys made by women over the same period was 14.8 percent—and anecdotal evidence suggests a significant rise in female and "family" migration since then.

If migration is shaped by understandings of appropriate female behavior, it is equally, if less obviously, informed by expectations of appropriate *masculine* conduct. Megoran has described "hegemonic Uzbek masculinity" as conceiving men first as "dutiful sons and then heads of families and providers for their own wives and children."[31] This formulation is useful for thinking about Sokh masculinities too, since it highlights the complex (and, in situations of migration, often competing) demands between these different roles. A good Sokh man must, first and foremost, show respect toward his own parents, manifest not just in material provisioning, but also in regular social visits, in the provision of practical help, and

30 While this data does not include those (small number) of households from which nobody was present to respond to the survey, some of which potentially include families from which both husband and wife are absent, it is fair to note that migration is highly gendered in Sokh and is spoken of as such.

31 Megoran, "Framing Andijan, Narrating the Nation: Islam Karimov's Account of the Events of 13th May 2005," 22.

often simply by being *available*—to participate in communal labor projects (*hashar*) on behalf of the family, for instance; to drive fellow family members to social gatherings; or to represent the family at mahalla meetings. Such obligations figured centrally in the survey responses from male householders who had decided *not* to leave for Russia in search of work. Yet a son is also expected to provide materially for his family, typically including his parents as well as his wife and children. Stories of successful trips circulated vigorously in Sokh, and my interlocutors would often chart them by pointing out material changes to households (a second floor added, a satellite dish jutting out from a roof, a car parked in a courtyard), by noting changes to young men themselves (more confident, more skilled, more worldly, and more fluent in Russian), or by noting the good deeds that money earned abroad had enabled a son to perform: contributing to the costs of a wedding, holding a feast (*toi*) to celebrate a son's circumcision, contributing to the costs of a funeral, or enabling an elderly relative to attend the Hajj.

Migration as a Field of Potential

A period of work abroad (or, more accurately, several successive seasons' work) has the potential, if successful, to enable a change in social standing and, as the Osellas noted in Kerala, to "accelerate an individual's progress along a culturally idealized trajectory towards mature manhood."[32] This was often spoken of in terms of a shift in bodily comportment or habitus. Mutabar-opa, whose 15-year-old son Nurullo made his first trip to Russia in the spring of 2005 after completing nine grades of school, responded to my questions later that summer about the impact that this trip had had upon him by pointing to changes in Nurullo's appearance: she said he was "stronger" now, less thin, less shy, and he had come to "know the meaning of work." Men who had travelled to Russia themselves noted changes in styles of dress and demeanor. "We learned the smell of money in Russia," Valijon told me smiling, before pointing out the number of men now sporting leather jackets in the district. "I remember the first time I came back. I was one of the first to buy a leather jacket there and I bought an umbrella to protect it from the snow. An umbrella! People here would laugh at me, but they just have no idea that if you want something to

[32] Osella and Osella, "Migration, Money and Masculinity in Kerala," 118. I explore this theme in more detail in M. Reeves, "Black Work, Green Money: Remittances, Ritual, and Domestic Economies in Southern Kyrgyzstan." Slavic Review 71, no. 1 (2012): 108–134.

last, you have to protect it. They just don't think of the future like that. But there I was, taking care of my jacket, and now every second man here has one."

The capacity for migration to "mark a difference" was particularly true in those instances where a young man had accumulated sufficient savings to cover the costs of his own wedding, or to finance a neighborhood celebration for a son's or nephew's circumcision. Such occasions enabled, most obviously, a very public performance of material success and neighborhood responsibility. Parents would often praise sons who had demonstrated their worldliness and readiness for adult life by meeting the costs of family celebrations. Gifts and cash from Russia figured prominently during the ritual exchanges that such occasions entailed, and videos of the celebration would enable success to circulate and be noted by visitors and guests.

Communal celebrations—and the traces they left—also served to re-embed men, who might be absent for nine months of the year, in webs of communal solidarity and participation. As Fog Olwig has extensively documented in relation to West Indian migration, mobile livelihoods may go hand in hand with a vigorous performance of belonging *to* place—indeed, may render such performances all the more important.[33] In the case of Sokh men, weddings and other communal celebrations were not just expressions of material success and popular magnanimity. They also served to articulate and produce very real physical connections—to *this* piece of ancestral land in *this* mahalla—in the face of prolonged absence.

Migration as a Source of Risk

Migration, then, could act as a transformative "coming of age" moment. Yet, crucially, it is also fraught with risks. The potential for failure in Russia is very high, and I encountered numerous, often tragic accounts, of men who had failed to leave Russia because they had not made enough money to justify the costs of their departure and who could simply not afford to return. Most Sokh men undertake work that is poorly paid and

[33] K. Fog Olwig, "Cultural Sites: Finding a Place in a Deterritorialised World," in K. Fog Olwig and K. Hastrup, *Siting Culture: The Shifting Anthropological Object* (London: Routledge, 1997), 17–37.

structurally precarious:[34] undocumented, uncontracted, and open to abuse from employers, as well as from the police and from the intermediaries who secure informal construction contracts. Moreover, the longer one stays beyond the three months permitted to holders of temporary residence registrations, the more illegalized one risks becoming. Migrants who meet obstacles in Russia can thus find themselves in extended cycles of debt, paying a significant proportion of their income to local officials to keep their presence invisible to systems of stately accounting and legibility. There are more existential risks, too. Bribes and theft on the journey home are frequent; accidents are not uncommon, and since the vast majority of employees are uninsured, the costs of treatment or return in the case of accident typically fall to the migrant himself, and his immediate relatives and close friends.[35]

The constraints of life and labor—being precarious, poorly paid, and liable to unexpected termination (or being "thrown" (*kidat'*) as the Russian idiom would have it)—profoundly restrict the kinds of gender performance that are possible. One informant put this particularly bluntly when he observed that migration meant that men took on women's roles, and women, men's—the disruption to "proper" ways of behaving here calibrated through a reversal of gender roles. Kurban, who shared a railway wagon on a building site in Irkutsk with several other men from his mahalla, told me about his decision to make his own bread in Russia rather than buying it each day, and his subsequent embarrassment when it turned out "like a brick," hard and tasteless. In a similar anecdote, 19-year-old Rakhmatullo described how he would wash his clothes at

[34] Survey results suggest that earnings in Russia were significantly higher for those Sokh men who are able to engage in private trade than for the majority who worked in construction. Reported monthly earnings ranged from 1,200 rubles to 30,000 rubles, though the latter is an outlying sum indicated by a wealthy trader of dried fruits. The mean monthly earning was 6,200 rubles ($230), with the vast majority of reported earnings in 2005 clustered between 5,000 and 9,000 rubles ($185–330).

[35] In the context of Uzbekistan's tight control over migration data, it is extremely hard to estimate the scope and scale of such tragedies. During my period of research, I came to know of three fatal accidents—two on building sites, one, mysteriously, on the long journey through Kazakhstan to southern Siberia—and virtually everyone with whom I spoke could name somebody who had died or been seriously injured in Russia. I was also told of an informal system of mutual "insurance" to meet the substantial costs of repatriation should any person from a given mahalla die in Russia. On the "cost of dying abroad" for Central Asian labor migrants, see A. Sarkorova and J. Abdrakhmanova, "The Cost of Dying Abroad for Central Asians," *Reporting Central Asia*, no. 494, Institute for War & Peace Reporting, June 5, 2007.

night while his co-workers slept to avoid the embarrassment of being seen by them to be doing "women's work." Privacy was minimal and the most basic activities—sleeping, washing, cooking, eating, shaving, defecating—entailed complex routines and careful negotiations over their timing and visibility. Life on the building site, in short, could make a man of you; but it could also threaten the very things that make one human.

Testing Friendships

If ideas of manliness in Sokh are bound up with expectations concerning the proper performance of kinship roles—of father, son, and husband—they are also importantly shaped by the demands of friendship, neighborliness, and shared school experience. Friends and former classmates are absolutely crucial in helping new migrants to secure work, and a first-time migrant can expect help, just as he can expect to be asked for assistance in due course. The role of such ties emerges strikingly from the Sokh survey data. In finding their first employment, fewer than 5 percent of survey respondents who had worked in Russia relied on any kind of assistance that did *not* originate in Sokh, whether in the form of Russian intermediaries (*posredniki*), adverts, newspaper announcements, or commercial agencies. Moreover, over half of the returned migrants surveyed indicated that they were in turn able to invite someone to take up work, with 20 percent of respondents inviting one person and 38.3 percent inviting two or more.

Sokh sociality inflected life in Russia in other ways too. Most Sokh men reported sharing living space with others from their mahalla, an arrangement that could foster an intense sense of "barracks camaraderie." Men would often accompany their accounts of life "in town" with photographs from impromptu birthday celebrations around tablecloths squashed between bunk-beds in the railway wagons, shipping containers, or outhouses that typically served as home. I was often told that only under such constraints did "true friendship" emerge, and of the lengths to which men had gone to help colleagues, friends, and neighbors in trouble.

But these conditions could also strain social relations to their limit. During one winter lunch break, Kobil, a 45-year-old chemistry teacher who, as a child in the 1970s, had travelled to Moscow to participate in an Olympiad for talented schoolchildren, spoke of the multiple shocks that he experienced upon returning to Russia 30 years later in very different circumstances. "They treat you like you aren't fully human, you know?"

he said of his work as a painter and decorator on a private building site. "My boss was shocked when he found out I had a degree. He would ask me: 'Isn't there any work for you in your motherland?' Well, it was our motherland too!" Kobil described the indignation he felt at being promised one sum for a complex piece of decorative work and then being paid less when he found out an ingenious way to complete the job in half the time, unscrewing and refitting the wooden panels that required painting. He recounted his shock at being given bunks to sleep on without mattresses and sheets: "Did they think we were going to bring our own mattresses with us from Uzbekistan?" And he described the jarring contrast to the authority that he enjoyed in Sokh as a teacher when, in Russia, people referred to him as *churka*, a term of abuse for Central Asians with connotations of being "thick" and socially naive.

It was the pain of friendships strained, however, which eventually led Kobil to give up his work in Russia and return to teaching, for a fraction of the salary that he was making in Irkutsk. He described the decisive moment:

> Your best friend here won't even recognize you in Russia. That's a tragedy. I lost one of my best friends that way. He has been working in Russia for ages. He is still there at the moment, and I turned up in Irkutsk with the hope that he would help me out. I helped him out here in Sokh so many times! But there people's thinking changes. He had a birthday party, he was sitting there with two Russian friends, and he didn't invite me. Well... it wasn't the lack of invitation itself [that bothered me] so much as what it symbolized—I mean you can sit around with three friends, or you can sit around with five on your birthday, what difference does it make? But I think he wanted to make the point to me that here he didn't consider me his friend. He had his circle of friends there—Russians—and he didn't want me there to join him. He had found his niche there, he was working, and I had just showed up. And he wanted to remind me that he had power over me there.

Later in the conversation he elaborated on why such constraints also meant that, following "damaged" social relations, it was often easier to stay in Russia rather than face the embarrassment and demands of mahalla sociality in Sokh:

> There people are in a totally different world. They forget about life in Sokh, about their relatives, about their family and friends, and the fact that some day they will have to come back and confront you or your relatives in the mahalla again, and will have to deal with the shame of having rejected you there. We have a saying, you know, that you find your real friends in times

> of difficulty. Well, it's really true. I got drunk and told that guy that I would never consider him my friend again.

The demands of Sokh sociality was a recurrent theme, and was often used to explain why some men—a minority, but a significant proportion nonetheless—seemed to sever all ties with wives, parents, and children in Sokh. Mutabar-opa, who had earlier celebrated the return of her young son, Nurullo, from his first period of work abroad, commented on the tragedy of young brides who barely had the chance to get to know their husbands before they are left alone, awaiting their return. "They [the men who have departed] reach a stage where they have second wives there, families, and his wife *here* is sitting, waiting, sucking her cheeks. He doesn't write, doesn't send money, but yet he's ashamed to come back. [He knows] people would talk!" For *kelin*s left to live with in-laws, waiting was, indeed, often a long and uncertain process—and one shot through with the tensions of being in a position of powerlessness in the control of household budgets. Remittances, if a family is lucky enough to receive them in a man's absence, are typically sent to fathers and brothers rather than wives—with the result that the absent man's wife and children might be the last to see any of the remitted cash. For migrants themselves, meanwhile, the dilemma of whether to "stay and save" or to return at the end of a season was also shot through with a sense of the burden of family expectations: to come back empty-handed after a 9 or 21-month absence would be no return visit at all.

Migration, Marriage, and the Specter of "Second Wives"

Perhaps unsurprisingly given these contexts, migration also figured centrally in discussions concerning sexuality, fidelity, and the demands of long-distance marriages. The strain that prolonged male absence can pose to marital relationships has become a regular feature of news reporting on migrant life in Russia. Recent news articles have documented, for instance, the increasing use of "divorce by text message" by Tajik men in Russia,[36] the obstacles faced by women in asserting their legal right to property if

[36] "I Divorce U," RFE/RL Tajik Service, September 8, 2009, www.rferl.org/content/I_Divorce_U_/1818070.html.

they have been abandoned by husbands who are abroad,[37] and the threats posed to sexual health by the growing prevalence of AIDS and other sexually transmitted diseases brought home by returning migrants.[38]

Such themes also figured, albeit in more muted fashion, in discussions in Sokh concerning migration and its consequences for family life. Most women I spoke to assumed that absent husbands had extra-marital relationships in Russia with "European" (i.e., Russian) women. "Every man from here has got his Galochka, his Tanyushka in Russia," 30-year-old Sayora put it to me, conjuring, with the affectionate, diminutive form of these decidedly Russian names, a realm of intimacy from which she was excluded.[39] Others queried whether I, as somebody visibly "European," had ended up in Sokh having been brought back to the district as a "second wife." While not uncommon such extra-marital relationships are, however, probably less widespread than the densely circulating stories about them in Sokh would indicate. The realities of six or seven-day working weeks in Russia, exploitative rates of pay, and lack of privacy on building sites and in railway wagons mean that opportunities for any kind of intimacy are minimal, and men often depict the working "season" as a period in which all human needs and desires are subordinated to the uncompromising demands of earning, saving, and keeping out of the way of the local police. For Sokh men who are undocumented in Russia, without a *propiska*—a temporary residence registration affirming their legal presence in the city—travel "off site" is kept to a minimum and visits to commercial sex workers are fraught with risks. Keeping a "second wife," meanwhile, is largely confined to the relatively small group of more-established migrants: those who feel at home in the city, who enjoy the privacy of an apartment, and whose earnings allow them some degree of material comfort and security.

Whatever the real scale of such relationships—a question that I did not seek to establish in the survey research—what is significant here is the way in which perceptions of Russia as a site of particular sexual and emotional

[37] M. Odinaeva and L. Olimova, "Marriage vows not always enough in Tajikistan," *Institute for War and Peace Reporting Report on Central Asia*, no. 564, January 30, 2009.

[38] "Tajikistan-Russia-AIDS: Tajik migrant workers bring back money, gifts and often AIDS from Russia," *Agence France-Press*, December 14, 2003.

[39] Very occasionally, such relationships were visible in Sokh too. I was once invited to the home of Hakim, a wealthy Sokh trader who had recently returned to his mahalla accompanied by Lena, a middle-aged Russian woman from Novosibirsk. Hakim introduced Lena as his "second wife," but, as it emerged during conversation, she was also his landlady and the intermediary who secured his trading stall at one of Novosibirsk's markets.

possibility came to inflect local concerns, for those who remained behind, about the practical and moral entailments of marriage. Recent literature has illuminated how migration to distant cities may enable new patterns of consumption, as well as new forms of social and sexual experimentation, for the men and women who depart.[40] Correspondingly less attention, however, has been focused on the way in which such encounters can mediate a reassessment, for those who remain behind, of the parameters of their own modernity. In Sokh, the fact of widespread male absence to a place that is considered at once more "advanced" and more permissive than home has come to serve as a powerful site for exploring and debating differences in social obligations and sexual mores. The Russia that figured in the accounts of Sokh women whose husbands were abroad was characterized by a mixture of opportunity and moral risk: a place of tall, beautiful, skimpily clad, and sexually experienced women who knew, as Sayora put it, how to "satisfy" men; a place where women are autonomous, but also shockingly unconcerned with the welfare of their parents and siblings. Above all, the Russia that figured in such accounts was a place tolerant of sexual promiscuity and little concern for wives left sitting and waiting back home.

If migration has contributed, along with the soap operas and music videos that have been made accessible through the proliferation of satellite dishes, to fostering a particular image of Russia and Russians, it has also, in important ways, prompted new kinds of commentary on the regulation of sexual relations in Sokh. For wives who were left "waiting," uncertain whether a husband would ever return or not, the dilemmas were particularly acute. Mehrigul, a half-Tajik, half-Tatar mother of four, spoke of her anger at being left without money because earnings were being spent on a lover in Russia instead, and the pain of harmful "talk" after her husband had failed to arrive home for the fourth winter in a row. But even in those instances where a *kelin* knew that her husband would return for three months of the year, the emotional pressures could be considerable. One young bride, who was married in December 2005, spoke of her sense of failure at "delaying" her husband's departure for Russia because, by the following May, she had not yet fallen pregnant. She was taken for costly

---

40 M. Beth Mills, for instance, has shown how for young, unmarried women from rural Thailand, migration to Bangkok allows them "to pursue a level of personal autonomy unavailable to them in the village, while at the same time allowing them to uphold their obligations to their families." M.B. Mills, "Contesting the Margins of Modernity: Women, Migration and Consumption in Thailand," *American Ethnologist* 24, no. 1 (1997): 44.

ultrasound scans in Ferghana, and her (in)fertility became a topic of considerable family commentary: should her husband leave, nonetheless, in order not to miss more months of the building season that was already well underway? Or should the couple continue to try for a child? Women also complained about the domination of the local medical establishment by men (the sole female gynecologist to whom Sokh women had access was over the border in Kyrgyzstan), and the lack of information about sexually transmitted diseases. As one middle-aged woman noted, laughing at her own "ignorance," the first time she heard about the risks of AIDS (*SPID* in Russian) at an NGO-sponsored seminar, she thought she was being told about the dangers of alcohol (Russian *spirt*) and wondered why, as a woman who didn't drink, she had been invited to such an event.

Besides crystallizing concerns about the state of medical care in the district, the (perceived) prevalence of extra-marital affairs in Russia fed into a more general discourse of Sokh's own "backwardness." Far from criticizing husbands for lack of faithfulness, many women attributed the prevalence of such liaisons to the "ignorance" and "shyness" of Sokh women. Migration, in other words, was leading to new kinds of critical reflection concerning the regulation of sexual relations at home. One particularly stark example of such discourse came early during my fieldwork from Mutabar-opa, the 50-year-old mother of Nurullo. We were chatting on the bench near the water-pump that served her street, when a young *kelin* walked past us on her way back home from the water-pump. The young woman was struggling with two large pails of water, and was stooped over in an effort to prevent the water from spilling as she climbed uphill. She was dressed in the typical work clothes of a *kelin* who had stepped out briefly from the family courtyard, with a faded green overcoat wrapped around a long grey dress, black plastic galoshes on her feet, and her hair tied up in a scarf. Mutabar-opa and I had been talking about something else entirely when the sight of the young woman struggling with her water pails led Mutabar-opa to change subject suddenly. With the unfortunate *kelin* still in earshot, she launched into an impassioned commentary on the "un-culturedness" (*nekulturnost'*) of Sokh women, leaving me struggling for an adequate response:

> Look at her bent over like an old woman! If you look at her from behind, you wouldn't know whether she was 20 or 50. Our women have no idea how to dress, how to make themselves beautiful, how to make a man feel good. Even in bed they behave like cows, they'll just turn over on their sides to let their husband relieve his urges, and then roll straight back over!

Mutabar-opa then linked this to a previous conversation we had had about migration from Dekhkonobod, her mahalla:

> Do you think it's any surprise that when our boys are in Russia they each pick up a blonde [*vziali po odnoi blondinkoi*]? They've never seen a woman's body like that before. Our women have no idea how to show affection. They just sit there like this, averting their eyes!

Mutabar-opa's discourse was no doubt shaped by the fact that, as someone who had married in to Sokh from a much more industrialized area of northern Tajikistan, she perceived herself to be considerably more worldly and "cultured" than the younger generation of women in her mahalla. But this kind of self-abasing commentary was far from unique. Gossip about women left "sitting" at home, especially if they had not borne any children, could be sharp and wounding. In a context where a woman's respectability depends on marriage and where her authority within the household accrues to the extent that she bears children, the moral censure surrounding male infidelity could easily come to rest upon the presumed "failings" of his wife.

Sokh women, then, could find themselves in the paradoxical situation of being expected at once to conceal their sexuality, as *so'xchilik* required, while at the same time subject to social commentary of the kind undertaken by Mutabar-opa for not being "attractive" enough to their husbands. Colette Harris has interpreted a similar dynamic in the Khatlon region of Tajikistan in terms of a patriarchal logic of control. Harris argues that despite the fact that the men who have migrated to Russia for work have "learned to enjoy more open relationships in Russia, which makes them complain of boredom with their Tajik marriages," they nonetheless "refuse to allow either their wives or their daughters greater mobility or exposure to the outside world. For all their grumbling, the last thing they actually seem to want is for their Tajik wives to become Russified."[41]

My sense is that the actual dynamic in question is rather more complex than this narrative of male dominance would suggest. Control over female sexuality is, indeed, bound up with expectations of appropriate masculine behavior, and many men may refuse their wives and daughters freedom to "continue their relatively comfortable domestic situation," as Harris suggests. But this is not the whole story. Expectations of male and female behavior are each the product of a complexly constituted social order that

---

[41] Harris, *Control and Subversion: Gender Relations in Tajikistan*, 148.

is marked as much by generational hierarchies as by a simple binary of male control over women. In discussing why they could not contemplate allowing women more "freedom" (not least by allowing their wives to travel with them, and work in Russia), men often responded in terms of their own obligations to their parents: a *kelin*'s behavior was the index of a son's respect for his parents, perhaps especially in his own absence.

There is a second factor, moreover, which complicates an explanation framed in terms of patriarchy alone. This is the fact of obligations to a mahalla community beyond the immediate family, such that individual identity is profoundly shaped—indeed, is understood to be *constituted* by—membership in this community. The role of the mahalla in regulating social life, materially and morally, was a constant refrain during fieldwork, and has been extensively documented in literature on the region. I was often told that it was "better to lose one's religion than to lose one's community"[42]—the rhetorical equation here signaling that to lose *either* of these would effectively be to lose one's identity. And it is the mahalla, with its capacity to celebrate or condemn, to judge or gossip, which polices social conformity. Harris is not wrong, then, to see the control of female sexuality as importantly constitutive of Tajik masculinities. But we need to situate this dynamic within a much broader social system. It is precisely because ideas of manliness in Sokh are profoundly constituted by expectations of filial duty and mahalla membership that young men participate so actively in keeping women "in place."

* * * * *

Seasonal and long-term migration to Russia is fostering a new degree of reflexivity, for men and women alike, about the demands of so'xchilik and the entailments of long-distance marriage. These demands, I have argued in this chapter, are complex and contradictory: a successful season of work in Russia can, in important respects, consolidate the status of a young man as a fully-fledged member of his community, by enabling him to provide for his family and to acquire the skills, habits, and social recognition that earlier generations of men would have acquired through service in the Soviet military. But the experience of work that is precarious and poorly paid, in conditions that can be exploitative and marked by forms of ethnicized discrimination that undermine precisely the "manliness" of Central Asian men, mean that the stakes of migration are high

---

[42] In Sokh dialect, *az jamiyat buromadana, az din buromadan nagztar.*

indeed. The chapter has sought to document this complexity in order to enrich our understanding of the range of considerations—that extend far beyond the narrowly economic—that can shape a decision to leave for Russia or not.

In so doing, however, it has also sought to explore Central Asian masculinities beyond the rather inflexible categories in which they are typically framed. In Uzbekistan, ideals of "proper" manly behavior are shaped by a host of modernizing discourses, projects of religious reform, and state institutions including, most consequentially, the army. Presidential writings, as Megoran has demonstrated, have fostered an image of the Uzbek male as defined by virility, filial duty, *and* unflinching loyalty to the state.[43] There is, indeed, no shortage of public images that would reinforce the rather one-dimensional account of male identity that figures in the presidential corpus, and juxtapose it with an equally "thin" account of female identity. And yet, explored ethnographically, what emerges is precisely the mutability of gender roles, and their position within complex fields of power. For contemporary Sokh men, the demands of being a good son, husband, father, friend, mahalla member, elder, and citizen are considerable—and not necessarily easily reconcilable with one another. The expectations of respectful performances of filial care often stand in tension with the need to provide materially for families, and the role of gifts "from town" in demonstrating friendship and affirming community membership.

Attending to these complexities can help us to gain some analytical purchase on the way in which large-scale male departure for Russia is transforming gender roles in rural Central Asia—but also on the *limits* of such transformation. Migration is leading to new forms of awareness of, and local commentary about, how gender roles and family relations are different "over there." But we would be wrong to read migration, as news reports are wont to, as producing the wide-scale "breakdown" in marriage, or as leading to significant shifts in the conduct of sexual relations at home. To understand why, as I have suggested, we need an explanation that moves beyond "patriarchy" or the inherent "conservatism" of rural society to explore both the inter-play of gender and generational hierarchies, and the role of community and family membership in articulating ideals of Sokh manhood today.

---

43 Megoran, "Framing Andijan, Narrating the Nation: Islam Karimov's Account of the Events of 13th May 2005."

TRANSITION, MIGRATION, CAPITALISM: FEMALE UZBEK SHUTTLE TRADERS IN ISTANBUL

Luisa Piart

Since independence, the development of shuttle trade and the mushrooming of open-air bazaars in Uzbekistan illustrate tendencies common to the transitional economies of the post-communist world.[1] Starting during the perestroika period between 1986 and 1991, the gradual collapse of the state distribution system left an institutional vacuum that gave rise to a hitherto unprecedented scale of private commercial activities.[2] Various figures existing for neighboring countries indicate that goods brought to Uzbekistan by shuttle traders accounted for between 20 and 48 percent of gross imports in the early 2000s.[3] During the 1980s a commercial marketplace was also set up in Istanbul's Laleli district. In close proximity to the Grand Bazaar, Laleli became a major destination in the 1990s for petty traders coming from former Soviet countries and Eastern Europe. The first commuters to Laleli sold or bartered subsidized goods. Subsequently, commercial activities in Laleli specialized in clothing and shoes. In its heyday in 1996, Laleli may have yielded the equivalent of up to 60 percent of Turkish gross exports. In 2011, profits from the shuttle trade in Turkey were worth more than $4 billion.[4]

---

[1] C. Humphrey and R. Mandel, eds., *Markets and Moralities. Ethnographies of Postsocialism* (Oxford, New York: Berg, 2002).

[2] E. Sik and C. Wallace, "The Development of Open-Air Markets in East-Central Europe," *International Journal of Urban and Regional Research* 23, no. 4 (1999): 699.

[3] According to a Kyrgyz parliamentary commission, the shuttle trade made up for 48.7 percent of imports to this country in 2001. H. Bal, "Geçiş Ülkelerinde Yolsuzluk ve Kayıtdışı Ekonomi: Kırgızistan Bavul Ticareti Örneği" *Manas Sosyal Bilimleri Dergisi* 5, no. 9 (2004): 186, http://yordam.manas.kg/ekitap/pdf/Manasdergi/sbd/sbd9/sbd-9-10.pdf. In comparison, in Kazakhstan this figure may be 25 percent, and in Russia it constituted a third of all imports in the late 1990s. S. Yessenova, "Hawkers and Containers in Zarya Vostoka: How 'Bizarre' Is the Post-Soviet Bazaar?" *Research in Economic Anthropology* 24 (2006): 57; A. Yakovlev, "Russian 'Shuttle' Traders and Dynamics of Integration into Global Markets," *Fourth CEEISA Convention*, University of Tartu, 2006, 1, http://www.ceeisaconf.ut.ee/orb.aw/class=file/action=preview/id=166497/yakovlev.doc.

[4] According to the Central Bank of Turkey, which has produced figures on the shuttle trade since 1996. M. Eder, "From 'Suitcase' Merchants to Organized Informal Trade? The Case of Laleli District in Istanbul," *4th Mediterranean Social and Political Meeting*, European University Institute, Robert Schuman Centre for Advanced Studies, 2003, 9.

Referred to as a "modern avatar of peddling,"[5] shuttle trade is practiced by small-scale economic actors who take advantage of price differences between one country and another, and who characteristically transport their merchandise themselves in "suitcases," which are actually large patched-up plastic bags. In Turkish, *bavulcu* literally means someone making money from his or her suitcase (*bavul*).[6] This neologism appeared in Istanbul to name the traders from former communist countries who started to overrun the Laleli district in the early 1990s. Although its historical origin differs, the Russian word *meshochnik* is also used to designate these actors, similarly characterizing someone who transports merchandise in, and sells goods from, a sack. Another and more widespread Russian term stresses the shuttle traders' constant movement between two or more destinations: a *tchelnoki* is someone who commutes to and from, like a shuttle on a weaver's loom. Thus, "suitcase trade" and "shuttle trade" describe the two skills necessary to succeed in this commercial activity: the ability to conclude business deals, or to empty and refill the suitcase, and the ability to circulate with some degree of regularity between several destinations.

According to data from the Turkish Embassy in Tashkent, Uzbeks travelling officially to Turkey as *bavulcu* numbered between 800 and 900 in 2005. Eighty-five percent of them were women.[7] In Laleli, traders from other countries of the former Communist bloc are mostly women as well. Although similar commercial circulations exist elsewhere, they are rarely so strongly gendered.[8] Thus, in the post-Soviet transition, it is typically a woman that comes to mind when speaking of a shuttle trader. The aim of this chapter is to question this femininity both in practice and discourse. The material presented here was collected in 2005 and 2006 during

---

[5] M. Peraldi, "Aventuriers du nouveau capitalisme marchand. Essai d'anthropologie de l'éthique mercantile," *Working Paper Series, Ramses* 2, 2007, 4, http://ramses2.mmsh.univ-aix.fr/Publications/Commerce-a-la-valise.pdf.

[6] In Turkish the suffix *–ci/cu/cü/cı* marks the profession. A *çiçekçi* is a florist (from *çiçek*, flower).

[7] From June 2003 to July 2007, Uzbek nationals traveling to Turkey had to obtain a visa before their departure. This data is derived from the questionnaire and documents required to request a visa in 2005. It was provided by the Ambassador of Turkey in Uzbekistan, Ms. Gaye Öyüncü. My most sincere thanks go to her for her assistance.

[8] D. Yükseker, "Trust and Gender in a Transnational Market: The Public Culture of Laleli, Istanbul," *Public Culture* 16, no. 1 (2004): 47–65. Commercial circulations have been well-researched in the Mediterranean region, notably in Marseille and Naples. M. Peraldi, *Cabas et containers. Activités marchandes informelles et réseaux migrants transfrontaliers* (Paris: Maisonneuve & Larose-MMSH, 2001); A. Tarrius, *La mondialisation par le bas: les nouveaux nomades de l'économie souterraine* (Paris: Balland, 2002).

extensive fieldwork undertaken in Istanbul and Uzbekistan, both in Tashkent and Samarkand.[9] The Uzbek shuttle traders form only a minority of the "colorful" Laleli crowd. Nevertheless, they were easy to identify in Istanbul, where the fieldwork started, and subsequently 50 Uzbek shuttle traders were systematically interviewed in Turkish in the two countries where they shop for and sell Turkish goods.[10]

After only a few weeks in the Laleli district, it became clear that the Uzbek shuttle traders rarely recognized themselves according to the designations conferred on them, like bavulcu or tchelnoki. I was often asked to specify by the traders themselves what was meant by these terms, which are nonetheless pervasive in political discourses and in the media in Turkey and Uzbekistan.[11] A semantic fuzziness predominates when actors name their own activity. This paradox reflects two issues at stake in this chapter. First, shuttle trade carries with it a suspicious reputation and, as such, many feel uncomfortable to identify with it. Negative views about female shuttle traders are indeed prevalent and ubiquitous in both Turkey and Uzbekistan, where they are associated with prostitution. Second, this paradox reflects the extreme diversity of practices and careers of Uzbek shuttle traders traveling to Istanbul. Accordingly, the goal of the fieldwork presented here was not to discover if a certain person was a shuttle trader or not according to a preset definition, but rather to adopt a non-normative approach to this mobile trade, finding relevance to the analysis also in what people *do* and what they *say* (or what others say) about the trade.

---

[9] Since Uzbek border and trade regulations evolve constantly, it is important to stress that most of the information on these issues presented here dates from the fieldwork period.

[10] My thanks go to the Institut français des études sur l'Asie centrale (IFEAC) in Tashkent and the Institut français d'études anatoliennes (IFEA) in Istanbul, which provided two short-term grants to carry out fieldwork from January to July 2005 in Istanbul, and from March to May 2006 in Uzbekistan (Tashkent and Samarkand). Most of the Uzbek shuttle traders coming to Istanbul have at least a basic command of the Turkish language because of its similarities with the Uzbek language.

[11] For Turkey, see J.-F. Pérouse, "Irruption et éclipse des navetteurs 'russes' à Istanbul (1988–1999): remous et rumeurs dans la mégapole," *Slavica Occitania*, no. 8 (1999): 273–312. For Uzbekistan, see Kamp, "Gender ideals and income realities: Discourses about Labor and Gender in Uzbekistan," *Nationalities Papers* 33, no. 3 (2005): 419; "Uzbek Border Row Introduces New Element of Tension in Central Asia," *Eurasianet*, January 27, 2003, http://www.eurasianet.org/departments/business/articles/eav012703.shtml; M. Tokhtakhodjaeva, "Traditional Stereotypes and Women's Problems in Post-Soviet Uzbekistan: A Survey of the Mass Media," *WLUML Dossier*, no. 22 (1999): 32–42.

The choice to engage in shuttle trade is a decision to leave home with the hope of returning with the means for a better life. Shuttle trade involves accepting the risk of trying one's luck abroad with the hope of improving one's personal economic situation. Therefore, even if it is not a decision for long-term departure or settlement in another country, shuttle trade resembles a mobility strategy. While some traders build their careers on these commercial circulations, others resort to them only temporarily. Nevertheless, the activity constitutes the most mobile part of what are dense and complex migration networks existing between Turkey and Uzbekistan. Commercial circulations play a key role in their cohesion. To understand why shuttle trade has acquired above all a feminine face, it is necessary to take a closer look at mobility strategies and the place of commuters within migration networks. Among the new destinations accessible since 1991, Turkey—and especially Istanbul—is a popular destination for Uzbeks willing to migrate. If their "Turkishness" can ease their entry, more importantly Uzbek migrants both participate in and take advantage of the emergence of Istanbul as a major crossroads for international migrations.[12]

Cross-border shuttle has been described as the most characteristic form of East European post-communist mobility.[13] The situation in post-Soviet Central Asia differs noticeably from this context, since many restrictions still constrain freedom of movement.[14] However, from a gender point of view, shuttle trade is as significant in Central Asia as it is in Eastern Europe. It is argued that the Uzbek female shuttle traders, through their knowledge of the migratory field and their experience, are indeed true

[12] A community who fled the sovietization of Turkestan is settled in Istanbul. The Uzbek newcomers are seldom in contact with this established community. See A. Bentzin, "Zwischen türkischer, turkestanischer und usbekischer Identität? Usbekische Migranten in Istanbul," in B. Pusch and T. Wilkoszewski, eds., *Facetten internationaler Migration in die Türkei: Gesellschaftliche Rahmenbedingungen und persönliche Lebenswelten* (Würzburg: Ergon Verlag, 2008), 235–248. M. Aslan and J.-F. Pérouse, "Istanbul: le comptoir, le hub, le sas et l'impasse. Fonctions dans le système migratoire international," *Revue Européenne des Migrations Internationales* 19, no. 3 (2003): 173–204. For an overview on migration issues in Turkey, see A. İçduygu and K. Kirişci, eds., *Land of Diverse Migrations. Challenges of Emigration and Immigration in Turkey* (Istanbul: MiReKoç-Bilgi University Press, 2009).

[13] M. Morokvasic, "La mobilité transnationale comme ressource: le cas des migrants de l'Europe de l'Est," *Cultures et conflits* 33–34 (1999): 105–122.

[14] M. Reeves, "Travels in the Margins of the State: Everyday Geography in the Ferghana Valley Borderlands," in J. Sahadeo and R. Zanca, eds., *Everyday Life in Central Asia. Past and Present* (Bloomington: Indiana University Press, 2007), 284.

"mobility experts."[15] In order to both understand why Uzbek shuttle traders going to Istanbul are mostly women and scrutinize the assumption, I will first sketch portraits of three female shuttle traders, illustrating the diversity of practices and initiatives among women. Second, an analysis of how the activity started and developed will help differentiate male and female shuttle trade practices. Finally, relations between migrants and shuttle traders will be investigated.

Portraits of Female Shuttle Traders

Uzbek women who travel to Istanbul as suitcase traders share common practices that define them as a group. They come to buy the same kinds of products, mainly clothes and shoes. They arrive by plane and find accommodation in a number of hotels located in Laleli. Beyond these few shared characteristics, their actual commercial activities in Istanbul provide reasons to differentiate their commercial trips. These differences manifest themselves in the quantities of goods bought, the means and routes of shipment chosen, whether or not they own the goods they buy, the degree to which they are acting on their own initiative (in the sense of enterprise and determination in one's own actions), and how their abilities and skills develop in the course of their individual experiences and according to their biographical backgrounds. Through precise portraits of female traders, it is possible to chart the evolutions and turns of the shuttle trade, a phenomenon that has been ongoing for approximately two decades.

Zuleikho, a 48-year-old woman, was one of the first female shuttle traders that I met in Istanbul in 2005.[16] A widow since the mid-1980s, she was the only one in her family from Samarkand living in Tashkent.[17] Since 1992, she had been going to Istanbul in order to sell Uzbek handicrafts and to buy Turkish clothes in small quantities, which she then resold back

---

[15] S. Potot, "Le réseau migrant: une organisation entre solidarité communautaire et 'zone de libre échange,'" *Migrations Société*, nos. 105–106 (2006): 49–74.

[16] In order to protect the anonymity of the people mentioned, their names have been changed.

[17] That is to say that she is registered as a Tashkent resident, according to the Soviet *propiska* system still in force. The traders usually recognized themselves as Uzbek, specifying their city of origin. In this chapter, the term "Uzbek" is thus used to refer to the citizens of the Republic of Uzbekistan. According to the Turkish Embassy in Turkey, 90 percent of *bavulcu* live in Tashkent, 7 percent in Samarkand, and 3 percent in Dzhizzak, Andijan, Kokand, and Ferghana.

in Tashkent or Samarkand.[18] Before she began her career as an "entrepreneur without an enterprise," she worked as a Russian school teacher.[19] At the beginning of the 1980s, she had lived in Moscow for three years with her son and her Belarusian husband. She started in the suitcase trade by chance while travelling with a friend to Istanbul who had been to Laleli once before. She recalled her first trip with a smile: "With the Turks, you have to be careful! At the beginning you are not able to count your money very well, the different currencies . . . the quality, the goods, you get everything stolen, you don't understand what happens to you!" She was a regular in Laleli when I met her. She even had a *sevgili* (darling) there, Mustafa, a Kurd from Diyarbakir who sold Uzbek handicrafts in the Grand Bazaar. But besides storing her merchandise when she could not sell all of it before returning to Uzbekistan, he did not support her in any other way and, in any case, she did not trust him in matters of money.

The main worries of Zuleikho concerned border transit and the sale of goods. Problems transpired in both countries because she did not collect orders before buying goods in Istanbul, nor in Tashkent or Samarkand. Additionally, she did not own a shop or stall in the bazaar where she could sell her goods. This precarious situation increased the risks, and each trip was a commercial gamble. Thus, she could only buy merchandise in small quantities and relied on her network of relatives and friends. In Uzbekistan, she made the majority of her sales at home and at get-togethers of women that combined friendly discussion with commercial sale. Despite her long experience in Istanbul, her negotiations with the Turkish salespersons in the Grand Bazaar were tough. Her business partners knew that she had to sell her stock of handicrafts during her stay because she needed the money. As a rule, she managed to travel from Uzbekistan to Istanbul once a month and stayed one or two weeks. These trips yielded 500 dollars each if she was lucky. In 1996, she even stayed for a whole year in Laleli and opened a small clothing shop. On the contrary, however, she did not go to Istanbul for two consecutive years in 2002 and 2003. At the time of the interview in 2006, she was considering settling in Laleli again. Yet it seemed increasingly unlikely that she would do so because she had

---

[18] Most of the products that are sold in Laleli are made in Turkey. Laleli widely took advantage and contributed to the development of the apparel sector in Istanbul. S. Dedeoglu, *Women Workers in Turkey. Global Industrial Production in Istanbul* (London, New York: Tauris Academic Studies, 2008), 58–70.

[19] Expression from Clifford Geertz, "*Peddlers and Princes. Social Change and Economic Modernization in Two Indonesian Towns*" (Chicago-London: The University of Chicago Press, 1993 (original edition 1963), 28.

accumulated debts since the customs regime in Uzbekistan tightened in 2002. Moreover, her main concern was for her son. She expressed her intention not to leave for a longer period of time until he had married or had found a job to support himself.

Zuleikho's family situation was a difficult one not only because she was a widow, but also because her 26-year-old son, her only child, was still single and without a stable job in Uzbekistan. I met her son, Zafer, in Istanbul, where he had stayed for a year in 2005 and worked in a tiny apparel sweatshop in Laleli. This turned out to be a short-term endeavor, however, since his boss did not pay him regularly, and no other job opportunities opened up. When we met again in Samarkand in 2006, he was jobless and seemed to be about to leave for another destination. I asked why Zafer did not engage in the shuttle trade himself. He answered that "it is a women's thing; I don't know anything about clothes." On a different occasion, his mother insisted that shuttle trade was not possible for men: "They can get beaten at customs. With the women, they don't dare. They ask for money. We can reach an agreement." The success of female traders would therefore seem to stem from the perceived "weakness" of their sex. According to what is a well-established consensus, men are not to use violence against women, who are regarded as being "naturally" defenseless. Of course, ill-intentioned rumors about prostitution twist this argument and spread the idea that women "offer" sexual favors instead of money. "Why do you think there is always a younger woman in their groups [of female shuttle traders]? You think it's a coincidence? At customs, it helps them, that's clear." In the same vein, the female traders insist on the fact that they transport very few products: "Barely some suitcases. If we have problems, we tell them we didn't know and that we won't do it again." In order to receive favorable treatment, or at least be tolerated, by customs officers, and consequently by society, female shuttle traders downplay their activities as unimportant and amateurish.[20]

However, Zuleikho seemed to have been acting more on her own initiative. This was not the case with Czarina. My seatmate on a flight from Istanbul to Tashkent full of Uzbek shuttle traders, she lived in Samarkand and was a 33-year-old mother of three children aged 11, 8, and 5. Her sister

---

20 At a different economic level, Alexei Yurchak describes similar strategies. Russian business women "mix the role of a weak woman (involved in a 'woman's business') with the role of a self-sufficient entrepreneur (involved in 'true business')." A. Yurchak, "Russian Neoliberal: The Entrepreneurial Ethic and the Spirit of 'True Careerism,'" *The Russian Review* 62, no. 1 (2003): 88.

took care of the children while she was abroad, which was a regular occurrence. The agenda of Czarina's "shopping tours," as she called them, was busy and well organized. She rotated between three destinations: Istanbul, Beijing, and Dubai.[21] Her purchases were used to supply different stores in Samarkand, especially a children's store that her husband owned and where she worked when she was not abroad. The goods she imported were diverse, with clear specifications for certain destinations: computer equipment in Dubai, clothes for children in Istanbul, and a mix of different small domestic appliances in Beijing whose only common feature, according to Czarina, was that they were cheap. She made purchases in impressive quantities: she talked in terms of container loads of merchandise. Yet, her role as a shuttle trader was dominated by other family members and in-laws, who had sway in the decision-making over her activities. If her self-initiative was strong during her first trips that were conducted on a small scale with a suitcase, her activities at the time I met her consisted more in managing the shipment of goods than in making important commercial decisions.

Unlike Zuleikho and most female traders that had been going to Istanbul for a long time, Czarina spoke only a few words of Turkish. She used Russian instead; a large number of other Russian-speaking traders frequent the same marketplaces that she visited, where Russian is used as the lingua franca. Czarina was a customer of Uzbek travel agencies that booked her flights to Istanbul and completed the procedures at the Turkish Embassy for obtaining visas. She also used the services of freight companies to transport her goods. Interestingly enough, she was among the few female shuttle traders I met who told me she was a *tchelnoki*. It seems that female shuttle traders recognize themselves as *tchelnoki* only when their practices are well-trodden and regular, as was the case for Czarina. This can be linked to the fact that she did not work before independence and therefore did not have another professional identity. On the contrary, Zuleikho, who was a teacher before 1991, frequently repeated to me that she had no job: "*İşim yok!*" (I do not have

[21] Istanbul is indeed only one of the Uzbek shuttle trade destinations. See P.H. Loughlin and C.W. Pannell, "Growing Economic Links and Regional Development in the Central Asian Republics and Xinjiang, China," *Post-Soviet Geography and Economics* 42, no. 7 (2001): 469–490; E.H. Thomas, "Delivering Dogs to Delhi: Uzbek Women Launch into International Trade," *Central Asia Monitor*, no. 3 (2000): 5–6.

a job!).[22] In response to my persistent questions regarding what she called her commercial activities, Zuleikho simply said she was "traveling." When I asked Czarina why none of her male family members went abroad, she insisted that they lacked the discipline necessary for commercial exchanges: "Men cannot successfully handle money, when they see they have so and so much, they end up drinking and there's nothing left when they come back home."

The third main interviewee was Saida, who was one of the most successful female shuttle traders in Istanbul. What singles her out from other traders is that she had risen to a position of some prominence in her business. Whereas Zuleikho and Czarina were anonymous shuttle traders, Saida had acquired the reputation of being a self-made woman. In Laleli, she was called "*Doktor Hanım.*" Those involved in the Uzbek shuttle trade were all familiar with her; in fact, I learned more about her from others than I did from her. The Turks spoke about her with a mixture of respect, fear, and anger. The female Uzbek shuttle traders, meanwhile, related to her with jealousy. Nobody knew about her marital status, but it was clear that she provided a large part of her family's income. Fifty-nine years old, she lived in Samarkand and came frequently to Istanbul with her daughter, Nargiz, who lived in Tashkent and who, too, was in the "suitcase business." She was one of the only female traders that I met who owned a cell phone with a Turkish number. Like Czarina, Saida's trade was a family business, with the difference being that Saida was firmly at the head of the enterprise. In fact, Saida perfectly fulfills the criteria of the energetic post-Soviet woman taking charge of her family's survival. Unsurprisingly, she was already involved in the black market before 1991. This sector was particularly developed in the Soviet Republic of Uzbekistan, and it is likely that women played a key role in it.[23] The case of Saida is, however, a rare one, and it would be an undue simplification to equate female shuttle traders with the "speculators" of the Soviet era.

In Soviet times, Saida worked as a trained gynecologist. She astutely took advantage of the opportunities that opened up when trade regulations

---

22 Similar remarks have been noted in the Lodz region (Poland). F. Pine, "Retreat to the household? Gendered domains in postsocialist Poland," in C.M. Hann, ed., *Postsocialism. Ideals, ideologies and practices in Eurasia* (London: Routledge, 2002), 95–113.

23 G. Mars and Y. Altman, "The Cultural Bases of Soviet Central Asia's Second Economy (Uzbekistan and Tajikistan)," *Central Asian Survey* 5, no. 4 (1986): 195–204. On the involvement of women in the black market, see F. Heyat's case study, "Women and the Culture of Entrepreneurship in Soviet and Post-Soviet Azerbaijan," in Humphrey and Mandel, *Markets and Moralities. Ethnographies of Postsocialism*, 19–31.

were relaxed at the end of the 1980s, and she started selling carpets and Uzbek handicrafts in Laleli. When she gradually consolidated her network of contacts (notably at customs), her range of merchandise consequently widened. Unlike in Czarina's case, support from her family was always a result of her own initiative. Shuttle trade toward Turkey made her a rich woman and, accordingly, she was able to build up a business empire. She not only headed a medical clinic in Samarkand, but she also owned a hotel with a restaurant and a shop selling Turkish jewelry. At the time of the meeting, she only did business in Istanbul, on a similar scale as Czarina's family. While she still traveled to Laleli from time to time, the Turkish bazaar traders who knew her said that these personal trips were no longer her main source of income. She was in the position instead to hire a growing number of female shuttle traders to go on these trips in her place. In thus doing, she either employed people with a profile like Czarina, who are not the sole and direct owners of the goods they carry, or she took advantage of female shuttle traders in desperate situations, such as Zuleikho when she could not sell her goods.[24]

As the above examples demonstrate, it would appear that there are a wide range of initiatives according to the shuttle traders' ages and family situations.[25] The activities of the younger female traders are in line with a strategy that is more familial than individual (the profile of Czarina). The older women like Zuleikho and Saida, on the other hand, display a stronger individual initiative, but their family and social statuses are more marginal or exceptional than those of the younger women.[26] Shuttle trade is strongly embedded in social structures. It follows that for the younger traders, the initiative is determined by "strong family ties" and for the older by "weak ties," to use Granovetter's terminology.[27] How to understand this

---

[24] From this distinction between the owner of the goods and the risk-taker, Markus Kaiser distinguishes two types of economic actors in the Uzbek bazaars: "proprietors" and "realisators." M. Kaiser, "Informal Sector Trade in Uzbekistan," *Working Paper of the University of Bielefeld*, no. 218 (1997): 23–28.

[25] According to the Turkish Embassy in Uzbekistan, the Uzbek female shuttle traders travelling to Turkey are on average 35 years old. The fact that the three female traders are from Samarkand is a coincidence.

[26] This differentiation of initiatives according to the age of female shuttle traders adopts a distinction that Camille Schmoll and Véronique Manry have made between female shuttle traders from Algeria and Tunisia. V. Manry and C. Schmoll, " 'Le bizness des femmes': de nouvelles figures de la mobilité maghrébine dans l'espace euro-méditerranéen," *Mobilités au féminin*, Seminar in Tanger, 2005, 9–13, http://halshs.archives-ouvertes.fr/docs/00/23/92/80/PDF/ManrySchmoll_Tanger2006.pdf.

[27] M. Granovetter, "The Strength of Weak Ties," *American Journal of Sociology* 78, no. 6 (1973): 1360–1380.

distinction? It could result from a logical scheme of career advancement, the trade corresponding to an activity enabling the start of a commercial career. In the case of the older women, engaging in shuttle trade would be a marginal occupation since it is a tiring and risky activity that should be reserved for younger people. But according to my interviews, the older women, who have more initiative and familial autonomy, were in the same position when they were younger. If one considers that women of any age potentially have a similar need for income provided by the shuttle trade, it seems that for younger female shuttle traders the only way to overcome rumor and stigmatization is to embed their activity within a strong familial network. Female shuttle trade, spread widely in post-Soviet countries, could be interpreted as a sign of "emancipation" since it involves unaccompanied women traveling abroad alone. But in the Uzbek case, it seems rather to be part of the country's social "re-traditionalization."

Resourceful Women and Professional Men: The Changing Strategies of Shuttle Trade

To understand why Uzbek shuttle traders are mainly women, this section scrutinizes the "feminine" and "masculine" practices of shuttle trade. It questions whether Uzbek shuttle traders are women because adverse conditions pushed them into this business,[28] or because specific practices and skills deter men from becoming involved. A closer look at the shuttle trade system between Uzbekistan and Turkey shows that it can best be described as a stable feminine economic niche. According to shuttle traders, it was Uzbek women who began trading with Turks during the perestroika period. A description of this period will emphasize the importance of Uzbek handicrafts in establishing trade links. The way shuttle trade is currently organized will also be described and explained. There have been significant changes since the end of the 1990s—most goods bought in Laleli are no longer transported in suitcases, but are shipped in a more conventional way. Whereas the district is still labeled as the marketplace of the suitcase trade, new services like freight companies have increasingly appeared on the scene.

---

[28] In Uzbekistan, the opinion that women suffered more than men from the transition is widespread. See Kamp, "Gender Ideals and Income Realities: Discourses about Labor and Gender in Uzbekistan," 414.

According to collected personal histories, the first suitcase exchanges between Turkey and Uzbekistan can be traced back to the perestroika years, when Istanbul's antique and handicrafts merchants discovered a newly accessible hunting ground in Central Asia. Turks went to the Soviet republics of Uzbekistan and Turkmenistan to buy carpets, *kilims, ikats, suzani, chapans*, and antique jewelry. The Grand Bazaar in Istanbul has long functioned as a redistribution platform for these kinds of goods.[29] But from the late 1980s onward, according to Turkish carpet sellers, there were more Uzbek *suzani* and antique Turkmen carpets in Istanbul than in Central Asia. Samarkand was the destination of choice for these purchases.[30] Whereas in Turkey commercial sale is an activity reserved exclusively for men, the contacts they established in Uzbekistan to access handcrafted pieces were mainly with women. Asked about this issue, the Turks implied that the laziness and inclination of Uzbek (or Soviet) men to alcoholism were major obstacles to concluding business deals with them. A repeated explanation was that "Men over there don't do anything besides drink."[31] Yet the prevailing role of women, both in the production and knowledge of artisan products in Central Asia, and supposedly in black market activity, has surely been the decisive factor in the low involvement of men in this type of trade.[32] After the independence of Uzbekistan, antique handicrafts became scarcer, and Turkish merchants gradually stopped going to Uzbekistan.

It seems that the first Uzbek women who traveled to Istanbul were those who had been in close contact with Turks in Uzbekistan. The women continued selling antique—as well as those of more recent manufacture—

---

[29] C.-J. Charpentier, "Three commercial sectors: Some structural observations in the bazaar of Istanbul," *Zeitschrift für Ethnologie* 99, no. 1 (1974): 224–253.

[30] Besides the particular availability of handicrafts in this town, these Turks were of Kurdish origin and evoked the widespread use of Tajik, and its similarity with the Kurdish language, in order to explain their choice of Samarkand.

[31] Generally, a litany followed on the Uzbek conditions of hygiene and property, which Turks considered lamentable. This topic of cleanliness seems to be recurring in Turkish impressions of the post-Soviet world. S. Shami, "Prehistories of Globalization: Circassian Identity in Motion," *Public Culture* 12, no. 1 (2000): 187.

[32] In Central Asian pre-Soviet households, the task of women was to sew and embroider traditional clothes. S. Akiner, "Between tradition and modernity: the dilemma facing contemporary Central Asian women," in M. Buckley, ed., *Post-Soviet Women: from the Baltic to Central Asia* (Cambridge: Cambridge University Press, 1997), 265–66. During the Soviet period, many Uzbek women did not work in the formal sector but participated in the family economy, notably through the commercialization of textile goods that they produced. Kamp, "Gender Ideals and Income Realities: Discourses about Labor and Gender in Uzbekistan," 412–13.

traditional handicrafts to them. Until 1994, the suitcases of Uzbeks were rarely empty, and when artisan products were not directly bartered in Istanbul, the money earned in sales (in dollars or deutschmarks) enabled the Uzbek women to supply themselves with Turkish goods before returning home.[33] At the same time, the commercial marketplace of Laleli started to become more organized. A hotel infrastructure developed and prices of plots soared.[34] More and more people came to Laleli, and those markets that had emerged on the Turkish borders with countries of the former Eastern bloc in the late 1980s, lost their importance.[35] An increasing number of Uzbeks, men and women, travelled to Istanbul with the sole intention of purchasing goods. Today at the Grand Bazaar, only a few women from Samarkand continue to sell Uzbek artisan products, which are much prized by Western tourists. These goods are mainly carpets (*kadife* or *suzani*) of recent make. Some of the women organize the production in Uzbekistan, and sometimes they manage to get orders directly from Turkish merchants.[36] Sales take place either in one of the Laleli hotels, where the women usually accommodate themselves whilst in Istanbul, or directly in the Grand Bazaar itself.[37]

The practices of those responsible for initiating shuttle trade networks between Turkey and Uzbekistan highlight important features of the activity: namely, bargaining and negotiating, both of which women seem best able to lead. Shuttle trade is subject to the vicissitudes of changing visa regulations of the different countries whose borders are crossed, as well as being dependent on personal contacts at the customs offices, and

---

[33] P.S. Blacher, "Les shop-turisty à Tsargrad ou les nouveaux russophones d'Istanbul," *Turcica*, no. 28 (1996): 29.

[34] For a brief history of the district, see Ç. Keyder, "A Tale of Two Neighborhoods," in Ç. Keyder, ed., *Istanbul. Between the Global and the Local* (Lanham, Boulder, New York, Oxford: Rowman & Littlefield Publishers, 1999), 173–186.

[35] The best-known case is the one of Sarp on the Georgian border. C. Hann and I. Hann, "Samovars and Sex on Turkey's Russian Markets," *Anthropology Today* 8, no. 4 (1992): 3–6; F. Bilici, "Une réalisation concrète avant la lettre: la coopération en mer Noire orientale," *Cahiers d'Études de la Méditerranée Orientale et du Monde Turco-Iranien (CEMOTI)*, no. 15 (1993): 168–183; C. Aktar and N. Ögelman, "Recent Developments in East-West Migration: Turkey and the Petty Traders," *International Migration* 32, no. 4 (1994): 343–354.

[36] The latest fashion in the Grand Bazaar is for boots and handbags made from Uzbek *kadife* (manufactured in Istanbul with embroidered velvet cloth brought from Central Asia). According to my own observation, the number of stalls in the Grand Bazaar selling Central Asian handicrafts more than tripled between 2005 and 2008. Kyrgyz felt, Afghan wooden boxes, Uzbek *suzani*, and chapans are ubiquitous.

[37] The same phenomenon exists for Turkmen women who find accommodation in other hotels in Laleli.

on the availability of financial capital. Since the late 1990s, Uzbekistan and Turkey have tightened their legislation concerning handicrafts and antiques.[38] In order to circumvent the tighter restrictions, women opt for longer itineraries that see them cross less controlled borders. Possible routes cross through Kyrgyzstan and Kazakhstan, with whom Uzbekistan has a free visa-regime, on the way to Istanbul. Once they have arrived in Istanbul, if their products are impounded at Atatürk airport—as happens quite often—they can make multiple roundtrips to other nearby destinations that do not necessitate additional visas (in 2005, Northern Cyprus or Moscow). Then, each time they reenter Turkish territory, they are allowed to claim the impounded goods at Atatürk airport in authorized quantities. In contrast, male shuttle traders do not seem to face similar constraints. Seldom interested in handicrafts, they tend to trade on a much larger scale than women. This forces them to adopt different strategies. The male traders that I met rented one or more storage rooms in the main bazaars of Tashkent (Ippodrom, Chorsu, or Alayskii) in order to sell goods bought in Turkey. This is a luxury that women can rarely afford. In addition, male traders are more likely than women to resort to services, which first appeared in the late 1990s, designed to simplify commercial shuttle trade—namely, travel agencies and freight companies.

The development of these services follows a general trend existing in Laleli.[39] As of 2006, at least five Uzbek travel agencies offered booking flights to Istanbul as well as assistance acquiring Turkish visas.[40] Four freight—or *cargo*—companies based in Laleli and in Tashkent transported Turkish goods bought by traders, thus obviating the need for suitcases.[41] Paradoxically, those traders such as Czarina not transporting their goods in suitcases identified themselves more easily as *tchelnoki*. In Laleli, the activity remains branded as *bavul ticareti* (suitcase trade), even though most of the traded goods are shipped through freight

38 Uzbekistan pays particular attention to the protection of its cultural heritage. Besides its Museum of Decorative Arts, it is one of 19 countries that took part in the first UNESCO Proclamation of Masterpieces of Oral and Intangible Heritage in 2001; M. Lerch, *Zwischen Handwerkstradition und globalem Markt. Kunsthandwerker in Usbekistan und Kirgistan* (Berlin, Schwarz, 2011).

39 Yakovlev, "Russian 'Shuttle' Traders and Dynamics of Integration into Global Markets," 2–3.

40 For the first shuttles, the agencies also take care of the hotel reservations for a small additional fee.

41 To give a ballpark figure, "in February 1998, the responsible of the Treasury of Istanbul estimated the cargo-companies officially established in Laleli to be 42." Pérouse, "Laleli, giga-bazar d'Istanbul. Appréhender les caractéristiques et les mutations d'une place commerciale internationale," 310.

companies. In Istanbul, the introduction of cargo services was seen to mark the end of the suitcase trade, or at least as a "normalization" of commercial exchanges that had previously been widely associated with illegality and the informal economy.[42] However, in Uzbekistan the situation is somewhat different. The existence of very strict customs rules and a policy of state protectionism that limits commercial exchanges to very low levels does not allow for such a normalization.[43]

More than changing the structure of shuttle trade as such, travel agencies and freight companies serve to delegate certain risks and hazards. After Uzbekistan implemented a restrictive customs tax in 2002, cargo companies started to play a crucial role. For approximately a year after the introduction of the new tax, suitcase trade came almost entirely to a halt, thus affecting traders such as Zuleikho. Subsequently, it was the cargo companies that found ways to circumvent the tax. These companies are based in Istanbul with intermediaries working in Tashkent. Each of the partners works independently, traders paying them upon deposit and delivery of the goods. In 2005 and 2006, the price paid for shipments in Istanbul was two dollars per kilo when sent by air freight and $0.70 per kilo when sent by truck, a journey which takes about two weeks.[44] In Tashkent, the cargo intermediaries I met were women who had previously been shuttle traders themselves. They adjust their fees according to the money they have to pay at customs. These fees depend on current customs regulations as well as on the strength of their relations with the customs officers. After 2002, goods were not shipped directly by plane to Tashkent but rather sent to Shymkent (Kazakhstan) or Bishkek (Kyrgyzstan) and then transited through one of the 20 official depots located around Tashkent. According to the *kargocu* (people working for a cargo company), negotiations between officials and customs go more smoothly

---

[42] *Ibid.*, 325–27.

[43] In spring 2002, the taxes on imports rose 100 percent with the official intention to support national production. B. Abdullaev, "Uzbekistan: Shuttle Traders Curbed," *Institute for War and Peace Reporting, RCA*, no. 129, July 12, 2002, http://iwpr.net/report-news/uzbekistan-shuttle-traders-curbed. These measures were followed by others in 2003 and 2004, which also affected the shuttle trade. G. Bukharbaeva, "Uzbek Authorities Mount Witchhunt after Unrest," *Institute for War and Peace Reporting, RCA*, no. 325, November 9, 2004, http://iwpr.net/report-news/uzbek-authorities-mount-witchhunt-after-unrest. Though 2011 was the "year of small business and entrepreneurship," several bazaars have been shut down or destroyed and new taxes implemented. See "Uzbekistan: Tashkent's Flat Tax Crushing Small Businesses," *Eurasianet*, July 21, 2011, http://www.eurasianet.org/node/63927.

[44] In 2008, the prices had almost doubled, and one of the four cargo companies sending goods from Istanbul to Uzbekistan shut down.

in these depots than at the airport.[45] Female traders who transport their merchandise themselves have adopted similar itineraries, but their contacts at customs or at the borders are not as reliable as those of the cargo companies. Therefore, the success of trips undertaken individually is less predictable.[46]

Developments after 2002 underline the fact that the involvement of cargo companies and travel agencies did not necessarily, in the Uzbek case, translate into the economic activity of shuttle trade undergoing a process of normalization. Rather, it seems that the institutional and legislative vacuum that initiated the development of shuttle trade in the first place was replaced by excessive state regulation. In June 2005, a Turkish employee of a cargo company described the problem as follows: "There are so many different regulations for the goods: the customers don't even know them! It's not possible to respect all of them because nobody ever does." Strategies developed both as a reaction against constraints introduced by the Uzbek state and as a result of individual initiatives and arrangements.

The following example describes the biggest cargo company's handling of shipments of Turkish goods to Uzbekistan. Aged in her fifties, Gulmira had been the Tashkent intermediary of this company since 1994. Gulmira explained to me that, as a shuttle trader, her Turkish goods had often been impounded at Tashkent airport. She therefore decided she had to do something and contacted a person by the name of Cem in Laleli, with whom she subsequently set up a business. Cem, a Kurd from Tunceli and a fluent speaker of Uzbek and Russian, knew most of the Uzbek shuttle traders.[47] The company became successful because they managed to secure a network of contacts at customs and among the shuttle traders. Several times a week, Cem goes to Istanbul's Atatürk airport to welcome Uzbek shuttle traders and to take them to their hotels in Laleli. The traders pay for this service, which is organized in accordance with the

[45] The majority of goods imported transit through the capital, where the most important bazaars of the country are located (Ippodrom and Chorsu). Though bigger, Dordoy and, above all, Zarya Vostoka play a similar role in Kyrgyzstan and Kazakhstan. Bal, "Geçiş Ülkelerinde Yolsuzluk ve Kayıtdışı Ekonomi Kırgızistan Bavul Ticareti Örneği," 187–191; Yessenova, "Hawkers and Containers in Zarya Vostoka: How 'Bizarre' Is the Post-Soviet Bazaar?"

[46] It is possible that part of the negotiations between the cargo companies and the customers in Tashkent consist of agreeing to "discourage" the traders to use another cargo services or to transport their goods themselves.

[47] Since the 1990s, Kurds from Eastern Turkey have arrived en masse in Istanbul. They form a growing number of workers in Laleli, having gradually replaced people coming from the regions of Erzincan and Kayseri, who themselves replaced Turks from the Balkans.

hotels where they find accommodation. While escorting them to their hotels only generates a small income, it nonetheless enables Cem to connect with the incoming traders and to advertize his and Gulmira's shipment services to them.

The analysis of female and male practices of shuttle trade would be incomplete without underlining the disproportionate visibility of female bavulcu in Laleli. Uzbek female shuttle traders usually travel in groups of three to five persons. They think that as a group, they can better bargain wholesale prices for the Turkish goods they buy and also ease their passage through the customs office in Tashkent. They also share hotel rooms. Although they are more numerous than male shuttle traders, traveling in groups makes women even more visible compared to the men, who generally travel alone. The shuttle trade thus forms an economic niche where women are in the majority numerically and dominate symbolically. This economic niche is the result of constraints as much as opportunities. Not only did many women lose their jobs after 1991, but they also do not have access to higher economic spheres in Uzbek society.[48] The commercial practices of men enable them to engage in greater and further reaching enterprise than women. For men, the shuttle trade potentially opens doors to import-export enterprises. However, in Uzbekistan, men without a job do not regard the shuttle trade as a viable option, while women are considered to be more adept at bargaining and negotiating.

Fortune, Plight, and Hierarchies in Uzbek-Turkish Migration Networks

For Uzbek migrants, Laleli is often the first point of arrival in Istanbul.[49] The majority arrive with a three-month tourist visa and then overstay after its expiration. Staying on illegally, they take care to be discreet so as to avoid intensifying police surveillance. Laleli offers numerous jobs,

[48] M. Tokhtakhodzhaeva, *The Re-Islamization of Society and the Position of Women in Post-Soviet Uzbekistan* (Folkestone: Global Oriental, 2008).

[49] The current Uzbek emigration could represent up to 20 percent of the active population, similar to the situations of its Central Asian neighbors. A. Ilkhamov, "Geographic Mobility of Uzbeks: The Emergence of Cross-National Communities Vs. Nation-State Control," paper prepared for NBR Conference, Generational Change and Leadership Succession in Uzbekistan, March 2, 2006; M. Schmidt and L. Sagynbekova, "Migration Past and Present: Changing Patterns in Kyrgyzstan," *Central Asian Survey* 27, no. 2 (2008): 111–127; C.M. Becker, et al., "Short-Term Migration Responses of Women and Men during Economic Turmoil: Lessons from Kazakhstan," *Eurasian Geography and Economics* 44, no. 3 (2003): 228–243.

and it structures the networks of diverse groups of migrants in Istanbul.[50] Although its activities have been threatened by recent municipality policies, the district embodies the role of Istanbul as "a switching point in the complex system of international migrations, mobility, and circulations, ensuring the change from one form of mobility to the other, the restructuring and the interaction of the actors of the system, as well as offering multiple comparative advantages."[51] In Laleli, the migrants can be hired in shops and hotels to make use of their linguistic skills, or in small workshops. The transit of numerous foreigners generates additional activities: daily labor markets, companies organizing the placement of women as domestic employees, illegal transit to Europe, and prostitution. The district is associated with all kinds of trafficking, of which the female suitcase traders are only the most visible. It is worth noting that they are often stigmatized as "Natashas," the local appellation for prostitutes coming from the former Communist bloc.[52]

On Thursday evenings, part of the Uzbek community of Istanbul used to gather in the Otel Özbekler of Laleli. Domestic employees taking a break from their workplaces in the distant suburbs for a few hours, construction workers between two contracts, and suitcase traders passing through the city—all were regular participants at these gatherings. For them, the meetings were an occasion to get together and eat *plov* (the traditional Uzbek rice dish with meat and vegetables), to exchange news, and to express hopes and hardships.[53] For me, these meetings were a chance to

---

50 As a Moroccan who had been set up in Istanbul for ten years (and without documents) said, "Here [in Laleli] we are fine: I can eat fresh fish in Kumkapı [in the South of Laleli], for the Friday prayer, I can choose between ten historical mosques, catch up with friends passing by, play soccer near the fortification... Taksim [a popular entertainment district in Beyoğlu, on the other side of the Golden Horn]? Why should I go there? It's dangerous."

51 Aslan and Pérouse, "Istanbul: le comptoir, le hub, le sas et l'impasse. Fonctions dans le système migratoire international," 174. Since the 1990s, the AKP (*Adalet ve Kalkınma Partisi* or Party of Justice and Development) has tried to relocate in specific peripheral locations the handicrafts and small industries traditionally located in the historical peninsula. The most important operations are Giyimkent, Tekstilkent, and Kuyumcukent. Laleli, situated near the touristic spot of Sultanahmet, clashes directly with these policies.

52 On this topic, see A. Bloch, "Victims of Trafficking or Entrepreneurial Women? Narratives of Post-Soviet Entertainers in Turkey," *Canadian Women Studies/Les Cahiers de la Femme* 22, no. 3–4 (2003): 152–58; L. Gülcür and P. Ilkkaracan, "The 'Natasha' experience: Migrant sex workers from the former Soviet Union and Eastern Europe in Turkey," *Women's Studies International Forum* 25, no. 4 (2002): 411–421.

53 The shuttle traders often find accommodation in the cheap hotels in the southern part of Laleli between Ordu Avenue and the Marmara Sea. It is normally possible to arrange self-catering in them.

understand some of the general factors that influenced their choices and changes of employment. The constraints that pushed them to leave were stressed by a number of migrants, among them the typical following assertions: "I didn't have the choice"; "I had no money"; "the kids had to be sent to school." The recurrence of these discourses from people in very different economic positions was puzzling. Without denying the severe social and economic difficulties of Uzbekistan, one has to keep in mind that people with the fewest resources are unable to leave.[54] In addition, despite the similar nature of their complaints, the Uzbek migrants organize their different commercial activities according to a hierarchy.

This hierarchy is organized along several lines—start-up capital, experience and skills. In order to enter the suitcase trade, one needs more money than is needed to work abroad as a laborer. Additionally, starting capital is higher for male traders than for female shuttle traders.[55] The female and male migrant laborers I met at the Thursday gatherings were hired by companies (*firma*) that provided them with plane tickets. The companies confiscate their passports upon arrival and the migrants have to refund the company's initial financial outlay during their first months in Istanbul. Thus, migrant laborers are in a more precarious and vulnerable situation than the shuttle traders who provide for themselves. Beyond the benefits derived from the sales, female suitcase traders can also profit from the frequency of their tours and travel experience. On the one hand, their experience confers on them an aura of authority in Uzbekistan on migration issues. They frequently give advice and provide contacts to people willing to leave.[56] On the other hand, their shuttling enables them to play a role as intermediaries between the migrant laborers in Istanbul and their families in Uzbekistan.[57] At the Thursday gatherings, they exchanged news since the traders had been to Uzbekistan more recently than the others. Female shuttle traders also accept the transmission of cash remittances against a commission. Even if not all of the female

---

54 This lack of resources among the poorer strata of society prevents them from exploiting potential mobility to improve their situation. J. Gertel, "Mobility and Insecurity: The Significance of Resources," in J. Gertel and I. Breuer, eds., *Pastoral Morocco. Globalizing Scapes of Mobility and Insecurity* (Wiesbaden: Reichert Verlag, 2007), 11–30.

55 According to my own estimations, the figure is around 700 dollars for women and 1,000 dollars for men. This starting capital should suffice for paying for the Turkish visa ($80), the cost of the round-trip flight ticket ($500), the hotel in Laleli (between $10–20 per night), and the purchase of goods in the desired quantities.

56 In Laleli, it is said that a female shuttle trader has used this trust to feed prostitution networks. On this topic, see the work of Gulnara Kuzibaeva.

57 The cargos can transmit remittances and packages from the migrants as well.

suitcase traders play the role of intermediaries, men never fulfill this function. Male shuttle traders are not compelled to do so because they mobilize more "financial capital" rather than "social capital" during their trips.[58]

Start-up capital, experience, and skills: these elements structure the migration networks according to a hierarchy that strictly designates which sectors of the labor market are engaged in by which gender. The economic role of the female shuttle traders has no male equivalent. This hierarchy does not form a linear scale on which the individual biographies are distributed. In the course of one's career, circumstances may change. Moreover, there are several factors which may disorder this hierarchy—pleasure and reputation—that must be taken into account. Indeed, many suitcase traders compared their activity to an addiction; the pleasure of travel or flair for business is often mentioned as a way to explain or excuse the choice to trade. On the other hand, some female migrant laborers told me they had tried to start in the suitcase business but had not been successful, although they had had the necessary financial capital. I learned afterward that they were said to be thieves or unreliable payers. Such a reputation, rightly or wrongly assigned to individual shuttle traders, can be more powerful in determining their success or failure than any business acumen. In Laleli, one has to make quick decisions, and commercial deals are based on the given word. To build up one's reputation or to spread rumors about competing traders is one way to feel more secure in this risky environment. Female shuttle traders are not only highly visible in the public space of Laleli but also frequently absent, their absence making them vulnerable to *dedikodu* (gossip in Turkish). Voluntarily or not, they feed rumors and quarrels that stretch from Tashkent all the way to Istanbul and vice versa. In spite of this, because they transmit remittances and provide information, their frequent shuttling back and forth also places them in a position of strength among the migrants.

* * * * *

Between Tashkent and Istanbul, Uzbek women loaded with suitcases catch the eye, and provoke negative gossip and hostile rumors. In analyzing the femininity of the shuttle trade, this chapter has strived to articulate

[58] P. Bourdieu, "Les trois états du capital culturel," *Actes de la Recherche en Sciences Sociales* 30, no. 1 (1979): 3–6. This function of intermediaries is a strategy which male traders do not need because they engage in the activity on a different scale than female traders.

the discourses concerning it. These discourses mainly invoke female skills in contrast to the male inability and/or disinterest in the activity. To recapitulate the main discourses, shuttle traders are women for the reason that they have a particular acumen for this activity. They "know how to talk with customs officers," for instance, which is connected to the "weakness" of their sex or with black market practices inherited from Soviet times. Moreover, women are better acquainted with the products that are exchanged in Istanbul because these are related to the domestic realm (handicrafts and clothes). The shuttle traders are also women because men are supposedly unable to practice this activity due to laziness, alcoholism, irresponsibility, and their incapacity to "keep accounts"; not only that, but no man would be interested in being a *bavulcu*. It follows that men are not forced into the trade because they have more lucrative or "noble" professional activities than shuttle trade, which is regarded as "degrading." The fact that men cannot or do not wish to partake in the shuttle trade both explains and excuses the involvement of women.

Female Uzbek shuttle traders travelling to Istanbul occupy an economic niche that has no male equivalent. Before the collapse of the Soviet Union, many of these women worked as professionals and state employees. Their generation paid the price of the post-Soviet transition.[59] They have been forced by necessity to trade and are condemned to the suitcase business for lack of anything better. Indeed, the customs law of 2002 and the more restrictive legislation that followed it partly "liquidated the merchant class, the only popular social class that benefited from the economic evolution of the country since independence."[60] In Uzbekistan, the higher echelons of the labor market are reserved for men rather than women. Although this economic niche is the structural product of post-Soviet constraints, it has nevertheless been invested with specific practices thought to be feminine, and thus made it in turn inaccessible to men. Constraints and skills have reinforced each other to establish and consign female shuttle traders to the lower economic levels. The shuttle trade is indeed an activity of small actors "doomed" to bargain and negotiate. Success stories like that of Saida are the exception rather than the norm. In this regard, it is not only the product of the post-Soviet transition and of Uzbek customs

59 Alexei Yurchak calls them the "last Soviet generation."

60 M. Laruelle and S. Peyrouse, *Asie centrale, la dérive autoritaire* (Paris: Autrement, 2006), 113. The Andijan events in June 2005 started with the arrest of bazaar traders and seem to have been a tragic replay of the previous "bazaars' riots" (notably in Kokand in November 2004).

protectionism. Shuttle trade occupies a specific place in the economy that did not appear in 1991. Likewise, it is highly unlikely to suddenly disappear.

In gender discourses, Uzbek women are both recognized as victims of the transition and strongly stigmatized if they engage in shuttle trade. The question of gender is (re)placed at the center of attention, as if women must make up for the post-Soviet disorder. The goal of this study thus has been to "articulate the discursive construction of the social world with the social construction of discourses."[61] The key to success for the female shuttle traders is to remain discreet. Invisible in official statistics, they try to make themselves inconspicuous at the customs offices and borders. In the public space of Laleli, among the migrants, and in the rumor mill between Istanbul and Tashkent, they are, on the contrary, extremely conspicuous. The shuttle trade is an activity made up of contrasts and intermittences: between here and there, absence and presence, discretion and attention. As opposed to ordinary female migrant laborers, who are likely much more numerous, female shuttle traders stand out more and garner more attention—whether positive or negative. Neither victims nor queens by virtue of their resourcefulness, they embody the complexity of social change and epitomize the difficulties facing Uzbek society.

[61] R. Chartier, *Au bord de la falaise. L'histoire entre certitudes et inquiétude* (Paris: Albin Michel, 1998), 129.

THE FEMINIZATION OF TAJIK LABOR MIGRATION TO RUSSIA

Nafisa Khusenova

Independent since 1991, the Republic of Tajikistan had over six million inhabitants in 2000. That same year, between 630,000 and 1.2 million Tajikistanis were working abroad.[1] In light of statistical inaccuracies, the range given for 2006 was even larger; between 200,000 and 1 million migrants were estimated to have left the country to find work abroad, especially to Russia and Kazakhstan.[2] The reasons for such large-scale labor migration are mainly economic in nature. After the collapse of the Soviet Union, Tajikistan spiraled into a serious economic crisis, which was then aggravated by the devastating civil war that lasted from May 1992 to June 1997. One of the only survival strategies left to people was to go abroad to find work. Since then, massive labor migration has played a major role in the national economy. A driving force in the fight against poverty and in the reduction of social and economic tensions, labor migration is a safety valve that contributes greatly to the stability of the country. Indeed, possibilities to earn a proper living remain scarce in Tajikistan, where the average monthly salary was 49 dollars in 2006.[3] Although an increase from 1998, when it was just 11 dollars,[4] it remains small.

While mostly dominated by males at the outset, there has been, since 2003, a steady increase in the number of women migrating for work, despite the unconducive social, cultural, and political barriers to them doing so. This leads to the question of whether this increased feminization creates new social tensions, especially within families, among children, and in gender relations; and whether it also contributes to changing the socially constructed and "traditional" status of women in Tajikistani society. To answer these questions, this chapter will first describe the general

---

[1] S. Olimova and I. Bosc, *Trudovaia migratsiia iz Tadzhikistana* (Dushanbe: International Organization for Migration, Sharq, 2003), 20.

[2] D.C. Amonova, "Osobennosti trudovoi migratsii naseleniia Respubliki Tadzhikistan," in *Problemy trudovoy migratsii i puti ikh resheniia* (Dushanbe: Irfon, 2007), 31.

[3] V. Mukomel', "Novaia migratsionnaia politika Rossii: shag vpered ili nikuda," in V. Tishkov and E. Fillipova, eds., *Etnicheskaia situatsiia i konflikty v stranakh SNG i Baltii. Ezhegodnyi doklad* (Moscow: RAN, 2006), 34.

[4] *Country Economic Review. Tajikistan* (Asian Development Bank, April 2000), 5.

characteristics of labor migration from Tajikistan. Then it will present the reasons for its increasing feminization, before analyzing its structure and modus operandi in Tajikistan's post-conflict context. Finally, the impact of labor migration on the national and household economies will be assessed, including on the social status of women in post-Soviet Tajikistan.

The Characteristics of Contemporary Labor Migrations

According to a survey conducted in 2002 by Saodat Olimova and Igor Bosc, the goal of almost all (nearly 98 percent) Tajikistani migrants going abroad to work was to seek an improved standard of living.[5] For many years migration had been only seasonal and temporary (for less than 12 months), but the number of those migrating on a more permanent basis started to rise from around 1997.[6] The principal destination for 84 percent of Tajikistani migrants is Russia, a near-monopoly that can be explained by several factors. First, the common Soviet past and knowledge of the Russian language allow the majority of migrants to arrive in a country they are already culturally familiar with.[7] The visa exempt regime between Tajikistan and Russia also lifts some of the administrative barriers and facilitates migration flows.[8] Tajikistani migrants can rely, too, on the presence of a significant community of compatriots who have fled to and settled in Russia since the civil war, which is not the case in other countries. Most of these refugees work in the agricultural and construction sectors, especially in the south of Russia. Their established presence facilitates the integration of new migrants.

The above notwithstanding, the principal factor in migration remains the possibility to earn a good living in Russia. In 1996, the average salary in Russia was 30 times higher than in Tajikistan.[9] Two main reasons account for the high demand for foreign workers in Russia. The first is

[5] Some go abroad to study or to visit relatives. Olimova and Bosc, *Trudovaia migratsiia iz Tadzhikistana*, 21.

[6] A.G. Mughal, *Migration, Remittances, and Living Standards in Tajikistan* (Dushanbe, 2006), 112–14. I would like to thank the author, who gave me this unpublished manuscript during my field research in Moscow in July 2007.

[7] According to Olimova and Bosc, 78.4 percent of migrants speak Russian in addition to Tajik or Uzbek. Those who do not speak Russian are mostly young people and women.

[8] Originally, this visa exemption was part of the agreement signed in Bishkek in October 1992 by Russia, Belarus, Ukraine, Moldova, Armenia, Tajikistan, Uzbekistan, Turkmenistan, Kyrgyzstan, and Kazakhstan. It was renewed on a bilateral basis in 1999.

[9] Olimova and Bosc, *Trudovaia migratsiia iz Tadzhikistana*, 25.

Russia's demographic decline, which is due to low birth rates combined with high mortality rates. Between 1992 and 2002, the Russian population decreased by over three million inhabitants.[10] The second reason is that the Russian economy has been growing since 1998. After the economic recession in the beginning of the 1990s, and following the 1998 financial crisis, GDP increased by 5.4 percent in 1999, and by 10.2 percent in 2000. From 2001 to 2006, growth fluctuated between 4.7 percent and 7.3 percent per year.[11] Russia's workforce demand is primarily in construction, metallurgy, mechanical construction, the energy sector, agriculture, trade, and services. It is precisely in these sectors that one finds the main migratory flows from Tajikistan. Fifty-one percent of Tajikistani migrants work in construction, 34 percent in trade and services, and only 1 percent in the education and health sectors. Others work in the gas and oil sectors, manufacturing industries, catering, and agriculture.

The age structure of migrants can be divided into two groups. The first includes migrants between 20 and 29 years of age ("sons"), who go abroad to earn money needed for their weddings. The second group includes migrants between 40 and 49 years of age ("fathers"), who need additional income to buy an apartment or a house for their children, to pay for family parties (weddings or circumcisions), make repairs to a house, or to start a small business. However, the majority of fathers go abroad in order to feed their families. More than half of the migrants in Russia do not have any professional skills; this is especially the case for young men between 18 and 29 years of age who work in construction and represent 35 percent of all workers in this sector. They usually do hard, unskilled, and poorly paid work. The most skilled persons are migrants between 35 and 49 years of age who received a higher education and technical qualifications during the Soviet period. Their professional profiles are therefore more diverse. They are engineers, doctors, heads of companies, teachers, farmers, administrative employees, or construction workers. While they generally work in state or private enterprises in Russia, their actual occupation rarely corresponds to the profession in which they originally qualified.

[10] The Russian population has fallen from 148.3 to 145.2 million (a decrease of 2.1 percent). Zh. Zaionchkovskaia, "Pochemu Rossii neobkhodima immigratsionnaia politika," in Zh. Zaionchkovskaia, I. Molodikova, and V. Mukomel', eds., *Metodologiia i metody izucheniia migratsionnykh protsessov* (Moscow: HESP OSI, UNESCO, 2007), 114.

[11] J. Sapir, "Quel bilan économique pour les années Poutine en Russie?" *CEMI Working Document*, 2007, 15, http://cemi.ehess.fr/document.php?id=981.

The huge scale of these migratory flows is striking. Almost all Tajikistani families have sent at least one member abroad since independence.[12] Migration flows soared in 1995, during the worst of the economic crisis, and peaked in 1999. They have continued to increase since 2001, but not as quickly as before, which can be explained by the slow recovery of the national economy. In this dramatic social and economic situation, demographic growth remained high and unemployment soared. The population increased from 5.09 million inhabitants in 1989 to 6.12 million in 2000,[13] while the official unemployment rate rose from 0.6 percent in 1993 to 30 percent in 2001.[14]

According to the Customs Committee of Tajikistan, 1.2 million Tajikistanis were working in Russia in 2001. However, official figures have to be viewed cautiously because statistical data is not always reliable, especially in Tajikistan. The inadequacies of data collection are not the only factor explaining this lack of reliability; there is also confusion between different types of data. Indeed, measures do not always differentiate between temporary and permanent migrations, and between stock and flow variables.[15] The figure of 1.2 million Tajikistanis working abroad is a stock measure. In terms of flow, 632,000 Tajikistanis would have left their country between 2000 and 2002 in order to work abroad.[16] Abdul-Gaffar Mughal thinks that this number is an exaggeration, however, and instead puts forward a maximum figure of 370,000 migrants in 2005.[17]

The Feminization of Labor Migrations

As part of this cheap workforce to meet labor demands in Russia is a growing proportion of women, the number of which has increased since 2002,

---

12 "Republic of Tajikistan: Selected Issues and Statistical Appendix," *IMF Country Report* (Washington, D.C.: The International Monetary Fund, no. 05/131, 2005), 51.

13 R. Rowland, "National and Regional Population Trends in Tajikistan: Results from the Recent Census," *Eurasian Geography and Economics* 46, no. 3 (2005): 206.

14 *Country Economic Review. Tajikistan* (Asian Development Bank, April 2000), 24; International Crisis Group, *Tajikistan: an Uncertain Peace*, December 24, 2001, http://www.crisisgroup.org/~/media/Files/asia/central-asia/tajikistan/Tajikistan%20An%20Uncertain%20Peace.pdf, 20.

15 Mughal, *Migration, Remittances, and Living Standards in Tajikistan*, 119.

16 Olimova and Bosc, *Trudovaia migratsiia iz Tadzhikistana*, 22.

17 This figure was obtained by an extrapolation from a study conducted only in the region of Khatlon. Mughal acknowledges the limits of this extrapolation. Mughal, *Migration, Remittances, and Living*, 115.

when 85 percent of Tajikistani migrants were men and 15 percent women.[18] However, migration is far from an easy solution for Tajikistani women who have not gained a high social status, despite the Soviet "emancipation" policy, and who still come up against social and cultural obstacles. Nevertheless, through force of circumstance, women have become increasingly involved in the labor market since independence, and a growing number of them end up migrating as well.

As a result of the Soviet so-called emancipation policy, women entered the labor market as early as the 1930s. To promote the Soviet social and economic model in a "traditional" Central Asian society, the Soviet authorities launched the *hudjum* campaign in 1927, aimed at emancipating women.[19] It hoped to take women out of *purdah* (confinement to private spaces) and to make them participate in social, economic, and political life. However, in practice, although some women managed to enter the Party system, employment policy in Central Asia encouraged them to work in the social sphere and above all in agriculture.[20]

Although women entered the Soviet public sphere, their "emancipation" was rather formal and superficial. Their economic status remained far inferior to that of men, since the guarantee of material support to the family continued to depend on the head of the family—always a man. Very often, women were engaged in unskilled and poorly paid work, particularly in the countryside, where they worked in the fields and constituted 53 percent of *kolkhoz* members. The average income of a woman was 25 percent lower than that for a man and served only as a complementary resource.[21] Cultural pressures remained strong and some women were compelled by their husbands or families to change their occupation, making it a point of honor to preclude the chance of any promiscuity

18 Olimova and Bosc, *Trudovaia migratsiia iz Tadzhikistana*, 32–40.

19 A declaration on education in the Autonomous Soviet Socialist Republic of Tajikistan and a document "on the rights of Tajik women workers and the necessity to fight for their emancipation" were adopted on December 1, 1926, at the constituting First Congress of the Soviets. Special attention was paid to Muslim women, who were granted the same civic, family, and land rights as men. S. Kasymova, *Gendernaia sistema tadzhikskogo obshchestva: put' k modernizatsii (Sovetskii period)* (Dushanbe: Irfon, 2004), 132–159, http://www.genderstudies.info/social/so6.php.

20 In the absence of a proletariat in this region of the Soviet Union, and due to a relative lack of workforce, women were to play the role of a surrogate proletariat. O. Roy, *La nouvelle Asie centrale ou la fabrication des nations* (Paris: Seuil, 1997), 131.

21 S. Kasymova, *Polozhenie zhenshchin na rynke truda i v sfere zaniatosti: puti sokrashcheniia bednosti v Tadzhikistane* (Dushanbe: Swiss Agency for Development Cooperation in Tajikistan, 2005), 9.

with men at the workplace.[22] Furthermore, the tradition of having large families—the average family size in Tajikistan was 6.6 persons—rarely gave women the possibility to work full time. Soviet policy thus brought little influence to bear on entrenched patriarchal gender relations and the division of labor in the private sphere.

In spite of the above, the economic crisis of the 1990s saw the head of the family lose the capacity to meet the needs of his family by himself. Different situations compelled women to seek work: becoming a widow (often due to the death of a husband during the civil war) in a situation where the extended family could not help financially; having an unemployed husband, or a husband who could not or did not want to go abroad for work; having a husband who emigrated but did not manage to send enough money back; or having a husband who emigrated but disappeared (because of a work accident or crime) or started a second family in the recipient country. When caught in these situations, women could not help but work or otherwise be doomed to poverty. Responsibility for providing for their families has pushed them to emigrate. Many of them are called by their husbands or their close relatives to help them work abroad, especially in agriculture. In 2002, almost 44 percent of migrant women met their husband, or another member of the family, with the aim of working intermittently with them abroad.[23] It may also occur that women go to Russia to find their missing husbands only to eventually settle there for work purposes, either because they cannot find their husband or because he has started a new family, as was the case with one of my interviewees below:

> Four years ago, my husband went to Russia for work in order to increase our quality of life. But he has never sent money or news. I have two children, four and six years old. It was very difficult for me to find a job in Tajikistan to feed my family. I then decided to leave my two children with my sister and to go to Russia to earn my living. One day I met my husband in Moscow; he had married another woman. He asked me to go back home. I told him, 'You have deserted your family; you have absolutely no right over me!' I have been working here for a year in two different places: four days a week I clean the streets and three days a week I work at the bazaars. Life is very tough here; luckily, I have two other sisters here who support me (Interview with Olmakhon in Moscow, July 14, 2007).

22 *Ibid.*, corroborated by my personal experience in Uzbekistan.

23 Olimova and Bosc, *Trudovaia migratsiia iz Tadzhikistana*, 31.

Like men, the age structure of female migrants generally ranges from 20 to 49 years.[24] These women are in most cases divorced, abandoned, or widowed; sometimes they have a husband who has been unemployed for years. On average, they have between two and four children who live in Tajikistan and who are brought up by their grandparents or close relatives.

According to research conducted in 2003 by the office of the International Organization for Migration in Dushanbe, 74.5 percent of Tajikistani female migrants work in shuttle trade (*chelnoki*),[25] 14.5 percent in catering, groceries, services, and subordinate positions at hospitals, 5.5 percent in agriculture, and 3.6 percent in construction work.[26] During my own field research in Moscow, I noticed that many female migrants worked in catering and the retail trade. In the majority of cases, they had been hired by men—either their compatriots or representatives of other national minorities in Russia, notably Azeris and Armenians—who had often migrated long ago and were better organized than Tajikistani migrants in the Russian markets. These female migrants occupy very much subordinate positions, be they sellers in the markets, dish-washers, waitresses, or cooks in restaurants. They generally cook Central Asian cuisine intended for migrants working at the markets and not for Russian customers.[27] Some of them also work as cleaners at supermarkets or private enterprises, or on assembly lines, notably in food-processing. Most of them have professional qualifications unrelated to their current job; they had previously been teachers at secondary schools, nurses, and university graduates.

The majority of the women interviewed work from dawn to dusk, every day of the week, for a maximum monthly salary of 500 dollars in the markets and 300 dollars for services. They work in markets exposed to bad weather, suffering heat in the summer and cold in the winter. They often live in unhealthy conditions, regularly catching infectious and gynecological diseases. Tuberculosis is widespread. The duration of stay of these female migrants varies widely and each case is specific. Unlike men, who work seasonally in construction or agriculture, female migrants do not return to Tajikistan every winter; rather they return only sporadically, such as on the occasion of their children's weddings or their relatives' funerals.

---

24 *Ibid.*, 29. This is also what I noticed amongst the female migrants I met in Moscow in July 2007.

25 Female traders involved in the shuttle trade buy goods in one region and resell them in another on a regular basis.

26 Olimova and Bosc, *Trudovaia migratsiia iz Tadzhikistana*, 30–31.

27 Referred to here are the *sambusakhona, nonvoikhona*, and cheap restaurants preparing dishes of *plov, manty*, and so on.

All of these women hold the thought of returning to Tajikistan once they have succeeded in saving enough money to carry out their projects: building a house or buying an apartment, financing their children's weddings, or starting a small business. However, some women have been working in Russia for more than ten years and still cannot afford to return.

The Self-Organization of Labor Migrations

The Tajik state was slow to adopt measures to help its citizens find work abroad. At the beginning of the 2000s, it created within the Ministry of Labor and Employment a directorate for external relations, which is in charge of exporting workforces. However, in 2003, only 0.8 percent of migrants found work via this state structure.[28] In 2002, the president of Tajikistan signed a decree regulating the allocation of citizens taking positions abroad (and vice versa for foreign citizens taking positions in Tajikistan). Nonetheless, in 2006, there were only a dozen state and private agencies in the whole country that had the legal capability to draft contracts between migrants and Russian companies.[29] Given the inefficiency of the state in the organization of labor migration, Tajikistani migrants, be they men or women, rely largely on themselves or family and regional networks to find work abroad; some migrants also turn to middlemen when they do not have the necessary family networks.

The organization of labor migration networks is based on traditional social institutions (*avlod, toyfa, qawm*, and so on), which merchants and mountain dwellers have used for their seasonal migrations since the nineteenth century. They have since regained in importance. The avlod, a patrilineal line of descent, constitutes a very strong linkage in Tajikistani society, in particular in the countryside. It plays a decisive role in the organization of migrations, including in the choice of the date of departure and of destination, the search for means to finance departure and work abroad, and in support provided to families staying behind in Tajikistan.

---

[28] Almost 7 percent of migrants found work through advertisements, while 45 percent found work through friends, 21 percent through relatives, 23 percent by themselves, and 3 percent on the black market. See Olimova and Bosc, *Trudovaia migratsiia iz Tadzhikistana*, 65. For a comparative analysis of migratory policies in the CIS, see G. Vitkovskaia, "Novaia migratsionnaia politika Rossii: vzgliad MOM," 14; the manuscript was given to me by the author during an interview on July 19, 2007.

[29] M.S. Khamraeva, "Problemy trudovoi migratsii i puti ikh resheniia," in *Problemy trudovoi migratsii i puti ikh resheniia* (Dushanbe: Irfon, 2007), 51.

Usually, the departure of the would-be migrant is discussed within the family; elder members of the avlod, especially the oldest representative of the line, are required to give their consent.[30] Indeed, wielding the highest social authority means that all important decisions concerning the lives of its members are made with his agreement. He also decides where the family of the migrant will live during his absence, distributes responsibilities between the members of the family staying, and gives his blessing to the migrant upon departure. If several young men in the same family are of age to migrate, they wait their turn to leave and place their family and children under the responsibility of another man in the family. In this case, the migrant can stay abroad for several continuous seasons.

Once the first migrant has left, several conditions must be met before other members of the family can also be sent abroad. First, the avlod needs proof that the work engaged in abroad is efficient, such as if the migrant manages to send to his family members part of the money he has earned, either as gifts or directly to finance a family ceremony, or to buy agricultural equipment or cattle. The "pioneer" migrant thus plays a structuring role. After returning home to his family in Tajikistan, he then leaves again but this time with other selected kinship members. Thanks to the experience he has gained (generally two to three years), he provides accommodation and money to the newcomers, ensures their registration with the appropriate state authorities, finds them work, and is the guarantor of their safety. Between 2000 and 2002, more than half (66 percent) of Tajikistani migrants found work through their relatives already settled in the recipient country.[31]

Although some cheating and swindling does occur between the group members, the avlod remains the main network for the organization of migration. In principle, labor migrants create in the recipient country a stable and closed group, based on the family (kinship) and the village (neighbors). However, the development of individualism and the uprooting of rural populations which are transplanted to unfamiliar urban environments can lead to the weakening of family relationships.

This community organization is not particular only to men; some special features exist also in female migrations. Like men, women have at least one contact person in Russia, thanks to their family or larger solidarity

---

30 In the cities, the oldest member(s) of the avlod have often lost their predominant role.

31 Olimova and Bosc, *Trudovaia migratsiia iz Tadzhikistana*, 65.

networks, but their work is not necessarily arranged and guaranteed upon their arrival. The key actor facilitating their migration remains the departure organization, in particular in obtaining basic financial support, the fostering of children by family members, and the guarantee of accommodation in the recipient country. Once in the recipient country, their network is supposed to help them to find work. However, it can also happen that female migrants are unable to reach their contact person in Russia.[32] Then they end up alone in Moscow, without accommodation and in very vulnerable situations. They are compelled to fend for themselves and to find new contacts in markets or huge shopping centers. In some extreme cases, they are forced to turn to prostitution to earn enough money to survive. While this may be on a sporadic basis at first, for the lack of another means of income, they may then become "full time" prostitutes.[33]

The organization of labor migration is often strengthened by communication between the family network and a wider solidarity network based on local and regional affiliations. Both local and regional solidarities are a critical social phenomenon in Tajikistan. They exist at the center of a strong and united society built on mutual aid between people from the same locality or region. While this kind of localism or regionalism is an age-old phenomenon, it intensified during the civil war, which led people to trust and rely only on their own community. Therefore, it is not surprising that labor migrant groups in Russia are structured according to local and regional origin. For instance, the association "Badakhshan" in Moscow helps mainly migrants from this region of eastern Tajikistan. These family and regional solidarity linkages ensure the quick formation of migration networks and also play a key role in money transfer mechanisms. Given the lack of help offered from both their own country and from the recipient country, in this case Russia, these linkages also constitute a system of support, adaptation, and social welfare for migrants.

Departure and return from and to Tajikistan are sources of major difficulty for migrants. Whereas there are three means of transportation to Russia—plane, train, and bus[34]—these cannot meet the full demand for

---

[32] There are two scenarios: either the female migrant has an incorrect phone number, which can be the result of human error or deceit, or her contact refuses to answer to avoid taking charge of the newcomer.

[33] Interview with Gavkhar Zhuraeva, director of the association "Fond Tadzhikistan," in Moscow on July 12, 2007.

[34] There are four weekly Dushanbe–Moscow flights and two weekly Khudjand–Moscow flights, as well as other air links with major cities of Russia such as Yekaterinburg, Krasnoyarsk, Novosibirsk, Samara, Ufa, and St. Petersburg. The main rail links between the two

travel, in particular during March and April, the high season for departures, and the returns in November and December. The lack of available seats leads to a hike in prices, especially in the informal economic networks. Further, long journeys by train and bus increase the risks of extortion by customs officers in Central Asian transit states (Uzbekistan and Kazakhstan), by traffic police, and also by drivers and transportation controllers.[35] As a consequence, traveling by bus and train is more expensive than traveling by plane. The risks are even higher for women, who prefer traveling by plane, even if the price is very high.[36]

The difficulties of the journey, the lack of security, and extortion have contributed to the creation of a new job: the organizer-attendant. This type of middleman helps labor migrants to organize their departure, accompanies them during the journey, and assists them in obtaining a job abroad, in return for a fee amounting to 20 percent of the migrant's first three months of salary.[37] Contrary to official agencies, which are concentrated in the capital city, middlemen can be found in every city of Tajikistan. Usually a middle-aged man or woman, the beneficiary enjoys the protection of a local official to conduct his activity and cooperates with mahalla dwellers, traders, or other professional channels to find clients. An experienced traveler, the middleman has contacts in the recipient country and has a reasonably good knowledge of migratory formalities. He resorts to patronage relationships to get travel tickets that are generally difficult to obtain; nevertheless, he sometimes makes use of fake documents. His job also consists of keeping the documents, passport included, of the migrants he accompanies, and maintaining good relations with border guards through "gifts" and other means. Upon arrival in the recipient country, the middleman sets up migrants with people from their region and helps them to register. It also falls to him to find the first job for them via the contacts he has with local employers. However, some dishonest organizer-

countries are Dushanbe–Volgograd and Dushanbe–Astrakhan. The main bus routes are Dushanbe–Krasnoyarsk, Khudjand–Novosibirsk, and Isfara–Yekaterinburg. These routes go through Uzbekistan, Turkmenistan, and Kazakhstan prior to entering Russia.

[35] Even when migrants do have their documents in order, customs officers extort money from them. If migrants do not pay, they can be held at the border post for several days, and endure psychological and physical abuse.

[36] All the female migrants I met in Moscow had come to Russia by this means of transportation.

[37] This information is derived from my interviews with female migrants in Moscow, July 2007. Olimova and Bosc do not present any data on this issue.

attendants cheat their customers by failing to keep their promises or even abandon migrants during the journey.

A second type of unofficial middleman resides already in Russia. Thanks to his experience and contacts, he mainly offers to find migrants jobs, dealing little with the organization of the journey from the city or village of departure. Like the organizer-attendant, this middleman is not always reliable. Several women respondents to this study obtained their jobs upon arrival, but were not paid for the first two months or received a lower salary compared to the one advertized by the middleman.

> After the death of my parents, I decided to go to Russia for work. I was 22 years old, single, and I had to earn my living. Before leaving for Moscow in November 2006, I was working as a waitress in a restaurant in Khudjand. But the salary was too low to survive there. Once in Moscow, a Pamiri *brigadir* [middleman] found me work in a supermarket. He told me that I would earn 9,000 rubles [360 dollars] per month, but I got paid only 3,000 rubles [120 dollars] during the three first months and I received no salary for my last two months. I sought the help of the head of the association "Fond Tadzhikistan" to obtain my salary, but it was in vain. I then stopped working and hoped to find something else. But since the law on regulating migrations came into force in January 2007, it is no longer possible to work without a permit. I then approached the Russian administration to get the permit, but I failed because I did not pay a bribe. Another middleman proposed to get a work permit for me for 8,000 rubles [300 dollars]. I paid the fee but the middleman disappeared. What hurts me the most is that we get ripped off by our own fellow citizens; the two middlemen I resorted to were from my region [Gorno-Badakhshan]! Luckily, I have met Pamiri women with whom I am now living and who support me a lot while I am looking for another job (Interview with Nisso in Moscow, July 21, 2007).

The Impact of Migrations on National and Family Economies

The huge migratory flows from Tajikistan have major economic repercussions for the country. According to Alexei Kireyev, the case of Tajikistan is unique: "No other country has seen its workforce decline by around 20 percent in a decade, nor see flows of remittances reach around 50 percent of GDP."[38] Tajikistan thus exports its main commodity of comparative advantage, cheap labor. The volume of remittances that migrants transfer

[38] A. Kireyev, "The Macroeconomics of Remittances: The Case of Tajikistan," *IMF Working Paper*, WP/06/2, 2006, 3.

each year to their homeland is difficult to estimate with accuracy. This is mainly due to the fact that migrants resort extensively to informal means (such as *perekidka* or *hawala* systems) to transfer remittances, that statistics in Tajikistan lack reliability, and that individual imports of goods are not counted. Given these uncertainties in calculations, it is estimated that remittance inflows represent anywhere from 20 to almost 50 percent of Tajikistan's GDP.[39] It should be noted that even the lower figure of 20 percent is very high by international standards. It is comparable to Moldova (25 percent of GDP) and exceeds the annual levels of remittances received by Lesotho (19 percent), Jordan (18 percent), and Albania (15 percent) in 2005.[40] It is therefore unsurprising that this massive inflow of money plays a major role in national and familial economies.

At the macro-economic level, remittances have enabled the recovery of Tajikistan's economy.[41] Their income multiplier effect is all the more important because the level of unemployment is and remains high. Remittances also constitute a stabilizing factor for the economy, which faces cyclical fluctuations. They contribute to improving the balance of payments, benefit the banking system (when they are transferred via formal channels), give Tajikistani importers access to foreign currencies, and stimulate demand in local consumption.[42] At the micro-economic level, remittances play a key role in the fight against poverty. Indeed, they raise the standard of living of the migrants' families by increasing their incomes and also by diversifying sources of income. Thereby, they reduce vulnerability to unexpected shocks and events. According to Olimova and Bosc, remittances are one of the principal sources of income for 81.7 percent of migrants' families.[43]

Labor migrations have nevertheless had some negative impacts on the national economy, at least in the medium and long terms. For one, Tajikistan has lost much of its skilled labor force. Some key sectors, like education and health, are lacking in competent personnel to ensure that basic services such as the latter function properly. This situation has been aggravated by the growing number of women departing, as women have largely staffed these two sectors since the Soviet period. The departure of

---

[39] *Ibid.*, 5.
[40] *Ibid.*
[41] Mughal, *Migration, Remittances, and Living*, 67–68.
[42] Olimova and Bosc, *Trudovaia migratsiia iz Tadzhikistana*, 105.
[43] To compare, the salary earned at a state company is a main source of income for just 42.5 percent of migrants' families. *Ibid.*, 109.

unskilled migrants also delays the creation of national industries, in particular in the manufacturing sector. Although women have been invited to take part in national economic activity in order to compensate for the departure of young men, a large part of the most productive labor force in the country is still absent.[44] Moreover, the relatively skilled migrants who migrate to Russia often lose their qualifications when they are compelled to accept work that does not correspond to their training, as in the case of Mavjuda quoted below. Resuming their former professional activities after months or years of migration proves to be almost impossible.[45]

> I have been working in Russia for 11 years [selling food to migrants working in the big mall nearby]. My husband has been unemployed for years and refuses to leave to find work abroad. Before coming to Russia, I was working as a nurse at a hospital, but our standard of living was constantly declining in the 1990s. I then decided to go to Moscow. Thanks to my work here, I have bought a house in Dushanbe and my daughter married. I plan to return home at the beginning of August when my son marries, but I will stay only ten days. I will not be able to stay longer because August corresponds to the season when it is possible to earn a good living in Moscow. If I came back home for good, I would spend all my money very quickly. This is why I continue in spite of the harsh living and working conditions here (Interview with Mavjuda, Izmailovskii market, July 27, 2007).

The remittances sent by migrants to their families are first allocated to procuring basic necessities (food, clothes, and urgent medical expenses), and then to the repayment of debts. In 2002, 32.9 percent of migrants used the money to ensure that their families were properly fed, 22.5 percent to purchase clothing, and 22.7 percent to pay for medical services for themselves and family members.[46] When significant amounts of money can be saved, they are used to buy a house or an apartment, for undertaking renovations in a house or flat, purchasing household electrical appliances, organizing ceremonies such as weddings or circumcisions, covering non-urgent medical expenses, paying for children's educations, and financing minor business activities. This last investment, however, is less frequent.[47]

---

[44] *Ibid.*, 105–6.

[45] S. Kasymova, "Meniaiutsia li muzhchiny Tadzhikistana?" *Bisnes i Politika*, no. 36 (2001): 2.

[46] Olimova and Bosc, *Trudovaia migratsiia iz Tadzhikistana*, 123.

[47] According to Olimova and Bosc, only 3.8 percent of migrants started a business, and 16.2 percent managed to save money in order to do so. The businesses created by migrants are generally small ventures such as shops (mainly grocery stores), cafes, and small restaurants, but sometimes also construction companies.

The migrants who can afford more expensive purchases typically work in retail trade, in particular in shuttle trade, where they earn relatively more and are more self-sufficient in their activities. Therefore, labor migrations and remittances constitute a "survival strategy" for the migrants' families rather than a real "development strategy" for the country as such.[48]

Housing is particularly important in terms of the object of migrants' savings.[49] The majority of women I met in Moscow who had been working there for more than six or seven years, often in the retail trade, had bought a house or flat in Tajikistan. Investing in housing is essential because it enables them to visibly demonstrate a degree of social success. It also provides a certain security in a country where the future seems uncertain; also, compared to a small enterprise, housing represents a safe investment. Owning property also allows for the realization of a dream and compensation for exile; it symbolizes roots in the country of origin. Besides, the house must correspond to the latest demands of comfort in terms of its conditions, furniture, and design. It is women who usually initiate the overhaul of a house and its furniture, as private space is considered to be primarily a feminine domain. Women are therefore said to be the best placed to gauge the new household needs of their families still living in Tajikistan.[50]

In addition, remittances enable families to finance rites of passage. In the countryside as in cities, the cost of a wedding often amounts to several years' salary for parents. Migrants' financial contributions are thus essential to minimize these debts.[51] The experience of labor migration also makes migrants understand how important education is for their

---

48 E. Sadovskaia, "Denezhnye perevody trudovykh migrantov: dinamika, rol' v migrantskikh domokhoziaistvakh i soobshchestvakh Tsentral'noj Azii," in V. Tishkov and E. Fillipova, eds., *Etnicheskaia situatsiia i konflikty v stranakh SNG i Baltii. Ezhegodnyi doklad* (Moscow: RAN, 2006), 58.

49 According to Olimova and Bosc, 5.5 percent of migrants bought or built a house or flat for the whole family, 5.2 percent bought a flat or flats for their children, 37.2 percent completely renovated the house or flat, 0.3 percent bought land, while 50.8 percent did not succeed in improving their housing conditions. *Trudovaia migratsiia iz Tadzhikistana*, 124.

50 S. Monqid, "Les Femmes émigrées vecteur de modernisation? Le rôle occulté des femmes émigrées dans le développement du pays d'origine: le cas marocain," *Passerelles: revue d'études interculturelles*, no. 28 (2004): 60. This is corroborated by my own personal experiences in Uzbekistan and in Tajikistan in 2006.

51 In 2002, 24.7 percent of migrants entirely financed their children's weddings, and 14 percent of migrants saved up for a wedding. Olimova and Bosc, *Trudovaia migratsiia iz Tadzhikistana*, 110.

children, and thus how crucial it is to allocate money toward it.[52] Survival priorities, however, sometimes subordinate investment in education, whether primary or secondary, to that of a peripheral concern. Not only this, but cultural factors also hamper investment in higher education in a situation where the marriage of one's children is traditionally given priority over their studies. Sharifa, below, is a case in point in terms of her priorities:

> I came to Moscow for work seven years ago in order to enhance our standard of living and in particular to buy a house for my family. I am married and have two children aged 16 and 17. My husband does nothing and stays at home. I managed to leave Tajikistan and find work thanks to my two brothers who have been working in Moscow for several years. At the beginning we were selling dry fruits from my region [Konibodom, in northern Tajikistan] in one of the markets of Moscow. Currently, this market is undergoing repairs; this is why I am working here [in the Tioplyi Stan market], for an Azeri, as a seller. I sell fruits and vegetables. With my new job, I am earning only 500 dollars a month, while I was earning a lot more with my brothers. With the money earned with them, I was able to buy and equip a house. This has allowed us at last to leave the house of my in-laws, where we had lived for several years. Now we have our own house. I will continue to work here with the goal of financing the weddings of my children (Interview with Sharifa, Tioplyi Stan market, July 19, 2007).

The Consequences of Labor Migration for Gender

While improving families' standard of living and reducing social tensions fed by economic crisis, labor migration also produces new cultural disbalances, which stem especially from the growing participation of women in the economy. These tensions impact the family structure, women's status (migrant or not), and gender relations, developments which are explored below.

Labor migration disrupts the family structure and entails its reorganization. A significant element is the strong renewal of traditional social institutions. To survive in harsh socioeconomic conditions, people have returned to traditional modes of production and rely on the enlarged family as a solidarity network. In the regions that were most severely affected by the civil war (Khatlon, Hissor, Gharm, and Badakhshan), the avlod have

[52] Almost 33 percent of migrants invested money in their children's education (from primary to secondary school) in 2002.

become the central social institution and labor migrations have consolidated their importance.

Another change concerns the composition of families. The number of households consisting of two or more marital units has increased in almost all regions of Tajikistan, implying the decreasing role of the nuclear family. According to the study by Olimova and Bosc (2003), 28.8 percent of migrant households comprised of two or more conjugal units in 2002, compared to 20 percent for all families in Tajikistan in 1989.[53] This phenomenon is particularly striking in the countryside, where almost all men of working age have left to find work. In such a situation families may be composed of the migrant's elderly parents, his wife and children, and possibly one or more of his brothers, along with their wives and children. One can also find migrants' families spanning three or four generations, the members of which are only women and children.

There is also another kind of family reorganization that is not linked to the extended family. A migrant who has left to find work in Russia may get married to another woman while maintaining his first wife and children back in Tajikistan. This second marriage receives traditional validation through a religious wedding (*nikoh*), but is not recognized under state law since polygamy is officially forbidden in Tajikistan. Families thereby are recomposed and enlarged under economic pressure. Serious tensions can ensue when the first wife refuses to recognize her husband's second wedding. In the case of households having several marital units, migrants face heavy financial burdens. In 2002, according to Olimova and Bosc, 54.2 percent of migrants were providing financial assistance to relatives living in separate households, and 13 percent of migrants were supporting several related households at the same time.[54] Shahnoza, below, was the case of an interviewee who had married a migrant who already had a wife in Tajikistan and provided support to her family:

> I have been working in Moscow for six years. I am divorced and have two children that I have entrusted to my mother in Samarkand. I got married again [through a traditional and religious wedding] here to Saidjon, who already has a wife and four children in Tajikistan. His family is aware of our relationship and accepts it. On the contrary, my family knows nothing about it, even though Saidjon provides them with financial assistance, through me. I am not really sure that Saidjon will stay with me, even though he reassures me every day that he won't leave me and that he will introduce me to

53 Olimova and Bosc, *Trudovaia migratsiia iz Tadzhikistana*, 114.

54 *Ibid.*, 114–15.

> his family one day…I don't dare to announce my wedding to my relatives because if we do separate, I fear being considered badly by society (Interview with Shahnoza, July 17, 2007).

Labor migrations also have negative consequences for the education and upbringing of children. The long-term absence of the father often creates a problem of authority for the mother. If the latter is compelled to migrate herself, she generally leaves her children with her relatives. But children are often left to their own devices. Once they return, parents often find that they have lost authority over their children because of their protracted absence. More than a third of migrants (36.6 percent in 2002)[55] noticed a deterioration in their children's education. The children are even more affected in the case of marital tensions or divorce provoked by labor migration.

The increasing role played by women in the economy, either by working in Tajikistan or by migrating, tends to modify gender relations. Migrations change the "traditional" female role based on motherhood and housekeeping. Women leave the home and become the main breadwinner for the family, which strengthens their authority as the de facto family head.[56] Their decision-making powers then cover not only the economic sphere, but also, and increasingly, birth control.[57] Moreover, their long stays abroad, as in the case of Mahbuba below, push their husbands to take care of the housekeeping and to be fully responsible for the education of children. The number of households headed by women is increasing and, according to official statistics, represents 21 percent of Tajikistani households.[58]

> I am married and have two children. My husband is unemployed and has stayed with the children in Tajikistan. True, there is no work at all in our region [Gorno-Badakhshan], but my husband refuses to go and work elsewhere. This is why I was compelled to come here for work. I earn around 500 dollars a month, which is good revenue for us. My husband accepts the situation, even though it is not easy for him, psychologically speaking. It has been going on for five years. I think we got used to living like this. When I go back home, I can see that my husband has now mastered the housework

---

[55] *Ibid.*, 115.

[56] This also applies to economically active women who remain in Tajikistan with an unemployed or missing husband.

[57] This change is occurring both in cities and in the countryside, but women are still far from having full birth control. S. Kasymova, *Transformatsiia gendernogo poriadka v tadzhikskom obshchestve* (Dushanbe: Irfon, 2007), 211.

[58] *Ibid.*, 210.

> and he sometimes does it better than I do. But we hope that one day we will get back to our former way of living (Interview with Mahbuba, Moscow, July 13, 2007).

The increasing role that women play in the economy is not without provoking strong reactions from society, in particular from men. The situation is paradoxical. On the one hand, women are slowly gaining a place in the economy, which even the men accept as a fundamental contribution to socioeconomic survival. In the countryside, with the support of international organizations and the consent of their families, women no longer hesitate to apply for micro-credit schemes (to buy a sewing machine or a baking oven, for instance) or to oversee the farming of lands rented from the state, which they then plough, sow, and harvest themselves.[59] Their involvement in the shuttle trade also preceded that of men. (There is one particular reason for this: compared to men, women are under less suspicion of being traffickers or "terrorists." This is why they are entrusted with goods and money which they find it easier to pass through customs with. Cooperation and sharing of responsibilities between men and women is thus accepted.) On the other hand, society is not yet ready to fully accept women as the head of a family, even if they demonstrate their ability to simultaneously carry out the roles of mother and housekeeper, which are traditionally assigned to them. In the family, gender-driven socialization remains very strong. Parents and relatives prepare boys and girls for their respective social roles. Male work is always given more value than female work, and women generally have no professional prospects after their weddings. Defined as the pillar of the family by their system of values, men have great difficulties accepting the reversal of roles and the concomitant deterioration of their status, especially when they are confronted with unemployment.[60] Overall, this results in increased marital violence, which was already high, and the social humiliation of men who remain at home and often fall victim to alcoholism, drug use, or even suicide. According to recent studies, the number of suicides is increasing more quickly among men than women in Tajikistan.[61] In the northern city

---

59 Nevertheless, women are very often assisted in this difficult work by their children, who compensate for the lack of labor force, but to the detriment of their education.

60 Anecdotally, each and every male migrant I met in Moscow in July 2007 told me that the woman's place was in the home.

61 Kasymova, "Meniaiutsia li muzhchiny Tadzhikistana?"

of Khudjand, for example, 40 of the 66 suicide cases recorded during the first three months of 2005 involved men.[62]

Even if female migrants and women working in Tajikistan manage to become more independent through their multiple tasks and responsibilities, they do not always succeed in imposing their new role and simultaneously maintaining good relationships with their extended family. Therefore, they prefer keeping up appearances to ease social relationships. Women securing the survival of their families often keep a low profile and act discreetly, while their husbands, even while unemployed, still enjoy the symbolic status as the head of the family.

In addition, the fact that women do not necessarily seek to change their position in society does not contribute to the evolution of their socially constructed role. On the one hand, working women, female migrants in particular, are vectors for social change. They introduce material innovations to the household, enhancing comfort and efficiency. They also bring new ways of doing things, new ideas, and behaviors regarding different domains (architecture, design, and *art de la table*). However, some of these women continue to promote the idea that a woman's traditional place is in the home as an accepted and internalized social norm. Female migrants often hope that their work abroad or in their country will be only temporary. All those I met in Moscow emphasized that they came for work not by deliberate choice, but through the force of circumstances. They think that remittances should allow them to stay at home with their children rather than work. Furthermore, women, whether they migrate or not, do not always see other female migrants in a positive light. Their judgment is a moral one and concerns reputation. Women are suspected of losing their virtue when they leave the household and go abroad alone, even when with another (non-male) member of the family. Therefore, the great majority of female migrants hope their daughters will not follow their example and instead encourage them to stick to and reproduce the social model of early marriage and bearing children.

* * * * *

Labor migration plays a major role in the economy of Tajikistan, especially in poverty reduction in the countryside as well as in cities. Despite

---

[62] M. Sayfidinova, "Zhenshchiny berut Tadzhikistan pod svoi kontrol'," *Zona.kz*, June 15, 2005, http://zonakz.net/articles/9047.

harsh working and living conditions in Russia, Tajikistani migrants will be compelled to work abroad in Russia as long as the Tajik economy does not provide adequate work opportunities for the economically active population. However, even if labor migration enables a strategy of survival and adaptation to difficult economic circumstances, it does not constitute a strategy of economic development for the migrants' households in Tajikistan, unlike in other countries such as in Central America.

The phenomenon of migration has important social consequences. It affects almost all Tajikistani families and creates strong tensions within this institution, which is at the core of the social structure. The massive migration of men and the growing migration of women disrupt the family structure and lead to its reorganization along larger configurations. Migration also greatly affects relations between parents and children, and the education of the latter. However, the changes entailed do not necessarily lead to changes in the socially constructed roles of women. Gender and power relations in Tajikistani society are changing slowly, but much more fundamentally than during the Soviet period, when the Soviet regime tried to impose change from above. Just as in European societies, where war was a prerequisite to the promotion of the role of women to that equal with men, the civil war in Tajikistan and economic crisis enabled women to take on more of a leading role as economic actors. It now remains to be seen how the status of women will evolve as a result of the pressures emanating from the socio-economic context as well as the actions of the authorities and external actors.

PROJECTS AND MIGRATORY STRATEGIES OF WOMEN BELONGING TO THE TASHKENT INTELLIGENTSIA

Stéphanie Belouin

While the new Uzbekistani nation-state is built on the reappropriation of Islam and Uzbek traditional values, globalization reformulates the issue of identity and questions the function of societies at the local level. It is therefore a dual challenge and one which is not without serious paradoxes in Uzbekistani society. Since the country became independent in 1991, joint ventures and foreign agencies have arrived in Tashkent. The capital city, which until then had existed more or less in isolation, benefited from the emergence of international economic and cultural openings. Whereas before perestroika migration was almost only confined to the Soviet Union,[1] today destinations and poles of attraction have diversified, and the country's difficult economic transition has also contributed to pushing segments of the population to migrate.

Scholarly knowledge concerning these new mobilities in Central Asia is developing with an increase in research on the subject. Despite the difficulties in quantifying migratory flows, studies show that Uzbekistan has become an important point of departure. Faced with the "Uzbekization" of the higher echelons of society, since the 1980s ethnic minorities have progressively left the country, resulting in the loss of the intellectual elite,[2] such as doctors and professors. At the same time, the most underprivileged social groups have also migrated, usually on a temporary or seasonal basis, in search of jobs or higher wages. To meet the needs of their families, many men leave the country to work as construction workers in the United Arab Emirates or in former Soviet republics, like Russia and Kazakhstan. Uzbek networks of "shuttle traders" have also been created, predominantly in Russia, Turkey, and South Korea.

However, a sociological profile of female migration, social networks, and the evolution of gender relations remains to be established. Upon

---

[1] A. Vichnevski and J. Zaiontchkovskaia, "L'émigration de l'ex-Union soviétique: prémices et inconnues," *Revue Européenne des Migrations Internationales* 7, no. 3 (1991): 5–29.

[2] C. Poujol, *Ouzbékistan. La croisée des chemins* (Paris: Belin, 2005).

examining statistics published by the Uzbek state,[3] foreign consulates in Uzbekistan, and European ministries, it appears that the significance of female migration from Uzbekistan is far from negligible. Moreover, these official figures do not include illegal or unrecorded departures.[4] These "invisible" flows will not be discussed in this chapter, which instead focuses on the legal migrations of skilled, unaccompanied women.

Despite the fact that women of the ex-intelligentsia remain a minority within Uzbekistan's migratory flows, their specific mobility constitutes a means to understand the state of society since independence, especially the situation of the post-Soviet intelligentsia. While their degrees are largely unrecognized outside of the Commonwealth of Independent States (CIS), these women possess mastery of one or more foreign languages and have the capacity to learn what is needed for quick adaptation to foreign university programs and labor markets. Contrary to some analyses that present women in migration as victims and use reductive representations of "Slavic women," this study aims to underline the power of decision that these women wield in their migratory paths. Although the degree of "female emancipation" in the former Soviet Union remains difficult to define relative to the evolution of gender relations in the West, one shall see that these skilled migrants consciously and rationally increase the value of their cultural capital in order to build a life more befitting of their aspirations.

It is partly through the personal discourses of these women, who plan and organize their departures, that one can understand the political, economic, and social issues facing the independent state of Uzbekistan. From here common questions, which will tie this analysis together, can be posed: why do these women try to leave despite belonging to a comparatively favored social group? How do they build their migratory projects and their strategies for leaving Uzbekistan? What are the links between these migrations and the ongoing social recombining that has occurred since independence?

[3] In 2005, women represented 53.8 percent of registered migrants (132,550 people), meaning those who received from Uzbek authorities a visa to leave the country and changed their residence permit. This figure only reflects a small part of current migrations from Uzbekistan. Source: State Committee of the Republic of Uzbekistan on Statistics in *Women and Men of Uzbekistan, Statistical bulletin* (Tashkent, 2007).

[4] On this subject, see *Central Asia: Special Report on Human Trafficking*, United Nations Integrated Regional Information Network, October 21, 2003; I. Bosc, *Trafficking in Persons: A Form of Social Exclusion* (Washington, D.C.: The World Bank, 2002).

The migratory projects of these women will be analyzed using a qualitative approach. This study is based on a survey conducted in Tashkent, between March and May 2008, with 21 skilled Uzbekistani women. Ten of them had already experienced migration; the remaining respondents expressed their desire to leave Uzbekistan and were making concrete plans to go abroad. The analysis will be presented in three sections: an introduction of the methodology used during the survey, including detailed profiles of the women and their families; an examination of how the women articulated their various migratory strategies in preparation for their departure; and a conclusion that places these migrations in perspective with actual social transformations underway in Uzbekistan.

Fieldwork and Analysis of the Sample

Methodology

The goal of this fieldwork consisted in analyzing the intentions and practices of an urban elite composed of women possessing important cultural capital (mastery of one or more foreign languages as well as academic and professional skills), and who increase the value of these assets through their migratory projects. With some rare exceptions, I intentionally chose to interview women with whom I had already established links through research.[5] The subject of this survey was a delicate one to tackle. Migration is not a subject about which people speak freely in Uzbekistan, as leaving implies that they are not fully satisfied with the situation of the country. Explaining the real motivations for migration is sometimes incompatible with the maintenance of positive discourse on the future of Uzbekistan and the policies pursued there since independence. Posing questions of a personal nature were also needed for analysis of some migratory strategies, especially those concerning marriage. I therefore preferred to interview people who had known me for some time, hoping that they would feel more at ease, and free to speak about the social, economic, and political situation of their country, as well as their personal lives. My work was based on the collection of life stories in order to place a person's migratory project in a spatiotemporal context and make it more comprehensible; that is, identifying who their parents were, whether the family

[5] The author worked for the French embassy in Tashkent for three years before enrolling on a doctoral program.

had a history of migration, and which specific events had left a mark on the individual's life. As far as it was possible, I tried to initiate informal conversations with their close circles (men and women in their family and among their friends) so as to study how the intentions and practices of these women were received in Tashkent. I gathered testimonies from women already "in migration," who I had previously met between 2004 and 2007, through telephone conversations or e-mail exchanges. This method also allowed me to reconstruct migratory courses by gathering different chronological stages of migration (departure from Tashkent, settlement in the host country, developments in professional life, and marriage).

Finally, I conducted exploratory interviews with three matrimonial agencies and one recruitment agency that sends workers abroad, allowing me to better understand their function and evaluate their importance in the migration of the women. I also met with different representatives of consulates and foreign cultural centers in Tashkent.

Presentation of the Surveyed Women and their Families[6]

All of the women surveyed held Uzbekistani citizenship, but belonged to different ethnic groups. Nine of them had at least one parent belonging to a Central Asian ethnic group (Uzbek and Tajik). Twelve belonged to a foreign-born minority (Russian, Korean, Tatar, and Armenian), with the majority being Russian-speakers. Fourteen of the interviewees were Muslim and seven were Orthodox Christians. In fact, being part of an ethnic or religious group seems to play an important role in the primary motivations for, and progress made in, migration. With some exceptions, notably the Koreans, women belonging to Russian-speaking ethnic minorities often explained their departure in terms of "not feeling at home" in Uzbekistan. They all declared an inability to speak Uzbek. Their families seemed to understand their decision to migrate and were supportive of it. The Central Asian women tended also to justify their intention to migrate with a denunciation of the patriarchal society and its effects on their lives as women, particularly with regard to marriage.

[6] The results of this qualitative survey cannot exhaustively represent all of the migratory experiences of qualified women since independence. Nevertheless, they constitute a primary tool of analysis in regard to this population's migratory behaviors. As a consequence, the examples and accounts set out in this study should not be generalized. For reasons of privacy, the names of the interviewees have been changed.

The age of the interviewees was mostly between 20 and 30 years old, which generally corresponds to the period when these urban women would make their major life choices (marriage and career). It is also at this age that the majority of the surveyed women made the decision to migrate. Nine of the women were older than 30 and were mostly divorced (a quarter of the women in the sample were divorced); six of them already had children and explained that their decision to migrate was also to give them a "better life." The fact that a quarter of the interviewees were divorced contrasts with the low number of divorces recorded each year in Uzbekistan.[7] Urban populations are more likely to divorce than rural populations, but the high proportion in the sample here shows the degree of self-sufficiency already acquired before migration. As of May 2008, 8 of the 21 women interviewed were single, 8 were married, and 5 were engaged or cohabitating. Of the 13 women in relationships, 10 were together with a foreign man. Here one can see the importance of the linkage between international couples and migration. Dating a foreign man can cause one to make the decision to migrate or, conversely, the decision to migrate can cause one to date a foreign man.

Five interviewees had already migrated internally by leaving the provinces to establish themselves in the capital city, Tashkent. The decision to do so was anticipated and had been prepared for by the women and their families for a long time, with all of them being aware of the greater opportunities available in the capital. Two young women from Russian-speaking ethnic groups came from *kolkhozes* in the region of Tashkent, moving to the capital at the age of 17 to study. In their cases, their parents, who had studied in the capital, helped them to realize this internal migration, notably by maintaining a flat in Tashkent. Two other women who had migrated internally had been born in Samarkand; one came for higher education purposes while the other had found a job in Tashkent, having previously worked for a foreign organization in Samarkand. She wanted to leave her city because of the social pressure imposed by her mahalla due to her status as a single woman (she was over the age of 25). The fifth woman was from Bukhara and had received a promotion at the age of 26, allowing her to settle in Tashkent. The three provincial women mentioned above had no permanent *propiska*, or residence permit, allowing them to live in Tashkent, although they did have a job or were registered

[7] In 2005, out of a population of 26 million, only 16,392 divorces were counted. Source: State Committee of the Republic of Uzbekistan on Statistics in *Women and Men of Uzbekistan, Statistical Bulletin.*

at a Tashkent university. Paradoxically, therefore, international migration can represent an easier way to settle outside of these provincial cities than migration to Tashkent. Nevertheless, internal migration to the capital city corresponds, in the short term at least, to these women's expectations. They all harbored a feeling of non-belonging and felt uneasy living in the provinces and were desirous of escaping the social controls there that they considered challenging and problematic.

The only common denominator among the surveyed women was that they were all highly qualified, although some were still students at the time of the investigation. Five had more than a master's degree, 13 had a master's degree, and 3 had a bachelor's degree. Moreover, most of them had benefited from an elite education since the beginning of their schooling. Eighteen interviewees had studied in "Russian schools," where the level of instruction is known to be better than in Uzbek schools.

Some of the women were overqualified in comparison with the type of positions they held in Uzbekistan or abroad (for instance, as waitresses, cleaning women for expatriates, or beauticians in luxury hotels). But, nevertheless, these jobs allow them to earn better wages than being employed in the public sector in Uzbekistan.[8] Those who finished their studies highly qualified and who knew English and/or another foreign language already earned relatively good wages before leaving Uzbekistan (between 500 and 1,000 dollars per month compared to the average wage in Tashkent estimated at 100 dollars per month). They worked as secretaries, switchboard operators, and accountants in foreign firms and international organizations. It was noticeable that even before migrating, the surveyed women already tended to reject the local labor market in favor of better paid positions as "local employees" of foreign companies or institutions. However, in spite of the good wages in this international labor environment, women complained about being confined to assistant tasks. As they started at the bottom, few of them succeeded in acquiring a position with responsibilities, like consultant or project manager, which would correspond more to their professional aspirations.

Many of their families had histories of being mobile, primarily for the reason that the Soviet intelligentsia regularly migrated in order to study or work (to Tashkent, but also to Moscow and Leningrad). Nine interviewees had at least one parent who had emigrated for a long-term stay in

[8] Such as teachers, nurses, and administrative employees in ministries; women mostly occupied these types of posts during the Soviet era.

another Soviet republic. Their children therefore seemed to also take on this "tradition" of international mobility, their academic and social capital now allowing them to study or work beyond the Iron Curtain. Moreover, for non-Central Asian ethnic minorities, family backgrounds are characterized by a history of migration: Korean, Armenian, and Tatar families were deported to Central Asia, while Russian families are descended from settlers. Sometimes, this specific past gives rise to a feeling of being able to adapt abroad as Anna, one of the respondents, testified:

> I was born here, from Russian parents, I always lived between two worlds. It seems difficult to say just like that, but for us, it is a wealth, the Russians who arrived here adapted themselves to Central Asia, and, in a way, they are more open than the Russians of Russia. By living here, I understand how Eastern people react, and how, with my Russian roots, I react. From that, I always succeed in adapting to whoever, to any situation… You just have to be a 'good psychologist.' The Europeans also, I know how they think, what is necessary to say and do with them (Anna, Russian, 21 years old, student).

Many of the women surveyed, furthermore, were not the only ones in their family to have migrated since independence. Thirteen of them had parents, cousins, or sisters abroad. These families therefore operate within the same dynamic of mobility. The links between the interviewees and their families abroad is explored further in the section on the role of social networks in migratory strategies.

The Diversity of Migratory Strategies

According to my observations, women in Uzbekistan have more opportunities than men to leave for the European Union and North America, and especially to establish themselves there permanently. However, data on this is incomplete, with visa services not having the same system to record departures and registrations; also, some national immigration statistics fail to distinguish the gender of migrants. Figures from the French Interior Ministry[9] show, for instance, that from 1997 to 2002, Uzbekistani women were almost twice as likely than Uzbekistani men to acquire a permit for work in France. From the German embassy in Tashkent,[10] I also

[9] French Ministry of the Interior. *Les titres de séjour des étrangers en France. Rapport établi en application de l'article 45 de la loi du 11 mai 1998.*

[10] The German embassy in Uzbekistan, among all the EU members' representations in Tashkent, is the one that gives out the highest number of Schengen visas.

gathered data on female Uzbekistani migrants to Germany in the period from January 1, 2003, through December 31, 2007. The embassy issues different types of visas according to the purpose of the trip. Only the "D-type" of visa allows a person to legally immigrate; it can be renewed in the country and authorizes work in Germany. It is issued to students, scientists, au pairs, and to those who want to get married to a German citizen. In the case of those who successfully requested D-type visas, women were slightly more numerous than men (ranging from 52 to 56 percent according to the year).

Due to the more restrictive migratory policies now applied in destination countries, migrating abroad is far from a quick and simple matter for these women. On the contrary, the decision to migrate is well planned and organized in advance according to set strategies aimed at finding opportunities for departure and optimizing living conditions once abroad.

Constitution and Promotion of Cultural Assets

These educated women have cultural assets and learning tools that they seek to exploit in migration. They are aware of their skills and do not hesitate to further enrich their curriculum vitaes by acquiring new competences. The women under study were perfect Russian speakers and almost always preferred to express themselves in this language, although some of them had Uzbek or Tajik as their mother tongue. This knowledge of Russian puts them at an advantage over those who speak and understand only Central Asian languages. Indeed, the international press, scientific works, language methods, and Internet sites are frequently available in Russian, but very few are translated into Uzbek or Tajik.

These educated women are also characterized by their excellent knowledge of one or more foreign languages. Most have mastered English as well as a second European (German, French, Italian, Spanish) or Oriental (Japanese, Korean, Turkish) language. An essential tool for the migrant, foreign language ability is beneficial to their social trajectory, conditioning the migrant for departure to and integration in the host society. From early on, the women surveyed had acquired good linguistic knowledge by specializing in languages in school and university, or by attending elite Uzbek universities in the fields of economics, law, and political science, where instruction is also focused on foreign languages. Others registered at foreign cultural centers or in private language institutes. Some successfully learned a language by themselves, without the help of a professor, thanks to simple audio recordings downloaded on the Internet. The study of a language is a first step and essential precondition in the construction of a specific migratory strategy—whether it be studying or working abroad, becoming an au pair, or marrying a foreigner.

Students interviewed during the survey all wished to study abroad in order to improve their curriculum vitae, better their linguistic competence, or sometimes to purse specialized training not readily available in Uzbekistan (management or international finance, for instance). Many complained about the loss of value of degrees in Uzbekistan, as well as growing corruption during exams, poor lesson content, and the repeated absences of teachers. Many of the interviewees were aware they live in a region that was isolated and closed in the past, and underlined the necessity of discovering other parts of the world:

> I want to live in Europe or the United States because it is there that things take place, that everything is decided (Irina, Korean-Tatar, 32 years old, student).
>
> Studying in Germany, for me, it is the opportunity to have really interesting lessons, to learn a new way of thinking (Anna, Russian, 21 years old, student).

Those who had already worked in international firms or institutions in Tashkent adapted themselves to new working methods and discovered professional opportunities outside their country. To rid themselves of their "local staff" status and increase their chances of being employed in more professional capacities abroad, they found it necessary to develop more technical competences beyond simply translation or administration. The validation of foreign degrees allowed them to "open doors" that were hitherto closed. Eight of the women returned to higher education where, at the time of the study, they had either finished or were in the process of earning master's degrees in business, economy, law, or development, and were envisaging a change in professional occupation. In their view, these types of degrees, combined with mastery of Russian, were good assets on the international labor market.

Use of Migratory Opportunities

However, in spite of their skills, these women cannot rely on a short trip abroad to find a job and gain the same level of social acceptance as, for instance, European citizens with similar qualifications. The possession of an Uzbekistani passport and their relatively low financial resources complicate their mobility. It is therefore necessary for them to exploit opportunities which guarantee the legitimacy of their departure and provide them with acceptable living conditions in their new country.

Some foreign embassies in Tashkent offer opportunities to study in their respective countries; in general, they help students register at universities. Certain countries also organize large-scale outreach programs in Tashkent to promote their higher education systems to Uzbekistani students, as is the case for South Korea and Malaysia. Every year, hundreds of grants are offered for study abroad, in most cases by the U.S., German, French, and Swiss governments. Foundations like George Soros' Open Society Institute and the Aga Khan Foundation also fulfill such a role. These programs are intended to reinforce bilateral cooperation or to support development by trying to push a "democratization" agenda on the country through the training of intellectual elites abroad. While these students are supposed to return to Uzbekistan at the end of their studies, according to the representatives of these programs the majority remain abroad. Selection takes place on the basis of an exam or written application. Those who are not selected choose sometimes to finance their studies abroad, in general through the support of their families. For Schengen destinations, they must prove that they have a minimum of 8,000 dollars in their bank account, as well as a level of language proficiency that grants them entry into university. These criteria automatically disqualify many candidates. Moreover, as I have observed, this type of family financial investment in regard to studies is more likely to be made in the case of sons than daughters.

An alternative solution lies in registering on the websites of au pair agencies. Although in principle not exclusively reserved for women, it appears in practice to be a female migratory strategy. By becoming an au pair, young women commit to living with a family and taking care of their children for an academic year. At the same time, they can register at a university because their schedules are especially tailored for study. As the au pair stay does not cost money, it helps some young ethnic Central Asian women to acquire the parental consent they need to leave on their own. The fact that they are under the supervision of a family reassures some parents, traditionally reluctant to let their daughters out of their social control. Moreover, au pairing is a rather efficient strategy to migrate to Europe or the United States, where immigration is strictly controlled. Once the foreign family is found and the process of hiring has been started, the consulate of the country in question can hardly refuse a visa to the young woman. When the au pair stay ends, it is possible to extend the residence permit by registering as a student; but one must first solve the problem of financial resources to afford housing, for which it is often necessary to find a part-time job (typically as a waitress, saleswoman, or babysitter). In spite of these difficulties, the European consulates in Tashkent interviewed confirmed that about 80 percent of au pairs do not come back to Uzbekistan, or at least extend their stay abroad. This strategy of departure can constitute a first step for young women in their migratory plans.

Some women can also choose to work abroad by going through the services of international recruitment agencies, which are flourishing in Tashkent. These agencies offer fixed-term employment contracts. Here one can speak of temporary migrations, in which workers alternate between working abroad and in Uzbekistan. Uzbek legislation, however, forbids any private agency from sending a labor force abroad; only the Ministry of Employment is authorized to exercise this authority. In this regard, the Uzbek government has signed a few bilateral labor agreements, notably with South Korea and Russia. Therefore, these agencies identify themselves instead as "advice offices" and offer "consultation" for those intending to work abroad. During the field survey, I attempted to interview the representatives of agencies found in local newspapers or on the Internet. But of eight agencies found, three had disappeared by changing their address and telephone number and only one agency granted an interview. Their activities are regularly monitored by the Ministry of Interior, which mainly checks that the women do not leave for prostitution. The only agency that would talk opened in 2003.[11] It sends Uzbekistani men and women under contract to Gulf countries, which, faced with significant waves of rich former Soviet tourists, are searching for Russian-speaking staff to work in the reception, service, and salon sections of hotels. The monthly wage in these hotels is about 400 dollars per month, with accommodation and food included in the contract. The team managers, also recruited in Uzbekistan, are paid around 900 dollars per month. About 250 people leave every year through this agency, of which 40 percent are women and 60 percent men. These proportions vary according to destination. Few women go to Saudi Arabia because it is necessary to wear the *hijab*, while in Dubai they are more numerous in light of the laxer application of *sharia* law. The agency mainly attracts potential recruits by word of

[11] See www.sobsmv-brain.com.

mouth.[12] The future employees leave in groups and must give up their first month's wage to the agency. One of the companies that has contacted this agency is Emirates Airlines, which was seeking to recruit flight attendants. Nine women and four men were subsequently recruited by the company, for a wage of 1,000 dollars per month. Unlike the other contracts offered by the agency, the employees signed a long-term agreement.

Recruitment is based on fulfilling definite criteria. The candidates must be unmarried with no children. Work experience in the hotel industry is not obligatory but desirable. The employers in the Emirates also attach particular importance to good physical appearance, and also to Russian and English language skills. The agency therefore searches for candidates that belong to the urban and skilled strata of the population:

> As these are jobs in contact with customers, they do not tolerate acne, gold teeth ... Today, the problem is that at least half of the persons who come to see us to find a job are not from Tashkent—they come from Kashkadarya or Surkhandarya. They have never worked in hotels or luxurious restaurants because their regions do not have a lot of tourist appeal. People are poor; there are no jobs, and therefore no money. They have no means to dress well. Few of them really know English. And with their accent and grammatical mistakes in Russian, it is even worse. Thus, of course, we have people who remain registered here for more than two years and still have found nothing. They systematically fail ... Three or four years ago, it was simpler for us to offer good candidates to the recruiters. We had mostly people from Tashkent and Russians who have a pleasing appearance, with a good level of English. Today we receive less and less of them. They all left for overseas (Interview with the representative of Sobmsv-Brain agency in Tashkent).

Getting married to a foreigner can also be a migratory strategy. Agencies exploiting international marriages have been recently created in Tashkent. Only one of the surveyed women met her husband through a matrimonial agency. A so-called mail-order bride,[13] she explained her situation as follows:

> He is a divorced man. Like me, his children are grown up. We corresponded for six months before meeting. We spoke about this and that, about our lives. The week before his arrival, I was really stressed, I wondered if [what I had done] was very serious, if I had not made a big mistake. And then he came to Tashkent. I showed him the city. I thought he was a real gentleman,

[12] One of the surveyed women left for Dubai in August 2008, through a friend who had been previously recruited by this agency.

[13] R. Vartti, "Equal Partners Online? German Matchmaking Web Sites and Trafficking in Women," in M. Morokvasic, U. Erel, and K. Shinozaki, eds., *Crossing Borders and Shifting Boundaries, vol. 1: Gender on the Move* (Opladen: Leske and Budrich, 2003), 177–206.

> and then I trusted [him] (Ekaterina, Tatar, 56 years old, project manager for an NGO).

According to consular representatives, every year there are numerous marriages through matrimonial agencies:

> It is a very significant phenomenon here. I spend my time regulating this type of request. People meet on the Internet, through agencies. Everything takes place very fast. I pointed out that all the women who get married to Belgian citizens are more qualified than their husbands, who are in general men who earn low wages in Belgium (Extract of a dialogue with the Consul of Belgium).

I was able to meet with three agencies in Tashkent. All were "tourism" agencies that simultaneously managed a small matrimonial agency. During interviews, however, I noted that numerous phone calls concerned assistance in acquiring multi-month visas to the European Union or Israel. It would seem that the boundary between marriage, tourism, and migration is rather blurred in the case of these agencies. The information I obtained showed that about 70 percent of customers were trying to marry a foreigner. For 15 euros a year, the women publish a photo and their personal information (age, occupation, and the profile of the type of man they are seeking) in a catalogue. According to the agencies, the number of registered women varies between 300 and 400. Fifty-two to 65 percent of the women were divorced. About 70 percent of the women belonged to Central Asian ethnic groups, ranging in age from 18 to 60.

These Tashkent agencies are linked with a network of foreign agencies in Italy, Greece, Germany, Belgium, Spain, France, Israel, Australia, South Korea, Canada, the United States, India, the United Arab Emirates, Egypt, and Turkey. None of the representatives agreed to disclose the names of their partner agencies. Foreign men pay a fee in their country to browse the Tashkent catalogues. They then communicate by mail with the women of their choice and, if desired, come to Uzbekistan on a tourist visa to meet them in person. The Tashkent agencies organize the trips of these foreign men, furnishing the necessary invitation letters for visa support, accommodation, translation of documents, and administrative support to get married in Uzbekistan. The selection criteria change according to the nationality of the customers:

> The men of the Arab countries and the Koreans do not want divorced women because of tradition. Also, they do not accept women that already have children. With the Europeans, on the contrary, it is not a problem (Extract of an interview with a representative of a matrimonial agency in Tashkent).

The Korean men come to search exclusively for ethnic Koreans from Uzbekistan or other Central Asian women. They do not want to meet Russians or Tatars due to a so-called unsuitability between the mentality of these women and the traditions of Korean society. According to the matrimonial agents, the Central Asian women seem to adapt to Korean society without any problem. The question of religion is also important:

> The women who get married to men from the Emirates agree to wear the *hijab* because they already read the Koran and preferred getting married to a Muslim rather than to a European. Some Arab men choose Russians, but then they [the women] have to convert.
>
> The men come to search for spouses here because they have heard that Uzbekistani women are very nice, have a pretty face. They are not depraved, they take care of the house very well, they are obedient.
>
> I have already been several times to Russia to find a woman, but I am now disappointed. It is not the same there anymore; the women are overdemanding and want money first of all. While in Uzbekistan, women are also beautiful, there is a nice mixity. And they are pure, less corrupted, the Muslim religion helps (Extract of a dialogue with a European "tourist" in Tashkent).

Use of an International Social Network

In parallel to the migratory devices listed above, women make use of their own networks outside of Uzbekistan. These social networks consist of Uzbekistani migrants or foreigners met in Tashkent or through the Internet. Thirteen of the women interviewed had family members or friends abroad, who were able to give them advice or some material assistance. Zamira, a young student who was just about to get married to a European, had an aunt in England and a grandmother in the United States:

> When she was young, my aunt smoked in front of all the mahalla neighbors, she liked to provoke them, just for fun. She always refused to get married to somebody she didn't love, and remained single until she was more than 30 years old! And then she met her boss, an English man with whom she worked in Uzbekistan for several years. They got married, she left more than 15 years ago and there she went back to university. She is divorced now, but earns good wages and brings up her son alone … I have already visited her there [in England] (Zamira, Uzbek, 20 years old, student).

These trips to England allowed her to discover Europe at a rather young age. Thus, deliberately or not, this aunt enabled her to become more "internationally aware." Zamira also explained how her grandmother sent her remittances:

> It is my grandmother who paid for my air ticket in order so I could see my boyfriend in Europe again, and now she has just sent me from the United States different presents for our wedding.

Friends from Uzbekistan can also turn out to be "key persons" in encouraging migration. Observing a group of classmates, one can notice a dual phenomenon of emulation and mutual aid. In 2006, when Anna was still living in Tashkent and was cohabitating with a European man, she encouraged her friends Vika and Aliona to migrate. She introduced them to expatriate friends, sometimes trying to play matchmaker. She recommended that they chat on Internet forums. Anna was partly at the helm of her friends' migratory projects: "I did not want them to stay in Tashkent, they deserved better than this." One year later, Vika left to work in India, thanks to an agent recruiting musicians for a hotel, and Aliona followed her after a few months.

For these women, the fall of the Iron Curtain and the arrival of foreigners in Tashkent constitute a real opportunity:

> If the Soviet Union still existed, I would have never been able to meet my husband in Tashkent, seeing that foreigners were not allowed to come! (Zamira, Uzbek, 20 years old, student)

Indeed, the professional and academic environment in Tashkent that the women of this study move in is conducive to contact with expatriates and thus the forging of international networks. Many of them worked with foreign colleagues or, in the case of students, benefited from lessons given by foreign professors. Some were invited to embassy cocktail parties or to participate in international seminars. As the expatriate sphere is very small, in a country where English is not widely spoken, these women enjoy special privilege in being able to establish contacts with foreigners, especially those that do not speak Russian. In associating with expatriates, these women burnish their "Western" credentials and aspirations. In my interviews with them, there was frequently a form of identification to what represents the West and Russia in terms of values and references, in opposition to the Eastern character of independent Uzbekistan:

> You see, I am like you, I am European. I feel closer to French than Uzbek people (Vera, Armenian, 29 years old, teacher).
>
> I have never felt Uzbek. To be Uzbek, it means knowing how to cook and get dressed in a way other than my own. My friends at the university, they are all Russian, I get on better with them (Zamira, Uzbek, 20 years old, student).

Some expatriates also share the feeling that these women are not representative of the country; that they are very "Westernized":

> I don't have the impression that these girls were born and lived in Uzbekistan. There is a gap between the modernity that they have in their mind and the fact that they come from the back of beyond (Julien, 24 years old, French expatriate).

They consequently frequent the same places in Tashkent: trendy bars and clubs, Italian restaurants, Irish pubs, and sushi bars. These places and this "Western microcosm" are also the instruments of a new modernity in Tashkent and contrast sharply with the *chaikhana*, the traditional Uzbek teahouse. The "trendification" of the city has recently developed, partly thanks to investment from Gulnara Karimova, the daughter of the president, herself representative of a certain post-independence modernity.

Some of the young women who go frequently to these "expatriate places" in Tashkent are also searching for a foreign husband. A lot of these women know one another, talk, and compare themselves:

> I do not understand why Nastia succeeded in getting married with X while Y [names substituted] did not want to marry me. I did everything as was needed. Perhaps it's me who did not understand anything about the way European men think... I am sure that one day I will do as the others, I shall succeed in leaving. Everybody should achieve this aim. At the moment I do not see my life in another way (Marianna, Tatar, 29 years old, secretary).

These women are not always perceived positively by those who mix with them:

> Those who leave by getting married, they are all prostitutes! You should see them hanging around in cocktail parties, conferences... My daughter could go and do the same thing but she does not dare to go out with us anymore on these evenings for fear of being associated with these unrespectable girls (Natalia, 40 years old, Korean married to a German living in Tashkent).
>
> The women that I met here were very interested, I do not feel that they are sincere (Henrich, German expatriate, 25 years old).

The Internet is also an established and efficient means of creating an international network. Twelve of the women interviewed had turned to using online meeting forums. For those Central Asian women reluctant or unable to go to cafés or nightclubs, this serves as an alternative way to get to know men:

> Here it is not common to go out with boys. If you do this once, just for talking, the following day everybody thinks that you are going to get married. That's why in this country, men and women do not know each other.

> At least with the Internet, I have time to get to know them, without anyone watching what I do behind my back (Shakhzoda, 30 years old, Tajik, professor).

The women I questioned never formed serious relationships with the men they met on online forums, but some of these foreigners came to Uzbekistan to meet the women in person. One of the women also received presents; but she already had several expatriate boyfriends in Tashkent and, according to her, these virtual contacts were more of a game:

> This allowed me to receive a DVD reader, some clothes ... they all wanted to come to see me but I refused (Anna, Russian, 21 years old, student).

Moreover, "social networks" on the Internet allow Uzbekistani women to not only keep in touch with their acquaintances abroad, but also to establish new links with unknown persons on a worldwide scale. Eleven of the women use the social networking site Facebook, its motto being to "give people the power to share and make the world more open and connected." Others use *Moï mir* on Mail.ru, a Russian-speaking equivalent. As part of a migratory plan, these sites constitute a useful and free tool to maintain a social network abroad.

The end of Soviet rule has allowed women to successfully organize their migrations abroad through utilizing migratory devices on a local level (international recruitment agencies, matrimonial agencies, and academic exchange programs) and also by establishing international networks prior to migration (Internet and expatriate friends). The borders of Uzbekistan are now "half-open" with flows of people and information; however, government-led protectionnist policies have slowed down the freedom of movement. These two opposing logics of opening and closing are emblematic of the period of transition that the country has experienced. The aspirations of educated women to make a career abroad as well as to get married with a foreigner must be questioned and placed in the greater context of the Uzbek society. Migration constitutes a personal response to the end of the Soviet Union and the Uzbek government's isolationist stance. On the one hand, these skilled migrants find themselves amidst social transformations that are rather disadvantageous for women, and on the other, they are able to exploit new opportunities for departure. Indeed, the political orchestration of a return to a traditional society aims at deeply transforming gender relations and the place of women in Uzbekistani society. Some of these women are finding it difficult to locate their place in the new society. On the labor market, they are more affected by unemployment than men[14] and do not often get jobs with responsibilities:

> I graduated from the University of Diplomacy, but as a woman, it is impossible to make a career in the ministries. I shall always remain a secretary, in spite of my degree (Feruza, Tajik, 25 years old, student).

Finding a husband in Uzbekistan has also become a recurrent problem for this category of women. Some of them see marriage to a foreigner as the only way to find a husband who can meet with their expectations. The scarcity of husbands, real or fantasized, came up frequently in the discourses of the women, as well as the unsuitability of men in their close circles, due to the mass exodus of Russian-speaking minorities, or the retraditionalizing of relations between men and women:

> During my last trip to Moscow, the city was full of young and really nice people, with whom I talked. It was great, I felt very good there. But here, where are the Russians? I do not see them, I do not know any of them. All young Russians, Tatars, they left to work abroad (Marianna, Tatar, 29 years old, secretary).
>
> Before I thought, I shall find a husband among those who had left to study abroad. I thought that their mentalities would differ. But not at all, as soon as they come back, it is even worse. They follow even more traditions than the others! They get married very quickly to 18-year-old girls who have seen nothing yet… Nobody wants me as an official spouse, they just offer me to be the second wife, to pay a flat and to keep me (Shakhzoda, Tajik, 30 years old, professor).

* * * * *

The migratory plans and strategies of these women are therefore based on social, professional, and matrimonial stakes. They will search elsewhere for that which they do not or cannot find in Uzbekistan. These migratory movements constitute, thus, an alternative, or even a rejection, of the current societal model, which fails to satisfy these women. In reference to Arjun Appaduraï's theory,[15] through migratory practices these women reveal a progressive substitution of national references, linked to territory, to the advantage of the appropriation of a "transnational" space. Theoretically, at least, this would place them at the forefront of the globalization of

[14] "Women in Uzbekistan," *ADB Briefing Paper* (Tashkent: Asian Development Bank, 2005).

[15] A. Appadurai, *Après le colonialisme. Les conséquences culturelles de la globalization* (Paris: Payot, 2005).

the Uzbekistani society. At present, these skilled women may try to transcend borders, but it remains uncertain if the phenomenon will persist in the coming decades. New generations of Uzbekistani women are growing up in a country that is undergoing profound changes. It is thus difficult to forecast whether they will have the same access to higher education and qualified jobs. In short, the question is whether these migrations should be interpreted as traces of the communist past, destined to disappear, or as a deeper process of social transformation, destined to continue.

BIBLIOGRAPHY

2003 UNHCR Statistical Yearbok: Tajikistan Fact Sheet; 2004 Statistical Yearbook; 2005 UNHCR provisional data.

Abazov R., "Economic Migration in Post-Soviet Central Asia: The Case of Kyrgyzstan," *Post-Communist Economies* 11, no. 2 (1999): 237–252.

Ablezova M., Botoeva G., et al., *Pokolenie v opasnosti?! Detskaia bednost' v Kyrgyzstane, CHIP Report no. 15* (Bishkek: Research Center of Childhood Poverty and Policy Development, 2004).

Abramzon S., *Kirgizy i ikh etnogeneticheskie i istoriko-kul'turnye sviazi* (Frunze: Kyrgyzstan, 1990).

Adelkhah F., and Olszewska Z., "Les Afghans iraniens," *Les études du CERI*, no. 125, April 2006.

Afanasyan S., *L'Arménie, l'Azerbaïdjan et la Géorgie de l'indépendance à l'instauration du pouvoir soviétique, 1918–1921* (Paris: L'Harmattan, 1981).

Aktar C., and Ögelman N., "Recent Developments in East-West Migration: Turkey and the Petty Traders," *International Migration* 32, no. 4 (1994): 343–354.

Alekseenko N.B., and Alekseenko A.N., *Naselenie Kazakhstana za 100 let (1897–1997 gg)* (Ust'-Kamenogorsk: Vostochno-Kazakhstanskii tekhnicheskii universitet, 2000).

Alymbaeva A., "K voprosu of urbanizatsii Kyrgyzstana," *Voprosy istorii Kyrgyzstana*, no. 1 (2008): 65–77.

Amonova D.C., *Problemy trudovoy migratsii i puti ikh resheniia* (Dushanbe: Irfon, 2007).

Analiticheskii otchet o sotsiologicheskom issledovanii "Politicheskie vzgliady naseleniia Kazakhstana" (Almaty, Moscow: Institut Giller, 1998).

Anderson B., *Imagined Communities: Reflections on the Origin and Spread of Nationalism* (London, New York: Verso, 2006).

Anderson B., and Hancilová B., "Migrant Labour in Kazakhstan: A Cause for Concern?" *Journal of Ethnic and Migration Studies* 37, no. 3 (2011): 467–483.

Anderson M., *Frontiers: Territory and State Formation in the Modern World* (Cambridge: Polity Press, 1996).

Antebi-Yemini L., Berthomière W., and Sheffer G., eds., *Les diasporas: 2000 ans d'histoire* (Rennes: Presses universitaires de Rennes, 2005).

Appadurai A., *Après le colonialisme. Les conséquences culturelles de la globalization* (Paris: Payot, 2005).

——, *Modernity at Large. Cultural Dimensions of Globalization* (Minneapolis: University of Minnesota Press, 1996).

Arel D., "Démographie et politique dans les premiers recensements post-soviétiques: méfiance envers l'Etat, identités en question," *Population-F* 57, no. 6 (2002): 791–820.

Asanov U., and Asankanov A., eds., *Kyrgyz Taryhy: Entsiklopediia* (Bishkek: 2003).

Aslan M., and Pérouse J.-F., "Istanbul: le comptoir, le hub, le sas et l'impasse. Fonctions dans le système migratoire international," *Revue Européenne des Migrations Internationales* 19, no. 3 (2003): 173–204.

Babetskii I., Kolev A., and Maurel M., "Kyrgyz Labor Market in the late 1990s: The Challenge of Formal Job Creation," *Comparative Economic Studies*, no. 45 (2003): 493–519.

Badie B., Brauman R., and Decaux E., *Pour un autre regard sur les migrations. Construire une gouvernance mondiale* (Paris: La découverte, 2008).

Basch L.G., Schiller N.G., and Blanc C.S., *Nations Unbound: Transnational Projects, Post-Colonial Predicaments, and Deterritorialized Nation-States* (Amsterdam: Gordon and Breach Publ., 1994).

Becker C.M., Musabek E.N., Seitenova S. Ai-Gul, and Urzhumova D.S., "Short-Term Migration Responses of Women and Men during Economic Turmoil: Lessons from Kazakhstan," *Eurasian Geography and Economics* 44, no. 3 (2003): 228–243.

Becker H., *Tricks of the Trade: How to Think About Your Research While You're Doing It* (Chicago: The University of Chicago Press, 1998).

Bekturganova B., *Vnutrenniaia migratsionnaia orientatsiia sel'skikh kyrgyzov vo vtoroi polovine 90kh godov XX veka (Po materialam etnosotsiologicheskogo issledovania)* (Ph.D., Bishkek: Kyrgyz State University, 2002).

Bichsel C., Hostettler S., and Balzer S., *"Should I Buy a Cow or a TV?* Reflections on the conceptual framework of the NCCR North-South Based on a comparative study of international labour migration in Mexico, India and Kyrgyzstan," *NCCR North-South Dialogue Working Paper* (Berne: NCCR North-South, 2005).

Bilici F., "Une réalisation concrète avant la lettre: la coopération en mer Noire orientale," *Cahiers d'Études de la Méditerranée Orientale et du Monde Turco-Iranien (CEMOTI)*, no. 15 (1993): 168–183.

Blacher P.S., "Les shop-turisty à Tsargrad ou les nouveaux russophones d'Istanbul," *Turcica*, no. 28, (1996): 11–50.

Bloch A., "Victims of Trafficking or Entrepreneurial Women? Narratives of Post-Soviet Entertainers in Turkey," *Canadian Women Studies/Les Cahiers de la Femmes* 22, no. 3–4 (2003): 152–158.

Blum A., *Naître, vivre et mourir en URSS (1917–1991)* (Paris: Plon, 1994).

Borbieva N., *Development in the Kyrgyz Republic: Exchange, Communal Networks, and the Foreign Presence* (PhD Dissertation, Harvard University, 2007).

Bordes-Benayoun C., and Schnapper D., *Diasporas et nations* (Paris: Odile Jacob, 2006).

Borob'eva O.D., *Migratsiia naseleniia*, vyp. 6 (Moscow: Migratsiia v Rossii, 2001).

Bosc I., *Trafficking in Persons: A Form of Social Exclusion* (Washington, D.C.: The World Bank, 2002).

Bourdieu P., "Les trois états du capital culturel," *Actes de la Recherche en Sciences Sociales* 30, no. 1 (1979): 3–6.

Boyd M., "Family and Personal Networks in International Migration: Recent Developments and New Agendas," *International Migration Review* 23, no. 3 (1989): 638–670.

Brettell C.B., and Hollifield J.F., eds., *Migration Theory: Talking across Disciplines* (New York and London: Routledge, 2000).

Brown R., Olimova S., and Boboev M., *A Study on International Migrant Remittances in Central Asia and South Caucasus: Country Report on Remittances of International Migrants in Tajikistan* (Manilla: Asian Development Bank, 2008).

Brubaker R., "The 'Diaspora' Diaspora," *Ethnic and Racial Studies* 28, no. 1 (2005): 1–19.

——, *Nationalism Reframed: Nationhood and the National Question in the New Europe* (Cambridge: Cambridge University Press, 1996).

——, "Nationhood and the National Question in the Soviet Union and Post-Soviet Eurasia: An Institutionalist Account," *Theory and Society* 23, no. 1 (1994): 47–78.

Bruneau M., *Diasporas et espaces transnationaux* (Paris: Anthropos, 2004).

Bruno A.-S., and Zalc C., eds., *Petites entreprises et petits entrepreneurs étrangers en France (XIXe–XXe siècles)* (Paris: Publibook Université Editions, 2003).

Brusina O., "Migranty iz Srednei Azii v Rossii: etapy i prichiny priezda, sotsial'nye tipy, organizatsii diaspor," *Vestnik Evrazii* 40, no. 2 (2008): 66–95.

Buckley C., "Rural/urban differentials in demographic processes: The Central Asian States," *Population Research and Policy Review*, no. 17 (1998): 71–89.

Buckley M., ed., *Post-Soviet Women: from the Baltic to Central Asia* (Cambridge: Cambridge University Press, 1997).

Çağla C., "Les fondements historiques de l'Etat-nation en Azerbaïdjan," *Cahiers d'études de la Méditerranée turque et orientale (CEMOTI)*, no. 31 (2001): 89–109.

Carrère d'Encausse H., *Decline of An Empire (The Soviet Socialist Republics in Revolt)* (New York: HarperCollins, 1981).

——, *L'Empire éclaté: la révolte des nations en URSS* (Paris: Flammarion, 1978).

Cassarino J.-P., "Theorising Return Migration: The Conceptual Approach to Return Migrants Revisited," *International Journal on Multicultural Societies* 6, no. 2 (2004): 253–279.

Castles S., "Guestworkers in Europe: A Resurrection?" *International Migration Review* 40, no. 4 (2006): 741–766.

Castles S., and Miller J.M., *The Age of Migration: International Population Movements in the Modern World* (London: Macmillan, 1993).

Central Asia Human Development (Washington, D.C.: UNDP, 2005).

Cerny A., "Going where the Grass is Greener: China Kazaks and the *Oralman* Immigration Policy in Kazakhstan," *Pastoralism* 1, no. 2 (2010): 218–247.

Chaliand G., and Rageau J.-P., *Atlas des diasporas* (Paris: Odile Jacob, 1991).

Chanudet-Lentz E., *Du plov et des blinis. Les Slaves d'Ouzbékistan: de minorité dominante à minorité dominée* (Paris: Institute of Political Studies, Master Thesis, 1998).

Charpentier C.-J., "Three commercial sectors: Some structural observations in the bazaar of Istanbul," *Zeitschrift für Ethnologie* 99, no. 1 (1974): 224–253.

Chartier R., *Au bord de la falaise. L'histoire entre certitudes et inquiétude* (Paris: Albin Michel, 1998).

Chislennost' Naseleniia Respubliki Uzbekistan na 1.1.2005 (Tashkent: Goskomstat, 2005).

Choate M.I., "Sending States' Transnational Interventions in Politics, Culture, and Economics: The Historical Example of Italy," *International Migration Review* 41, no. 3 (2007): 728–767.

Chopra R., Osella C., and Osella F., eds., *South Asian Masculinities: Context of Change, Sites of Continuity* (New Delhi: Women Unlimited, 2004).

Chupik V.V., and Alimov K.Z., *Trudovye migranty iz Uzbekistana v iuzhnykh regionakh respubliki Kazakhstana* (Almaty: International Organization for Migration, 2005).

Chuvin P., Létolle R., and Peyrouse S., *Histoire de l'Asie centrale contemporaine* (Paris: Fayard, 2008).

Cohen R., *Global Diasporas. An Introduction* (Seattle: University of Washington Press, 1997).

Connell R.W., *Masculinities* (Cambridge: Polity Press, 1995).

Cornelius W., and Tsuda T., eds., *Controlling Immigration. A Global Perspective* (Stanford: Stanford University Press, 2004).

Cornwall A., and Lindisfarne N., eds., *Dislocating Masculinities: Comparative Ethnographies* (London: Routledge, 1994).

Country Economic Review. Tajikistan (Manilla: Asian Development Bank, 2000).

Danenova A., and Formanek A., *Sravnitel'nyi opyt integratsii immigrantov v zarubezhnykh stranakh i Kazakhstane* (Almaty: International Organization for Migration, 2004).

De Rudder V., Taboada-Leonetti I., and Vourch F., *Stratégies d'insertion et migration* (Paris: CNRS-IRESCO, 1989).

De Tinguy A., *La Grande Migration. La Russie et les Russes depuis l'ouverture du rideau de fer* (Paris: Plon, 2004).

Dedeoglu S., *Women Workers in Turkey. Global Industrial Production in Istanbul* (London, New York: Tauris Academic Studies, 2008).

Degtiar M., "The Jews of Uzbekistan—The end of the epoch," *Central Asia and the Caucasus*, no. 4 (2001): 176–181.

Demograficheskii ezhegodnik Kyrgyzskoi Respubliki 2001–2005 gg. (Bishkek: National Committee of Statistics, 2006).

Deniel R., *De la savane à la ville* (Paris: Aubier-Montaigne, 1968).

Diatlov V., *Sovremennye torgovye men'shinstva: faktor stabil'nosti ili konflikta? (Kitaitsy i kavkaztsy v Irkutske)* (Moscow: Natalis, 2000).

Dicken P., *Global Shift. Mapping the Changing Contours of the World Economy* (New York, London: The Guilford Press, 2011, 6th edition).

Diener A.C., "Homeland as Social Construct: Territorialization among Kazakhstan's Germans and Koreans," *Nationalities Papers* 34, no. 2 (2006): 201–235.

——, "Kazakhstan's Kin-State Diaspora: Settlement Planning and the *Oralman* Dilemma," *Europe Asia Studies* 57, no. 2 (2005): 327–348.

Donnan H., and Wilson T.M., *Borders: Frontiers of Identity, Nation and State* (Oxford: Berg, 1999).
Dorigo G., and Tobler W., "Push-Pull Migration Laws," *Annals of the Association of American Geographers* 73, no. 1 (1983): 1–17.
Dudoignon S., and Jahangiri G., eds., *Le Tadjikistan existe-t-il? Destins politiques d'une nation imparfaite, Cahiers d'études de la Méditerranée turque et orientale (CEMOTI)*, no. 18 (1994).
Dufoix S., *Diasporas* (Berkeley: University of California Press, 2008).
——, *Les Diasporas* (Paris: PUF, 2003).
Durand J., Parrado E.E., and Massey D.S., "Migradollars and Development: A Reconsideration of the Mexican Case," *International Migration Review* 30, no. 2 (1996): 423–444.
Duvell F., "Crossing the Fringes of Europe: Transit Migration in the EU Neighbourhood," COMPAS Working Paper 06–33, 2006.
Eberstadt N., "Russia's Peacetime Demographic Crisis: Dimensions, Causes, Implications," *NBR Report*, May 2010.
Ekonomicheskie i pravovye problemy garmonizatsii zakonodatel'stva v oblasti zashchity prav i obespecheniia interesov lichnosti v usloviakh globalizatsii: teoriia i praktika stran SNG (Almaty: Kazakh State University, 2005).
Erofeeva I.V., Masanov N.E., Abylkhozhin Z.B., et al., *Istoriia Kazakhstana: narody i kul'tury* (Almaty: Daik-Press, 2001).
Eshamanova E., "Tendentsii i puti sotrudnichestva Kazakhstana i Rossii v reshenii problem trudovoi migratsii iz stran Tsentral'noi Azii," *Informatsionno-analiticheskii tsentr izucheniia obshchestvennykh politicheskikh protsessov na postsovetskom prostranstve*, March 5, 2008.
Fassin D., "Une double peine—La condition sociale des immigrés malades du sida," *L'Homme*, no. 160 (2001): 137–162.
Fathi H., *Femmes d'autorité dans l'Asie centrale contemporaine. Quête des ancêtres et recompositions identitaires dans l'islam postsoviétique* (Paris: Maisonneuve & Larose—IFEAC, 2004).
Fawzi El-Solh C., and Mabro J., eds., *Muslim Women's Choices: Religious Belief and Social Reality* (Oxford: Berg, 1995).
Ferrando O., "Déplacements de populations et identités dans la vallée du Ferghana: les limites du paradigme ethnique," *Cahiers d'Asie Centrale*, no. 19–20 (2011): 177–212.
——, "Manipulating the Census: Ethnic Minorities in the Nationalizing States of Central Asia," *Nationalities Papers* 36, no. 3 (2008): 489–520.
Finko A., "Ukraine, the Turkic World, and Central Asia," *Central Asia and the Caucasus* 56, no. 2 (2009): 102–112.
Flanagan W.G., *Urban Sociology: Images and Structure* (Needham Heights: Allyn & Bacon, 1999, 3rd edition).
Flynn M., *Migrant Resettlement in the Russian Federation: Reconstructing "Homes" and "Homelands"* (London: Anthem, 2004).
Fog Olwig K., and Hastrup K., *Siting Culture: The Shifting Anthropological Object* (London: Routledge, 1997).
Fumagalli M., "Ethnicity, State Formation and Foreign Policy: Uzbekistan and 'Uzbeks abroad,'" *Central Asian Survey* 26, no. 1 (2007): 105–122.
——, "Framing Ethnic Minority Mobilization in Central Asia: The Cases of Uzbeks in Kyrgyzstan and Tajikistan," *Europe-Asia Studies* 59, no. 4 (2007): 565–588.
Gadwani V., and Sivaramakrishnan K., "Circular Migration and Rural Cosmopolitanism in India," *Contributions to Indian Sociology* 37, no. 1–2 (2003): 339–367.
Ganiev S., Ismoilov S., and Ergashev A., *Rapid Response Group (RRG) For Prevention Of Torture In Uzbekistan. The Government Of Uzbekistan Should Change Its Policy On The Uzbek Labor Migrants Abroad*, December 2007.
Gertel J., and Breuer I., eds., *Pastoral Morocco. Globalizing Scapes of Mobility and Insecurity* (Reichert Verlag, 2007).

Ghoussoub M., and Sinclair-Webb E., eds., *Imagined Masculinities: Male Identity and Culture in the Modern Middle East* (London: Saqi Books, 2006).
Globalization and socio-cultural adaptation. Proceedings of the II Congress of Kazakhstan Sociologists (Astana: Kazakhstan Sociologists' Association, 2006).
Gonon E., and Lasserre F., "Une critique de la notion de frontières artificielles à travers le cas de l'Asie centrale," *Cahiers de Géographie du Québec* 47, no. 132 (2003): 433–461.
Gossiaux J.F., *Pouvoirs ethniques dans les Balkans* (Paris: PUF, 2002).
Granovetter M., "The Strength of Weak Ties," *American Journal of Sociology* 78, no. 6 (1973): 1360–1380.
Guild E., and Mantu S., eds., *Constructing and Imagining Labour Migration. Perspectives of Control from Five Continents* (Farhnam: Asghate, 2011).
Gülcür L., and Ilkkaracan P., "The 'Natasha' experience: Migrant sex workers from the former Soviet Union and Eastern Europe in Turkey," *Women's Studies International Forum* 25, no. 4 (2002): 411–421.
Hammar T., eds., *International Migration, Immobility and Development: Multidisciplinary Perspectives* (Berg, 1997).
Handrahan L., "Hunting for Women: Bride-Kidnapping in Kyrgyzstan," *International Feminist Journal of Politics* 6, no. 2 (2004): 207–233.
Hann C., and Hann I., "Samovars and Sex on Turkey's Russian Markets," *Anthropology Today* 8, no. 4 (1992): 3–6.
Hann C.M., ed., *Postsocialism. Ideals, ideologies and practices in Eurasia* (London: Routledge, 2002).
Harris C., *Control and Subversion: Gender Relations in Tajikistan* (London: Pluto Press, 2004).
Haugen A., *The Establishment of National Republics in Soviet Central Asia* (New York: Palgrave MacMillan, 2003).
Hohmann S., "Le narcotrafic en Asie centrale: enjeux géopolitiques et répercussions sociales," *Revue internationale et stratégique*, no. 64 (2006): 110–119.
Humphrey C., and Mandel R., ed., *Markets and Moralities. Ethnographies of Postsocialism* (Oxford, New York: Berg, 2002).
İçduygu A., and Kirişci K., eds., *Land of Diverse Migrations. Challenges of Emigration and Immigration in Turkey* (Istanbul: MiReKoç-Bilgi University Press, 2009).
ICG, "Tajikistan: an Uncertain Peace," *International Crisis Group Asia Report*, no. 30, 2001.
Iglicka K., "The Migration of Ethnic Poles from Kazakhstan to Poland," *International Migration Review* 32, no. 4 (1998): 995–1015.
Ireland P., *Becoming Europe: Immigration, Integration and the Welfare State* (Pittsburgh, PA: University of Pittsburgh Press, 2004).
Istoriia Kirgizskoi SSR (Frunze: Izd. Akademii Nauk, 1986).
Itogi edinovremennogo obsledovaniia naseleniia v iule 2006 g. Zaniatost', bezrabotitsa, trudovaia migratsiia (Bishkek: National Committee of Statistics of the Kyrgyz Republic, Committee of Migration and Employment of the Kyrgyz Republic, 2007).
Jha R., and Dang T., "Vulnerability to Poverty in selected Central Asian Countries," *The Australian National University Working Paper*, no. 10, August 2008.
Jones L., Black R., and Skeldon R., "Migration and Poverty in Tajikistan," *Working Paper C11*, Development Research Centre on Migration, Globalisation & Poverty, 2007.
Kaiser M., "Informal Sector Trade in Uzbekistan," *Working Paper of the University of Bielefeld*, no. 218 (1997): 23–28.
Karmysheva B.Kh., *Ocherki etnicheskoi istorii iuzhnykh raionov Tadzhikistana i Uzbekistana* (Moscow: Nauka, 1976).
Kasten, E., ed., *Rebuilding Identities. Pathways to Reform in Post-Soviet Siberia* (Berlin: Dietrich Reimer Verlag, 2005).
Kasymova S., *Gendernaia sistema tadzhikskogo obshchestva: put' k modernizatsii (Sovetskii period)* (Dushanbe: Irfon, 2004), 132–159.
——, *Polozhenie zhenshchin na rynke truda i v sfere zaniatosti: puti sokrashcheniia bednosti v Tadzhikistane* (Dushanbe: Swiss Agency for Development Cooperation in Tajikistan, 2005).

Kay R., *Men in Contemporary Russia: The Fallen Heroes of Post-Soviet Change?* (Aldershot: Ashgate, 2006).

Kelly L., "Fertile Fields: Trafficking in Persons in Central Asia," Vienna: International Organization for Migration, 2005.

Keough L., "Globalizing postsocialism: Mobile mothers and Neoliberalism on the margins of Europe," *Anthropological Quarterly* 79, no. 3 (2006): 431–461.

Kertzer D.I., and Arel D., eds., *Census and Identity: The Politics of Race, Ethnicity, and Language in National Censuses* (Cambridge: Cambridge University Press, 2002).

Keyder Ç., ed., *Istanbul. Between the Global and the Local* (Lanham, Boulder, New York, Oxford: Rowman & Littlefield Publishers, 1999).

Khamraeva M.S., *Problemy trudovoi migratsii i puti ikh resheniia* (Dushanbe: Irfon, 2007).

King C., and Melvin N.J., eds., *Nations abroad. Diaspora Politics and International Relations in the Former Soviet Union* (Oxford: Westview Press, 1999).

Kireyev A., "The Macroeconomics of Remittances: The Case of Tajikistan," *International Monetary Fund Working Paper*, January 2006.

Klimova T., "Tendentsii migratsionnykh protsessov v respublike Kazakhstan," *Tsentral'naia Aziia i Kavkaz*, no. 3 (2001): 204–215.

Kolstoe P., *Russians in the Former Soviet Republics* (London: Hurst, 1995).

Komatsu H., Obiya C., and Schoeberlein J., eds., *Population in Central Asia: Its History and Current Problems: Population Movements in the modern world from the JCAS Symposium Series 9* (Osaka: The Japan Center for Area Studies, National Museum of Ethnology, 2000).

Koser K., and Salt J., "The Geography of Highly Skilled International Migration," *International Journal of Population Geography*, no. 3 (1997): 285–303.

Kosmarskaia N., *"Deti imperii" v postsovetskoi Tsentral'noi Azii: adaptivnye praktiki i mental'nye sdvigi (russkie v Kirgizii)* (Moscow: Natalis, 2006).

Kratkie itogi perepisi naseleniia 1999 goda v respublike Kazakhstan (Almaty: Agentstvo respubliki Kazakhstan po statistike, 1999).

Kudabaev Z.I., and Denisenko M.B., eds., *Naselenie Kyrgyzstana* (Bishkek: National Statistic Committee, 2004).

Kuenhast K., *Let the stone lie where it has fallen: Dilemmas of gender and generation in Post-Soviet Kyrgyzstan* (PhD dissertation, Department of Anthropology, University of Minnesota, 1997).

Kuznetsov I.M., and Mukomel' V.I., *Adaptatsionnye vozmozhnosti i setevye sviazi migrantskikh etnicheskikh men'shinstv* (Moscow: Institut sotsiologii RAN, 2005).

Kyrgyz Republic Poverty Assessment, volume II: Labor Market Dimensions of Poverty, Report No. 40864-KG (Washington, D.C.: The World Bank, 2007).

Landau J.M., and Kellner-Heinkele B., *Politics of Language in the ex-Soviet Muslim States* (London: Hurst, 2001).

Laruelle M., ed., "Les Russes de l'étranger proche et la question de la 'diaspora,'" *Revue d'Études Comparatives Est-Ouest* 39, no. 1 (2008).

——, "Central Asian Labor Migrants in Russia: The 'Diasporization' of the Central Asian States?" *The China and Eurasia Forum Quarterly* 5, no. 3 (2007): 101–119.

——, "Les 'Russes de l'étranger proche': le thème diasporique et ses lobbies en Russie," *Revue d'études comparatives Est-Ouest*, no. 4 (2008): 5–28.

Laruelle M., and Peyrouse S., *Asie centrale, la dérive autoritaire* (Paris: Autrement, 2006).

——, *Les Russes du Kazakhstan. Identités nationales et nouveaux États dans l'espace post-soviétique* (Paris: Maisonneuve & Larose—IFEAC, 2004).

——, *The 'Chinese Question' in Central Asia. Domestic Order, Social Changes, and the Chinese Factor* (New York, London: Columbia University Press, and Hurst, 2012).

Le Borgne-David A., *Les Migrations paysannes du Sud-Brésil vers l'Amazonie. Le salariat plutôt que la malaria* (Paris: L'Harmattan, 1998).

Lebedeva N.M., *Novaia russkaia diaspora. Sotsial'no—psikhologicheskii analiz* (Moscow: RAN, 1997).

Levitt P., *The Transnational villagers* (Berkeley: University of California Press, 2001).

Liu M.Y., "Hierarchies of Place, Hierarchies of Empowerment: Geographies of Talk about Postsocialist Change in Uzbekistan," *Nationalities Papers* 33, no. 3 (2005): 423–438.

——, *Recognizing the Khan: Authority, Space and Political Imagination among Uzbek Men in Post-Soviet Osh, Kyrgyzstan* (PhD Dissertation, Department of Anthropology, University of Michigan, 2002).

Liu S., *Passage to Manhood: Youth Migration, Heroin, and AIDS in Southwest China* (Stanford: Stanford University Press, 2010).

Loughlin P.H., and Pannell C.W., "Growing Economic Links and Regional Development in the Central Asian Republics and Xinjiang, China," *Post-Soviet Geography and Economics* 42, no. 7 (2001): 469–490.

Lucas R.E.B., *International Migration and Economic Development: Lessons from Low-Income Countries* (Northampton: Edward Elgar, 2005).

Luntsev V.A., ed., *Mezhdunarodnaia migratsiia: ekonomika i politika* (Moscow: TEIS, 2006).

Makarenko A.F., *Ukraintsy* (Almaty: Bilim, 1998).

Malabaev J., *Bishkek—stolitsa Kyrgyzstana* (Bishkek: Erkin-Too, 2002).

Managing Labour Mobility in the Evolving Global Economy (Geneva: International Organization for Migration, 2008).

Mansoor A., and Quillin B., eds., *Migration and Remittances: Eastern Europe and the Former Soviet Union* (Washington, D.C.: The World Bank, 2006).

Mars G., and Altman Y., "The Cultural Bases of Soviet Central Asia's Second Economy (Uzbekistan and Tajikistan)," *Central Asian Survey* 5, no. 4 (1986): 195–204.

Marsden M., "All-male sonic gatherings, Islamic reform, and masculinity in northern Pakistan," *American Ethnologist* 34, no. 3 (2007): 473–490.

Massey D.S., Arango J., Hugo G., Kouaouci A., Pellegrino A., and Taylor J.E., *Worlds in Motion. Understanding International Migration at the End of the Millennium* (Oxford: Clarendon Press, 1998).

Megoran N., "Framing Andijan, Narrating the Nation: Islam Karimov's Account of the Events of 13th May 2005," *Central Asian Survey* 27, no. 1 (2008): 15–31.

Mendibaev N., *Novye poselencheskie obshchnosti: Sotsial'nie problemy* (Turkestan: International Kazakh Turkish University, 2000).

Migration and Development in Tajikistan. Emigration, Return and Diaspora (Geneva: International Labor Organization, 2008).

Migration and Development. Proceedings of Moscow State Lomonosov University International Conference (Moscow: Moscow State Lomonosov University, 2007).

Migratsiia SNG i Baltii: cherez razlichiia problem k obshchemu informatsionnomu prostranstvu (Moscow: Adamant, 2001).

Migratsiia v Tsentral'noi Azii: problemy i perspektivy (Almaty: Daik-Press, 2005).

Mills M.B., "Contesting the Margins of Modernity: Women, Migration and Consumption in Thailand," *American Ethnologist* 24, no. 1 (1997): 37–61.

Monografiia i atlas Respubliki Tadzhikistan po dannym Vseobshchei perepisi naseleniia 2000 g. (Dushanbe: Goskomstat Respubliki Tadzhikistan—UNFPA, 2005).

Monqid S., "Les Femmes émigrées vecteur de modernisation? Le rôle occulté des femmes émigrées dans le développement du pays d'origine: le cas marocain," *Passerelles: revue d'études interculturelles*, no. 28 (2004): 59–68.

Morokvasic M., "La mobilité transnationale comme ressource: le cas des migrants de l'Europe de l'Est," *Cultures et conflits* 33–34 (1999): 105–122.

Morokvasic M., Erel U., and Shinozaki K., eds., *Crossing Borders and Shifting Boundaries*, vol 1: Gender on the Move, (Opladen: Leske and Budrich, 2003).

Mughal A.G., *Migration, Remittances, and Living Standards in Tajikistan* (Dushanbe, 2006).

Naselenie Kyrgyzstana. Itogi pervoi natsional'noi perepisi naseleniia Kyrgyzskoi Respubliki 1999 goda v tablitsakh II (1) (Bishkek: National Committee of Statistics, 2000).

Naselenie Kyrgyzstana: Resul'taty pervoi natsional'noi perepisi naseleniia Kyrgyzstana 1999 goda v tablitsakh II (Bishkek: National Statistical Committee, 2002).

Naumkin V.V., ed., *State, Religion and Society in Central Asia: a Post-Soviet Critique* (Reading: Ithaca Press, 1993).

Nazpary J., *Post-Soviet Chaos: Violence and Dispossession in Kazakhstan* (London: Pluto Press, 2001).

Nyberg-Sørensen N., Van Hear N., and Engberg-Pedersen P., "The Migration-Development Nexus: Evidence and Policy Options," *International Migration* 40, no. 5 (2002): 49–73.

Olcott M.B., *The Kazakhs* (Stanford: Hoover Institution Press, 1987).

Olimova S., *Migratsiia v gornykh regionakh stran Tsentral'noi Azii (Tadzhikistan, Kirgiziia)* (Dushanbe: Sharq, 2005).

Olimova S., and Bosc I., *Labour Migration from Tajikistan* (Dushanbe: International Organization for Migration, 2003).

——, *Trudovaia migratsiia iz Tadzhikistana* (Dushanbe: International Organization for Migration, Sharq, 2003).

Olimova S., and Kurbonova R., *Povedencheskoe issledovanie sredy trudovykh migrantov iz Tazhikistana i chlenov ikh semei po voprosam VICH i IPPP* (Dushanbe: International Organization for Migration, 2006).

Olimova S., and Quddusov J., *Families of Migrants in Tajikistan: Problems and Ways of Their Solution* (Dushanbe: Irfon, 2007).

Omarov N., *Migratsionnye protsessy v Kyrgyzskoi Respublike v gody nezavisimosti. Itogi desiatiletiia* (Bishkek: 2001).

——, "Etnicheskaia situatsiia i migratsionnye protsessy v postsovetskom Kyrgyzstane," *Etnograficheskoe obozrenie*, no. 3 (2005): 75–82.

Osella F., and Osella C., "Migration, Money and Masculinity in Kerala," *The Journal of the Royal Anthropological Institute* 6, no. 1 (2000); 115–131.

Ostergaard-Nielsen E., *International Migration and Sending Countries, Perceptions, Policies and Transnational Relations* (Basinkstoke: Palgrave MacMillan, 2003).

Ouzgane L., *Islamic Masculinities* (London: Zed Books, 2006).

Paugam S., *La Disqualification sociale: essai sur la nouvelle pauvreté* (Paris: PUF, 2000).

Pécoud A., and De Gutcheneire P., eds., *Migration without Borders. Essays on the Free Movement of People* (Oxford, New York: Bergham Press, 2007).

Peraldi M., ed., *La fin des norias? Réseaux migrants dans les économies marchandes en Méditerranée* (Paris: Maisonneuve & Larose—MMSH, 2002).

——, "Aventuriers du nouveau capitalisme marchand. Essai d'anthropologie de l'éthique mercantile," *Working Paper Series, Ramses 2*, 2007.

——, *Cabas et containers. Activités marchandes informelles et réseaux migrants transfrontaliers* (Paris: Maisonneuve & Larose—MMSH, 2001).

Pérouse J.-F., "Irruption et éclipse des navetteurs 'russes' à Istanbul (1988–1999): remous et rumeurs dans la mégapole," *Slavica Occitania*, no. 8 (1999): 273–312.

Pétric B.M., *Pouvoir, don et réseaux en Ouzbékistan post-soviétique* (Paris: PUF, 2002).

——, "Uzbekistan ne iavliaetsia obshchestvom, osnovannym na printsipe etnichnosti. No mozhet takovym stat'," *Etnograficheskoe obozrenie*, no. 1 (2005): 87–91.

Peyrouse S., "Les flux migratoires des Russes d'Asie centrale vers la Russie," *Espace, Populations, Sociétés*, no. 1 (2007): 47–57.

——, *Turkmenistan. Strategies of Power, Dilemmas of Development* (Armonk: M.E. Sharpe, 2011).

Pierret J., *Vivre avec le VIH. Enquête de longue durée auprès des personnes infectées* (Paris: PUF, 2006).

Pilkington H., *Migration, Displacement and Identity in Post-Soviet Russia* (London, New York: Routledge, 1998).

Popkov V., *Fenomen etnicheskikh diaspor* (Moscow: Institut sotsiologii RAN, 2003).

Portes A., ed., *The Economic Sociology of Immigration. Essays on Networks, Ethnicity and Entrepreneurship* (New York: The Russell Sage Foundation, 1995).

Portes A., Guarnizo L.E., and Landolt P., "The Study of Transnationalism: Pitfalls and Promise of an Emergent Research Field," *Ethnic and Racial Studies* 22, no. 2 (1999): 217–237.

Potot S., "Le réseau migrant: une organisation entre solidarité communautaire et 'zone de libre échange,'" *Migrations Société*, no. 105–106 (2006): 49–74.
Poujol C., ed., *Dictionnaire de l'Asie centrale* (Paris: Ellipses, 2001).
——, *Ouzbékistan. La croisée des chemins* (Paris: Belin, 2005).
——, "Les Polonais du Kazakhstan entre l'intégration et la Patrie rêvée," *Espace, Populations, Sociétés*, no. 1 (2007): 91–100.
——, "Santé mentale et société en Asie centrale post-soviétique ou comment tenter de diagnostiquer un mal-être social?" *Outre-Terre*, no. 16 (2006): 367–380.
Poutignat P., and Streiff-Fenart J., *Théories de l'ethnicité* (Paris: PUF, 1999).
Pusch B., and Wilkoszewski T., eds., *Facetten internationaler Migration in die Türkei: Gesellschaftliche Rahmenbedingungen und persönliche Lebenswelten* (Würzburg: Ergon Verlag, 2008).
Reeves M., *Border Work: An Ethnography of the State at its Limits in the Ferghana Valley* (PhD dissertation, Department of Social Anthropology, University of Cambridge, 2008).
"Republic of Tajikistan: Selected Issues and Statistical Appendix," *IMF Country Report*, International Monetary Fund, No. 05/131, April 2005.
Resnik J., and Benhabib S., eds., *Migrations and Mobilities: Citizenship, Borders, and Gender* (New York: New York University Press, 2009).
Riaux G., "La radicalisation des nationalistes azéris en Iran," *Cahiers d'études de la Méditerranée turque et orientale (CEMOTI)*, no. 27 (2004): 15–42.
——, "Les relations entre l'Azerbaïdjan et l'Iran: des représentations conflictuelles à l'apprentissage du realism," *Eurorient*, no. 28 (2008): 53–71.
——, "The Formative Years of Azerbaijani Nationalism in Post-Revolutionary Iran," *Central Asian Survey* 27, no. 1 (2008): 45–58.
Röhner I., "National and International Labour Migration. A Case Study in the Province of Batken, Kyrgyzstan," *NCCR North-South Dialogue Working Paper* no. 8 (Berne: NCCR North-South, 2007).
Rowland R.H., "National and Regional Population Trends in Tajikistan: Results from the Recent Census," *Eurasian Geography and Economics* 46, no. 3 (2005): 202–223.
Roy O., "Tadjikistan : structures d'un conflit," in *Laïcité(s) en France et en Turquie, Cahiers d'études de la Méditerranée turque et orientale (CEMOTI)*, no. 19 (1995): 445–452.
——, *La nouvelle Asie centrale ou la fabrication des nations* (Paris: Seuil, 1997).
Rubin B.R., and Snyder J., eds., *Post-Soviet Political Order. Conflict and State Building* (London: Routledge, 1998).
Ruget V., and Usmanalieva B., "Citizenship, migration and loyalty towards the state: a case study of the Kyrgyzstani migrants working in Russia and Kazakhstan," *Central Asian Survey* 27, no. 2 (2008): 129–141.
Rumer B.Z., *Soviet Central Asia: 'a Tragic Experiment'* (Boston: Unwin Hyman, 1989).
Ruth Gimbaud M., *The Kitchen Spoon's Handle: Transnationalism and Sri Lanka's Migrant Housemaids* (Ithaca: Cornell University Press, 2000).
Sadovskaia E., "Chinese Migration to Kazakhstan: a Silk Road for Cooperation or a Thorny Road of Prejudice?" *The China and Eurasia Forum Quarterly* 8, no. 4 (2007): 147–170.
——, "Denezhnye perevody trudovykh migrantov i ikh rol' v migrantskikh domokhoziaistvakh Tsentral'noi Azii," *Central Asia and the Caucasus*, no. 3 (2006): 109–123.
——, "Kitaiskaia migratsiia v Kazakhstane: sovremennye tendentsii i perspektivy," *Analytic*, no. 6 (2007): 33–45.
——, *Migratsiia v Kazakhstane na rubezhe XXI veka: novye tendentsii i perspektivy* (Almaty: Galym, 2001).
——, "Remittances and their role for labor migrants' households in the Republics of Central Asia," *Central Asian Affairs*, no. 3 (2006): 36–40.
——, et al., *Trudovaia migratsiia v stranakh Tsentralnoi Azii, Rossiiskoi Federatsii, Afganistane i Pakistane* (Almaty: European Commission, International Organization for Migration, 2005).

Safonova E.I., ed., *China in the Regional and World Politics* (Moscow: The Far East Institute of the Russian Academy of Sciences, 2009).

Safran W., "Comparing Diasporas: A Review Essay," *Diaspora* 8, no. 3 (1999): 255–291.

Sahadeo J., and Zanca R., eds., *Everyday Life in Central Asia: Past and Present* (Bloomington: Indiana University Press, 2007).

Savoskul S.S., *Russkie novogo zarubezh'ia. Vybor sud'by* (Moscow: Nauka, 2001).

Sayad A., *La double absence, des illusions de l'émigré aux souffrances de l'immigré* (Paris: Seuil, 1999).

Schmidt M., and Sagynbekova L., "Migration Past and Present: Changing Patterns in Kyrgyzstan," *Central Asian Survey* 27, no. 2 (2008): 111–127.

Schnapper D., *La France de l'intégration, Sociologie de la nation en 1990* (Paris: Gallimard, 1991).

Shaffer B., *Borders and Brethrens: Iran and the Challenge of Azerbaijani Identity* (London: MIT Press, 2002).

Shami S., "Prehistories of Globalization: Circassian Identity in Motion," *Public Culture* 12, no. 1 (2000): 177–204.

Sheffer G., ed., *Modern Diasporas in International Politics* (London: Croom Helm, 1986).

Shlapentokh V., Sendich M., and Payin E., eds., *The New Russian Diaspora: Russian Minorities in the Former Soviet Republics* (Armonk: M.E. Sharpe, 1994).

Shokamalov Ju.K., "Demograficheskoe razvitie Kazakhstana: sostoianie i perspektivy," *Informatsionno-analiticheskii tsentr izucheniia obshchestvennykh politicheskikh protsessov na postsovetskom prostranstve*, March 10, 2009.

Shterenshis M., "Jews in Central Asia: The Past for the Present," *Central Asia and the Caucasus*, no. 1 (2001): 189–200.

Sik E., and Wallace C., "The Development of Open-Air Markets in East-Central Europe," *International Journal of Urban and Regional Research* 23, no. 4 (1999): 697–714.

Smith G., "Transnational Politics and the Politics of the Russian Diaspora," *Ethnic and Racial Studies* 22, no. 3 (1999): 500–523.

Snizhenie riskov trudovoi migratsii i torgovli liud'mi (Almaty, Eretpes NGO seminar materials, 2009).

Spencer S., ed., *The Politics of Immigration* (Malden: Blackwell, 2003).

Stalker P., *Workers without Frontiers* (Boulder: Lynne Rienner, 2000).

Suzhikov M., ed., *Mezhnatsional'nye otnosheniia v Kazakhstane* (Almaty: Gylym, 1993).

Swietochowski T., and Collins B., *Historical Dictionary of Azerbaijan* (Lanham: Scarecrow Press, 1999).

Tadzhikistan: 15 let gosudarstvennoi nezavisimosti, Statisticheskii sbornik (Dushanbe: Goskomstat, 2006).

Tadzhikistan: problem trudovoi migratsii i vozmozhnye podkhody k formirovaniiu politiki (Dushanbe: Panorama, 2004).

Tajikistan Policy note: enhancing the development impact of remittances, World Bank Report No 35771-TJ April 2006.

Tajikistan: Human development report 1998 (Washington, D.C.: UNDP, 1998).

Tarrius A., "Au-delà des Etats-nations: des sociétés de migrants," *Revue des migrations internationales* 17, no. 2 (2005): 37–61.

——, *La mondialisation par le bas: les nouveaux nomades de l'économie souterraine* (Paris: Balland, 2002).

The International Migration Agenda and the World Bank. Managing Risks, Enhancing Benefits (Washington, D.C.: The World Bank, 2006).

The Population of the Republic of Tajikistan in 2000 (Dushanbe: State Committee on Statistics, 2002).

The World Bank Migration and Development Brief, November 11, 2008.

Thieme S., "Living in Transition: How Kyrgyz Women Juggle their Different Roles in a Multi-local Setting," *Gender, Technology and Development* 12, no. 3 (2008): 325–345.

Thorez J., "Enclaves et enclavement dans le Ferghana post-soviétique," *Cahiers d'Etudes sur la Méditerranée et le Monde Turco-Iranien (CEMOTI)*, no. 35 (2003): 28–39.

—— "Itinéraires du déracinement—L'essor des migrations de travail entre l'Asie centrale et la Russie," *Espaces, Populations, Sociétés*, no. 1 (2007): 59–71.

——, "*Khorosho gde nas net.* L'émigration des 'Russophones' d'Asie centrale," *ÉcoGéo*, no. 9, 2009.

Thual F., *La crise du Haut-Karabakh: une citadelle assiégée?* (Paris: PUF, 2003).

Tishkov V., and Fillipova E., eds., *Etnicheskaia situatsiia i konflikty v stranakh SNG i Baltii. Ezhegodnyi doklad* (Moscow: RAN, 2006).

Tishkov V.A., "Russkie v Srednei Azii i Kazakhstane," *Issledovaniia po prikladnoi i neotlozhnoi etnologii*, no. 51 (Moscow: RAN, 1993).

Todaro M.P., and Smith S.C., *Urbanization and Rural-Urban Migration: Theory and Policy in Economic Development* (Washington, D.C.: The George Washington University and Prentice Hall, 2012).

Todoroki E., Celik K., and Kholmatov M., *Alternative Remittance Systems in Kazakhstan* (Washington, D.C.: The World Bank, 2011).

Tokhtakhodzhaeva M., *The Re-Islamization of Society and the Position of Women in Post-Soviet Uzbekistan* (Folkestone: Global Oriental, 2008).

Tololyan K., "Rethinking Diaspora(s): Stateless Power in the Transnational Moment," *Diaspora* 5, no. 1 (1996): 3–35.

Transparency International, *Korruptsiia i nezakonnaia migratsiia* (Almaty: Transparency International, 2005).

Triandafyllidou A., and Gropas R., eds., *European Immigration. A Sourcebook* (Aldershot: Ashgate, 2007).

Trudovaia migratsiia iz Kyrgyzstana (Bishkek: International Organization for Migration, 2008).

Trudovaia migratsiia v stranakh Tsentral'noi Azii, Rossiiskoi Federatsii, Afganistane i Pakistane (Almaty: International Organization for Migration, 2005).

Tsuda T., ed., *Diasporic Homecomings: Ethnic Return Migration in Comparative Perspective* (Stanford: Stanford University Press, 2009).

Tyner J., *Made in the Philippines: Gendered Discourses and the Making of Migrants* (London: Routledge, 2004).

U.S. Committee for Refugees, "World Refugee survey 1997—Tajikistan," in *HCR Refworld 2006*, 15th edition, 2006.

Umarov Kh., and Ulmasov R., *Vneshniaia trudovaia migratsiia v Tadzhikistane (prichiny, problemy, posledstviia, regulirovanie)* (Dushanbe: Irfon, 2006).

Ushakin S., "Chelovek roda on: futliary muzhestvennosti," *Voprosy filosofii*, no. 7 (2005): 34–56.

"Uslovia i sostoianie sotsial'noi reabilitatsii trudovykh migrantov—grazhdan Kirgizskoi Respubliki, posle vozvrashcheniia na rodinu" (Bishkek: Social Research Center of the American University of Central Asia, PACT, 2007).

Uzbekistan: problemy trudovoi migratsii i vozmozhnye podkhody k formirovaniiu politiki (Tashkent: Center for Human Resources Development, 2004).

Van Gennep A., *Les rites de passage. Etude systématique des rites* (Paris: A.J. Picard, 1981).

Vertovec S., ed., *Migration. Critical Concepts in the Social Sciences* (London: Routledge, 2009).

Vichnevski A., and Zayontchkovskaya Zh., "L'émigration de l'ex-Union soviétique: prémices et inconnues," *Revue Européenne des Migrations Internationales* 7, no. 3 (1991): 5–29.

Vichnevski A., "Migrations et croissance démographique en Russie," *Migrations Société* 17, no. 101 (2005): 129–142.

Vitkovskaia G., ed., *Migratsiia russkoiazychnogo naseleniia iz Tsentral'noi Azii: prichiny, posledstviia, perspektivy* (Moscow: Carnegie Endowment for International Peace, 1996).

——, ed., *Sovremennye etnopoliticheskie protsessy i migratsionnaia situatsiia v Tsentral'noi Azii* (Moscow: Carnegie Endowment for International Peace, 1998).

Vorob'eva O.D., ed., *Migratsiia naseleniia. Trudovaia migratsiia v Rossii* (Moscow: RAN, 2001).

W stepie dalekim: Polacy w Kazachstanie, V stepi dalekoi: Poliaki v Kazakhstane (Poznań, Almaty: Wystawa, 1997).

Weber F., *Le travail au noir: une fraude parfois vitale?* (Paris: Ed. Rue d'Ulm, 2008).

Werner C., "Bride abduction in post-Soviet Central Asia: marking a shift towards patriarchy through local discourses of shame and tradition," *The Journal of the Royal Anthropological Institute* 15, no. 2 (2009): 314–331.

Wettig G., ed., "No Future for the Ethnic Germans in Kazakhstan?" *Aussenpolitik* 44, no. 2 (1993): 153–162.

World Migration Report 2010. The Future of Migration: Building Capacities for Change (Geneva: International Organization for Migration, 2010).

Yakemtchouk R., *Ouzbékistan: puissance émergente en Asie centrale* (Paris: L'Harmattan, 2003).

Yap Kioe Sheng, "Urbanization and Internal Migration," *Population Studies Series No. 158: Fifth Asian and Pacific Population Conference's Selected Papers* (Bangkok: UNESCAP, 2003).

Yessenova S., "Hawkers and Containers in *Zarya Vostoka*: How 'Bizarre' Is the Post-Soviet Bazaar?" *Research in Economic Anthropology* 24 (2006): 37–59.

——, "Routes and Roots of Kazakh Identity: Urban Migration in Post-Socialist Kazakhstan," *The Russian Review*, no. 64 (2005): 661–679.

Yükseker D., "Trust and Gender in a Transnational Market: The Public Culture of Laleli, Istanbul," *Public Culture* 16, no. 1 (2004): 47–65.

Yurchak A., "Russian Neoliberal: The Entrepreneurial Ethic and the Spirit of 'True Careerism,'" *The Russian Review* 62, no. 1 (2003): 72–90.

Zayonchkovskaya Zh., *Demograficheskaia situatsiia i rasselenie* (Moscow: Nauka, 1991).

——, ed., *Migratsionnaia situatsiia v stranakh SNG* (Moscow: Kompleks-Progress, 1999).

——, ed., *Trudovaia migratsiia v SNG: Sotsial'nye i economicheskie effekty* (Moscow: Adamant, 2003).

Zayonchkovskaya Zh. A., ed., *Zashchita prav trudiashchikhsia—migrantov v stranakh CBE i SNG i perspektivy prisoedineniia k Konventsii OON 1990 g.* (UNESCO, 2005).

Zayonchkovskaya Zh., Molodikova I., and Mukomel' V., eds., *Metodologiia i metody izucheniia migratsionnykh protsessov* (Moscow: HESP OSI, UNESCO, 2007).

Zevelev I., *Russia and its New Diasporas* (Washington, D.C.: United States Institute of Peace, 2001).

Zhorobekov Zh., *Etnodemograficheskie protsessy v Kyrgyzstane (vchera, segodnia, zavtra)* (Bishkek: 1997).

INDEX

www.ingramcontent.com/pod-product-compliance
Lightning Source LLC
LaVergne TN
LVHW011106300926
849160LV00008B/294

9789004226814